By Joe H. Ferguson

© 2021 Fund Forwarding LLC
All rights reserved.

No part of this book may be reproduced in any form whatsoever without prior written permission from the author.

Note: The opinions expressed and images selected herein are those of the author and his alone. No other person, publisher, nor organization bears responsibility for these opinions.

The Church of Jesus Christ of Latter-day Saints does not endorse this work. The opinions and views expressed herein belong exclusively to the author. Permission for the use of images, photos and sources is also solely the responsibility of the author.

ISBN-13: 978-0-9985443-4-2

Version 1.1

Preface

Purpose and Organization of this Book

By violating the Constitution and pursuing its own agenda, the Supreme Court constitutes a major threat to the survival of America and to Christianity. This book can be used as a handbook for the patriot fighting for liberty and the restoration of the Constitution, or by the Christian defending Christian principles from assaults from the Supreme Court, the media and other sources.

We as the people of America are in grave peril. Many Americans sense that something is seriously wrong, but they do not know the cause.

The purpose of this book is to explain the causes, expose many of the people responsible for the problems and explain the course that we should take to protect ourselves, our families and our nation. There is much information in this book for the patriot who wants to defend his country, for parents who want to help their children through these troubled times, for the serious Christian that wants to protect himself, his family and his faith from the many assaults being waged against it. The focus of the book is found in Section Two, which deals with the corrupted Supreme Court and the damage that it has done and is doing to Christianity and to America.

I also explain what Marxism really is. You will be surprised at how much of the American government is now Marxist.

In organizing this book, I have been faced with a HUGE dilemma. The first is that many readers will want to focus mainly on the Supreme Court chapters, Section Two. However, to fully understand the information in Section Two, one must have some prerequisite preparation. That information is found in Section One. But then I realized that many readers will feel bogged down reading all through Section One before getting to the heart of the book. So, I give you the option of reading all of Section One, then going to Two, or skimming through One and going right to Two. I strongly recommend that you read all of Section One before going to Two. At least read Chapters 4 and 8. But that is up to you. (I strongly believe in free agency.)

Section One is comprised of **Chapters One through Nine** and serves as a prerequisite to Chapters Ten through Fourteen. Since American law has (or had) a foundation in the Ten Commandments, it is impossible to separate the law from religion. (Although many in the legal field desire to.) So when the law is corrupted, it also has a corresponding corrupting influence on the people. This section is important in understanding the corruption of American law and the degradation of morality in our culture and in our people. This section will be very helpful to the American who wants to combat the forces attacking Americanism and Christianity.

Section Two comprises **Chapters Ten through Fourteen** and deals with the subversion of the law and of the Supreme Court. Two explains how the Supreme Court (SCOTUS), in violating the Constitution, violates our rights instead of protecting them. And how they are actively converting our Republic into a Marxist (yes, Marxist) dictatorship. This is in preparation for merging America into a world government. Since the American legal system has been corrupted by professionals, it is understandable that everything presented in Section Two will be at variance with the prevailing consensus among many professional lawyers and judges. **But the information in Section Two will be true and compatible with the Constitution, which is, truthfully, supposed to be the Supreme Law of the Land.**

Section Three, **Chapters Fifteen through Twenty**, discusses how to understand and deal with the destructive and subversive forces in our society today. We are in great peril. All three branches of the federal government are under the control of people who want to diminish, then destroy, the Constitution and our liberties. They also want to destroy our souls. All throughout the book and especially Section Three, I will present information that will be helpful to you to prepare to fight the enemies of America and of Christ and to protect yourselves and your families. This fight is going to get MEAN. And we will not survive it **without the direct intervention of the Lord.** We are living in the last days. And things are going to get VERY INTERESTING.

If you choose to skip right to Section Two, I do recommend that you read Chapter 4 on Gramsci and Chapter 8 on Marxism before proceeding to Section 2 on the law and the Supreme Court.

Introduction by the Highest of Authorities

Dear Fellow Christian American: Thank you for being interested in this subject, threats to our religious liberties and in my book. This is my gift to you in the cause of liberty. In this introduction, instead of presenting recommendations from well-known contemporaries, I am presenting the messages from some prophets, ancient and modern, on the subject of whether conspiracies exist. There are powerful and influential voices that encourage us to ignore and to disbelieve the warnings of these prophets.

To disbelieve these prophets is to do so at our peril. You will notice that some of them address threats to liberty and not specifically to religious liberty. Just be aware that **all totalitarians and tyrants hate Christianity.** When you see a message from a prophet regarding a threat to our political liberties, you can be certain that that threat is also a threat to our Christian liberties.

I have chosen to begin this book by emphasizing the need for more understanding of this subject by presenting the profound but not widely published declarations of former leaders of the Church of Jesus Christ of Latter-day Saints. I hope that you find the statements of these prophets to be enlightening and convincing and my book interesting and valuable. Joe

From 2nd Timothy 3 (Emphasis added):

1. This know also, that in **the last days** perilous times shall come.
2. For men shall be lovers of their own selves, **covetous**, boasters, proud, blasphemers, disobedient to parents, **unthankful**, unholy,
3. Without natural affection, trucebreakers, **false accusers**, incontinent, fierce, <u>despisers</u> **of those that are good.**
4. <u>Traitors</u>, heady, high minded, lovers of pleasures more than lovers of God.

1941 First Presidency

J. Reuben Clark - Public Domain Image

George Albert Smith - Public Domain Image

David O. McKay - Public Domain Image

In September 1941, the First Presidency of the Church of Jesus Christ of Latter-day Saints expressed serious doubts about the need for America's involvement in the war in Europe and the Church refused to support the government's highly promoted War Bond drive. Responding to a letter from the U. S. Secretary of Treasury, here are excerpts from two letters from the First Presidency, shown above: L to R: President J. Reuben Clark, Jr., President Heber J. Grant, President David O. McKay:[1]

> **We believe that our real threat comes from within and not from without and** it comes from the **underlying spirit** common to Naziism and Communism, namely, the spirit which **would array class against class,** which would set up **a Socialistic state** of some sort, which would **rob the people of the liberties** which we possess under the Constitution and would set up **such a reign of terror as exists now in many parts of Europe.** (Letter to U. S. Treasury Sep 30, 1941) (Emphasis added.)

And in the following letter:

> …but this much we feel we can definitely say, that **unless the people of America forsake the sins and the errors, political and otherwise**, of which they are now guilty and return to the practice of the great fundamental **principles of Christianity and of Constitutional**

---

1. These two letters are to be found in the Marriner Eccles Collection at the University of Utah Library. They are also found published by Conner Boyack, Libertas Institute, November 16, 2009.

government, there will be no exaltation for them spiritually and politically we shall lose our liberty and free institutions. (Letter to U. S. Treasury dated Oct 11, 1941) (Emphasis added.)

President David O. McKay: President McKay's *Statement on Communism* in 1966 contains eternal truths. It is timeless. It tells us much regarding our fight for Christian liberty. Here are some excerpts:

…The position of this Church on the subject of Communism has never changed. We consider it **the greatest satanical threat to peace, prosperity and the spread of God's work among men that exists** on the face of the earth…

…The entire concept and philosophy of **Communism is diametrically opposed to everything for which the Church stands-belief in Deity,** belief in the dignity and eternal nature of man and the application of the gospel to efforts for peace in the world. Communism is militantly atheistic and is committed to the destruction of faith wherever it may be found…

…**No member of this Church can be true to his faith, nor can any American be loyal to his trust, while lending aid, encouragement, or sympathy** to any of these false philosophies; for if he does, they will prove snares to his feet. (President David O. McKay, Priesthood, April 9, 1966) (Emphasis added.)

Ezra Taft Benson- Public Domain

David O McKay- Public Domain

President McKay's statement is powerful. It merits our serious consideration. It has some especially valuable clues to help us in defending attacks against Christianity. "…The entire concept and philosophy of Communism is diametrically opposed to everything for which the church stands…" WOW!!! That is powerful!!!

President Ezra Taft Benson: I testify that Lucifer was also in the council of heaven. He sought to destroy the agency of man. He rebelled. (See Moses 4:3.) There was a war in heaven and a third of the hosts were cast to the earth and denied a body. (See Rev. 12:7–9; D&C 29:36–37.) Lucifer is the enemy of all righteousness and seeks the misery of all mankind. (See 2 Ne. 2:18, 27; Mosiah 4:14.)...

President Ezra Taft Benson: I testify that wickedness is rapidly expanding in every segment of our society. (See D&C 1:14–16; D&C 84:49–53.) It is more highly organized, more cleverly disguised and more powerfully promoted than ever before. Secret combinations lusting for power, gain and glory are flourishing. **A secret combination that seeks to overthrow the freedom of all lands, nations and countries is increasing its evil influence and control over America and the entire world.** (See Ether 8:18–25.)... (October, 1988 Conference address.) (Emphasis added.)

J. Reuben Clark, Jr. - Public Domain

President Ezra Taft Benson: Communism introduced into the world a substitute for true religion. It is a counterfeit of the gospel plan. The false prophets of Communism predict a utopian society. This, they proclaim, will only be brought about as capitalism and free enterprise are overthrown, private property abolished, the family as a social unit eliminated, all classes abolished, all governments overthrown and a communal ownership of property in a classless, stateless society established.

Since 1917 this godless counterfeit to the gospel has made tremendous progress toward its objective of world domination. Today, we are in a battle for the bodies and souls of man. It is a battle between two opposing systems: freedom and slavery, Christ and anti-Christ. The struggle is more momentous than a decade ago, yet today the conventional wisdom says, "You must learn to live with Communism and to give up your ideas about national sovereignty." Tell that to the millions—yes, the scores of millions—who have met death or imprisonment under the tyranny of Communism! **Such would be the death knell of freedom and all we hold dear.** God must ever have a free people to prosper His work and bring about Zion. (*Ensign,* Nov 1979, 31, "A Witness and a Warning") (Emphasis added.)

President J. Reuben Clark, Jr. — President Clark served as counselor in three first-presidencies, was a former U.S. ambassador, a recognized constitutional scholar and a seasoned analyst of foreign affairs. As you can see, he was many years ahead of what we now see as routine propaganda. America was badgered by fake news long before anyone had ever heard of Donald Trump. During the same general conference of April, 1944, he addressed the cause of America's plight:

> We are in the midst of the greatest exhibition of propaganda that the world has ever seen. Just do not believe all you read and hear.

And do not think that these usurpations, intimidations and impositions are being done to us through inadvertence or mistake; **the whole course is deliberately planned and carried out; its purpose is to destroy the Constitution** and our constitutional government; then to bring chaos, out of which the new Statism with its slavery is to arise, **with a cruel, relentless, selfish, ambitious crew in the saddle, riding hard with whip and spur, a red-shrouded band of night riders for despotism.** (Emphasis added.)

Just who might those "night riders" be? And what is the "despotism" of which President Clark has spoken? That is exactly the subject we will be addressing herein.

Notice that President Clark used the expression "deliberately planned." Isn't that what today's mocking moguls call a "conspiracy theory?" If I, Joe Ferguson, had first said that terrible word "conspiracy" I would face ridicule in Twitter, Facebook and every fake news channel from Maine to California. But President Clark is my celestial witness, safely beyond the reach of the media cynics. His dire predictions are, as anyone can see, right on. The only thing is, the situation has worsened since he made that statement in 1944.

Moroni speaks (on behalf of the Lord) to us in Ether 8 (Emphasis added.):

> 23 Wherefore, O ye Gentiles, it is wisdom in God that these things should be shown unto you, that thereby **ye may repent of your sins and** suffer not that these murderous combinations shall get above you, which are built up to get power and gain—and the work, yea, even the work of destruction come upon you, yea, even the sword of the justice of the eternal God shall fall upon you, to your overthrow and destruction **if ye shall suffer these things to be.**
> 24 **Wherefore, the Lord commandeth you,** when ye shall see these things come among you that ye shall awake to a sense of your awful situation because of this secret combination which shall be among you; or wo be unto it, because of...
> 25 For it cometh to pass that whoso buildeth it up seeketh to overthrow the freedom of all lands nations and countries; **and it bringeth to pass the destruction of all people,** for it is built up by the Devil, who is the father of all lies;...

Note: In verse 23, the Lord tells us, "…that thereby ye may repent of your sins,…" What sins? The people reading this book are not sinful people.

I suggest that this is the answer: That we have been sinning by either participating (even unknowingly) in the building up of these secret combinations or we have been passive and acquiescing to their buildup.

Note: In verse 24, the Lord "commandeth" us…This is the only place in the Book of Mormon of which I am aware where the Lord *commands* us. So this must be a very special message in these verses.

On July 3, 1936, the First Presidency published this warning to Church members:

> Communism is not a political party nor a political plan under the Constitution; it is a system of government that is the opposite of our Constitutional government. …
>
> **Since Communism, established, would destroy our American Constitutional government, to support Communism is treasonable to our free institutions and *no patriotic American citizen may become either a Communist or supporter of Communism*. …**
>
> We call upon all Church members completely to eschew [shun] Communism. The safety of our divinely inspired **Constitutional government and the welfare of our Church imperatively demand that *Communism shall have no place in America*"** (signed: Heber J. Grant, J. Reuben Clark, Jr., David O. McKay, The First Presidency, in *Deseret News,* 3 July 1936; (emphasis added.)

President Marion G. Romney:

> Communism is Satan's counterfeit for the gospel plan and … it is an avowed enemy of the God of the land. **Communism is the greatest anti-Christ power in the world today** and therefore the greatest menace not only to our peace but to our preservation as a free people. **By the extent to which we tolerate it, accommodate ourselves to it, permit ourselves to be encircled by its tentacles and drawn to it, to that extent we forfeit the protection of the God of this land**

Marion G. Romney - Public Domain

(*Ensign,* , Sept. 1979,p.5). (Emphasis added)

President Ezra Taft Benson:
The truth is, we have to a great extent accommodated ourselves to Communism—and we have permitted ourselves to become encircled by its tentacles. Though we give lip service to the Monroe Doctrine, this has not prevented Cuba from becoming a Soviet military base, ninety miles off our coastline, nor has it prevented the takeover of Nicaragua in Central America, the surrender of the Panama Canal, **or the infiltration by enemy agents within our American borders...**

...Never before has the land of Zion appeared so vulnerable to so powerful an enemy as the Americas do at present. And our vulnerability is directly attributable to our loss of active faith in the God of this land, who has decreed that we must worship Him or be swept off. Too many Americans have lost sight of the truth that God is our source of freedom—the Lawgiver—and that personal righteousness is the most important essential to preserving our freedom. **So, I say with all the energy of my soul that unless we as citizens of this nation forsake our sins, political and otherwise and return to the fundamental principles of Christianity and of constitutional government, we will lose our political liberties, our free institutions and will stand in jeopardy before God**...(Ensign, Nov 1979, P 31) (Emphasis added.)

The statements of the above prophets, powerful though they are, go mostly unheralded and ignored. Nevertheless, let the nature of their messages speak to you the importance they deserve.

The very future of our nation, our freedoms and our souls, with the souls of our children and all posterity, depends on whether we understand them and act upon them.

There are some messages in this life that go unheralded, with no emphasis, yet are extremely important. We must dig for them. We must suspect that this is part of the test to which we are put in this mortal life. Are we willing to **search for these truths** and **then study them** until we understand them? I submit that this is one of the most important tests to which we are being put.

My study of this subject for the past 56 years convinces me that this subject is one of extreme importance and that the messages of the prophets on this subject, ignored, ridiculed and rejected though they might be by some, contain wisdom of extreme value.

You will find that practically all of the contents of this book are contrary to what is taught in education. That is exactly why this book needed to be written, read and understood. Herein you will find wisdom.

Table of Contents

Purpose and Organization of this Book 2
Introduction by the Highest of Authorities 4

SECTION ONE *14*
Chapter One - A Caveat or Two 15
Chapter Two - The Value of Christianity in Civilized Society 26
Chapter Three - Clues, Suspects and Motives and "Qui Bono"? 37
Chapter Four - Gramsci's Long March Through the Institutions 43
Chapter Five - Christianity, Secular Humanism, Evolution and Marxism 52
Chapter Six - Evolution, Humanism, Marxism, Globalism and Public Education 66
Chapter Seven - *Never* Trust the Main Stream Media 81
Chapter Eight - Marxism—What it IS NOT and What it REALLY IS 101
Chapter Nine - Communist/Leftist/Globalist Tactics and Tricks 135

SECTION TWO *174*
Chapter Ten - Corrupting the Law to Persecute Christians 175
Chapter Eleven - The *Everson* Case and "Separation of Church and State" 194
Chapter Twelve - *Obergefell* Another Attack Against Christianity and the U.S. Constitution 243
Chapter Thirteen - That Awful Crime of Discriminating 257
Chapter Fourteen - The SCOTUS-Greatest Threat to Christianity and to America 270

SECTION THREE *282*
Chapter Fifteen - Warnings of Ancient Prophets Regarding Our Day 283
Chapter Sixteen - The 2020 Election and the Blocking of Justice 287
Chapter Seventeen - The Deep State 293
Chapter Eighteen - Defense and Counterattack - Exposing and Defeating a Communist Front 303

Chapter Nineteen - Defending Christ and His Words 311

Chapter Twenty - The Constitution is the Solution 323

APPENDIX *327*

    Appendix A: Obergefell 328

    Appendix B - How Obergefell Threatens Religious Liberty, America and Civilization 330

    Appendix C - George Washington's Farewell Address 332

    Appendix D - How to Study the Constitution 334

    Appendix E - Excerpts from the *Declaration of Independence* 336

    Appendix F - The Fourteenth Amendment 341

    Appendix G - The Bill of Rights 343

    Appendix H - Congress Supposed to Regulate the Supreme Court 345

    Appendix I 346

    Appendix J - The Doctrine of the Lesser Magistrate 346

    Appendix K - Attacks on Religion by Politicians 351

    Appendix L - Judging the United States Supreme Court by Utah Chief Justices A. H. Ellett and J. Allen Crockett 354

    Appendix M - Sample Letter to Send Your CongressmenError! Bookmark

    Appendix N - Communist /Leftist/Globalist/Marxist Fronts and RIOTS .... Error! Bookmark not defined.

    Appendix O - Organic Law Definition .... Error! Bookmark not defined.

    About the Author 355

SECTION ONE

Chapter One - A Caveat or Two

Note: This chapter is vital to understand the times in which we live and what the Lord's prophets have said about the subject matter of this book.

First of All—Be of Good Cheer

In this book, we will be addressing some of the most cunning, devious, evil people and forces on earth.

The fact that some of them have attained positions of high power and authority in the government of our beloved America, over decades and centuries, is most disturbing.

But do not let this depress you. They exist, whether or not we recognize their existence and understand their workings. And it is far, far better that we recognize and understand them than to be ignorant of their workings and thereby be vulnerable to falling under their control.

The Lord allows evil people and evil forces to exist on this earth in order that we may be tested and that we may prove ourselves. However, he does not leave us defenseless. He gives us the ability to see, to hear and to think. He gives us the power of reason.

Then, he gives us clear, explicit information about these evil forces so that we may prepare our defenses against their wicked wiles. Yes, these evil forces conspire to take control of us…both body and soul.

These forces are directed by the Devil himself. But we are led, if we choose to follow, by the Lord Jesus Christ and his living prophets on this earth. When we are enlightened by the information available to us, we can make ourselves much more potent than those who are determined to capture and destroy us.

So be ye of good cheer. We are launching on an adventure of information gathering. We shall be seeking and finding sources of light in this world of darkness.

The Lord warns us in 2nd Nephi 15:

> 13 Therefore, my people are gone into captivity, **because they have no knowledge;** and **their honorable men are famished** and **their multitude dried up with thirst**.

We are not left without knowledge. There is an abundance of it. However, in this time of information abundance, we are deluged with **a certain amount**

that is false, pernicious and sometimes very alluring. The Lord warns us also, in 2nd Nephi:

> 20 Wo unto them that **call evil good and good evil**, that **put darkness for light** and **light for darkness**, that put bitter for sweet and sweet for bitter..

We will identify this false information as "disinformation," about which more later. The enemies of religious liberty, in fact of all liberty, constantly call evil good. They put darkness for light and light for darkness. They put bitter for sweet and sweet for bitter. **In their every move, there is trickery and deception.**

Our challenge in life is to always call good "good" and evil "evil" and to be honest in all things. In this book, we are going to learn some tricks of the Devil's trade and how he makes evil appear to be good and darkness appear to be light. We are going to expose his trickery so that we can help others understand it. We are going to do as the Lord instructs us in D&C 123:

> 13 Therefore, that **we should waste and wear out our lives in <u>bringing to light all the hidden things of darkness</u>**, wherein we know them;...

And never lose sight of the fact that even though there is corruption in the government, we still love America and the principles upon which it was founded.

Be Ye of Good Cheer

I am going to bring to your attention, for your use and benefit, some very select messages on this subject from our Lord and Savior through His prophets, the most reliable source of information available to mankind.

Be ye of good cheer! If reading about all of these evil and powerful people starts to get you depressed, just remember-while we are learning about them and their tricks; we are learning about how to defend ourselves and how to, ultimately, to defeat the bad guys. And look at the bright side. Look at the temples we are building all over the world and at the number of missionaries we have out. Our numbers are increasing. And furthermore, the most powerful force in the universe is on our side! Personally, I like the odds.

Let us be aware that the knowledge that we are gaining about the works of darkness, about the works of evil people, about the combinations of the Devil serves to confirm the accuracy and the truthfulness of the gospel of Jesus Christ. For in His gospel, we are warned of these evils by His prophets ancient and modern. Our observations of modern-day evil confirm these prophetic warnings.

While we are gaining truthful knowledge and experience from opposing evil forces, we are accumulating wisdom. That is what we are on earth for, is it not?

Remember, all through this book-BE YE OF GOOD CHEER!

A Silent But Deadly War

A great war is raging. Under threat are our country, homes, automobiles, motorcycles, horses, dogs and shotguns. Yes, and even our children and their souls are at stake. This war is, in some ways, a silent war. So many do not even know that it is raging. It is definitely a war between the good guys and the bad guys. It is Christ and His forces on one side and Lucifer and his followers on the other. We have been warned about this war by the most reliable authorities-the Lord's prophets, both ancient and modern. But, for many reasons, its notice has escaped many of the good people who should be engaged on our side. I wish this book to assist the messages of the prophets to take life and become very, very visible in today's cacophony of life's distractions. It is also to help those on our side to understand the enemy and know how to counterattack when Christian liberties are threatened.

Elder Neal A. Maxwell (1926-2004) Could See This Situation Developing as Far Back as 1978, When He Stated:[2]

Neal A Maxwell Public Domain

We are now entering a period of incredible ironies. Let us cite but one of these ironies which is yet in its subtle stages: we shall see in our time a maximum if indirect effort made to establish irreligion as the state religion. It is actually a new form of paganism that uses the carefully preserved and cultivated freedoms of Western civilization to shrink freedom even as it rejects the value essence of our rich Judeo-Christian heritage.

M. J. Sobran wrote recently:
"The Framers of the Constitution . . . forbade the Congress to make any law 'respecting' the establishment of religion, thus leaving the states free to do so (as several of them did); and they explicitly forbade the Congress to abridge 'the free exercise' of religion, thus giving actual religious observance a rhetorical emphasis that fully

---

2. Maxwell, Neal A., "Meeting the Challenges of Today," BYU Devotional, 10 Oct, 1978

accords with the special concern we know they had for religion. It takes a special ingenuity to wring out of this a governmental indifference to religion, let alone an aggressive secularism. Yet there are those who insist that the First Amendment actually proscribes governmental partiality not only to any single religion, but to religion as such; so that tax exemption for churches is now thought to be unconstitutional. It is startling to consider that a clause clearly protecting religion can be construed as requiring that it be denied a status routinely granted to educational and charitable enterprises, which have no overt constitutional protection. Far
from equalizing unbelief, secularism has succeeded in
virtually establishing it.

[Sobran continues:] "What the secularists are increasingly demanding, in their disingenuous way, is that religious people, when they act politically, act only on secularist grounds. They are trying to equate acting on religion with establishing religion. And—**I repeat—the consequence of such logic is really to establish secularism**. It is in fact, **to force the religious to internalize the major premise of secularism**: that religion has no proper bearing on public affairs." [Human Life Review, Summer 1978, pp. 51–52, 60–61]

[Elder Maxwell now speaks] Brothers and sisters, irreligion as the state religion would be the worst of all combinations. Its orthodoxy would be insistent and its inquisitors inevitable. Its paid ministry would be numerous beyond belief. Its Caesars would be insufferably condescending. Its majorities—when faced with clear alternatives—would make the Barabbas choice, as did a mob centuries ago when Pilate confronted them with the need to decide. Your discipleship may see the time come when religious convictions are heavily discounted. M. J. Sobran also observed, "A religious conviction is now a second-class conviction, expected to step deferentially to the back of the secular bus and not to get uppity about it" (*Human Life Review,* Summer 1978, p. 58).

This new irreligious imperialism **seeks to disallow certain opinions** simply because those opinions grow out of religious convictions. Resistance to abortion will soon be seen as primitive. Concern over the institution of the family will be viewed as untrendy and unenlightened.

In its mildest form, irreligion will merely be condescending toward those who hold to traditional Judeo-Christian values. In its more harsh forms, as is always the case with those whose dogmatism is blinding, the secular church will do what it can to reduce the influence of those who still worry over standards, such as those in the Ten Commandments.

It is always such an easy step from dogmatism to unfair play. Especially when the dogmatists believe themselves to be dealing with primitive people who do not know what is best for them. It is the secular bureaucrat's burden, you see.

Please read the words of Elder Maxwell, above and also of M. J. Sobran, who Elder Maxwell quotes, **very slowly and very carefully** (above). Ponder them. They contain a powerful message.

What Elder Maxwell referred to as "irreligion" we can recognize as Secular Humanism, or Humanism and **we already have it today** as the de facto official state religion of the federal government of the USA and of all fifty states. Very few Christians seem to understand Secular Humanism or its threat to Christianity. In defending Christianity, it is imperative that we understand Secular Humanism. Therefore, Secular Humanism will be treated rather extensively herein. We shall see much more of the devastating work of the irreligionists in Chapters Ten, Eleven and Twelve.

The Prophets Are Right On

The two most important things that I wish to emphasize in this book are:

1. The prophets, ancient and modern, quoted in this book are right on for accuracy and,
2. The secret combinations that these prophets warn us about are very real and they are RIGHT NOW.

We Live in the Best of Times, We Live in the Worst of Times
Dickens might have been describing our times:[3]

> It was the best of times, it was the worst of times, it was the age of wisdom, it was the age of foolishness, it was the epoch of belief, it was the epoch of incredulity, it was the season of light, it was the season of darkness, it was the spring of hope, it was the winter of despair.

Times are good, as this is being written in early 2020. However, there are powerful and mostly unseen forces at work threatening to destroy us or to do us much harm. We live in a time of unprecedented information. Yes, and also unprecedented misinformation and disinformation. These are times of deception. Siren voices lull us into a sense of false security. We must exercise extreme caution in that which we choose to believe.

As we proceed, I strongly recommend the words of (then) Elder (later President) Ezra Taft Benson as he is addressing the very issues that will be presented herein:[4]

---

3. Dickens, Charles, A Tale of Two Cities 3
4. Benson, Ezra Taft, Conference Report, April, 1968

If America is destroyed, it may be by Americans who salute the flag, sing the national anthem, march in patriotic parades, cheer Fourth of July speakers — normally good Americans, but Americans who fail to comprehend what is required to keep our country strong and free — Americans who have been lulled away into a false security.

First of all, a Caveat

We shall address herein several forces that threaten Christianity. Emphasis will be placed on the threat of a rogue Supreme Court (SCOTUS).

Its nine members are comprised of five or more whose ideologies are hostile to Christianity and who render judgments based on their ideologies rather than the Constitution.

Although this threat has largely gone unrecognized by most Americans, its magnitude is so enormous and so overriding that, unless we get it resolved, all of the other threats will be relegated to insignificance.

You are no doubt aware of some of the attacks made against Christianity in the courts, the media, education, entertainment and elsewhere. Well, as Jimmy Durante used to say, "Youse ain't seen nuttin' yet!!!"

The intensity, sophistication, magnitude and frequency of these attacks are going to intensify. The purpose of this book is to help all Christians and other good people to be able to:
1. First to defend ourselves and our families from these satanic attacks and then to,
2. secondly,: to analyze, expose and counter them. It is not only our right but our duty.

Christ expects us to defend Him and His gospel. In St. Luke 9:

> 26 For **whosoever shall be ashamed of me and my words**, of **him shall the son of man be ashamed**, when he shall come in his own glory and in his Father's and of the holy angels. (Emphasis added.)

We must understand that the enemies of Christ often attack the gospel of Jesus Christ *one principle at a time*. So we must be ready to defend not only His gospel but each and every principle of His gospel.

Jesus Christ Artwork - Public Domain

Some of the misinformed praise the gospel of Jesus Christ but, unfortunately, ridicule or degrade some of the *principles* of the gospel.

It seems logical that we should stand to defend the words of Christ (the gospel of Jesus Christ) as well as Christ Himself. The enemies of Christ use intimidation extensively as one of their major weapons. So if we allow them to intimidate us into silence in the face of attacks upon Christ and His words, does that not make us guilty of being "ashamed of Him and His words?"

I encourage you to give your special attention to the words of those wise and honest men whose statements are found in the Introduction. I cannot claim that they agree with everything in this book, but I certainly do agree with them. I have endeavored to write everything in this book in congruity with their statements on this subject.

With Justice Kennedy retiring and Ginsburg passing and with Gorsuch, Kavanaugh and Barrett having been nominated and confirmed, it appears that we shall enjoy a reprieve; though a tenuous one. We are hopeful of Gorsuch, Kavanaugh and Barrett, but they have yet to be proven. If a justice will judge by the law (the Constitution) then he will judge in favor of Christianity. But if he/she judges otherwise[5], then that justice will be a domestic enemy of the Constitution and an enemy of Christianity.

The average American is just now becoming aware of the attacks against religious liberty in America. Yet, it is worldwide and in varying degrees. We need to clarify the targets of these attacks. They are not against all religions. Just specific religions. Those within the Christian category and to some extent, the Jewish category also. In fact, these attacks against the Christian religion seem to be coming mainly from five sources-the Secular Humanists, evolutionists, the Muslims, the Marxists and the Globalists (advocates of one-world government).

Secular Humanism is a strange religion in that it attracts the loyalty of many others who are either members of no specific denomination or might even be members of any one of the various denominations. This might be due to the fact that, when closely compared, **the characteristics of the Humanist religion turn out to be just about the opposite of the Christian religion**. So, if a person's religion is somewhat different from the Christian religion, his religion, knowingly or not, coincides with and lends support to the Humanist religion. Chapter Five contains a graph which compares the principles of Christianity with those of Secular Humanism.

Please take note that the Secular Humanist religion is **never under attack by the courts nor the media. Nor are the Muslims nor the Marxists. Only the**

---

5. For more on this, see The Quest, on website www.joehferguson.com, chapters VIII and IX.

Christians and the Jews are under attack. The media is very selective in its attacks on religious liberties. They attack mostly Christians and Jews, never Secular Humanists and seldom Muslims any other anti-Christian sect.

The SCOTUS (or some members thereof) obviously has/have an agenda whose course diverges from that of the Constitution, from Christianity and the best interests of the American people. This agenda is to render the Constitution invalid and useless so as to change the laws so that the United States can be merged, politically and economically, with Mexico and Canada and then with a world government. If this is too startling for you to accept, just keep reading. Solid evidence will be provided.

If you are interested in religion, religious liberty, the law, history, the future of America, human psychology, truth and/or justice, I believe that you will find the contents of this book to be interesting and most useful.

Foreign enemies of the Constitution. And DOMESTIC ENEMIES OF THE CONSTITUTION, also.

When I was sworn in as a second lieutenant in the U. S. Air Force, I took an oath to "...defend the Constitution of the United States against all enemies, foreign and domestic." Most oaths of allegiance to the United States contain this or similar language. We know what a foreign enemy is, but what is a domestic enemy to the Constitution? It is so seldom spoken of. It is, especially, when an officer of government whether President, Legislator, judge, or other, takes an action that is in conflict with the Constitution. He thereby makes of himself a domestic enemy of the Constitution and of America. The idea of a domestic enemy of the Constitution is seldom given any thought. But it is very serious. It is equal to treason. Its frequency of occurrence and the fact that little is thought of it is another sign of intellectual and moral decadence in our nation, especially in those of our governments.

While the U. S. Supreme Court is the focus of this book, others who are complicit in these attacks against Christianity will be exposed.

As we proceed, you might think at times that I have wandered far afield from the subject of protecting religious liberties. But all of the information contained herein is helpful in understanding our enemies and how to expose, oppose and neutralize them.

For example, the foundation of the philosophy of the anti-Christ is evolution, Secular Humanism and Marxism. To effectively defend Christianity, we need to understand these hostile philosophies. They also constitute the foundation of the Secret Combinations of the Devil, which will be addressed briefly herein.

Note: If you have read my previous book, *The Quest:*[6] *To Identify the Secret Combinations of the Devil,* you will notice that much of the material for this book came from that one. The reason is that the same material fits both subjects. Nevertheless, there is much new material in this book and the emphasis on defending Christian liberty and exposing the Supreme Court.

Four Different Ways of Acquiring Knowledge

It has been said that there are four ways to acquire knowledge:

1. The first is the Scientific Method,
2. the second is the Analytical Method,
3. the third is the Academic Method
4. and the fourth is the Divine Method.

Regarding matters presented herein, I suggest that you use any of the first three methods that apply and then, finally, apply the Divine Method *with emphasis.*

Take the matter to the Lord. Very few of those who disagree with the contents of this book would suggest that you take the matter to the Lord. That in itself tells you a lot. I want you to come to the truth. Those who oppose the contents of this book do not. Does that not tell you something?

Many are completely unaware that there is a gigantic battle raging between good and evil. Between the forces of Christ and those of the Devil. Even most of those who are aware of it do not understand the magnitude of it. It is HUGE. Our enemies plan to take from us not only ALL of our property but our very souls as well. Is there anything NOT at stake in this battle? Many believe that there is no God, that God is dead. They are also completely unaware that there is a Devil and that he is very aggressive. Well, he is real and he is very actively pushing his agenda. The LDS KJV Bible Dictionary says this of the Devil:

> **The Devil ...is the enemy of righteousness and of those who seek to do the will of God.**
>
> **...Latter-day revelation confirms the biblical teaching that the Devil is a reality and that he does strive to lead men and women from the work of God. One of the major techniques of the Devil is to cause human beings to think they re following god's ways, when in reality they are deceived by the Devil to follow other paths...**
>
> **...He is miserable in his situation and "stirreth up the children of men unto secret combinations of murder and all manner of secret works of darkness" (2 Ne 9:9)**...(Emphasis added.)

---

6. On website http://www.joehferguson.com/

That is what we are up against. We need to devise a strategy to defend ourselves and to defeat the Devil and his minions.

Obstructions to Learning or Believing the Truth

Few people give much thought to what causes us to accept certain things as being true and rejecting others that we believe to be untrue. Our adversaries certainly give serious thought to this, since they strive to influence what we believe and how we behave. Here are a few thoughts to help us in this battle against the most evil of adversaries.

1. Fear. If our adversaries can cause us to be fearful, he can manipulate our emotions and our thinking. If he can convince us that if we do not believe a certain thing, we will be looked down upon or considered inferior, we will tend to accept it, regardless of the evidence for not believing it.
2. Peer pressure. We are all, in varying degrees, subject to peer pressure. We tend to "go with the herd."
3. We are reluctant to let go of presently-held beliefs. If we believe in "A" and are presented with another idea, which we shall call "B", we will reject "B" without giving it much thought.
4. There are many more. And some of the above-mentioned tendencies can in certain cases work to our favor instead of our detriment. The point is that we should exercise caution in what we choose to believe. Use a reliable set of standards to judge every idea. For example, for ideas regarding morality, use the Ten Commandments. For political ideas, use the Constitution.

How do I Know My Conclusions Are Correct?

Here is the method that I use to test my conclusions in this book and why I am convinced that they are correct. In addition to having spent thousands of hours of study on this subject:

1. The foundation of all of my beliefs is that God exists and that He has a son, Jesus Christ. They provide us with the most reliable information available.
2. We are not left alone. God, through His prophets, has provided us with some very accurate information to help us with our decisions on tough subjects.
3. The prophets, both modern and those writing to us around two thousand years ago, have warned us that the Devil will have his soldiers build up secret combinations to threaten our freedoms and our souls.
4. With some study, we are able to detect the workings of these secret combinations today. Their workings are what we should expect from the Devil's soldiers. They lie, cheat and, especially, corrupt the law in order to advantage themselves financially and to persecute Christians.
5. The Constitution of the United States was crafted by wise men that God raised up for this very purpose. They gave to us the greatest government ever created by the minds of men. (See D&C 101:80).

6. The disciples of Christ strive to defend the Constitution. The soldiers of the Devil strive to violate and to destroy the Constitution. The form of government that they favor is Marxism. They think like Marxists, advocate Marxist ideas, defend Marxist ideas and scorn the Constitution of the United States. The majority of them deny that they are Marxists. They lie about other things, too.
7. With study and time, a person can learn to detect the workings of the secret combinations in our day.
8. I can detect these workings, can see the parallel of today's secret combinations with those in ancient times.
9. The secret combinations have developed their own religion. It is exactly the opposite of the gospel of Jesus Christ. Should we be surprised? The SCs have caused that their religion, by the force of corrupted law, be taught in our public schools and **adopted as the de facto official religion** of the United States government.
10. Our adversaries, the SCs, corrupt the laws of the nation and then use these corrupted laws against us. Is that not exactly what soldiers of the Devil would do? They also create administrative and regulatory agencies that operate outside of the framework of the Constitution to gain power over us. Is that not what the soldiers of the Devil would do? The above reasons are why I am convinced that the information presented herein is accurate.

Jesus Christ Artwork - Public Domain

Chapter Two - The Value of Christianity in Civilized Society

Noah Webster- Wikimedia Commons

The Christian religion, in its purity, is the basis, or rather the source of all genuine freedom in government....and I am persuaded that no civil government of a republican form can exist and be durable in which the principles of that religion have not a controlling influence.

(Noah Webster1758-1843)

Note: This chapter is important to understanding the actions of the Supreme Court as the anti-Constitutional rulings of the Supreme Court are undermining the foundation upon which our civilized society depends.

Christianity the Foundation of Western Civilization

The foundation of Western Civilization was laid only about 2,000 years ago. That was when Christ started His ministry with 12 disciples in the midst of the polytheism and paganism of the Roman empire.

> "The ancient triumph of Christianity proved to be **the single greatest cultural transformation** our world has ever seen...Without it the entire history of Late Antiquity would not have happened as it did." (Ehrman, Bart D., *The Triumph of Christianity: How a Forbidden Religion Swept the World.* Quoted in Vance, Laurence M, "The Triumph of Christianity," *The New American,* Jun 18, 2018, p 29.

If we are going to defend the Christian religion, we must know what we are fighting *for* and what and who we are fighting *against.* Those who do not know what they are fighting *for* quickly become confused, disheartened, weak and ineffective. Those who do not know what they are fighting *against* do not know how to erect a proper defense. We Christians have a weakness that could prove fatal if we do not correct it. That is, we are too timid when it comes to defending Christ and his teachings. We are too afraid to offend those who are attacking us. Our attackers take advantage of this. When we say something to defend Christianity, our attackers *pretend* to be sorely offended. Well, since we have no desire to offend anyone, we tend to back down, or yield. So they win the debate or the political battle or whatever. We indeed do not wish to unduly offend innocent people. But then we must at times stand as boldly as did General Moroni. If our attackers feign being offended, well, just let them be offended. *Pretending* to be offended is an old, old tactic of the political left.

George Washington Explains the Value of Christianity to Successful Government

Of all the dispositions and habits, which lead to political prosperity, **Religion and Morality are indispensable supports**. In vain would that man claim the tribute of Patriotism, who should labor to subvert these great pillars of human happiness, these firmest props of the duties of Men and Citizens. The mere Politician, equally with the pious man, ought to respect and to cherish them. A volume could not trace all their connexions with private and public felicity.

Let it simply be asked; **Where is the security for property, for reputation, for life, <u>if the sense of religious obligation desert the oaths</u>, which are the instruments of investigation in Courts of Justice?** And let us with caution indulge the supposition, that morality can be maintained without religion. Whatever may be conceded to the influence of refined education on minds of peculiar structure, reason and experience both <u>**forbid us to expect**</u>, that **national morality can prevail in exclusion of religious principle**. (Excerpted from his Farewell Address.) (Emphasis added.)

If You Take Away Religion, You Cannot Hire Enough Police

Professor Clayton M. Christensen, Harvard Business School, stated, **" If you take away religion, you cannot hire enough police."** (Emphasis added.)

Christians are extremely valuable to any free society. It is they who provide the stability and who produce the most, who invest and keep the wheels of commerce turning. Furthermore, we require the *very least amount of government expenditure*. We require the least amount of police to keep law and order. We exercise self-restraint. We do not require exterior restraint as we are restrained from within. Our prisons, on the other hand, are filled with millions who have violated one or more of the Ten Commandments that required them to be apprehended, tried, convicted, incarcerated and cared for. These are the irreligious.

Clayton Christensen- Wikimedia Commons

Furthermore, we require less government welfare, since we are more disposed to work and to carefully manage our resources than are the anti-Christians.

We all are born into this world with some proclivities for being civil and some for being uncivil. We all have carnal tendencies. However, our Creator has given us intelligence. So when we are taught about Christianity and that we should not steal, nor kill, nor bear false witness nor do anything malicious to other people, our intelligence and our desire to be civil will overcome the carnal nature. That is what makes us civilized. Without this restraint on our carnal nature, we tend to be uncivilized. Robert Winthrop, (1809-1894. Once a Speaker of the U. S. House of Representatives and a contemporary of John Quincy Adams and Daniel Webster) explains the importance of self-control like this:

> Men, in a word, must necessarily be controlled either by a power within them or by a power without them; either by the Word of God or by the strong arm of man; either by the Bible or by the bayonet.[7]

Zephaniah Swift (1759-1823) Explains the Value of Christianity:

> Indeed moral virtue is substantially and essentially enforced by the precepts of Christianity and may be considered to be the basis of it. but in addition to moral principles, the Christian doctrines inculcate a purity of heart and holiness of life which constitutes its chief glory. When we contemplate it in this light, we have a most striking evidence of its superiority over all the systems of pagan philosophy, which were promulgated by the wisest men of ancient times.[8]

The Dollar Value of Christianity to America

By one account, in 2018 there were 2,279,000 inmates incarcerated in local, state and federal prisons in the U.S. If the cost averages $ 30,000.00 per inmate, that comes to a total of nearly $68.5 billion per year. Few of these people are producing anything. They are merely consuming. That is a real drag on the economy and the working taxpayers. Here is some interesting counsel from Kelly Shackelford, President, Chief Counsel and CEO of First Liberty Institute:

> Noted social historian Dr. Rodney Stark[9] of Baylor University undertook a comprehensive analysis of the positive impact of religion in the United

---

7. Robert Winthrop, Addresses and Speeches on Various Occasions (Boston, Little, Brown & Co., 1852, p. 172)
8. Quoted in Barton, David, Original Intent, Wallbuilders, Aledo, TX p. 33
9. Shackelford, Kelly, Undeniable The Survey of Hostility to Religion in America, 2016 Ed., First Liberty, Plano, TX, p. 6.
10. Stark, Rodney, America's Blessings (West Conshohocken, PA, Templeton Press, 2012, Kindle ed. 85%)

States in reducing crime, improving education, bettering mental and physical health, increasing employment and reducing welfare. He conservatively estimated the benefit to be at least *$ 2.67 trillion per year.*[10] Other scholars confirm this overall assertion. Can we afford to ignore such research and toss away the blessings of free religious exercise? (Emphasis added.)

Christianity and a Stable Society

Here is a quote from Professor Carroll Quigley that I consider to bear on this subject. In any society, moral values, the result of Christian teachings, produce stability. In our country, we can presume that all of the crimes committed, including the riotings, are the result of a deficiency of the stabilizing influence of self-disciplining, which is the result of Christian teachings. Here is Dr. Quigley:

> The difference between a stable society and an unstable one is that the restraints in an unstable one are external. In a stable society government ultimately becomes unnecessary; the restraints on people's actions are internal, they're self-disciplined. (From A-Z Quotes. I presume from *Tragedy and Hope* but I do not have the page number.)

Christianity and Civilization

At this point, it will be helpful to examine the definition of "civilized," "uncivilized" and the relationship between Christianity and civilization. Here is my definition of "civilized:"

> **Civilized:** People who respect the lives, liberties and properties of all others. The self-restraint which prevents them from committing crimes against their fellow citizens comes from within. It is because of the values in which they believe and by which they live. Each person willingly respects the lives, liberties and properties of all others. They do this not because of coercion or of the fear of punishment for the violation of laws, but out of genuine respect for others. "Civilized" people seek not only knowledge but wisdom; the truth in all subjects and all areas of study. They seek also the ability to recognize all untruth and the courage to reject it. Is America Civilized or Uncivilized? (Joe H. Ferguson, June, 2020.)

While some might argue that Christianity is not necessary for a people to be "civilized," it is beyond argument that respect for life (Thou shalt not kill), respect for property (thou shall not steal) and honesty and integrity (Thou shalt not bear false witness) are all foundational to both Christianity and to being "civilized." A "civilized" person is also a sane person. He accepts, believes and deals with reality. The Lord would lead us to be 100% sane. The Devil would drive us insane, if we let him.

Definition of "Civilization:" A group of people who are "civilized." Such a people require a minimum of police since they are not disposed to crime. Each citizen willingly and willfully respects the lives, liberties and properties of all other citizens. The laws are designed to protect the lives, liberties and properties of the citizens. The laws are designed to suppress crime by punishing those who are convicted of committing criminal acts. None of the laws are designed to deprive any innocent citizen of life, liberty or property or to give advantages to one group of citizens at the expense of others. The officers of government take oaths of office to uphold the law of the land and do so willingly. In the judicial system and all throughout the government, the rule of law is absolute. (Joe H. Ferguson)

> The principles of Christianity are inseparable from the principles of civilization.

While some might deny that Christianity is the foundation of "civilization," it is undeniable that respect for life (Thou shalt not kill), respect for property (thou shalt not steal) and honesty and integrity (Thou shalt not bear false witness) are foundational to both Christianity and to "civilization." Every civilized society tends to degenerate towards being uncivilized. This is due to the carnal nature of man. To maintain being civilized, there must be a sufficient number in that society using intelligence and exerting good influence (called "civic virtue") to overcome the destructive, debilitating and evil influences. In a "civilized" society, the people rate high on the sanity scale. They accept, believe and deal with reality.

Definition of "Uncivilized:" A person who does not respect the lives, liberties and properties of others. He prefers to rob others rather than working and being productive. He does not have a set of values by which he lives that involve a control from within to cause him to respect others. This "uncivilized" person might be a thug who preys upon victims in the streets, one who cheats or defrauds others or a highly sophisticated and respected person high in the echelons of business or government. Such a person does not live by the Ten Commandments. He/she rates low on the sanity scale. He might be very sophisticated, wear the finest of clothes and be successful in a certain sphere of employment or in government. But because they do not respect the lives, liberties and properties of others they are to a large degree "uncivilized." The Devil would drive us and seduce us to be 100 % uncivilized. (Joe H. Ferguson)

Definition of "Uncivilized Society:" A society of minimally civilized or of "uncivilized" people. The government rules by brute force and the threat of force. The rule of law is minimal or non-existent. The top ruler tends to be the most brutal, albeit the most cunning, in the nation. The people have no inalienable rights. Since no government is perfect, every government on earth is partly uncivilized. Every civilized society tends to degenerate towards being uncivilized because of the carnal nature of man. The signs of degeneration of a civilized society are:

1. The diminishment of the influence of Christianity;
2. An increase in intensity and magnitude of attacks upon Christians and Christianity;
3. The sanity level of the people diminishes; they tend to believe in and act upon myths and fantasies rather than reality;
4. The increase of pagan and hedonistic influence;
5. A diminishment in civic virtue in the government, with an attendant increase in government corruption and
6. A breakdown in the rule of law in all levels of society and especially in the judicial system and all throughout government. (Joe H. Ferguson)

At this point I must "jump the gun" and insert a ruling of the SCOTUS that, I believe, has a direct bearing on the high number of crimes committed and the large number of people incarcerated. It is just one of the insane rulings issued by the SCOTUS, which forbade the posting of the Ten Commandments in school rooms:

If the posted copies of the Ten Commandments are to have any effect at all, it will be to induce the schoolchildren to read, meditate upon, perhaps to venerate and obey, the Commandments. *Stone v. Graham*, 449 U.S. 39, 42 (1980).[11] (Emphasis added.)

Note: Oh my goodness! The students might obey the Ten Commandments! This would mean that they would not rob, kill, lie nor defraud! They might even stay out of jail! This also shows the fanaticism that some SCOTUS justices have against the Christian religion.

How weird indeed! Those who are supposed to be enforcing the Law of the Land in order to protect the lives, liberties and properties of the innocent, are themselves violating the Supreme Law of the Land in order to attack Christians, the most law-abiding citizens of the country!

---

11. Barton, David, Original Intent, The Courts, the Constitution & Religion, 4th Ed., 1st printing, WallBuilders, Aledo, TX, p. 172
12. Shackelford, Kelly, UNDENIABLE The Survey of Hostility to Religion in America, 2016 Ed., Plano, TX, pp. 6, 7.

To be a Christian is to be civilized. We seldom see a comparison between being a Christian and being civilized, but the two have very similar characteristics. For example:

1. A Christian does not take other people's lives.
2. A Christian does not take other people's property.
3. A Christian does not abuse other people or their property.
4. A Christian does not lie.
5. A Christian obeys the laws of the land.
6. A Christian works and produces goods needed by others.
7. A Christian treats others as he would like to be treated.

The above characteristics are the same as those required for people to be civilized. Without these characteristics, a person is not truly civilized. Without these characteristics in its citizens, a nation is not completely civilized. This is how important Christianity is to any people, to any culture or to any nation.

All Freedoms Depend Upon Freedom of Religion

Just look at every Communist country where there is very little freedom of anything. Deprivation of freedom of religion goes along inseparably with the deprivation of all other rights. Also, look at the members of the U. S. House and the U. S. Senate and how they vote. Those who vote to restrict freedom of religion also vote to restrict the freedom of everything else. Here is how Kelly Shackelford, President, CEO and Chief Counsel for First Liberty Institute explains it[12]:

> **Third, freedom of religion is foundational to all other freedoms.** From the beginning of the colonies and continuing until today, immigrants came to America for religious freedom. Freedom of religious conscience is part of a person's core identity and is embedded in America's cultural DNA. Further, religious freedom is in the First Amendment because all other freedoms rest upon it. Without the concept of a higher authority to make government accountable to unchanging principles of justice, all other freedoms are at risk of being violated, redefined, or revoked by government. As the Declaration of Independence says, all men are "endowed by their Creator with certain unalienable Rights....That to secure these rights, Governments are instituted among Men."
>
> The good news is that the vast majority of the hostility to religion you will read in this survey is unlawful. It succeeds only because of its own bluff and the passivity of its victims. Hostility to religion can be defeated in the legal system—but only if challenged by Americans like you. When you stand up, First Liberty Institute and your fellow Americans will be standing with you offering legal assistance, research and decisive help.

(Kelly Shackelford, President, CEO and Chief Counsel for First Liberty Institute.)(Plano, Texas)

Most civil and criminal laws are designed to punish the evildoer after the fact. These are necessary and have a positive force in society. However, they do not do what is most desirable and that is to prevent the commission of crimes before they happen. This is exactly what the spirit of Christ does in people. It prevents them from even wanting to commit harm to others even if there were no threat of punishment therefore. There is no better crime-prevention force in society. And its cost in tax dollars is zero.

The strongest civil code is impotent against malicious behavior unless the heart itself can be restrained.

The First Amendment and its Priorities

The First Amendment is designed to protect five precious freedoms. The Framers of the First considered the freedom of religion to be so important that they made it the very first priority.

Laws of High-Quality Demand Legislators of High Moral Values.

> **Jay Liechty:**[13]Religion constitutes a major part of the foundation of government, because the religious beliefs of the individuals who are in power will be reflected in the government's attitude toward individual freedom. *Persons who make the rules cannot avoid reflecting their religious convictions when they enact laws and they cannot escape setting the moral tone for a nation through those laws.* The laws enacted and the moral tone set, inherently reflect the religious views of those persons who dominate government and their religious views define the moral values, motivations and acceptable behaviors for society and consequently the level of personal peace and domestic tranquility.

Please keep the above comments of Elder Maxwell and of Liechty in mind as we proceed to the issue of the decline of moral values. As we shall see in Chapter Twelve in the *Everson* case wherein the SCOTUS in 1947 violated the Constitution many times in order to oppress and persecute Christianity and Christians.

The mention of God, the Ten Commandments or anything else of Christian nature **was outlawed in the public schools and public discourse**. This has had a disastrous effect upon the moral values of Americans. Liechty[14]

---

13. Liechty, Jay, America's State Church, Calder Press, 1995, p. 23

14. Liechty, Ibid, p. 149. 14

compares data from two time periods, the first 1955 to 1960 and the second 1983 to 1990.

1. SAT scores dropped from 970 to 900,
2. Gonorrhea age 15-19 400 per 100,000 to 1200,
3. premarital sex activity girls age 18 from 22% to 70% and,
4. Divorce 2.2 per 1000 to 4.8.

Yes, Christian influence plays a very large part in the quality of life of a people.

Counterattack: We stand by to defend Christianity and its principles. To stand prepared and ready to rise to defend its virtues, to expose those evil forces and their objectives.

> **President Ezra Taft Benson:** I testify that Lucifer was also in the council of heaven. He sought to destroy the agency of man. He rebelled. (See Moses 4:3.) There was a war in heaven and a third of the hosts were cast to the earth and denied a body. (See Rev. 12:7–9; D&C 29:36–37.) Lucifer is the enemy of all righteousness and seeks the misery of all mankind. (See 2 Ne. 2:18, 27; Mosiah 4:14.) (Ensign, Nov 1988)

Examples of Attacks Against Christians

God, His Religion, His Government for Man and His kingdom	The Devil, His Religion, His Government for Man and His Kingdom
Adam and Eve created, with spirits, by our Creator Moses—The Ten Commandments Jesus Christ Birth, ministry, baptism, crucifixion, résurrection	Date unknown. Man emerged, presumably by accident. No intelligence involved. Man has no spirit. Date unknown. Woman appears. No explanation as to how the human race was propagated from the time that man appeared to the time that woman appeared. No spirit.
The Great Apostasy 1455 The Bible printed in English The Renaissance 14?? to 18??	

1776 The *Declaration of Independence* 1781 The *Constitution of the United States* The United States of America Individual Justice Freedom of Religion 1830 The Gospel of Jesus Christ Restored by God the Father and Jesus Christ through the Prophet Joseph Smith, Jr. 1830 *Book of Mormon* printed	May 1, 1776 Adam Weishaupt organized the Illuminati—secret organization. 1848 Karl Marx published *Communist Manifesto.* 1848-2020 Many secret organizations organized. 1859 Darwin pub *Origin of the Species.*
	1917 Bolshevik revolution in Russia. Russia became Communist. 1921 Council on Foreign Relations organized. Objective is to merge U.S.A. into Globalist (Marxist-like) government. 1933 *Humanist Manifesto I* published. John Dewey a signatory. Subsequent to 1933, Evolution, Secular Humanism, Marxism mutually supportive. ACLU organized 1920 NLG organized 1937 1937 Gramsci dies. Prison Notebooks published
1950 Joesph McCarthy's Congressional Hearings on Communism takes hold and becomes very popular in America. (NOTE: by this point the Communists had already infiltrated.) 1959 The John Birch Society	1945 United Nations organized by Communists to favor Communists. 1947-SCOTUS outlawed the ten Commandments and prayer from American schools and public discourse through corrupted ruling in *Everson.*

organized by Robert Welch to defend the *Declaration* and the *Constitution of the United States*.	Secular Humanism becomes, de facto, **official state religion**.
Through 2020 Greatest Nation ever created. Industrial growth. Prosperity. 2020 America threatened. Future in doubt. All liberties, especially Christian liberties, threatened by Marxist government. SCOTUS great threat to Christianity and to America. Christianity threatened due to its teaching having been outlawed in the public schools by the SCOTUS. Many anti-Christ groups organized and active. The media and public education are hostile to Christianity.	

For some examples of some of the idiotic and insane attacks that are being lodged against Christians today, please refer, at your convenience, to Attachment "K" in the back of this book. There is a message from Mat Staver, chief counsel for Liberty Counsel. That is what we are up against. And the signs of the times indicate that they are going to get worse.

Help All People Understand Who the Real Enemies Are

When anyone attacks Christian people or Christianity itself, they inevitably strive to show Christianity in a bad light and themselves as "the good guy" or "the innocent victim who has been abused/discriminated against.") Because of the positive influence that Christianity has on society, when a person attacks Christianity, he is attacking society itself as well as the foundation of civility.

Chapter Three - Clues, Suspects and Motives and "Qui Bono"?

Note: This chapter is important to understand the actions of the Supreme Court since its actions are so contrary to its obligations and responsibilities.

First-"Qui Bono?"

This chapter will help us to understand the motives of court justices who vote against the Constitution in their rulings. Why would a person do such a thing? To vote for a ruling that would constitute a violation of his oath of office and his duty to the American people? Whenever we see such a thing, we can ask ourselves, "qui bono?" (Who benefits?)

When any good detective launches an investigation into a crime, he begins with searching for clues, suspects and motives. In order to understand who might be launching attacks against us, we need to know; who would benefit from attacking the most honest and law-abiding people in America?

> The actions of those who participate in the attacks on Christianity today are akin to those who participated in the crucifixion of Christ.

The answer is that these are the same kind of people who participated in the crucifixion of Christ. Their object was power and gain. The same is true today.

Some of the people attacking Christianity today are some of the most wealthy in the country. They know that Christians are more likely to support honest and limited, i.e. constitutional, government, than are the non-Christians. Christians and corrupt, i.e., Marxist government are not compatible. Just as Paul said to the Corinthians, in 2 Cor, 3:17:

> Now the Lord is that Spirit; and where the Spirit of the Lord *is,* there *is* liberty.

The above speaks a powerful, comprehensive and immutable truth. Consequently, those who wish to corrupt our government and replace it with a Marxist one so as to increase their power must first render impotent or eliminate the Christians. Now, let us look for some clues as to those who might fall into this category.

The Clues
It stands to reason that, if Christ were going to anticipate attacks upon His

religion and His people, that He surely would give to His people some assistance, some clues, in helping to identify those doing the attacking. He has given us some excellent ones. We can safely assume that the attackers would be ideologically opposed to Christ, Christianity and to Christians. And it seems reasonable to assume that the bearers of these clues, or information, would be His appointed prophets. So let's start with a very important statement by President David O. McKay issued at the April General Conference of the Church of Jesus Christ of Latter-day Saints in April of 1966. It is entitled: "Statement on Communism and the Constitution of the United States."

This statement gives us some very powerful clues as to the identity of those

---

**Statement on Communism
and the
Constitution of the United States**
(Excerpts therefrom)
April, 1966
by President David O. McKay

...The position of this Church on the subject of Communism has never changed. We consider it the greatest satanical threat to peace, prosperity and the spread of God's work among men that exists on the face of the earth...

...The entire concept and philosophy of Communism is diametrically opposed to everything for which the Church stand's — belief in Deity, belief in the dignity and eternal nature of man and the application of the gospel to efforts for peace in the world. Communism is militantly atheistic and is committed to the destruction of faith wherever it may be found...

...The Russian Commissar of Education wrote: "We must hate Christians and Christianity. Even the best of them must be considered our worst enemies. Christian love is an obstacle to the development of the revolution. Down with love for one's neighbor. What we want is hate. Only then shall we conquer the universe..."

...No member of this Church can be true to his faith, nor can any American be loyal to his trust, while lending aid, encouragement, or sympathy to any of these false philosophies; for if he does, they will prove snares to his feet.

who might be ideologically motivated to attack Christians and Christianity, or would benefit there from. That is, those who believe in Marxism and its companion ideology, also the antithesis of Christianity, which is Secular Humanism. Note the quote from the Russian Commissar of Education that Communists must hate Christians and Christianity. This is embedded in Communist thought and policy. We can also include Secular Humanism (or "irreligion" as stated by Elder Maxwell) and evolution as one of the "false philosophies" that bolsters and empowers Marxism and Communism.

Note: In President McKay's Statement on Communism, we can read "Marxism" for "Communism," as Communism is founded on Marxism. Note also that President McKay stated, "…any of these false philosophies," not just the false philosophy of Communism. So he must have meant all of the false philosophies related to Communism.

The Deep Left: Communists, Socialists, Marxists, some "Liberals" and "Progressives" We must suspect **all on the deep Left** as being enemies of Christians and Christianity. That is just their nature. That is part of being of the ideological deep left. Marxism is the foundation of the Deep Left political ideology and Marxism contains built-in hatred for Christianity. So in our defense of Christian liberties, let's always keep this in mind.

Lest you think that I am being too critical of "liberals", just answer, for yourself, "have I ever seen a "liberal" defend a pro-constitutionalist American"? And, "Have I ever seen a "liberal" criticize a Socialist, Marxist or Communist"? The foundation of "liberal" thought is evolution, Humanism and Marxism.

Saul Alinsky, (1909-1972) a Communist community organizer in Chicago, leaves no doubt as to which camp the political Left belong. In his *Rules For Radicals*,[15] he states **his allegiance to Lucifer**:

> Lest we forget at least an over-the shoulder **acknowledgment to the very first radical**: from all our legends, mythology and history (and who is to know where mythology leaves off and history begins—or which is which), the **first radical known to man** who **rebelled against the establishment** and did it so effectively that **he at least won his own kingdom**—**Lucifer**.

Make no mistake about it-the attacks on Christianity have been coming from and will continue to come from, the political Left-the "liberals," "progressives," "Socialists," "Communists," "Globalist" crowd. Although

---

15. Alinsky, Saul D, Rules For Radicals, Vintage Books, New York, 1971, p. Introduction—no page no.

many fail to realize it, the ideological alignment of the far Left against Christianity is very, very real and it is permanent. The irreligious, Secular Humanists, etc go with corrupt government (socialism, Communism, Marxism, etc) and Christians go with honest government, justice and liberty. This scripture explains a lot (2 Cor 3:17:)

> **Now the Lord is that Spirit: and where the Spirit of the Lord is, there *is* liberty.** (Emphasis added)

So that is it, pure and simple, where the Spirit of the Lord is, there is liberty. Where the Spirit of the Lord is not, there is not liberty. (There is Marxism, etc.)

The ACLU One of the founders of the ACLU (American Civil Liberties Union) was John Dewey, who was also a signatory to the Humanist Manifesto I. He also had close ties with the top Communists of the Communist hierarchy of Russia as he was chosen to preside over the trial of Leon Trotsky in Coyoacan, Mexico in 1938 Trotsky was assassinated in 1940. The ACLU is a legal team which consistently is involved in cases that aids the causes of the Left and, especially, against religious liberties.

The LGBT This is an extremely sensitive subject, since many Christian families have members of the LGBT. However, we must face reality. It appears that the LGBT leaders have joined with the Marxists to obtain their objectives. It appears that the LGBT crowd will do anything to gain special privileges for themselves in the legislatures and in the courts. The political and cultural objectives of the LGBT are consistent in conflict with religious liberties. Please prove me wrong. Nevertheless, we must be aware of the fact that there are many in the gay and lesbian communities who are, in spite of their conditions, striving to lead Christian lives. These individuals deserve our compassion and consideration.

Committee for Separation of Church and State The best way to understand the agenda of this organization is to understand that they are for "separation..." as misinterpreted by the SCOTUS and NOT as intended by President Thomas Jefferson in his letter to the Baptists in 1802. That explains it all.

The United Nations or the United Religious Initiative We are justified in being suspicious of anything coming from the UN or the URI, as the UN is basically a pro-Marxist world government (Globalist).

The World Council of Churches (WCC) Pacepa (p 107) describes the WCC as being under KGB influence and explained that the general secretary of the WCC endorsed liberation theology and made it part of the WCC agenda. This makes, de facto, the WCC a front for the KGB.

World Peace Council (WPC) Former Romanian General Ion Pacepa identified the WPC (with branches in 112 countries)[16] as a Communist front organization. States Pacepa, on p. 41: "Even the money for the WPC budget came from Moscow, delivered by Soviet intelligence officers in the form of laundered American dollars to hide its Soviet origin. (In 1989, when the Soviet Union was on the verge of collapse, the WPC publicly admitted that 90 percent of its money came from the KGB.)

The World Federation of Trade Unions (With branches in 90 countries). Cited in Pacepa, p. 38.

The Women's International Democratic Federation (With branches in 129 countries). Cited in Pacepa, p. 38.

Here is another clue, given to us by Paul in Ephesians 6:

> 12 For we wrestle not against flesh and blood, but against principalities, against powers, against the rulers of the darkness of this world, against spiritual wickedness in high places.

And yet another, given to us in Alma 10:

> 27 And now behold, I say unto you, that the foundation of the destruction of this people is beginning to be laid by the unrighteousness of your lawyers and your judges.

Wow!! The above is right on the money in helping us to identify (certain) SCOTUS judges as enemies of Christ and of Christians. When we examine those who are attacking Christianity today, we will certainly find that many, if not most, are Marxists or Humanists (even if they deny it), they sit in high places where they commit wickedness. Some are in the SCOTUS and they definitely are laying the foundation of the destruction of this people. I would say that the Lord has given us some really good clues to start with. If lying and violating the Constitution constitutes wickedness and unrighteousness, then certain justices of the SCOTUS are certainly guilty.

Alma's warning, above, is certainly helpful in alerting us to the fact that there are *some* lawyers and *some* judges who are enemies of Christianity. The most positive means, however, is the examination of their behavior and court cases heretofore. When they deliberately corrupt the law and then deliberately use this corrupted law to suppress Christianity and to persecute Christians, this leaves little doubt that they choose to be enemies of Christianity, of Christians and of Christ.

---

16. Pacepa, Ion Mihai, Disinformation, WND Books, Washington, D. C., p. 38

Now, a word on "Communists" and "Marxists." The U. S. education system has been infiltrated and subverted and teaches much Marxism to the students without labeling it as such. Therefore, many students are led to believe in Marxist principles, programs and ideas without knowing it. They are being tricked. So the degree of culpability varies markedly from the hard-core conspiring Marxist to the young college kid who has been, unknowing to himself, taught a lot of Marxist poison. Hereinafter, we will talk of Marxists as those who understand what Marxism is and knowingly embrace it. Those who believe in Marxism unknowingly would probably identify themselves as "liberals" or "progressives".

In being alert to any person or organization that might do harm to Christianity, we should always keep the following in mind:

1. Those who are ideologically opposed to Christian principles.
2. Those who are in a position to warp our perceptions, to manipulate our thinking.
3. Those who are in positions of power in government who might attack us.
4. Those who might benefit in any way by harming Christians or Christianity.
5. Those who have declared hostility or antipathy toward Christianity, such as the Marxists, the Secular Humanists, the evolutionists and the Muslims.
6. Those organizations and persons that/who have been, historically, antagonists of Christianity.
7. Those organizations and persons that the prophets have warned us about who might wish to do us harm. Especially, Communists. Most people believe in parts of Marxism, albeit unknowingly, in varying degrees because such ideas are ubiquitous in education and in the media.

Chapter Four - Gramsci's Long March Through the Institutions

Takeover by Subversion and Ideological Dominance

> 38 ...the Nephites **did build them up and support them,** [secret combinations] **beginning** at the more wicked part of them, until they had **overspread all the land** of the Nephites and had **seduced the more part of <u>the righteous</u>** until they had come down to believe in their works and partake in their spoils and **to join with them** in their secret murders and combinations.
> 39 And thus **they did obtain the sole management of the government,**...(Hel 6)

Note: This Chapter is important to understand the actions of the Supreme Court since it is one of the prime institutions targeted to be taken over by our enemies. It has been, to a great deal.

Gramsci and the Supreme Court

To understand Gramsci is to better understand the Supreme Court turning against the American people. The Supreme Court is an American institution. Gramsci's mission was to facilitate the Marxists in taking over any country. To do so, they must convert the institutions of that country to be against the ideology upon which that country is based and the best interests of that country. They must convert those in positions of authority in those institutions to be anti-American, to be Marxists, to be "domestic enemies of the Constitution."

Gramsci and the Nephites

This chapter deals with evil forces seducing even the righteous to believe in their evil works so that an entire country can be captured and dominated. What Helaman described above is identical to what is happening to Americans in America today. It is as if Gramsci took lessons from the Nephite secret combinations.

Antonio Gramsci and the Secret Combinations

"What does Antonio Gramsci, an obscure Italian Communist theoretician, have to do with the Secret Combinations of the Devil and Religious

Antonio Gramsci- Creative Commons

liberties"? You are well justified in asking. The answer: Gramsci has affected the life of every American. While in prison, he wrote *Prison Notebooks* from which we learn about the "long march through the institutions" and "cultural hegemony."

When we learn about these, we begin to get an inkling about what has been happening to our culture, our education, our government and our legal system for the past 100 years. Let's start with the term, "cultural hegemony":

> In Marxist philosophy, cultural hegemony is the domination of a culturally diverse society by the ruling class (whether benevolent or malevolent, elected or otherwise) whose beliefs, perceptions, expectations, values and mores become <u>the accepted cultural norm</u>. This norm justifies the social, political and economic status as natural and inevitable, perpetual and presumably beneficial for everyone. (From Gramsci, modified by Joe H. Ferguson, March, 2017) (Emphasis added).

Gramsci's writings have become adapted by Communists and others (such as the Globalists who are planning to rule the world through a Marxist-like world government) throughout America and throughout America's institutions. Lenin, Stalin, Castro and Mao achieved Communism by militant force, mass murders and conquest. Gramsci's plan is entirely different, but no less effective and with near zero risk to the Marxist revolutionaries.

His plan is to surreptitiously **capture control of the institutions of a nation**. That is, of education, the media, religion, art, literature, entertainment, politics and, ultimately, the law and, especially, the courts. Gramsci's plan includes capturing the minds; the worldviews, of all those who hold positions in the legal system, from the deans of the law schools to the justices of the U. S. Supreme Court. I

n fact, it means capturing the worldview of all those involved in the other disciplines as well. Through the eyes of an honest American, this process would constitute subversion. Gramsci called it the **"Long march through the institutions."**

This process has been going on for well over a century in America. Its progress has been so gradual that we have been unaware of it or, at least, not alarmed. That is why we are now in the latter stages of a Communist/Globalist takeover of America. The Communists/Globalists and their useful idiots control a large portion of the positions of power. Fortunately, the greater portion of Americans still desire freedom, although they do not understand the principles of government that results in freedom.

Gramsci's ultimate concern was with, as with all Communists, how power works; how it is exercised by those in positions of power and how those who are out of power can wrest it from those who are in power. He realized that, ultimately, power is a reflection of the culture. Instead of conquering a people, Gramsci devised a plan to have the people *desire* **Communism. To believe** in

Communist principles and programs even though they might not realize where those principles and programs came from or to where they might take them.

While Gramsci was critical of Marx in areas, they were soul mates in their ultimate objective and in their hatred of Americanism and the Constitution. They were both enemies of freedom.

The foundation of Gramsci's plan calls for persuading the people to believe in the principles upon which Communist governments are built, while at the same time thinking that these principles will result in their freedom and prosperity. An example: convincing the workers of the world that they are "uniting to throw off their chains" while demonstrating in support of a Communist law or program.

The power of cultural hegemony lies in, among other things, its invisibility. Its power, without guns or the use of force, is unconsciously obeyed by those who live under it. Thus, by changing the culture, the beliefs and behavior of the populace can be changed. The culture can be changed by what is taught to the students in the schools and universities. It can be changed by what is presented to the people by the media. It can be changed by the nature of what is called entertainment. This change in the culture inevitably results in changes in the laws; in the government, especially in the courts.

> For the Communists or Globalists to take over America, they must first destroy the Christian Worldview and its Christian cultural hegemony. The Christian foundation of American culture and law.

Conversely, the worldviews of the people and consequently the culture can be changed by court rulings that take a departure from the established culture. Whether the law is good or corrupt, we are forced to alter our thinking and our behavior to comply with it. So, the Marxists realize that, by changing the law toward more Marxism, the people will be forced to comply with a corresponding change in their thinking and behavior. So a change in the hegemony can result in a change in the law and also a change in the law can result in a change in the hegemony. Much more on this later.

America was built on Christian principles. So, for Communists (or any other like group) to take over America, they must change or destroy the Christian worldview of the people and, consequently, its Christian culture. Its Christian cultural hegemony. The Christian foundation of American culture and law.

Changes in the culture are often gradual and insidious. The end results are certainly political and legal, but very few in the culture recognize it. They perceive the "new normal" after the change as merely "just the way things are". This makes changes a lot harder to recognize, much less resist. When the new culture becomes hegemonic, it becomes "comfortable" for the majority of the people. The laws can then be changed to fit the new hegemony without resistance from or even with the approval of the majority of the people.

The secret combinations are certainly committed to changing America to a Marxist dictatorship. They are very successful at it, mainly because very few Americans understand that this is taking place. For us to be able to prevent them from achieving their ultimate objective, we must understand their plan. If we do not understand it, they are surely going to win. And we are surely going to lose. **We and our posterity will lose freedom forever**. Freedom will be abolished. **Christianity will be outlawed**. This will be for an undetermined number of years. Or decades. Or centuries. As per Lucifer's ultimate plan for the people of Earth.

What Gramsci did not realize, nor do the millions of "liberals," "progressives," "Socialists," and "Communists" who are committing their lives and their souls to furthering the objectives of Gramsci, is that in building the government structure built on the Ten Points of the Communist Manifesto, the "Communist utopia," they are actually building the structure which the Secret Combinations of the Devil plan to eventually use to enslave us all, **including them**. It is the ultimate irony that the Communists are working to build a power structure to be controlled by the wealthiest of the elite capitalists. This will be explained more in the chapter on Marxism.

Briefly-the Communists and the "capitalist ruling elite" today are working to destroy our constitutional form of government. They are also both working to construct, in its place, a totalitarian Marxist dictatorship. Hold on. Don't drop out. Solid evidence of this will be presented hereinafter.

The Constitution was built on a Christian foundation. Communism is built on an atheistic foundation. So the Communist plan necessitates destroying the people's belief in Christianity or, at least, in the *principles* of Christianity, in order to change the culture, the cultural hegemony, the laws and the government. This is the main reason for the attacks against Christianity.

The hatred that we see in the rioters and in most Democrats is a hatred for a government built on a Christian foundation. This necessitates a hatred for Christianity itself and for Christians. Thus, the war against Christianity is being waged not only by the rabble in the streets but by the anti-American, super-wealthy and their puppets, the pro-Marxist (call them "liberal" or "progressive" if you wish—the result is the same) judges in the Supreme Court.

To measure the extent that Gramsci's "Long march…" has had on our institutions, consider Harvard and Yale. Harvard was founded in 1636 to educate students for the clergy. Yale was founded in 1701 by Congregationalist ministers. One faculty member said, about 1800, "Yale

College is a little temple; prayer and praise seem to be the delight of the greater part of the students." They used to be beautiful colleges, but as the song goes, "But Baby, look at them now!"

These rabble in the streets appear that they hate America, hate Americans, hate Christians, but they **do not have any understanding of why they do**. It seems like they have been programmed. Some way, some how, by somebody. General Pacepa's (about whom more later) reports indicate that it is highly probable that the KGB/ FSB of Russia has been active in America. Most of those people in the riots (this is being written in June of 2020, with much rioting around the country) appear to be very ignorant and uneducated and very emotional. Probably high on something, also. They would be easy prey for some KGB organizers.

This struggle that is being waged is not "merely" about freedom. It is not "merely" political. It is all that, but it is also a struggle **between the forces of Christ versus the forces of Satan**. There is no better application of our time and talents than to make sure that we are on the right side of this struggle. We must be very careful of what we choose to believe, whether it be in history, art, English, science, political science or law. Particularly the law.

Since Gramsci's long march suggests an army of soldiers, let us henceforth refer to those who push Gramsci's Marxist agenda, be they "liberals," "progressives," "Marxists," Globalists, secular humanists or whatever, as "Gramsci's soldiers" or "his soldiers."

The ultimate objective of this long march is a matter of altering worldviews and transferring allegiances. Allegiances from Christianity to Humanism and from Americanism (constitutionalism) to Marxism. The causative forces of this transference is at times subtle and at times violent. The people being affected usually are not aware of this transference of allegiances. They end up thinking and behaving like Humanists and Marxists but do not understand that they are doing so nor do they know why.

Now, let's see the devastation that Gramsci has left in America with his "Long March Through the Institutions."

Let's start with what I consider to be the three greatest hoaxes ever to afflict mankind, the theory of evolution, Secular Humanism and Marxism. We will then examine their effect upon our culture, our legal system and how they help the Secret Combinations.

Gramsci's "Long March Through the Institutions" consists mainly of converting the perceptions, or worldviews, of each individual and of all individuals (the cultural hegemony) collectively. Converting perceptions from Christianity, with Adam and Eve to evolution, from Christianity (the gospel of

Jesus Christ) to Secular Humanism and from Christianity (Liberty) to Marxism. It is astounding to see how effective his soldiers have been in this long march.

Definitions for "Sanity" and "Insanity" for Today's Political Environment

A quote attributed to Einstein is: "Insanity is doing the same thing over and over and expecting different results." Another definition of "insanity" might be:

> **Insanity**: the inability or the *unwillingness* to accept reality in one form or another.
> This definition might not be all-inclusive, but it is certainly accurate. This is the definition which I will apply to those who have fallen victim (as I had, in my youth) to any portion of the three hoaxes of evolution, secular Humanism or Marxism. Since all three of these are untrue, they are also unreal. (Joe H. Ferguson June 2020)

The opposite of insanity would be, of course, sanity, the definition of which would be:

> **Sanity:** The ability and willingness to accept reality in every form. (Joe H. Ferguson June 2020)

It is a sobering thought to perceive oneself as being insane. But think seriously. All of us perceive something in life differently than it actually is. I now acknowledge that I presently see some things much differently than I did fifty or sixty years ago. That means that I was partly insane back then. And, I admit, that I might be partially insane at present, although I am constantly seeking the truth in all matters. That is, to be able to perceive all matters as they actually are. Ask yourself if you do not perceive some things differently than you did one, five, ten or twenty years ago. Then you can realize that the way that you perceived them before was incorrect and that you are more sane now than way back then.

As a practical matter, what is the difference between a person being *unable* to accept reality and a person who is, because of unreal (false) ideologies that distort his worldview, *unwilling* to accept reality?

The reason that it is necessary to review the definitions of "insanity" and "sanity" is that we are dealing with people who are considered completely sane but who are unwilling or unable to accept reality in politics, law, various theories or whatever.

To believe something to be true when it is actually false is to believe something, due to inability or unwillingness, that is different than the truth. Just consider that if everything a person were to believe were to be false. Would not that person be insane? A person can get along fairly well being, say, 80% sane. That would be 20% insane. This definition of insanity brings us to the reality that the Devil, as he seduces us to believe his false philosophies, strives to drive us insane. Scary thought, huh? If the Devil can drive us insane, he can seduce us into supporting the principles of government that will eventually enslave us.

It does seem to me that if a person were to believe 100% truths, he would be 100% sane. If he believes 100% falsehoods, he would be 100% insane. What brought me to this belief is in listening to some politicians and political candidates. Some of the things they say are absolutely insane! They are totally false! They bear no resemblance to reality or to sanity! Some of these people believe lies for so long that they just cannot believe a truth. I believe strongly that truths beget truths and lies beget lies. It is true that some people with a high degree of insanity seem to get along in Washington, D. C. But then, there are a lot of insane people running around there. In D.C., they are considered to be the norm. Please inform me by email (at the close) what you think about my theory of sanity/insanity.

If the gospel of Jesus Christ is true, then its opposite must be untrue. So the Devil is constantly trying to believe what is not true, to drive us insane. Understanding and believing (100%) the gospel of Christ is total sanity and believing 100% the opposite is total insanity. That's the way I see it. Although, some people might think that I might be just a little bit *c r a z y*. But I am happy with striving toward understanding and believing the gospel a hundred percent.

Tragedy and Hope: Dr. Carroll Quigley, One of "Them", Exposes Conspiracies

Carroll Quigley- Public Domain

Extensive efforts have been expended to confuse the American people about the existence and influence of conspiracies. Some on the Left even advocate that anyone who believes in "conspiracy theories" are wacko. Here is some information about and from Professor Carroll Quigley that bears on the question.

Carroll Quigley (1910-1977) was a professor at Georgetown who had contacts with some of the ruling elite who hold memberships in some of the powerful secret combinations that are mentioned herein. Hardly anything gets done in U. S. politics without their approval. And when they want something, they get it. To show their power, the cabinet of every president - Republican OR Democrat - is ALWAYS filled with members of the CFR. That is POWER!!! At one time, three out of the nine justices on the SCOTUS were members of the CFR (O'Connor, Breyer and Ginsburg). Now, THAT IS POWER!!!

Quigley was very friendly with these people and managed to get access to some of their most confidential records covering about 1880 to 1963. While these people, like Rockefeller, operated in the tightest secrecy, Quigley thought their influence was of such importance that it should be made public.

In 1966, he published his 1348 page tome entitled *Tragedy and Hope*. It was exactly what the conservative crowd was looking for. It blew the lid off of the secrecy of these organizations. The first edition quickly sold out. Mostly to conservatives. In spite of its great success, there was no second edition. (At least not for a long time. They are again available). Somebody had put the clamps on the printing of the second edition.

Two books, *The Naked Capitalist,* by Cleon Skousen and *None Dare Call It Conspiracy* by Gary Allen and Larry Abraham were written taking excerpts from *Tragedy and Hope*. Both quickly became best sellers. *Tragedy and Hope* was the real deal. It was a HUGE help in helping to convince average Americans that these secret organizations did indeed exist and that their agendas were definitely counter to the best interests of America and to average Americans. Here are some quotes from Quigley, presumably from *Tragedy and Hope*. I do not have the page numbers, since I obtained these quotes not directly from the book but from AZ Quotes.com:

> The Council on Foreign Relations is the American branch of a society which originated in England ... [and] ... believes national boundaries should be obliterated and one-world rule established.~ (Carroll Quigley)

> For the first time in its history, Western Civilization is in danger of being destroyed internally by a corrupt, criminal ruling cabal which is centered around the Rockefeller interests, which include elements from the Morgan, Brown, Rothschild, Du Pont, Harriman, Kuhn-Loeb and other groupings as well. This junta took control of the political, financial and cultural life of America in the first two decades of the twentieth century. (Carroll Quigley)

> There does exist and has existed for a generation, an international Anglophile network which operates, to some extent, in the way the radical Right believes the Communists act. In fact, this network, which we may identify as the Round Table groups, has no aversion to cooperating with the Communists, or any other groups and frequently does so. I know of the operations of this network because I have studied it for 20 years and was permitted for two years, in the early 1960s, to examine its papers and secret record. (Carroll Quigley)

> I am now quite sure that *Tragedy and Hope* was suppressed although I do not know why or by whom. [Author Carroll Quigley, referring to the second printing of his book.]

Carroll Quigley explained, in *Tragedy and Hope,* how the CFR has, for an hundred years, contributed to the distribution of ideologies to weaken America and also effecting the strategic placement of its hand-picked people in high positions in most administrations since 1920. These CFR people have strongly influenced the presidents and the direction of this entire nation. It is probable that the CFR is the most powerful political force in the world. Yet, we hear nothing about it in the mainstream media.

Gramsci and Sun Tzu

Sun Tzu was a Chinese military general and strategist who lived about the sixth century B. C. His strategies were very similar to those of Gramsci. In his book, *The Art of War,* he states:

> "The supreme art of war is to subdue the enemy without fighting."
> "Victorious warriors win first and then go to war, while defeated warriors go to war first and then seek to win."
> "Know thy self, know thy enemy. A thousand battles, a thousand victories."
> "To fight and conquer in all our battles is not supreme excellence; supreme excellence consists in breaking the enemy's resistance without fighting."

We are being conquered by the Sun Tzu-Gramsci strategy. We are near the end of a Communist revolution. The enemy is working hard. Most Americans do not even realize that we are under attack and that we are losing the battle.

The objective of Gramsci is to convince Americans to believe, embrace and support beliefs and programs that are contrary to their own best interests. Crazy! Insane! But Gramsci is being very successful.

Chapter Five - Christianity, Secular Humanism, Evolution and Marxism

Ever learning and never able to come to the knowledge of the truth (2 Timothy 3:7)

> 2 Nephi 28:20: For behold, at that day shall he [Satan] rage in the hearts of the children of men and stir them up to anger against that which is good.
> 21 And others will he pacify and lull them away into carnal security, that they will say: All is well in Zion; yea, Zion prospereth, all is well—and thus the Devil cheateth their souls and leadeth them away carefully down to hell.
> 22 And behold, others he flattereth away and telleth them there is no hell; and he saith unto them: I am no Devil, for there is none—and thus he whispereth in their ears, until he grasps them with his awful chains, from whence there is no deliverance...
> 24 ...Therefore, wo be unto him that is at ease in Zion!

And

> 2 Nephi 26: 21: And there are many churches built up which cause envyings and strifes and malice.
> 22 And there are also secret combinations, even as in times of old, according to the combinations of the Devil, for he is the founder of all these things; yea, the founder of murder and works of darkness; and he leadeth them by the neck with a flaxen cord, until he bindeth them with his strong cords forever.

Note: To understand the decisions of the Court, it is very helpful to understand the various forces at work in the culture of the nation. A justice will perceive a case with a very different worldview if he is a Secular Humanist, an evolutionist or a Marxist than if he were a Christian. His worldview will very definitely affect what he perceives the ruling should be. There are many Court rulings where the Marxist or Secular Humanist influences are very evident.

Wickedness Never Did Engender Good Judgment; or Wisdom. A person whose worldview and behavior is what we would consider to be "wicked" will perceive any situation, its values and its judgments, much differently than will one with a Christian worldview and behavior. Likewise, the Holy Ghost will help a righteous person to learn all things pertaining to righteousness whereas he might not help the wicked with the same objective. Since this book addresses things of moral importance such as liberty and the Ten

Commandments, I suggest that the more righteous a person is who is studying this book, the more understanding he will gain.

My 57 years of involvement in this political battle convinces me that the wicked gravitate toward the political Left, consciously or otherwise and the righteous gravitate toward the Right. The Left seems to attract Socialists and Communists. The Right seems to attract lovers of constitutional government. Remember, righteous thought and behavior engenders good judgment and wisdom.

Also, if you are a parent, you will find this chapter to be especially helpful.

Identifying the Enemies of Christ

Wow! That's pretty serious stuff! But if the prophet Nephi said it, (Please refer back to the quotes from Nephi, above.) I believe it! And it can help us in identifying the enemies of Christ and of Christianity (the irreligious.) So Satan wants to pacify us and lull us into carnal security. That must mean that he wants to convince us that his secret combinations and the philosophies that support them do not exist. And how does he bind us with his strong cords forever? It must be that he binds us down with his false and anti-Christ philosophies. Let's take a serious look at this Secular Humanism to see how it fits in with the great scheme of things.

Secular Humanism an Anti-Christ Church

Many groups qualify as being anti-Christian. But it seems that any time some action is taken against the Christians, the Secular Humanist footprints are all over it. Let's take a serious look at the ideology of the Secular Humanists and see how it compares with Christianity. We are not left with speculation alone. We can take it from the Humanists themselves. They have published their *Humanist Manifesto I, II and III* for us to examine. Here are excerpts from *I and II*:

From *Humanist Manifesto I:*(1933)

> **First Point:** Religious humanists regard the universe as self-existing and not created.
> **Second Point:** Humanism believes that man is a part of nature and that he has emerged as a result of a continuous process.
> **Third Point:** Holding an organic view of life, humanists find that the traditional dualism of mind and body [body and spirit] must be rejected.
> **Fifth Point:** Humanism asserts that the nature of the universe depicted by modern science makes unacceptable any supernatural or cosmic guarantees of human values. [No God. No Creator. No Adam nor Eve. No Moses. No Ten Commandments. No Jesus Christ nor His gospel.]

Sixth Point: We are convinced that the time has passed for theism, deism, modernism and...

Tenth Point: It follows that there will be no uniquely religious emotions and attitudes of the kind hitherto associated with belief in the supernatural.

It is interesting to note that John Dewey (1859-1952), who was very influential in directing the path of early American education, was a signatory to the *Humanist Manifesto I.* He was also directly connected with the top Communists of Russia.

From *Humanist Manifesto II:* (1973)

FIRST Point: ...We believe, however, that traditional dogmatic or authoritarian religions that place religion, God, ritual or creed above human needs and experience do a disservice to the human species...As non-theists, we begin with humans not God, nature not deity, Nature may indeed...

SECOND Point: Promises of immortal salvation or fear of eternal damnation are both illusory and harmful. They *distract humans from present concerns, from… Modern science discredits such historic concepts as the"separable soul." Rather, science affirms that the human species is an emergence from natural evolutionary forces...There is no credible evidence that life survives the death of the body...* (Emphasis added).

SIXTH Point: In the area of sexuality, we believe that intolerant attitudes, often cultivated by orthodox religions and puritanical cultures, unduly repress sexual conduct. The right to birth control, abortion, [Roe v Wade] and divorce should be recognized...sexual behavior between consenting adults...individuals should be permitted to express their sexual proclivities and pursue their lifestyles as they desire.

Note: Re SIXTH above: When all restraints such as the Ten Commandments and our accountability to God are removed and Humanists encouraging sexual behavior as stated above and with the natural sexual drives built into men and women, Humanism encourages all kinds of sexual behavior, not excluding illicit, erotic and deviant. It accomplishes this by removing the internal restraint that causes a person to be civilized: Christianity, including the Ten Commandments.

Note that the Secular Humanist values do not exclude:
1. Sex outside of matrimony,
2. Sex between two or more of the same gender,
3. Adultery
4. Pedophilia or even
5. Bestiality and
6 Coprophilia.

Bringing it all into focus; let's examine a table contrasting the principles of Christianity with those of Secular Humanism:

Principles of Christianity and of Secular Humanism Compared

	Christianity	Secular Humanism
1	Man created by a Creator	Man evolved spontaneously
2	Adam and Eve, the first humans and who were created by our Creator.	Adam and Eve are myths.
3	The concept of a spirit-an extremely important component as to who we are.	Non-theists. Monism. Man is a body only. There is no such thing as a spirit.
4	The fall of Adam.	Adam is a myth. He never existed.
5	Laws given by the Creator (the Ten Commandments) by which man is to live.	Ten Commandments a myth. The laws of man are the highest laws. Nothing superior to the intelligence of man.
6	The existence of an adversary, usually called the Devil.	The concept of a Devil is a myth. Believe nothing supernatural.
7	Accountability to our Creator for our actions while in this mortal state.	No Creator and no accountability.
8	The concept of sin.	Concept of sin a myth.
9	Repentance and the need thereof.	Need for repentance not acknowledged.
10	The need for forgiveness.	No need for forgiveness.
11	The need for a savior.	Denies the reality of/need for a savior.
12	The necessity of baptism	Denies need for baptism.
13	The atonement.	No such thing as the atonement.
14	The Resurrection.	No such thing as a resurrection.

15	Salvation	No such thing as salvation.
16	Life after mortal death; eternal life.	Neither life nor judgment after mortal death

(Note re soul-spirit: We existed as spirits before being born into mortality, when our spirits took on our mortal bodies. At mortal death, our spirits separate from our bodies. At resurrection, our spirits reunite with our resurrected bodies and the resurrected body and the spirit comprise our soul. Our spirits and our bodies will never after that be separated.) (See D&C 18:15-17).

The above clearly shows that Humanism is definitely not neutral to Christianity. It is the exact opposite. It is as if the Devil himself decided to think up a religion to trick and trap us earth mortals and to bind us down with his strong cords forever. That does not necessarily mean that all Humanists want to be enemies of Christians. However, the actions of the leaders of the Humanist movement certainly make it clear that they do.

All throughout the SH Manifestos, it is made clear that they deny the existence of anything supernatural; They deny God. They deny Jesus Christ. They deny the Ten Commandments. They deny that man is comprised of a body and a spirit. They deny anything associated with Christianity. The Humanists reaffirm their belief in evolution as the origin of man. They also deny the Ten Commandments as a guideline for man to live by while in mortality. Their "god" is mankind. Their ethics are purely man-made. Nothing is superior to human intellect. They put the creature superior to the Creator. Humanism is completely congruent with the theory of evolution and with Marxism. We might liken the Humanists to very ambitious salesmen selling an inferior product. How have the Humanists managed to get their religion forced onto every American education system? (Coming up shortly.)

The Secular Humanist Manifestos also deny that there is a Devil. Whether the Humanists themselves realize that they believe in a religion that appears to be the Devil's own is not known.

Question: Is Secular Humanism a "Religion?"

One premise of this book is that Secular Humanism is a religion. The Humanists deny that they are a "religion." As we proceed, we will see that they must do so in order to achieve their objectives. But then, are they denying what they really are for: the definite purpose of gaining a strategic advantage in their war on other religions? I think so and here is why. The definition of "religion":

> As used in constitutional provisions of the First Amendment forbidding the "establishment of religion" the term means **a particular system of faith and worship recognized and practiced by a particular church, sect, or denomination.** "Reynolds v. U. S. . U. S. 98 (*Black's Law Dictionary*) (Emphasis added)

In the 1960s, the Court expanded its view of religion. In its 1961 decision Torcaso v. Watkins, the Court stated that the establishment clause prevents government from aiding "those religions based on a belief in the existence of God as against those religions founded on different beliefs." In a footnote, the Court clarified that this principle extended to "religions in this country which do not teach what would generally be considered a belief in the existence of God ... Buddhism, Taoism, Ethical Culture, Secular Humanism and others."

The Jan-Feb issue of *The Humanist Magazine* published an article by Humanist John Dunphy entitled, "A Religion For a New age". That seems to me evidence enough that the Humanists themselves consider Humanism to be a religion. They seem to be playing it cagey. Humanism has all of the characteristics of a religion, but the **Humanists do not want their religion to be recognized as a religion by the courts** for legal purposes. If it were, then it would be subject to the same restrictions as the Christian religions are. That would mean that their religion would be kicked out of the public schools. It seems that the courts are playing along with the Humanists in this game.

Humanists, Marxists and Globalists Have No Limits to Their Ultimate Quest For Control of America

The Humanists, Marxists and Globalists have combined to achieve their mutual objectives. In fact, it appears that most Humanists are Marxists and most Marxists are Humanists. Humanism and Marxism are totally compatible. The three ideologies overlap considerably in their political objectives to destroy constitutional government and merge the United States into a global government. All three are very aggressive in furthering their objectives. They are completely intolerant of Christians and Christianity. It is obvious that their objective is to increase the oppression of Christians until we are eradicated from the face of the earth.

The Humanists keep a very low profile. Very few Americans know anything about them. Yet, they are politically very powerful. Humanist footprints are all over various SCOTUS cases that negatively impact Christianity, such as those that hang on the corrupted version of "Separation of church and state" and *Obergefell v. Hodges.* When one reads these cases, he can see Humanist footprints all over them. In other words, it does appear that the judges who voted in the majority in those cases substituted the Humanist Manifesto for the Constitution.

Defense against Humanism:

First: Exposure. Explain to our friends, at town hall and school board meetings, how Secular Humanism is in conflict with Christianity. Explain how the SH have aggressively yet insidiously, with the complicity of the SCOTUS, have taken control of the public school system.

Second: Be aware of the subversion of our public school system so that we can teach our own children and grandchildren to recognize and beware of the false ideas taught to them.

Third: Support political candidates for all offices who will support the Constitution and will oppose Humanism and Marxism.

Humanism and the Law

Humanist Law Humanists are different from Christians also in the form of law that they advocate. Christians prefer absolutes. Like the Ten Commandments; like the Constitution. To the Humanists, there are no absolutes, so the law must be in a constant state of flux. To them, the law "evolves." Change in the law is not limited to those made by the amendments to the Constitution or by the Congress. It may be changed by the courts or by the chief executive. Constitutionally speaking, of course, this is called "usurpation." The importance of understanding this will become clear as we learn how the courts have favored Humanists by changing the law. Here is what David Noebel[17] says about Humanist law:

> The concept of evolution so permeates Humanist legal thinking that it can be stated, without contradiction, that evolution ultimately determines Humanistic legal principles. Man is evolving. Man is becoming. Everything is in flux. Nothing is permanent. There are no absolute legal standards. There are no permanent Ten Commandments; there is no permanent Constitution...

All schemers, liars and conspirators **hate absolutes**. Absolutes make it much more difficult for conspirators to convince their intended victims to believe their lies. It is much easier to detect a violation of an absolute, such as a commandment of God or the Constitution. That's the reason that they teach things like "everything is relative" in schools. Here is an example of the mindset of educator and Secular Humanist John Dewey in 1927:[18,19]

---

19. Quoted in David Barton, 2000, Original Intent, (Aledo, Texas, Wallbuilder Press, p. 228

The belief in political fixity, of the sanctity of some form of state consecrated by the efforts of our fathers and hallowed by tradition, is one of the stumbling-blocks in the way of orderly and directed change.

The above type of legal reasoning is perfectly congruent with a type employed in, "social justice." I believe that we can safely assume the probability that "social justice" originated with the Humanists, until someone provides us with a concise explanation of its origin: person, date and location.

The reason that the Secular Humanists support Noebel's explanation of Secular Humanist law and "social justice" is precisely because such law has no fixed limitations such as imposed by the Constitution. The Secular Humanist agenda is in direct conflict with the Constitution. The strict interpretation stands as a bar to the advancement of the Humanist agenda. So, when a case is presented to a court with a majority of justices who are either humanists or sympathetic to Humanism, such justices will ignore the Constitution and rule by the rules of "social justice."

Humanists prefer laws that are vague, nebulous, hazy and unclear. That way, when a Humanist judge ignores the Constitution and applies his own will to the ruling, it is more difficult for honest people to take notice.

Christianity and Evolution

No attempt will be made here to disprove the theory of evolution by some scientific argument.

> Evolution is an important part of the Marxists' arsenal since if a person believes in evolution, he is not likely to believe in that part of the Declaration of Independence that states that our rights are bestowed upon us by our Creator.

My only objective here is to show the conflict between Christianity and evolution and that evolution very definitely plays an important part in this battle between the forces of Christ and those of the anti-Christ.

In the education system, evolution is taught as some benign theory that has no correlation with Christianity either positive or negative. Such is not the case. Evolution is a dangerous weapon of our adversaries because of the simple fact that it is force-fed to every student in the public school

Charles Darwin – Public Domain

system and in nearly every university. When the SCOTUS ruled that nothing related to Christianity can be taught in the schools, this created a vacuum that was naturally filled by Secular Humanism, which includes the theory of evolution.

I realize that there are many Christians who believe in evolution. If you are one of those, I suggest that you give serious thought to the following.

Fundamentals of Christianity	**Fundamentals of Theory of Evolution**
A Creator.	No Creator
Adam and Eve, the first humans and who were created by our Creator.	No Adam nor Eve
The concept of a spirit. A spirit—an extremely important component as to who we are.	Man does not have a spirit.
The fall of Adam.	No Adam and no fall.
Laws given by the Creator (the Ten Commandments) by which man is to live	No Ten Commandments. Man—made laws only
The existence of an adversary, usually called the Devil.	No Devil
Accountability to our Creator for our actions while in this mortal state.	No Creator. No accountability.
The concept of sin.	Concept of sin is a myth.
Repentance and the need thereof.	Need for repentance not acknowledged.
The need for forgiveness.	No need for forgiveness
The need for a savior.	No savior and no need for a savior.
The necessity of baptism.	No need for baptism.
The atonement.	No such thing as the atonement.
Resurrection.	The concept of the resurrection is a myth.
Salvation.	No salvation.
Life after mortal death; eternal life.	No life after mortal death.

Evolution is an important part of the Marxists' arsenal since if a person believes in evolution, he is not likely to believe in that part of the Declaration of Independence that states that our rights are bestowed upon us **by our Creator**.

There is no Creator in evolution. So if there is no Creator, we cannot receive our rights from our Creator. In Marxist thought, there are really no natural rights. There are only privileges from the government called "rights". And if a person does not believe in the *Declaration,* he is not likely to believe in the *Constitution*. And if he does not believe in the Constitution and free agency, he will most likely be seduced into believing in Marxism.

Now, four very important things. The first is that Christianity and evolution are completely incompatible. See table below. Second, evolution is an integral part of Secular Humanism, which is the religion of the adversaries of Christianity. Third, evolution is an integral part of Marxist belief. Fourth, many evolutionists consider themselves to be intellectually superior to we who believe in Adam and Eve. Thus they scoff at Christianity and tend to support legislation and court actions that are damaging to Christian religious freedom. Whether these people realize it or not, they are enemies of Christ.

Evolution cannot possibly be a benign theory in this great war when it is part of the foundation of Secular Humanism and of Marxism.

See table (above) for the contrast between Christianity and Evolution.

Comparing Christianity with Evolution

In all of the above characteristics, it is clearly evident that **Christianity and the theory of evolution are exactly the opposite**.

In the evolution theory, there is **no room for one single fundamental belief of Christianity**. It is the **complete opposite of Christianity**. Looks like evolution might be a possible contender for being an ideology comprising the foundation of the secret combinations of the Devil. Looks like it was thought up by the Devil himself. I think that we are on the right track to identifying and understanding the three greatest hoaxes.

The fundamentals of Christianity include:
(1) The origin of man,
(2) The nature of man and
(3) The government of man.

The theory of evolution includes the origin of man and Secular Humanism and Marxism include:
(1) The origin of man;
(2) the nature of man and
(3) the government of man.

They are **the exact opposite** to those of Christianity.

Fundamentals of the Theory of Evolution

The theory of evolution comes from the writings of Charles Darwin (1809-1882.) While it has been modified to some degree, the Darwinism that is taught in the schools today has the following fundamentals:

(1) That all life on earth today descends from one single cell of life which appeared an unknown time ago from non-life. and,
(2) The event was spontaneous (not directed by any intelligence).

What About Our Spirits?

Let's give some serious thought to (3), in the table above, "the concept of a spirit." Nowhere in the teaching of evolution is there mentioned at what point, in these millions of years of presumed evolution, did the ancestors of modern man acquire a spirit. Without a spirit, what is a human being? Nothing but a mass of protoplasm, with no meaningful purpose, which ceases to exist at mortal death.

Considering that it denies the possibility of a spirit, how could evolution possibly be neutral toward, much less compatible with, Christianity?

The arguments for evolutionism are very sophisticated and very persuasive. It is understandable that many intelligent people, including Christians, have come to believe them. If you have never resolved the question of evolution vs. Christianity for yourself, you might start with asking yourself, "If evolution is true, when did man acquire a spirit?" and, "What about my spirit?" Every person should seriously question evolutionism until he can satisfactorily answer this one overwhelmingly important question. Also, "What about the spirits of my children and grandchildren?" As for me, I have answered the question. I have a spirit. My ancestors (yes, even the horse thieves and moonshiners) and I are descendants of Adam and Eve. What is your decision?

This study of evolution and Secular Humanism and their complete incompatibility with Christian principles brings into focus the importance of using Christian principles in evaluating many other areas of thought and activity, such as: literature, science (all areas), sports, medicine, psychology, government, politics, *(especially politics),* military strategy, statesmanship, agriculture, history, astronomy, animal science and, well…just about every area of human endeavor. We might be surprised the extent to which we would find the footprints of Gransci's soldiers in these various areas of endeavor. Here is what we are told about the value of the influence of Christ on just about every matter. From Moroni 7:

13 But behold, that which is of God inviteth and enticeth to do ^{a}good continually; wherefore, every thing which inviteth and ^{b}enticeth to do ^{c}good and to love God and to serve him, **is ^{d}inspired of God.**

14 Wherefore, take heed, my beloved brethren, that ye do not judge that which is ^{a}evil to be of God, or that which is good and of God to be of the Devil.

15 For behold, my brethren, it is given unto you to ^{a}judge, that ye may know good from evil; and the way to judge is as plain, that ye may know with a perfect knowledge, as the daylight is from the dark night.

16 For behold, the ^{a}Spirit of Christ is given to every ^{b}man, that he may ^{c}know good from evil; wherefore, I show unto you the way to judge; **for every thing which inviteth to do good and to persuade to believe in Christ, is sent forth by the power and gift of Christ**; wherefore ye may know with a perfect knowledge it is of God.

17 But whatsoever thing persuadeth men to do ^{a}evil and **believe not in Christ** and deny him and serve not God, **then ye may know with a perfect knowledge it is of the Devil**; for after this manner doth the Devil work, for he persuadeth no man to do good, no, not one; neither do his angels; neither do they who subject themselves unto him.

18 And now, my brethren, seeing that ye know the ^{a}light by which ye may judge, which light is the light of Christ, see that ye do not judge wrongfully; for with that same ^{b}judgment which ye judge ye shall also be judged.

I suppose that you remember, as I do, the chart on the wall of my elementary grade classroom of the renderings of figures starting from an ape on the left and progressing while evolving to a civilized man on the right. No date was given, but we presume that the time covered was several thousand or several million years. But wait—hold on—there was something missing. And no mention was ever made of this omission of the most important member of this scenario. This missing member of this scenario was **THE FEMALE. WHERE WAS THE FEMALE?**

WHERE WAS THE COMPLEX FEMALE REPRODUCTIVE SYSTEM?

Public domain image

Until the evolutionists can explain:

1. How the male was able to propagate the species over these millions of years **without the female companions** and
2. When and how, during these millions of years of evolution, did spiritless man acquire a spirit.

I will continue to consider the theory of evolution a very badly flawed theory. **A hoax and perpetuated for sinister purposes.**

Christianity and Marxism

Marxism is often thought of as an ideology of political affairs only. Not so. Closely woven all throughout Marxist ideology is a hatred for God, the Ten Commandments, Jesus Christ, the Bible and for all Christians. Marxism is very definitely a religion. Please refer back to Chapter One and the quotes of the early Church leaders. Also please see President Benson, which follows:

> **President Ezra Taft Benson:**[20] Communism introduced into the world a **substitute for true religion**. It is a counterfeit of the gospel plan. The false prophets of Communism predict a utopian society. This, they proclaim, will **only be brought about** as capitalism and free enterprise are overthrown, private property abolished, the family as a social unit eliminated, all classes abolished, all governments overthrown and a communal ownership of property in a classless, stateless society established.

---

20. Benson, Ezra Taft, "A Witness and a Warning," Ensign, Nov 1979 31

Since 1917 this godless counterfeit to the gospel has made tremendous progress toward its objective of world domination.

Chapter Six - Evolution, Humanism, Marxism, Globalism and Public Education

> Beware lest any man **spoil you through philosophy and vain deceit**, after the tradition of men, after the rudiments of the world, and not after Christ. (Col 2:8)

Note: This chapter will definitely help us to better understand the Supreme Court and its violations of the Constitution, since the violations of the Constitution by the Court benefits the Evolutionists, Secular Humanists, Marxists, Globalists, the Socialist educators and those (Council on Foreign Relations, Bilderbergers, Trilateral Commission etc.) whose agenda is to merge the United States into a world government. Such a merger would require that the Constitution of the United States be overturned, abolished or rendered impotent.

For parents, this chapter also helps us to understand the problems in education.

Control of Public Education Wrested from American People

The public education system no longer serves American parents and students. The control of it has been stolen by the U. S. Department of Education (hereinafter ED) and the National Education Association, (Hereinafter NEA.) in cooperation with the Secular Humanists, Evolutionists, Marxists and Globalists. They were aided by some U. S. Supreme Court Justices who violated the Constitution, their oaths of office and lied to hand down rulings which give those with these hostile ideologies a disproportionate amount of power over the rest of the American people. This is in spite of the fact that it is we who pay the taxes to support the educational system and whose children and grandchildren are being taught ideas that are alien and hostile to Christianity and to Americanism. Just how did all of this come about? It was brought about by surreptitious means and by very devious and dishonorable people.

When I told a lawyer friend of mine that I was going to write this book and accuse the SCOTUS of being the greatest threat to Christianity and to America, he disagreed. "It is the NEA and the ED," he claimed. He might be right. When the SCOTUS is comprised of 5 to 4 against us, (a rogue court) then it is a force to destroy America. When this is the case, then either the SCOTUS OR The NEA and ED are sufficiently powerful to destroy America. At this point, America is set on a course of self-destruction by several internal-anti-Christian, anti-American forces. Two of these forces are the SCOTUS and the public education system, comprised of the ED and the NEA combined with a rogue SCOTUS.

Maybe we should take the issue to court, with my lawyer friend arguing his case and me arguing mine. This could be interesting and informative.

The ED, the NEA and the rogue SCOTUSes all have almost identical agendas. Their agendas conform to the plan of the CFR (Council on Foreign Relations. About which more later) to destroy our constitutional government and to merge the United States into a Marxist, Globalist government. Note that they keep their real objective hidden. They never say that they advocate a Globalist *Marxist world-wide* government.

It is good to get an education. But we must beware of what we choose to believe. Learning "lots of things" that are **not true can be dangerous to our spiritual health**. Consider 2 Nephi, 9:

> 28 O that cunning [a]plan of the evil one! O the [b]vainness and the frailties and the [c]foolishness of men! When they are [d]learned they think they are [e]wise and they [f]hearken not unto the [g]counsel of God, for they set it aside, supposing they know of themselves, wherefore, their [h]wisdom is foolishness and it profiteth them not. And they shall perish.
> 29 But to be [a]learned is good if they [b]hearken unto the [c]counsels of God.

There are always various groups vying for the control of education. Some of them have the purest of motives. But the motives of the Dept of Ed, the NEA and the rogue justices on the SCOTUS are far from pure. In fact, I consider them to be evil. Downright evil. Plenty of evidence to support this position will be provided in Chapters Eleven through Fifteen.

Suppose You Were the Devil

In the previous chapter, Devil, we discussed your anti-Christ religion of Secular Humanism and before that, your anti-Christ theory of evolution. Now, let's back up to 1947. You would be so unhappy with the successes that the Christians are having up there on earth. You do have your soldiers, but they just are not making very good progress. You must devise some stratagem to make your religion more popular and Christianity unpopular. Your soldiers have not been doing very well with their proselyting. Those darn Christians are so stubborn! You just can't get your religion through their thick skulls! So you start scheming on how to get your religion more exposure and how to make it have more appeal. You have to find some way to show those Christians who's boss and that your religion is the law of the land and that Christianity is going out of style.

You look around and discover the perfect distribution system for your religion. Ah Ha!!! It is the public school system of America. But there are problems. There are a lot of really good teachers and they teach subjects in harmony with Christianity. You can't possibly get all those teachers converted over to your religion in a thousand years. And also, there are *laws* against what you want to do. Laws? Then you remember your disciple Langdell[21] and you observe his work. Ah yes! Perfect! Not only that, your soldiers have been busy getting some lawyers, trained in the "Langdell Method" and definitely sympathetic to your point of view, appointed to and confirmed to the U. S. Supreme Court. You get your plan all worked out.

You'll show those Christians, their Bible and their Constitution! You have waited long enough. Now, everything is in place. The year is 1947. You get one of your soldiers to bring a case to the U.S. Supreme Court. It is cited as: *Everson v. Board of Education*, 330 U.S. 1, 12 (U.S. 1947) Hyperlink to this case. –https://caselaw.findlaw.com/us-supreme-court/330/1.html

Secular Humanism: A Religion Hostile to and Subversive to Christianity and to Americanism

Secular Humanism (irreligion) is the Devil's own stealth nuclear submarine (Virginia Class), designed to torpedo American culture and its foundation, Christianity. And wherever Humanism goes, evolution and Marxism are sure to follow. Also, as we shall see later, following Humanism, evolution and Marxism comprise the foundations for secret combinations of the Devil. Humanism always leaves a trail of destruction in its wake. The destruction of belief in God and in Jesus Christ and in the Constitution and Americanism. Please keep this in mind as we proceed.

American parents and taxpayers have never been told by ED nor the NEA that, "We are going to teach your children and grandchildren to reject Christianity and the Constitution (Americanism), but that is exactly what they are doing. No person can believe in both Secular Humanism and Christianity nor can they believe in both Marxism and Americanism. Yet, the students in public schools are being taught to believe in the principles of Secular Humanism **WITHOUT THEIR KNOWING IT** and are being taught

> American parents and taxpayers have never been told by ED nor the NEA that, "We are going to teach your children and grandchildren to reject Christianity and the Constitution (Americanism), but that is exactly what they are doing.

---

21. Christopher Columbus Langdell—Dean of the Law School at Harvard 1870-1895. About whom more later.

the principles of Marxism **WITHOUT THEIR KNOWING IT**. They are being taught to believe Humanism and Marxism as if that is "just the way that things are."

The SCOTUS judges who voted to outlaw Christianity in public schools (about which more later) were educated in the public schools. The congressmen who vote for pro-Marxist and anti-Constitutional laws were educated in the public schools.

The division and conflict that we see in our country is due to the fact that the public schools have taught the students to believe in Marxist ideas and government programs (AS IF THEY WERE AMERICAN) and HAVE NOT taught them to understand the principles of the Constitution and the American system of free enterprise.

Humanism and the Public School System

All throughout the Manifestos, it is made clear that they deny the existence of anything supernatural; they deny God. They deny Jesus Christ. They deny that man is comprised of a body and a spirit. They deny anything associated with Christianity. They also deny the existence of the Devil. The Humanists reaffirm their belief in evolution as the origin of man.

They also deny the Ten Commandments as a guideline for man to live by. Their "god" is mankind. Their ethics are purely man-made. Nothing is superior to human intellect. They put the creature superior to the Creator. Humanism is completely congruent with the theory of evolution. We might liken the Humanists to a very ambitious salesman selling an inferior product. How have the Humanists managed to get their religion forced onto every American education system? Let's start with one of their own, one John Dunphy: [22]

> **John Dunphy:** I am convinced that the battle for humankind's future must
> be and won in the public school classroom by teachers who correctly perceive their role as the proselytizers of a new faith...These teachers...will be ministers of another sort, utilizing a classroom instead of a pulpit to convey humanist values in whatever subject they teach, regardless of the educational level preschool day care or large state university. The classroom must and will an area of conflict between the old and the new the rotting corpse of Christianity... and the new faith of Humanism, resplendent in its

---

22. John Dunphy, "A Religion for a New Age," Humanist Magazine, January/February 1983 issue.
23. Quoted also in Blumenfell, Samuel, "Is Humanism a Religion?" The New American, 23 Feb 2010

> promise of a world in which the never-realized Christian ideal of "love thy neighbor" will finally be achieved...

Dunphy made it very clear how the Humanists planned to spread their "gospel" through the classrooms of America. But how in the world would they manage to do that in a Christian (in spite of what Obama says) nation? Well, they have done it. And the history of how they did it certainly does involve, as Paul said, "...principalities, of wickedness in high places..."

In fact, Humanist editor Joe R. Burnett suggested as much in the Nov.-Dec. 1961 issue of *The Humanist* (p. 347) when arguing in favor of federal aid to education. He said:[23]

> Humanists obviously have a vital interest in the passage of a strong bill for federal aid to public education. Without wanting to push the analogy too far, *one might say that public education is the parochial education for scientific Humanism.* (Emphasis added)

Burnett's use of "parochial education" is clear evidence that the education that the Humanists plan for the public schools is to be religious in nature. *Their* religion and forced upon the American children through the public school system. Here is one definition of "parochial:"

Parochial school - Wikipedia   https://en.wikipedia.org/wiki/Parochial_school

> A parochial school is a private primary or secondary school affiliated with a religious organization and whose curriculum includes general religious education in addition to secular subjects, such as science, mathematics and language arts. (wikipedia.org/wikiParochial_school.)

So, the SCOTUS and the Humanists have turned our public schools into PAROCHIAL SCHOOLS and the religion taught in these parochial schools is Secular Humanism. It is well documented that the official policy of the Humanists is to use the public school system to do their proselytizing and educating, *while pretending to be opposed to that which they themselves are doing.* They condemn with their lips what they themselves do with their hands.

It is important to note the similarity of purpose of the Secular Humanists and the Marxists. The Tenth Point of the Communist Manifesto states: "10. Free education for all children in public schools." Of course, the Communists are not interested in the children's education. What they want is a government-operated school system so that they can infiltrate and control it.

Secular Humanists, Change Agents and the Public School System

When we examine the curriculums and textbooks used in the public school systems, we can certainly verify that the Humanists as a body have followed Dunphy and Burnett. What concerns us is the danger that our students are being indoctrinated to believe an entirely different set of values that we are told they are by the educators. These alien values with which we are concerned are evolution, Secular Humanism and Marxism. Essentially, that our students are being taught by change agents to believe a worldview or, in fact, a religion, that is contrary to and hostile to Americanism and to Christianity. Here is one definition of "change agents:"

> **Change Agents** are someone who are assigned or directed to intentionally change social attitudes, cultural values, thoughts, attitudes and morals of school children. TARGET: To change parental and church inspired morals, values and attitudes regarding life in general that is taught at home to destroy all PARENTAL INFLUENCE. Some teachers are change agents–trained to be change agents……..(http://newswithviews)

If our students enter the education system with Americanist and Christian worldviews and exit that system with Marxist and Secular Humanist worldviews, then we can know for a fact that **the system has changed their worldview** and that there must be **change agents** involved in the process.

The insidious and sinister part of this situation is that the educators never advise the parents nor the students that these change agents are going to be changing the worldview; the religions, of the students. Humanists Dunphy and Burnett, above, certainly make it clear that the Secular Humanists plan to use the teachers in the public school system as "change agents."

Students come out of the public school system with attitudes hostile to Christianity, to Americanism and in all too many cases to their parents. We now clearly understand why. The Humanists did it to them. With 3.3 million students graduating from public schools every year,[24] we can understand the extent of the negative impact that the public school system is having on our culture, our society, our politics and our government.

In 1933, the Secular Humanists published their *Humanist Manifesto I*. John Dewey, who played a leading part in shaping the direction of American education, was a signatory to this Manifesto. There can be little doubt that the influence that Dewey had on education was to force it to abandon its Christian base and to adopt the Secular Humanist ideology.

---

24. National Center for Education Statistics

This domination of the public school system by the Humanists constitutes a definite part of the war against Christians and Christianity that is being waged.

The Theory of Evolution and Public Education

The theory of evolution, which is an integral part of Secular Humanism and also of Marxism, is taught to the students in public schools as the *only* possibility for the origin of life and of man. Teaching any other possibility has been outlawed in this land of the free by the Secular Humanist and Marxist-loving SCOTUS in its rulings on "separation of church and state".

Through the years, this forced teaching of evolution has caused many millions of Americans to believe that, "Well, that must be the way it is." Thus, believing evolution, their worldview does not have room for the story of Adam and Eve nor much else of Christianity. This has got to be one of the major reasons for the decline in civility in our society.

No attempt will be made here to disprove the theory of evolution with scientific data. But if they evolutionists were more honest with their students, they would explain to them the caveat that Darwin himself stated regarding his own theory. Here is what Darwin himself confessed about his doubts regarding his own theory:

> Even Charles Darwin thought his own theory was "grievously hypothetical" and gave emotional content to his doubts when he said, "The eye to this day gives me a cold shudder." "To think the eye had evolved by natural selection," Darwin said, "seems, I freely confess, absurd in the highest possible degree." But he thought of the same about something as simple as a peacock's feather which, he said, "makes me sick." Of course, anyone who has knowledge of the intricacies of the human eye and other living structures immediately realizes the problem Darwin sensed. How could an organ of such intricate magnificence ever have originated via random chance? (Oller and Omdahl, p. 274.)

Today's evolutionists do not seem to put much credence in Darwin's caveat. For they still push evolution, albeit with their own modifications. It is because it serves their purposes. Evolution serves the purposes of the Secular Humanists in that it fits their ideology and it causes people to disbelieve the narrative of Adam and Eve. It serves the purposes of the Marxists in that if a person does not believe there is a Creator, he cannot believe that his rights come from his Creator as stated in the *Declaration of Independence*. Therefore, he tends to disbelieve and discredit the *Declaration* and the *Constitution* as a system of government. Rejecting the *Constitution*, he accepts the alternative, which is Marxism. See how that works?

Much more could be said about evolution. but let it suffice to say that it is in conflict with and hostile to Christianity, to civilization and to the *Declaration of Independence*.

Marxism and Public Education

You need not rely upon my word alone that the Marxists have control of or have great influence in the public school in America today I will present to you the words of the Marxists (Communists, Socialists, liberals, etc.) of their intent regarding American education. The first is from William Z. Foster,[25] (1861-1961), labor organizer, General Secretary of the Communist Party USA and said to be the most influential Communist in America in the first half of the 20th century:

William Z. Foster – Wikimedia Commons

> Among the elementary measures the American government will adopt to further the cultural revolution are the following: the schools, colleges and universities will be coordinated and grouped under a National Department of Education and its state and local branches. The studies will be revolutionized, being cleansed of religious, patriotic and other features of bourgeois ideology. ~ (William Z. Foster, *Inspiring Quotes*, p 67)

Foster's predictions have certainly come to pass. The cultural, educational and political revolution in America has proceeded just exactly as Foster had predicted, as the Communist Manifesto outlined and as Antonio Gramsci planned. Are we experiencing a revolution? Several indicators scream out a definite YES! Do we have a cultural revolution in our schools, colleges and universities? Do we have a centralized National Department of Education? President Jimmy Carter saw to that. Have the studies in all of our educational system been "revolutionized, being cleansed of religious, patriotic and other features of bourgeois ideology"? The SCOTUS of 1947 saw to that in *Everson*. So there we are. America IS being "Sovietized." Our freedoms are being taken away. The rule of law has been and is being destroyed. The constitutional government is being violated and destroyed and a Marxist, centralized and regionalized government is being reinforced and empowered in its place. The only logical view into the future is that the Constitutional government will be completely neutralized and the total government will be the centralized, regionalized government, with its power-hungry tyrants and its "red-shrouded band of night-riders, riding rough with whip and spur..." (Pres. J. Reuben Clark, Jr.) cruelly ruling over America.

Gramsci's soldiers have been very busy. And very successful.

---

25. Foster, William Z., Toward Soviet America, AZ quotes.com/quote/77

The Communist Manifesto is the Communist plan for converting a free country to a Marxist dictatorship. The Tenth Point of the *Communist Manifesto* reads, "Free education for all children in public schools…" Another lie promoted by the Marxists. There is no such thing as free education. Just as there is no such thing as a free lunch. Nothing is free. *Somebody* has to pay for it. And it is ridiculous to believe that the Marxists, who have been guilty of the misery and deaths of hundreds of millions of people, would be genuinely interested in the proper education of little children. What the Marxists really want is to control the education system so that the parents have no control and so that they can indoctrinate the children in the anti-Christian and anti-American ideologies of evolution, Secular Humanism and Marxism. Control is their objective and nothing else.

Let us all understand this one fact very clearly. It can be easily proven that the ideologies taught to the students in the public schools is based on Marxism, which results in the destruction of our constitutional government and its replacement with a Marxist dictatorship which is intended to enslave all of us. U. S. Senator William Jenner understood this very well. And it has been the public school system that has brainwashed the students to vote for Marxist politicians and even to them becoming Marxist politicians themselves. Hear it from Senator Jenner:

Senator William E. Jenner (1908-1970)[26] Foresaw Our Situation:

U.S. Senator William E Jenner- Wikimedia Commons

Today the path to total dictatorship in the United States can be laid by strictly legal means, unseen and unheard by the Congress, the President, or the people…Outwardly we have a Constitutional government. We have operating within our government and political system, another body representing another form of government, a bureaucratic elite which believes our Constitution is outmoded and is sure that it is the winning side…All the strange developments in foreign policy agreements may be traced to this group who are going to make us over to suit their pleasure….This political action group[27] has its own local political

---

26. Phoebe and Kent Courtney, America's Unelected Rulers: The Council on Foreign Relations (New Orleans: Conservative Society of 26 America, 1962) pp. 1-2.
27. This group to which Senator Jenner is obviously referring will be identified in Chapter VII.

support organizations, its own pressure groups, its own vested interests, its foothold within our government and its own propaganda apparatus.(Feb 23, 1954)

Much of the culpability for this situation **must be laid at the feet of the public education system**. The powers spoken of by Senator Jenner had been at work for over 30 years at the time of his statement. They have been at work constantly in the intervening 60 plus years. But-we have not heard a peep about this threat from the controlled MSM or by the controlled academia.

Enemies to the Constitution Foreign and Domestic

To understand the wisdom of Senator Jenner's Statement and the seriousness of it, please consider, in your mind, the specter of millions of foreign troops invading our shores and borders and attacking us. They overwhelm and destroy all of our military and police forces. They pronounce our constitutional government to be invalid. They establish their own form of government. State boundaries are abolished. This government controls all resources, commerce, communication and transportation from one central source. We Americans have no rights. The rulers are in no way accountable to We, the People. This was all done by foreign enemies of the Constitution.

Now carry Senator Jenner's warning to its logical conclusion. Slowly, over a period of decades, our constitutional government is bit by bit, ignored, violated and rendered impotent. Also, during this same period of time, a new type of government is created and superimposed over America. It is continuously strengthened, bit by bit. Under this new type of government, called "regional," and patterned after Marxist governments, the people have no rights. The rulers are not in any way accountable to the people. The administrators of these regions are appointed by the top ruler. This top ruler is an absolute dictator. During the process of diminishing the Constitution and building up the Marxist regional government, the good and honest people are eliminated from all government positions. In their places are a greedy, power-hungry and ruthless bunch. During this transitional process, the rogue POTUSes, the rogue Congresses and the rogue SCOTUSes call the new laws of the Marxist-regional government to be "constitutional." The rogue SCOTUSes declare various provisions of the Constitutional government to be "unconstitutional." The very worst in our society hold the top reins of power. The power that We, the People, possess has been severely compromised.

At a certain point, when "the powers that be," the conspirators, the secret combinations, accumulate sufficient power, they create a nationwide crisis. The people are confused and frightened. The conspirators move rapidly to consolidate their control. They implement a plan to eliminate all local police forces and to further strengthen the national police force and to disarm all law-abiding Americans. Anyone resisting will be imprisoned or shot. Then, the reign of terror begins, just as it has been done in all countries that have been overcome by the Communists. Just as President J. Reuben Clark warned, we would be ruled by: "…A red-shrouded band of night riders, riding hard with whip and spur." All this has been done by **domestic enemies of the Constitution,** be they the various presidents, the various SCOTUSes, rogue congressmen/women or the most humble voter. America will have fallen. Religion, especially the Christian religion, is outlawed. Freedom is destroyed for an unforeseeable period of time. And not for just America but for the entire world. The warnings of the prophets have come to fruition.

Public Education and Demagoguery

We are all aware of the scenes on the news about university students creating such disruptive demonstrations that Americanist-minded speakers were prevented from giving scheduled speeches. This is called demagoguery! The students had been taught by the Leftist professors to be so mean-spirited and closed-minded that they rejected the speaker's message even before they heard it. The students are so overwhelmed by their emotions that they refuse to listen to logic and reason. It must be Marxist professors who teach them to behave in such a manner.

Harvard Professor to Teachers: "Every Child…is Insane…Belief in a Supernatural Being…"

Addressing public school teachers in 1995, Harvard professor Chester M. Pierce told the teachers:

> Every child in America entering school at the age of five is insane because he comes to school with certain allegiances towards our founding fathers, toward his parents, toward a belief in a supernatural being…It is up to you teachers to make all of these sick children well by creating the International Children of the Future.[28]

I can only conclude professor Pierce is himself insane for accusing sane children of being insane. This professor definitely has a corrupting influence on education. He is doing a great service for the secret combinations. Unfortunately, his is not the only warped (or even "insane") worldview among public school educators.

In accusing public education of being corrupt, I must in the interest of fairness, explain that all of the fault is not that of the educators. I distribute the fault of this corruption to: 1. The U. S. Department of Education, 2. the NEA, 3. and last but by no means least, the U. S. Supreme Court. At any rate, we have a HUGE problem with corruption in our public education system.

---

28. Berit Klos, Brave New Schools, p. 161. Quoted in: Mathew Staver, Take Back America, New Revolution Publisher
29. Paracchini, Paul, "Saul Alinsky's Eight Steps to Socialism" 01/11/2016.

We realize that there are many very honest and loyal Christian teachers in the public school system. They just want to be teachers. They have nothing to do with the corrupting of the system. Having recognized that, we turn our attention to the system itself, the books and the curriculum. What is taught to the children? Is it consistent with Christianity and Americanism, as it was originally, or is it consistent with the theory of evolution, Humanism and Marxism, all three of which are hostile to Christianity and to Americanism?

This reminds us of the Tenth Point of the Communist Manifesto: "Free education for all children in government schools."

The National Education Association and Communist Organizer Saul Alinsky

Saul D. Alinsky (1909-1972) was a community organizer in Chicago and author of the books, *Rules for Radicals*[29] and *Rules for evolution.* At the beginning of his book, Alinsky paid tribute to a fellow radical and rebel-Lucifer. So Alinsky was not only a self-admitted radical (Communist? Marxist? Whatever?) but an admirer of Lucifer as well. Hardly the influence that we need in our educational system. But the NEA hired Alinsky to train their staff. [30] Of all people available, they hired Saul Alinsky! This certainly does emphasize the ideology prevailing in much of the educational system.

Alinsky's Eight Steps to a Communist Amerika

Although few Americans are aware of Alinsky, his plan has caught on BIG TIME with the Leftist crowd. Here are Alinsky's eight steps to transmogrify America into a Marxist dictatorship:

> 1. Healthcare - Control healthcare and you control the people.
> 2. Poverty - Increase the poverty level as high as possible. Poor people are easier to control and will not fight back if you are providing everything for them to live.
> 3. Debt - Increase the debt to an unsustainable level. That way you are able to increase taxes and this will produce more poverty.
> 4. Gun Control -Remove the ability to defend themselves from the Government. That way you are able to create a police state.
> 5. Welfare - Take control of every aspect of their lives (Food, Housing and Income).

---

30. Thompson, Arthur R., In the Shadows of the Deep State. Western Islands, Appleton, WI, p. 300, 303

6. Education -Take control of what people read and listen to — take control of what children learn in school.

7. Religion - Remove the belief in God from the Government and schools.

8. Class Warfare - Divide the people into the wealthy and the poor. This will cause more discontent and it will be easier to take (Tax) the wealthy with the support of the poor.

Lest one dismiss the importance of the influence of Alinsky, it is obvious that previous POTUS Obama followed Alinsky's program to a "T". Also, so does the Democratic Party and most of the Republican Party.

Barrack Obama and Hillary Clinton were both disciples of Saul Alinsky. Hillary wrote her college thesis on Alinsky. This proves the influence that Alinsky has had in American politics.

Presenting a lengthy evaluation of the public school system is outside the scope of this book. Just let it suffice to say that to the extent that evolution, secular Humanism and Marxism are taught, to that extent the public school system serves the Devil and is an enemy to Christianity and to Christians.

The U.S. Department of Education is a business operated by the government. That fits exactly the definition of Marxism. What should we expect to come from a Marxist bureaucracy? Should we expect that they would teach the students to believe in the free market system? In personal freedom? To understand, believe in and live by the Ten Commandments? To set a high set of moral standards for themselves? To understand and support constitutional government?

The honest teachers in the system have an awful struggle and a terrible dilemma. When an honest employee is fighting against a corrupt system, the system has the advantage. So—Good Luck to you honest teachers. May the Lord give you wisdom and strength to fight this evil.

Elder Maxwell, Senator Jenner and Helaman were Right

Senator Jenner and Elder Maxwell were right on in their statements. We are supporting an educational system and a political system to build a government to enslave us. Now consider the warnings of Helaman as he warns us of our predicament today, In Helaman 6:

> **38** And it came to pass on the other hand, that the **Nephites did build them [secret combinations] up and support them**, beginning at the more wicked part of them, **until they had overspread all** the land of the Nephites and had seduced **the more part** of the righteous until they had come down **to believe** in their works and partake of their spoils and **to join with them** in their secret murders and combinations.

39 And thus **they did obtain the <u>sole management</u>** of the government, insomuch that they did trample under their feet and smite and rend and turn their backs upon the *^a*poor and the meek and the humble followers of God.

40 And thus we see that they were in an awful state and *^a*ripening for an everlasting destruction.

In Summary

The theory of evolution teaches people to disbelieve in a Creator. So if there is no Creator, there is no God, no intelligence higher than man's. This leads to a deficiency of humility, which leads to arrogance and pride. Secular Humanism teaches that there is no God, therefore no restraints such as God's commandments placed upon man's behavior. No internal restraints upon behavior resulting from religious teaching. This leads to unrestrained sexual behavior, which we call sexual immorality. All of these leads to a diminution of spiritualism and a dominance of materialism. This leads to Marxism, which is corrupt government that man uses to enslave men. And themselves. Evolution, Secular Humanism and Marxism dominates our public educational systems today. It also dominates our Congress and has in the past dominated the SCOTUS and the POTUS. All of this indicates that we are on the path to self-destruction.

Some educators might try to deny their part of the blame for this situation. But there are 3 million members of the NEA (National Educators Association). With this many members and political clout, they could make some positive corrections to the problems in education. Evidently, the majority of the NEA does not have the will to do so.

Counterattack: Exposure, exposure and more exposure. Become involved with local and national groups to fight for honest education. **Consider home-schooling your children or grandchildren** or sending them to a good private school.

Suggested reading:
1. *Dark Agenda* by David Horowitz,
2. *Seven Men Who Rule the World From the Grave,* by Dave Breese,
3. *In the Shadows of the Deep State,* especially Chapter 25 on education by Art Thompson and, especially,
4. *Crimes of the Educators: How Utopians Are Using Government Schools to Destroy America's Children,* by Alex Newman.

At least, begin immediately with your own children and grandchildren to home-mentor them to counter the indoctrination being forced upon them in the public schools. **First, explain to them about evolution, about Secular Humanism and then about Marxism**. Teach them about <u>the value</u> of

Christianity to civilization. The material for that is found herein. Remember, there is nothing more valuable to us than the souls of our children and grandchildren. They are worth the effort.

Chapter Seven - *Never* Trust the Main Stream Media

It is Impossible For a Man to be Saved in Ignorance (D&C 131:6)

Note: This chapter helps us to understand the corruption of the media and the reason that the media has never informed us about the corruption of the Supreme Court.

A Corrupt Media and a Corrupt Supreme Court

This chapter helps us to understand how a powerful institution of the United States government can become so corrupted and do so much damage to the people and to the nation and yet not be exposed and reported upon by the mainstream media. This is something that most people cannot understand. This chapter will help you to understand.

The Propensity of the Media to Become Corrupt Over a Period of Time

Any means of influencing human thought, especially that of the masses, must be considered as *potentially* a weapon of our enemies to be subverted and used for their purposes.

Whenever a military commander is contemplating a mission against an enemy, the first thing that he plans is to disrupt the enemy's communication system, thereby throwing his enemy into a condition of confusion.

The mainstream media (MSM) is no friend of Christianity. Although the *First Amendment* is supposed to guarantee freedom of the press, the American press is definitely not free. The majority of all newspapers, radio and TV stations are owned by a small group of people, who are ideologically disposed toward Humanism. Marxism. and Globalism. Many of them are members of the CFR. Following is an explanation of how newspapers and media stations are more than likely to become owned by those who have agendas other than operating a business enterprise. Hidden agendas. Subversive agendas.

First, Consider the Propaganda Value of the Media in Dollars.

Let's just crunch some numbers to see why it is highly likely that the people who own the media -TV stations and newspapers- have agendas other than just wanting to operate a business. Consider that a TV station on the open market might be valued at a billion dollars. It makes an annual profit, just reporting the news objectively and taking revenue

> *The Propaganda $$$ Value of the Media to those with "Hidden Agendas."*

from advertising, of an hundred million. Considering it to be no more than a business venture, no one would be likely to pay more than the billion dollar value. But there are those individuals out there who have hidden agendas. In addition to the hundred million profit, the TV station would give them the opportunity to shape the public's thinking on some very important cultural, political and even religious subjects. This propaganda ability would be worth beaucoup bucks to somebody. Say a billion. So the bidders with "hidden agendas" would be willing to pay much more, say two billion, for the station.

They would consider one billion for the business and one billion for the ability to propagandize the public. So the bidders with the hidden agendas would outbid in every instance the honest entrepreneur looking at the station solely as a business venture. So over time, the honest bidders get squeezed out. This economic reality dictates that it is highly probable that, over time, those who have "hidden agendas" will gain and maintain control of all of the TV stations and newspapers. So, a little later, do not be surprised at the evidence that shows the **members of the CFR owning or controlling a cartel or cartels** that comprise a major portion of the media of the United States.

An Even More Attractive Scheme—Just Buy Control of the Editorial Policy

An even more attractive scheme to those with hidden agendas is to buy the control of the editorial policy of a newspaper, radio or TV station. Then, provide them with an editor of your own choosing to ensure that everything that is published or broadcast conforms to your agenda; to your political and cultural ideology. Jeff Bezos of Amazon bought political influence when he bought the *Washington Post.*

In this exposure of the corruption in the media, it will also be necessary to put the spotlight on some organizations, such as the Bilderbergers (BB), the Trilateralist Commission (TC), the Skull and Bones (Bones) and the Council on Foreign Relations (CFR), that belong also in the section about secret combinations, so keep this in mind.

I believe that we can all agree that the media has a tremendous effect upon the opinion-molding processes of the minds of the American people. The media might not be able to tell us what to think, but it can sure tell us what we are going to think *about*! Consider the tremendous power this represents. Is it not highly probable that some persons will gain positions in the media to exert some control that is more than just pure fact reporting; that diverges from the facts; that is contrary to the best interests of the readers/viewers?

Let me relate to you the distortions presented by the media and the contrasting facts as I personally knew them in one highly publicized case. It was a major incident of worldwide importance.

The Disappearance of Korean Airline Flight 007-An Unsolved Mystery

Active Measures, Disinformation and Agents of Influence

By profession, I was an airline captain prior to retirement. I was also a close personal friend of U. S. Representative Larry McDonald of Georgia. On the 1st of September, 1983, Congressman McDonald was on board Korean Airlines Flight 007 from Anchorage to Seoul. The flight strayed from its course (the reason has never been proven) and was attacked by a Russian jet fighter. The first report from a high-ranking FAA official in Washington to Congressman McDonald's office in Georgia was that KAL 007 had landed on Sakhalin Island, Russia and that KAL was sending two Boeing 747s to pick up the passengers and crew. (A tape recording of this conversation is in possession of Joe H. Ferguson.) Then, abruptly and without explanation, the narrative changed. The media began reporting, repeatedly and without variation, that KAL 007 had been hit by a missile and had been catastrophically destroyed at 35,000 feet, that it had plummeted in pieces from 35,000 feet to the sea and that all passengers and crew had perished.

I had an intense personal interest in this incident for three reasons: (1) I was a professional airline captain, (2) I was a personal friend of Congressman McDonald and (3) I was interested in the political ramifications of such an event. Consequently, I began an intense investigation of my own. Immediately after the shoot-down, President Reagan appeared on national TV night after night excoriating those mean old Russians but never once mentioned the name of Larry McDonald, a United States Congressman on board the flight. The strangeness of this is exacerbated by two facts: (1) Larry, although a Democrat, strongly supported the political position that President Reagan professed and (2) one day after the disappearance of 007, U.S. Senator "Scoop" Jackson, a liberal Democrat, of Washington state, died. President Reagan went on TV repeatedly praising Senator Jackson by name. *By name.* You can put your own interpretation on President Reagan's bizarre behavior and his motive. Or who might have been writing his script for him as he went on TV. Remember - all of his professional career, Ronald Reagan had been an actor. He played the script that someone else handed to him. Was he doing the same in the KAL 007 incident?

It does appear that someone in the shadows-the "Shadows of Power," was giving orders to President Reagan to not mention the name of Congressman Larry McDonald but to praise the name of "liberal" "Scoop" Jackson. It also appears that these same people "in the shadows" were giving orders to the entire federal government and to the media on how to handle the KAL 007 matter.

Robert W. Lee, Writing in *The New American* of September 10, 1991, Reports on KAL 007:

> Shortly after the attack, the Rome, Georgia office of U.S. Representative Larry McDonald, a passenger on the plane, received a number of calls from officials of Korean Air Lines and our Federal Aviation Administration (FAA) claiming that the jet had landed safely on Sakhalin. For instance, one call came from Mr. C. K. Suh, manager of the American regional office of Korean Air Lines in Los Angeles. Suh told McDonald's press aide, Tommy Toles, that he had "just called Korean Air Lines in Seoul" and that "the information I got from them is that [the] U.S. Embassy in Korea informed the Korean government, Minister of Foreign Affairs ... that the plane has landed in Sakhalin."
>
> But the most important (and pertinent) communication came from a spokesman for the FAA, who told Mr. Toles [his statement was tape recorded]:
>
>> This is Duty Officer Orville Brockman at FAA headquarters in Washington, D.C. We have just received information from our FAA representative, Mr. Dennis Wilham in Tokyo, as follows: He has been advised by the Japanese Civil Aviation Bureau headquarters, Air Traffic Division, Mr. Takano -- T-a-k-a-n-o -- who is his counterpart in Japanese aviation, as follows: Japanese self-defense force confirms that the Hokkaido radar followed Air Korea to a landing in Soviet territory on the island of Sakhalinska - S-a-k-h-a-l-i-n-s-k-a - and it is confirmed by the manifest that Congressman McDonald is on board. [A tape recording of this conversation is in the possession of Joe H. Ferguson.]
>
> Note that this confirmed report came from the Japanese self- defense force through the American FAA (not the CIA nor the MSM) and that radar "followed Air Korea to a landing." To follow it to what appeared to be a landing would mean, beyond any reasonable question, that KAL 007 was at the very least heading toward-rather than away from-Sakhalin. While radar may be fallible in certain other respects, it is unlikely to impossible that it could have misled air controllers regarding the direction in which KAL 007 was flying and its altitude. And how could the jet be heading toward Sakhalin unless it had reversed the direction in which it was flying when attacked (which was away from the island)?
>
> Yet shortly after, the scenario reported by the media reflected a sharp diversion from that reported by Duty Officer Orville Brockton of the FAA in Washington. The TV began reporting that 007 had been catastrophically destroyed at 35,000 feet and had fallen into the sea.
> *Time Magazine* of Sept. 12, 1983 depicted on its cover the 747 being blown to bits by a Soviet fighter. at 35,000 feet altitude. *Aviation Week* reported the same, as did *USN&WR* of Sept. 12.

Some time after the incident, I requested from the International Civil Aviation Organization (ICAO) in Montreal a copy of their report on this incident. The report stated that 007 had been tracked by Hokkaido (Japan) radar during and subsequent to the attack from 35,000 feet down to 6,000 feet. It took 007 four minutes to descend from 35,000' to 16,000' and eight minutes from 16,000' down to 6,000'. This told me that the crew of 007 had control of that airplane. It had not suffered catastrophic destruction.

The *Reader's Digest* article did not come out until the January, 1984 issue. The author was Viktor Belenko, a former Soviet fighter pilot[31] and probably the most highly qualified pilot in the West on the mindset of the Soviet military. However, Viktor did not avail himself of the ICAO Report. Nor, evidently, did he have access to the information from the Japanese CAB to FAA officer Brockton that was provided to Congressman McDonald's office.

Both of these constituted pivotal pieces of information regarding the probable fate of KAL 007. Viktor reported some interesting information about the mind of the Soviet military and of the Soviet defense system but failed to include in his evaluation the report from Hokkaido that 007 had been **tracked to a landing on Sakhalin**.

Therefore, he failed to allow for the possibility that the aircraft, crew and passengers survived the attack. It appears that Viktor took all of his information from media sources and failed to access the original official reports.

On the 24th of July, 1984, I rented a Boeing 747 flight simulator at United Airlines Training Department in Denver and with my good friend Captain Dick Fischel as co-pilot, simulated the 007 flight. We started at 35,000' and simulated an engine fire and emergency decompression. We initiated emergency descent for that situation. It took us 3 minutes and 45 seconds to descend from 35,000 to 16,000 (compared to four minutes for 007). We then retracted the gear, flaps and speed brakes and descended to 6,000 with three engines in idle and one shut down. This took us 7 minutes and 45 seconds (8 minutes for 007). We had full control of the simulator. This proved to me that the 007 crew had full control from 35,000 down to 6,000. And remember- Japanese radar on Hokkaido had reported to have followed 007 all the way to a landing on Sakhalin. The 747 had NOT been catastrophically destroyed as the media had reported. What happened to the aircraft, passengers and crew? A great mystery unsolved to this day. All of the information available indicated that the aircraft had probably survived and had a high probability of making a successful landing somewhere. That somewhere was most likely the island of Sakhalin, as was reported by Officer Brockton of the FAA.

---

31. The story of Viktor's defection is told in Mig Pilot: The Final Escape of Lt. Belenko, Reader's Digest, Jan 1980

Also, why did the people at the ICAO not publicly raise the issue of possible survival of 007? I talked with one of them and asked him that question. He said, amazingly, "We never thought of that." I later learned that the ICAO operates under the United Nations. That might explain a lot. Is the United Nations political? Does a duck quack? Why did the media fail to question the fate of 007 and its passengers and crew? Even the *Reader's Digest*, which I consider to be usually accurate and reliable, printed an article that repeated the "party line." Author Belenko merely accepted what was reported without doing any investigation. So I phoned John Barron, Senior Editor at the *Reader's Digest* and told him, "John-KAL 007 was not destroyed as you described in your article." He said, "Send your information to me." I did. John personally wrote a follow-up article asking some penetrating questions titled, *"KAL 007: The Hidden Story,"* in the November 1991 issue of *RD*. Nothing ever came of it. The fact that the U.S. government showed no interest in pursuing the matter when the facts were incontrovertible and which disproved the media reports is another one of those great mysteries of this life. I personally believe that 007 landed on Sakhalin and the crew and passengers were taken prisoner. But I have no way to prove it, of course. I believe that Officer Brockman reported the situation accurately. The flight data reported by Hokkaido radar supports Officer Brockman's report and completely disproves the scenario reported by *Time, USN&WR, Aviation Week, the Washington Post, the New York Times* and the rest of the media. This is a real mystery. Furthermore, neither the ICAO report nor the Hokkaido Radar report were ever discredited nor even challenged. They were never even mentioned. This is crucial.

Politicians lie. The media lies. The facts do not lie. For the above to have happened, it would have required the complicity of the President of the United States, the federal government of the United States, every tv station, every major newspaper in the United States and the government of Russia.

Bert Schlossberg's father-in-law was on 007. Bert has done extensive research on the subject and is probably the most knowledgeable man in the world on this subject. I consider Bert to be a very intelligent honest man. He has written a book on the subject, *Rescue 007*. He has also been interviewed on video by Alex Newman of *The New American* Magazine. Here is as link to that interview: - https://www.youtube.com/watch?v=_qkpWEUAe6Y

Were the "One-Worlders;" the Trilateralists and the CFR (about which more later) people so willing to get rid of Larry McDonald (who was very effective in exposing and opposing them) that they would sacrifice a 747, crew and passengers? Very possibly. For what other reason would they be fabricating such a false narrative relative to the event?

What was Reagan, the CFR-dominated media and the entire U.S. government covering up? Was Reagan, my favorite president, lying to us? Remember that George H. W. Bush (CFR, Bones and TC) was vice-president at the time. Still a mystery. I guess I will not know the answer until I get over on the other side and talk with Larry.

Even as late as 2012, congressmen were asking modern-day Russia about the whereabouts of the crew of flight 007. Including Larry McDonald.
(See: https://www.conservapedia.com/Larry_McDonald)

I hereby testify, as a seasoned airline captain who has researched this tragedy thoroughly, that the aircraft was NOT catastrophically destroyed at 35,000 feet as reported by the media and as maintained as the official line of the U.S. Government.

The point that I wish to emphasize is that the media has its own agenda and shapes, omits, distorts and "spins" the "news" to fit that agenda. And, as improbable as it seems, the various TVs and newspapers seem to all have the same agenda. They all report the same stories with the same spin.

Members of the CFR have almost total control of the TV stations. Yet not a peep about the fact that 007 was flying under control of the crew from 35,000 feet down to 6,000 feet. The CFR people **HAD** to have known what was going on.

Question: What was their motive in reporting what they did?
Question: Were they complicit in the whole affair? They were certainly complicit in the disinformation put out as "news."

I know from personal experience that the media favors collectivism (Marxism) over constitutionalism and will give collectivist (Marxist) politicians favorable treatment while demeaning conservative (constitutionalist, pro-American) politicians and candidates. The media also favors one-world government over United States sovereignty.

Corrupt Media Necessary to Cover for All Other Corrupt Entities

Just consider that none of the corrupting or corrupted entities listed below would be able to avoid exposure without a corrupt media. **No secret combination nor cabal would be able to operate if they were exposed by an honest media.**

U.S Rep Oscar Callaway Public

This might sound outrageous to you at first, but just keep this in mind as we proceed. In fact, the situation that threatens us could not exist without a corrupt media, a corrupt educational system, a corrupt federal government at all levels, especially the U.S. Supreme Court, a corrupt U.S. Congress, a corrupt President and with the corruption of all of them combined supporting the same agenda-the conversion of the United States to a Secular Humanist, Marxist dictatorship.

If just ONE link in this chain were to be broken, the SCs would be exposed and greatly dis-empowered.

In about 1915, a group set out to control the editorial content of the major American newspapers. I have never been able to determine the identities of those involved. However, I believe the report to be true. Here is what U.S. Representative Oscar Callaway (Oct 1872-Jan 1947) of Texas recorded in the Congressional Record:[32]

J.P. Morgan- Creative

In March, 1915, the J.P. Morgan Jr. [1867–1943] interests, the steel, shipbuilding and powder interests and their subsidiary organizations, got together 12 men high up in the newspaper world and employed them to select the most influential newspapers in the United States and a sufficient number of them to control generally the policy of the daily press...They found it was only necessary to purchase the control of 25 of the greatest papers. An agreement was reached; the policy of the papers was bought, to be paid for by the month; an editor was furnished for each paper to properly supervise and edit information regarding the questions of preparedness, militarism, financial policies and other things of national and international nature considered vital to the interests of the purchasers. Oscar Callaway (1872-1947) U.S. Congressman, D-TX 12, (1911–1917)

Hilaire du Berrier - Wikipedia

I believe it to be highly probable that it happened as Rep. Callaway testified. One thing for sure -if J. P. Morgan, Jr. was involved, the purchases were made for the sole purpose of controlling and influencing the news and the opinions of the American people. J. P. Morgan, Jr. was heavily engaged in politics. If J. P. was successful in his endeavor as alleged by Callaway (above), then what he created would be called a cartel of newspapers.

---

32. Congressional Record of February 9, 1917, page 2947, as entered by Representative Oscar Callaway of Texas
33. Fotheringham, Don, The President Makers, First Freedom Society, Colorado Springs, 2014, pp 58-6

We are going to be dealing in cartels of newspapers and of TV stations as we deal with how the secret combinations manipulates the thinking of the American people, so let's look at the definition of "cartel" here:

Cartel: A combination of producers of any product joined together to control its production, sale and price and to obtain a monopoly in any particular industry or commodity. (*Black's Law Dictionary*, 1979, West, St. Paul)

In the presidential election of 1912, the incumbent president and Republican Taft was expected to win. But J. P. Morgan and Co. persuaded former president Theodore Roosevelt to run on the Bull Moose ticket, knowing that it would split the Republican vote. It did. Democrat Woodrow Wilson won.[33]

During the election, Morgan's men bought the *New York Press*[34] so that Roosevelt would have a morning newspaper to help his election along. We can rest assured that the political information in the *Press* was slanted to favor Roosevelt. This purchase of a newspaper by Morgan to help elevate Roosevelt as a contender and siphon votes away from Taft is a clear indicator of the interest that Morgan took in owning newspapers in order to further his own agenda.

It also lends credence to the account of Congressman Callaway, above, about Morgan purchasing the editorial policies of various newspapers. This is how the big boys do it in order to manipulate the thinking of us peons.

Remembering that the wealthy who have political motivations are likely to spend double the business value of a TV station or newspaper also lends credence to Congressman Callaway's statement.

Remember that billions are spent during presidential election years. Must we be so naive as to believe that none of this money goes into the coffers of the media owners (or to the broadcasters), under the table, sight unseen, to influence a certain idea or to enhance the image of a certain candidate? For an excellent treatise on presidential elections and how they are financed, controlled and manipulated, I highly **recommend to you *President Makers* by Don Fotheringham. It is an eye-opener. I vouch for its accuracy.**

David Rockefeller, The Bilderbergers, Secret Combinations and a Complicit Media

---

34. Griffin, G. Edward, 1994, 2010, The Creature From Jekyll Island, 5th ed., American Media, Westlake Village, CA p. 453 34

David Rockefeller (Jun 1915-Mar 2017) was an extremely wealthy and politically powerful man. He was at one time (1970–1985) chairman of the Council on Foreign Relations (CFR), a politically very powerful group. At least, the combined members of the CFR are politically powerful, even though the CFR denies that itself is.

Rockefeller is or was also a member of the Bilderbergers, another group of very wealthy people who meet yearly in extreme secrecy and under heavy security. The meetings are always by very special invitation only. Here is a story that is germane to our quest. It might be second-hand, but I believe it to be valid. The late Hilaire du Berrier (1905-2002) had been, among other things, a WWI pilot, a spy and the editor of the very interesting newsletter *H du B Reports*. H du B, whom I met briefly on a couple of occasions, had some amazing sources for his news. On the two occasions that I visited with Hilaire, I considered him to be not only a very interesting fellow but an indefatigable hound always on the trail for news. Since Hilaire was a fellow aviator and also published a newsletter to which I subscribed, I took particular notice of him. I consider the following from H du B as highly probably accurate. Some information came to Hilaire regarding a statement by David Rockefeller which bears directly on the subject of manipulating public opinions. Here it is from H du B himself:

The Masks Are Coming Off
by Hilaire du Berrier

On June 5, 1991, a group of internationally important men converged almost furtively on Sand, a small German city near Baden. No newspaper announced their arrival but they were on their way to a Bilderberg meeting that lasted from Jun 6 to 8.

HILAIRE DU BERRIER LETS ROCKEFELLER'S CAT OUT OF THE BAG.

Mr. Rockefeller's opening speech should Give Americans a jolt. He told his listeners:"We are grateful to the *Washington Post*, the *New York Times*, *Time Magazine* and other great publications **whose directors have attended our meetings** and respected their promises of discretion **for almost 40 years**."

Analyze this: The Washington Post used duty to its subscribers to justify subverting a public servant to get the Watergate tapes and papers that destroyed a president and weakened the office itself. Yet for almost forty years, Mr. Rockefeller admits, its directors have participated, in a conspiracy to bring America into a Europe-dominated federation…

No paper has howled louder about government censorship, yet the most powerful newspapers in America, withheld information from its subscribers…without a qualm…

[Rockefeller continues:] "It would have been impossible **for us to develop our plan for the world** if we had been subject to the bright lights of publicity during these years. But the world is now more sophisticated (read: "more brainwashed by the press") he thanked and the professors his foundation supported) and **prepared to march towards <u>a world government</u>** which will never again know war but only peace and prosperity for the whole of humanity…" (*HduB Reports*, June 5, 1991, Paris, "The Masks are Coming Off," Vol 34, Letter 5, Sep 1991)

It seems that even the most cautious of conspirators occasionally slip up and let the cat out of the bag. Thank you, Mr. Rockefeller, for letting the cat out and thank you, Hillaire, for catching the cat and forwarding it on to us. [35]

Journalist Robert W. Lee analyzes the complicity of the media with Rockefeller's scheme:

Bilderbergers: A Deadly Alliance
by Robert W. Lee

As H du B points out, Rockefeller's comment amounted to formal acknowledgment that the same Washington Post responsible for leaking details that resulted in the Watergate investigation that "destroyed a President and weakened the office itself" has for nearly four decades "participated, under an oath of secrecy, in a conspiracy to bring America into a Europe-dominated federation." And the New York Times, which boasts of publishing "all the news that's fit to print," has had its directors and top editors "attending conspiratorial meetings of which they were pledged not to print a word." And Time, "the information bible of millions," has also had its sworn-to-secrecy participants "in the **secret activities of a cabal**," while "telling readers that anyone subscribing to the conspiracy theory was a kook." (Lee, Robert W., "Bilderbergers: A Deadly Alliance", *The New American*, August 24, 1992)

The fact that this meeting of some of the wealthiest and most powerful people in the world was never mentioned in any of the MSM in the United States is of itself most noteworthy. We all know that a *watchdog never barks at a burglar whom he recognizes to be a friend*. Thus, the MSM never reports to the general public on the conspiratorial doings of the super rich elite.

---

35. Considering that the BB was formed in 1954, its membership is comprised of some of the most wealthy and powerful people in the 35 world and yet the mainstream media NEVER publishes a peep about them.

The way in which Rockefeller's remarks were inadvertently made public ironically illustrates the power elite's chokehold on the mass media. Excerpts from Rockefeller's opening address were leaked to two independent French publications. They then came to the attention of H du B, who published them in his newsletter, *H du B Reports*. As he relayed Rockefeller's breathtakingly brazen admissions to his readers, H du B knowingly commented that he would "lay odds that not a word of Mr.

Rockefeller's speech will be reported in America." As far as the major media are concerned, H du B's prediction proved to be true. (Hilaire seldom missed.)

Here are names of some U.S. media people who have attended Bilderberger meetings and yet not a peep have we ever heard about them in the mainstream media: United States: William F. Buckley, Jr. (1996), columnist and founder of *National Review* (deceased), Charlie Rose (2008, 2010, 2011, 2012), Executive Editor and Anchor, 'Charlie Rose', George Stephanopoulos (1996, 1997), Former Communications Director of the Clinton Administration (1993-1996), now ABC News Chief Washington Correspondent. Fouad Ajami (2012), Senior Fellow, The Hoover Institution, Stanford University.

The Bilderbergers is comprised of some of the most wealthy and powerful people in the world. As a group, they probably own or control more wealth than any other group in the world. Yet we never hear anything about them from the mainstream media. We constantly hear about "the Republicans this" and "the Democrats that," but we never hear about the Bilderbergers.

Dead silence. Hmmmm. This gives us justification for *serious* suspicion! What must we think?

Bilderberg Hotel in Oosterbeek, Netherlands, Site of the first meeting of the Bilderbergers May 29-31, 1954. Creative Commons

The Bilderbergers must play some part in the secret combinations scheme of things. They must wield tremendous power and influence over the governments of the world, including, of course, ours. No doubt, David Rockefeller "rewarded" the owners of the media for keeping a lid of secrecy on the Bilderbergers. He certainly has the bucks and the motive, to do so.

The connections between the Big Four are not made public. We do know that David Rockefeller has played a major part in the BB, the TC, the CFR and the

Club of Rome. We know that there are never any major conflicts between the Big Four made public. All four seem to be working toward the same objective: 1. The dissolution of the Constitution and 2. The creation of a world government and (3) The subordination of the United States into that world government.

The above account about David Rockefeller is presented to prove how the media gives favorable treatment to certain people. It also serves to introduce us to the Bilderbergers. Considering the wealth and power of its members and the political designs of its leader, David Rockefeller, we must consider the group to play a part, perhaps a significant part, perhaps even a dominant part, in the secret combinations. Since we are well aware of the political objectives of David Rockefeller, we are safe to assume that those who follow him share those very same objectives. So that would include the majority of the Bilderbergers, the CFR and the TC. It is most important to remember that: 1. The Bilderbergers is comprised of some of the most wealthy and powerful 2. Participation is strictly controlled; it is by invitation only, 3. There is never anything ever reported about the Bilderbergers by the MSM and 4. The meetings operate by the "Chatham House Rule," to wit: "When a meeting, or part thereof, is held under the Chatham House Rule, participants are free to use the information received, but neither the identity nor the affiliation of the speaker(s), nor that of any other participant, may be revealed." With this much super-secrecy, must we not suspect that they are planning something that might be contrary to our best interests?

Carroll Quigley- Wikimedia Commons

Professor Quigley Lets More Cats Out of the Bag

Carroll Quigley (1910-1977) was a professor of history at Georgetown University and author. Quigley authored a book in 1966 entitled *Tragedy and Hope A History of the World in Our Time* that caused a sensation. One would not expect that a 1,348 page history book-like tome would become a best seller. But a few days after it hit the bookstores, there was run on it. The subject of the book was just what this book is addressing: secret combinations. The difference was that Quigley was an author with considerable credentials. He also had contacts with and on very friendly terms, some of the people that we are exposing in this book and whom we definitely consider the "bad guys". I have never ascertained whether Quigley was "one of them", one of the "bad guys." *Tragedy and Hope* was definitely not written to be an expose', but it certainly proved to be one. He laid bare the inner workings of the Council on Foreign Relations and others that we consider to be conspiratorial, secretive and malevolent...

Tragedy and Hope revealed such an amount of explosive information that two books taking off from it, were written for the conservative market, They were *The Naked Capitalist* by Dr. W. Cleon Skousen and *None Dare Call it Conspiracy* by Gary Allen and Larry Abraham Both of these books turned out to be best sellers as well.

Tragedy and Hope is as good a source as anyone could want to settle the issue of whether secret combinations exist, whether they plan a world government and plan to enslave us all. It removes all doubt.

Walter Duranty during WWI-
Stalin's apologist
Public Domain

Here is some very important information that serves to prove the validity of Quigley's message. The first printing sold out quickly. Surprisingly, there was no second printing (at least not for years). *SOMEBODY* had put the quietus on the second printing. Even Quigley himself was surprised at this and stated that he never knew who had done it. The fact that somebody shut down the second printing of this very fast-selling book serves to validate its accuracy.

The "Liberal" Media and the Starvation of Six Million Russian Kulaks

One of the most flagrantly malicious and erroneous pieces of reporting was by Walter Duranty in the *New York Times.* The year was 1932. The situation was Stalin had ordered all of the grain and other food supplies confiscated from the Kulaks, his own people, Ukranian-Russians The result was that six million Kulaks died of starvation. The people of the world wanted information about this tragedy. What they got from Duranty and the New York Times was pure disinformation. Here is an account of the tragedy by William F. Jasper in *The New American:*

> **Speaking the Truth About Communism**
>
> Throughout most of the last century, the Lenins, Stalins, Maos and Castros of world Communism were drenching the globe in blood, carrying forward a plan of world conquest and penetrating virtually all U.S. institutions. Yet instead of barking out loudly about these enormous crimes, the American press provided strategic cover.
>
> Over and over again, the U.S. media opinion cartel duplicitously assisted the Red commissars of Moscow, Beijing, Caracas and Havana and gravely deceived the American public. One of the most common tactics employed by the elite press is to "spike" facts, information and stories challenging or contradicting the Party Line. Spiking, in media argot, means to suppress, censor, or kill a story. Sometimes the spiking can be so pervasive and efficient that a complete "blackout" is achieved.

The case of Walter Duranty and the *New York Times* chillingly exemplifies the spike and blackout in operation over an extended period. In the 1920s, '30s and '40s, Duranty was one of the world's most famous journalists and undoubtedly the most influential writer on the Soviet Union. A Pulitzer Prize winner whose articles filled the *Times'* front pages with gripping stories from Mother Russia, he was the undisputed don of the Moscow correspondents. One of the most notorious acts committed by Duranty and the *Times* was the spiking of Stalin's mass-starvation genocide in the Ukraine during the early 1930s.

More than seven million Ukrainian men, women and children perished in that hideous Communist holocaust, while Duranty was singing Stalin's praises and insisting that FDR's plan to recognize the Soviet Union and establish diplomatic relations with Moscow was in America's interest. Without access to the truth, the American public failed to see through the rosy picture that the *Times* painted of Russia. Consequently, few opposed the pro-Stalin policies.

When British writer Malcolm Muggeridge and other reporters tried to tell the world of the massive death toll resulting from Stalin's orders, which they were witnessing with their own eyes, Duranty used his prestige to discredit their stories. Famine reports were "mostly bunk,""malignant propaganda," or "a sheer absurdity" he claimed, even though he had witnessed the horrific devastation himself. While millions were starving, Duranty told his worldwide reading audience of "village markets flowing with eggs, fruit, poultry, vegetables, milk and butter." He declared that "a child can see this is not famine but abundance." Similarly, he explained away Stalin's murderous purges and show trials. The *Times'* Insider management knew that Duranty was lying, yet continued printing his lies. Duranty and the *Times* continued covering for Stalin's crimes and were responsible for selling many of the pro-Soviet policies of the Roosevelt administration (and the administrations which followed) to the American public.
Unfortunately, the long Duranty epoch at the *Times*, nearly 30 years, was not unique; many other *Times* reporters followed his lead in covering Soviet Russia and the Communist revolutions in China, Poland,Yugoslavia, Cuba, Vietnam, Nicaragua and many other countries.

Time after time they, together with their editors and publishers, used the news blackout technique to hide the truth from the American people about Communist atrocities, torture, assassination, subversion, mass-murder, duplicity and betrayal. At the same time, they willingly transmitted Communist propaganda or fabricated their own lies to smear anti-Communist governments under Communist attack. Throughout the decades and up to the present, many of the other news organizations have replicated this *Times*-style deception. (William F. Jasper, "Speaking the

Truth About Communism," *THE NEW AMERICAN* • February 10, 2003, pp. 17-18).

Was Duranty acting as an agent of influence for Stalin? Or on orders from his superiors at the *Times?* No question that the *New York Times* served to cover Stalin's crimes against his own people and also served to cause the perception of the American people to be upside-down about Stalin. That was over 80 years ago, but the editorial policy of the *Times* has not changed much. The *Times* certainly did not report the truth about the disappearance of Korean Airlines Flight 007. And they had a million times more resources than I had to dig for the truth *if* they had wanted to. Obviously, *they didn't.*

Fidel Castro: "George Washington of Cuba" on Ed Sullivan TV show

I personally remember, in 1959, Communist Fidel Castro (1926–2016) being on the Ed Sullivan (1901-1974) TV show and hailed as the "George Washington of Cuba." CBS, I believe it was. It was disinformation like this that suppressed the anti-Communist resistance to Castro taking over Cuba, only 90 miles from America's shores. Was Ed Sullivan an "agent of influence" of Castro? Of somebody? There was certainly an "active measures" campaign in place at the time. With an abundance of disinformation carried to the American people that Castro was definitely NOT a Communist. In fact, most of the major TV stations and newspapers at that time played the same tune. To whose tune do these media people dance? I still have trouble believing it, even though I can clearly see it.

Communist Fidel Castro took over Cuba, even fooling some of those, like my Cuban friend Major Pedro Diaz Lanz (1926-1982), who was a major for a while in Castro's Air Force.[36] Castro slaughtered all political opposition. Thousands-maybe millions-of innocent anti-Communist Cubans died before Castro's firing squads.

CBS, Ed Sullivan, Most of the Media and the U. S. State Department were definitely complicit in helping the Communists take over Cuba and in the murder of many thousands (or millions) of innocent Cubans. We will include them in the "corrupt media" category. And lest we forget-the TV station was

Ed Sullivan– Public Domain

Fidel Castro- Public Domain

owned by the very wealthy. The evidence indicates that the TV stations and their owners were complicit in the propagation of disinformation to affect this active measures campaign.

The Council on Foreign Relations (CFR) And the Corrupt Media

We recounted above the part that J. P. Morgan had in the presidential election of 1912 and of buying a newspaper as well as the political policy of several others.

---

36. Major Pedro Diaz Lanz, after learning of Castro's true Communist identity, defected to the United States. While on a speaking tour in 36 Phoenix, I met him and he stayed in our home three nights. Very interesting fellow.

After J.P. Morgan's successful move to get Woodrow Wilson elected in 1912, the following took place:

1. The creation of the Federal Reserve,
2. The Sixteenth Amendment and the creation of the Internal Revenue Service (IRS) and, ultimately the implementation of the Marxist graduated income tax,
3. The passage of the Seventeenth Amendment **changed the method of the selection of U.S. senators.** This, in effect, deleted the senate which represented the states and created an additional house of representatives (Although still going by the title of "senate".) This was a great blow to the rights of the states and to keeping the United States a republic and
4. There was World War One. Morgan's investment to get Wilson elected paid off big dividends to Morgan in advancing his political objectives.

In 1921, J. P. Morgan, Jr. created the Council on Foreign Relations (CFR), which was destined to have a huge impact upon U.S. policy, both foreign and domestic. In our quest, J. P. Morgan, even though he is long dead, would certainly play a big part in the SCs. From 1970 until 1985, David Rockefeller was the chairman of the CFR, so that served to coordinate the forces of the **Bilderbergers, the TLC and the CFR.**

These **three** and the Bones, would determine the domestic and foreign policy of the United States. The CFR denies influencing the policies of the United States. Technically speaking, that is true. But the denial is very misleading.

For reasons unknown, Admiral Chester Ward, USN, was invited to join the CFR. He was a member for many years. Surprisingly, Admiral Ward was a true blue American and was shocked when he learned of the political ideology and operations of the CFR. Here is Admiral Ward explaining how the CFR operates, "without influencing the policies of the United States.":

> Once the ruling members of the CFR have decided that the U.S. Government should adopt a particular policy, the very substantial research facilities of CFR are put to work to develop arguments, intellectual and emotional, to support the new policy and to confound and discredit, intellectually and politically, any opposition.[37]

That's how it is done. Then, as soon as the CFR has developed the arguments to support a new policy, we should not be surprised that the CFR-dominated media should somehow mysteriously report favorably on this same policy. And the majority of politicians in Washington always suddenly champion the same line that the media is championing. Funny how that works. As early as in the FDR regime, the CFR supplied the direction for those in positions of

---

37. Quoted in James Perloff, Shadows of Power, Western Islands, Appleton, WI, 1988, p. 9 37 Also in Phyllis Schlafly and Chester Ward, Kissinger on the Couch, New Rochelle, NY, Arlington House, 1975, p. 151
38. Curtis Dall, My Exploited Father-in-Law, Action Associates, Washington, D. C. 1970, p. 185

power. Curtis Dall[38], son-in-law of President Franklin Delano Roosevelt, explained how CFR ideas were converted into official policy:

> For a long time, I felt that FDR had developed many thoughts and ideas that were his own to benefit the country, the U.S.A. But he didn't. Most of his thoughts, his political "ammunition," as it were, were carefully manufactured for him in advance by the CFR - One-world money group. Brilliantly, with great gusto, like a fine piece of artillery, he exploded that prepared "ammunition" in the middle of an unsuspecting target, the American people and thus paid off and retained his international support.

That's how it's done. The CFR does the planning and the research to present to politicians a plan that will serve the purposes of the CFR and with an accompanying narrative which would be palatable with the unsuspecting public. Then, the CFR uses its control of and influence over the media to present and popularize this plan to the unsuspecting public, at the same time attacking and demeaning any person who attempts to expose or oppose the plan. Concurrently, or shortly thereafter, this same information is distributed to the members of Congress. This "carrot and hickory stick" method works all too well.

So while the CFR itself might not take a "direct" hand in affecting U.S. policy, it certainly does do so indirectly. The CFR as a body determines the policy. Then the *members* of the CFR, acting as individuals, use their influence to get the policy implemented and the media, controlled by the *members* of the CFR, champions the policy and attacks or demeans any position in opposition to it. So by this method, CFR policy becomes official U.S. policy. Funny how that works.

With this much influence, the CFR can launch a nation-wide active measures campaign any time they wish and with unlimited amount of disinformation. The boys at the KGB must be suffering an inferiority complex. "Liberal" politicians always champion what is reported favorably in the media, so they go to work to get legislation passed in the Congress. So, that is how CFR policy becomes U.S. law.

We grassroots Americans fight to make some positive changes in our government. The CFR, the Trilateral Commission, the Bilder Bergers, the Bones and those under their influence and control prevent these changes from happening.

Here is the reason why:
1. Nixon had over 100 members of the CFR in his administration,

2. Carter had over 60,
3. Reagan had 75 CFR and TC,
4. GHW Bush had 350 CFR and TC and
5. Clinton over 25 CFR.

Whether a Democrat or Republican administration, They, the CFR, are in control and We, The People, always lose.

The above seems to me to constitute irrefutable evidence that:

1. A cabal (if you don't want to call it "conspiracy") of very powerful people does exist whose intent it is to monopolize the important positions of power of the United States government and
2. The media (all of the major TV and newspapers) are and have been for many years, complicit with the designs of this cabal.
3. The Department of Education, the NEA and the public school system of the United States and most universities (some more-so than others) are also complicit in this scheme. In fact, they play a major part.
4. It is obvious that all of the above are complicit in a design to eliminate Christianity from the United States and from the world and to destroying the freedom of all Americans and of all people.

Chapter Eight - Marxism—What it IS NOT and What it REALLY IS

In a time of universal deceit, telling the truth is a revolutionary act.
George Orwell.

Note: It is very helpful, perhaps necessary, to understand Marxism in order to understand the motives of some justices who vote to violate the Constitution. Therefore, this chapter will be very helpful in understanding chapters 10 through 14. Marxism means concentrated POWER. The corrupted rulings of the Court results in POWER being taken away from We, the People and transferred to a certain group in government.

The First Thing to Remember about Marxism and Marxists

The first thing to remember about Marxism is that it thrives on deception, disinformation and lies. Also, remember that Marxists/Communists NEVER admit to being Marxists/Communists. They claim to be "liberals" or "progressives" or something similar. They advocate Marxist ideas, they defend Marxists/Communists who have been exposed and possibly indicted. And they demean and excoriate Americans who stand for the Constitution and oppose Marxism. In fact, they hate them. But they will invariably deny being Marxists/Communists A strange but interesting phenomenon.

A Very Simple Explanation

Marxism is exactly the opposite of constitutionalism. Not complicated at all. The Constitution was designed to protect the lives, liberties and properties of the citizens. Near the end of this chapter, you will find a graph contrasting the characteristics of constitutionalism and of Marxism. They are the opposite in purpose, design and results. Marxist governments are designed to deprive the working people of their liberties and properties and, sometimes, their lives. Just look at every Communist country in the world.

In the arena of politics, which is quite often dominated by greed and contention, the principles of constitutionalism and those of Marxism become blurred. And the field of academia has been subverted so that the students are not taught to understand the principles of constitutionalism nor those of Marxism nor how to distinguish between the two. Just the opposite. Thousands of Marxist university professors spend semesters trying to convince their students that Marxism is something else, all the while demeaning the Constitutional system. We need to spend a little more time examining what Marxism IS NOT and what it REALLY IS. Because, when we get to chapters Eleven and Twelve, where we see the Court violating the Constitution, we will understand that when they do so, they are converting

America into a Marxist totalitarian state. Furthermore, they have a motive for doing so. An agenda.

Marxist Promises Distort Voters' Judgment

Marxist ("liberal" or "progressive") politicians always make promises that cannot be fulfilled. These promises cause the greed in the minds of the voters to crowd out the reality of the loss of rights, freedom and opportunity resulting from Marxist legislation. In addition, these politicians NEVER tell their constituencies the downside of Marxist legislation. Marxist professors are guilty of the same. This is how free countries are converted into Marxist ones. This is how people vote themselves into slavery. This is how America is being converted into a Marxist totalitarian state.

The structure and purpose of the government of the rich and mighty who are conspiring to merge the United States into a Marxist-like Globalist government is very similar to that of the rabble in the streets who riot against capitalism. In fact, when compared side by side, they are hardly distinguishable. Both the Marxist rabble and the super-elite Globalists are working for a centralized government that controls industry and the people in an arbitrary manner. In both cases, the rulers would have power over the people but would not be accountable to them. This supports the theory that the real intent of Marx was to create a theory that would produce the results that Marxism produces: the enslavement of the masses, with the wealthy ruling elite being their masters.

Usually, Marxist legislation proposed in the Congress has something to promise to the poor and something to promise to the rich. The cost of fulfilling these promises is never mentioned. The working class are usually the ones taxed to pay for the fulfillment of these promises.

Marxism-The Greatest Fraud Ever Perpetrated?

Marxism might well be the greatest fraud ever perpetrated against mankind. Marxism has its appeal to the poor as well as to the rich and it has its consequences, which are NEVER mentioned by those promoting Marxist ideas and programs. Karl Marx (1818 to 1883) based his writings on the promise of releasing workers from the bondage of poverty. "Workers of the world, unite! Throw off your chains!" was his cry. Redistribute the wealth. Feed the poor. These promises sound good. They have sounded good to millions. But the reality of Marxism has resulted in the starvation and deaths of approximately a hundred million people during this last century.

The purpose of Marxism is exactly the opposite of constitutionalism. The structure of Marxist governments is the opposite of our constitutional government (as originally intended.) Constitutional government is designed so that those in power are elected by and accountable to the people they govern. It is also designed to protect the liberties and properties of the people. It does this by restraining the powers of those in government.

> Marxism tricks people into supporting an ideology that will result in the development of a government that will enslave them.

Marxist government, on the other hand, is designed to give unlimited powers to the rulers. The rulers are not accountable to the people. The result is that the ruthless rulers of oppressive Marxist government occupy seats of self-perpetuating power. The government owns and controls the instruments of production, distribution and transportation. By doing so, it can and does confiscate the fruits of the labors of the working class. Not true? Just look at Russia, China, Venezuela and Cuba or any other Marxist country. Then why do Marxist governments continue to exist?

Marxist countries continue to exist by the use of promises, threats, deception, confusion, ignorance and brute force. After all, in Marxist countries, the government owns all the guns. The individual citizens own none. No matter how brutally they are treated, the people in Marxist countries cannot vote themselves out of slavery, neither can they organize to effect an overthrow. In Marxist countries, the Marxists control education and the media. The people who would like to change the government cannot get accurate information in order to be able to organize.

Just look at what the Democrats are doing today. One of their main efforts is to force the people to register all their firearms. After registration, confiscation is a simple matter.

Is there then no wealth in Marxist countries? Oh yes, indeed, there is. But it is accumulated and owned by the Nomenklatura, as they are called. The rulers of Marxist countries accumulated those riches at the expense of the workers who created them.

Do the Marxists Really Believe that Marxist Stuff?

The stark contrast between the theory of Marxism and the reality of Marxism makes one ask the above question. True, their minds, values, perceptions and worldviews are twisted and distorted. But I cannot think that the Marxist college professors, journalists and politicians who spout that Marxist stuff really believe it. It merely serves their purposes. They are not that stupid. They are so devoid of the spirit of civic virtue that they could not care less about what harm the Marxist government that they promote does to others.

The Best Way to Tell

Since there is so much confusion about what is constitutional and what is Marxism, why not refer to the very best way to tell the difference? That is, when there is a question, refer to the Constitution itself and to the Ten Points of the Communist Manifesto, which is presented hereinafter.

There are many reasons why there is so much confusion about what is constitutional and what is Marxist. Here are some:

1. The Congress passes Marxist legislation and calls it "constitutional."
2. This legislation goes to the President, who signs it and calls it "constitutional."
3. A case goes to court, and the SCOTUS pronounces Marxist legislation to be "constitutional."
4. Conversely, federal courts often pronounce perfectly constitutional laws to be "unconstitutional."
5. Professors, including law professors, teach that certain Marxist ideas and laws are "constitutional."
6. Furthermore, contrary to what we were taught in school and college, Marxist ideas and politicians are supported by some of the very wealthy. This adds to the confusion.

We live in a time and in a society in which corruption is so rampant that the only way to be sure on questions regarding this matter is to refer to the Constitution itself and to the Communist Manifesto.

Many of the university professors who expound Marxist ideas are no doubt compensated by wealthy foundations. Thus, while *pretending* to be interested in helping the poor and downtrodden, they are actually teaching their students to embrace a philosophy which will eventually enslave the working class and create a structure which the wealthy will rule and also be enriched by.

The Difference between Free Governments and Marxist Governments in a Nutshell

All of the volumes written about Marxism seem to be intended to confuse rather than to enlighten. Here, in a nutshell, is the difference between free governments and Marxist governments;

Governments and Laws in Free Countries are designed to protect the lives, liberties and properties of each and every citizen. They punish the perpetrators who are found guilty of damaging the lives, liberties and properties of innocent citizens. The Constitution of the United States contains provisions, such as the Bill of Rights, to prevent the federal government from infringing upon the rights of the citizens. Furthermore, the powers of government are limited to those delegated to it through the Constitution. Thus, freedom to all citizens is guaranteed because the government is not given the power to punish the citizens for exercising their freedoms, their right to choose, to make choices.

Governments and Laws in Marxist Countries are designed to force or coerce the subjects to perform, to think and to behave such as desired by the ruling elite. Thus, the laws are designed to punish the subjects for making choices and acting upon those choices. Such laws punish people for discriminating. The laws are designed to severely restrict the rights of the people to own property (See the First Point of the Communist Manifesto). Thus, the right to buy and to sell are severely restricted, as is the right to own and to manage a business. Thus, there is no free market, no free enterprise system and no prosperity. The powers of Marxist governments are, in effect, without limits.

It is SO Easy

It is SO easy to distinguish between freedom and tyranny, between constitutionalism and Marxism. Yet so very few Americans seem to be able to do so. So, many Americans who love freedom vote (unknowingly) for politicians who vote for Marxist legislation. Some Americans who love freedom tolerate and even praise judges who violate the Constitution, thereby moving us closer to a dictatorship. I suggest that the reason for this also is very simple.

It is because those who plan to rule over us have gained control over:
1. the media and,
2. education.

The media and education are the two main ways to control the thinking and behavior of the masses. The control of these two is necessary to convince and trick the masses to tolerate and even demand a government that will perform contrary to their own best interests.

I predict that by the time you finish reading this chapter and the next one, you will become an expert in being able to differentiate constitutional laws from Marxist/unconstitutional ones.

Also, since Marxism is the means to gain power over others for the benefit of themselves, it is just natural that people who want to benefit themselves by corrupt laws support Marxist legislation and Marxist politicians even though they do not consider themselves to be Marxists. (However, de facto, they are.)

The wealthy want to concentrate power in their hands, so they push for Marxist laws because Marxist governments are centralized. The rabble in the streets push for Marxist laws because they like the Marxist idea of redistribution of wealth. They think they are going to get something for nothing. So in a government that redistributes the wealth, who does the redistributing? The elitists in the government do. So we have certain wealthy people and then masses of poor all supporting Marxist laws.

> D&C 121: 39: We have learned by sad experience that it is the nature and disposition of almost all men, as soon as they get a little authority, as they suppose, they will immediately begin to exercise unrighteous dominion.

Considering the truthfulness of the above, the Framers of our Constitution constructed it so that the delegation of power is restrained, separated and specified. Those in power can be held accountable by those who are being governed. By contrast, the powers of government in a Marxist government are unlimited and unrestrained. Those being ruled are powerless to bring the rulers to account.

Now we are on the road to getting this tangled up mess untangled. We will learn what Marxism IS NOT and what it IS.

Marxism is NOT Constitutionalism. The Two are Totally Different and Incompatible

Every American needs to understand this because many politicians and judges call constitutional laws "unconstitutional" and unconstitutional laws "constitutional." Constitutional Government (What Marxism is NOT) is founded upon Christian principles, on the Ten Commandments. It is structured so that the rights to life, liberty and property of each and every citizen are considered to be bestowed upon them by their Creator and that the government is created to protect those rights. To do so, the federal government is divided from the states. This is to protect the liberties of the citizens from tyranny of the federal government. All matters relating to life, liberty and property are reserved to the states and to the people, respectively. Then, the powers of government are divided between the federal and the states.

> To understand the difference between constitutionalism (Americanism) and Marxism, study the Constitution and the Ten Points of the Communist Manifesto

The Ninth and Tenth Amendments constitute a barrier between any potential abusive powers of the federal government and the liberties of the people. To further prevent tyranny, the powers of the federal government are divided into three branches, the Legislative, Executive and Judicial. No branch shall exercise the powers delegated to the other two. **The above is what Marxism is NOT, since Marxism contains none of the characteristics of constitutional government and constitutional government contains none of the characteristics of Marxism.**

When attempting to determine whether a certain piece of legislation or act of government is constitutional or Marxist it is most important to rely not upon the words of judges, politicians or academicians, but to rely upon the Constitution itself and **its opposite**, the Ten Points of the Communist Manifesto.

Karl Marx (1818-1883) was born in Prussia and is the founder of Marxism. Marx claimed that his theories, his books and the movement that he created were to liberate the working man from poverty and capitalist slavery. His revolutionary cry was, "Working men of the world, Unite! You have nothing to lose but your chains!" Even today, millions believe Marxist theories and support Marxist movements in the belief that it will result in better lives for the working class and the poor. Hundreds of Marxist university professors spend the entire semester indoctrinating the students in a complicated process to convince their students of the glories of socialism and Communism.

But alas! As is the case in everything in which the Devil is involved, Marxism is trickery. Instead of liberating the working class, **Marxism enslaves the working class**. For proof, look at Russia since the revolution of 1917. Look at every country that Russia conquered after WW II. Look at China since the "Cultural Revolution." (Another lie. It was a bloody, murderous Communist revolution.) Look at Cuba. Look at Venezuela. Marxism does NOT produce the utopia that its proponents promise.

When one examines the Communist Manifesto, he finds that it produces a centralized government, with those at the top of government wielding total power over the people and yet are not in any way accountable to the people. They are not elected. There is no provision in Communist governments for the people to be able to remove abusive or corrupt government officials from their positions of power. Communist governments do not allow their subjects to (with very limited exceptions) own homes, or automobiles, or farms, or businesses or shotguns or dogs.

Especially shotguns. Communist governments do not allow their citizens to exercise freedom of speech nor to own and use private firearms. And, most importantly and most germane to the message of this book, Communist governments do not allow their citizens the free exercise of religion. At least, any religion that professes a belief in God and/or Jesus Christ.

What Marxism REALLY IS

First of all, let us recognize that Marxism is a religion. It is a false religion. It is the Devil's religion. Presidents Marion G. Romney, Ezra Taft Benson and David O. Mckay warned us of this fact:

President Marion G. Romney:

Communism is Satan's counterfeit for the gospel plan and ... it is an avowed enemy of the God of the land. **Communism is the greatest anti-Christ power in the world today and therefore the greatest menace not only to our peace but to our preservation as a free people.** By the extent to which we tolerate it, accommodate ourselves to it, permit ourselves to be encircled by its tentacles and drawn to it, **to that extent we forfeit the protection of the God of this land.**
(*Ensign,* , Sept. 1979,p.5). (Emphasis added)

Marion G. Romney- Public Domain

President Ezra Taft Benson: A Witness and a Warning:

Communism introduced into the world a substitute for true religion. It is a counterfeit of the gospel plan. The false prophets of Communism predict a utopian society. This, they proclaim, will only be brought about as capitalism and free enterprise are overthrown, private property abolished, the family as a social unit eliminated, all classes abolished, all governments overthrown and communal ownership of property in a classless, stateless society established.

Ezra Taft Benson – Public

Since 1917 this godless counterfeit to the gospel has made tremendous progress toward its objective of world domination. (Ensign, Nov 1979 31.) (Emphasis added.)

President David O. McKay Two Contending Forces:

I come with another theme this morning-Two Contending Forces..."In the beginning" they [the two forces] were known as Satan on the one hand and Christ on the other... In these days, they are called "domination by the state," on one hand, "personal liberty," on the other; Communism [read: socialism, Marxism, liberalism, globalism, etc.] on one hand, free agency on the other. (BYU, "Two Contending Forces," May 18, 1960), (Emphasis added.)

David O McKay- Public Domain

Marxism Causes <u>the Devil's Religion</u> to Become Institutionalized

A very important fact that is little known to the Christian world is that not all the forces acting against Christianity are acting at random. There are organizations whose agendas are to attack Christianity and the principles of Christianity. Furthermore, many people who despise Christianity have achieved influential positions in our government, especially in the courts and in education. This causes the religion of the anti-Christ to be not only organized but institutionalized.

Communism, (Socialism, Liberalism, Globalism, Etc.) <u>is a Religion</u>

The statements of Presidents Romney, McKay and Benson above are very clear. Most think of our enemy as merely a political force. But it is more. Much more. We are battling against, literally, the soldiers of Satan. This enemy wants to deprive us not only of our freedom and our assets but wants to capture us mentally and spiritually. Now, let us consider once more the words of the First Presidency in 1941: "**…that unless the people of America forsake the sins and the errors, political and otherwise, of which they are now guilty and return to the practice of the great fundamental principles of Christianity and of Constitutional government, there will be no exaltation for them spiritually and politically we shall lose our liberty and free institutions.**" (Letter to U. S. Treasury, Oct ll, 1941)

"…there will be no exaltation for them spiritually, …" This indicates that those who are on the wrong side of this political battle, even though good people otherwise, are in danger of losing their exaltation. What more do we need to prove that this battle is not only political but spiritual? It seems to me that the doctrine of the Secular Humanists fits all the criteria for being Satan's religion. And that Humanism would fit the criteria for being that kind of a religion that Satan would create for his followers. After all, when the principles of secular Humanism are compared with those of Christianity, they are exactly the opposite.

After all, what is this spiritual battle on earth all about? It is FREE AGENCY! It merely a continuation of the war for free agency in the pre-existence. The Constitution is designed to protect free agency. Marxism is designed to take away free agency.

It is amazing to realize that the majority of Americans, even the best educated, do not understand what Marxism is NOT and what Marxism REALLY IS. This is why Marxism is making such great strides in America. This is why we have a Marist-dominated U. S. Department of Education. This is why Americans elect Marxist politicians to the Congress and to the presidency.

To define and describe Marxism is very simple. Marxism is an ideology that produces a blueprint for a government that is structured so that there is a ruling elite that has total power over all industry, commerce, transportation, banking, communication, education, the people and everything else. This ruling elite is called the "nomenklatura." The ruling elite are not accountable to the working masses. That is to say, that the working masses have no way to control or remove those who rule over them. The government denies to the workers the right to own property. No farms, no ranches, no horses, no cattle, no tractors, no businesses, no trucks, no autos, no dogs and no shotguns. The government strictly denies to the workers the means to defend themselves from the brutality of gangsters, in or out of the government. No rifles, no pistols, no shotguns. No nuthin'!! It is noteworthy that all politicians who vote for Marxist (liberal? progressive?) legislation also hate the Second Amendment. They do not want Americans to have the means to defend themselves against the oppressive government that these leftist politicians plan to impose upon the people of America!

Marxism is the exact opposite of constitutionalism yet few Americans can distinguish between a Marxist law and a constitutional one. It's like the comparison between the submarine and the Boeing 747 in Chapter Three. The distinction between the two is very clear, yet many just can't seem to be able to see it. It is my objective in writing this to help you to: 1: Be able to distinguish between Marxism and constitutionalism and, 2; To understand the difference in the quality of life for all Americans which will be determined by the two different paths that Americans might choose to take. If we choose constitutionalism, it will be freedom and prosperity. If we choose Marxism, it will be despotism and poverty. We have been warned of the consequences of choosing Marxism by a man who is far wiser than I, so let me have him explain it:

President J. Reuben Clark, Jr. and the Reality of Marxism

J. Reuben Clark, Jr. (1871-1961) was a man of great wisdom. Perhaps, on this subject, he had no superior. He was an attorney, served many positions in the U. S. government and served in the first presidency of the Church of Jesus Christ of Latter-day Saints from 1934 to 1951. Here he warns us of the consequences of allowing Marxism to grow in America:

> **President J Reuben Clark, Jr.**: And do not think that all these usurpations, intimidations and impositions are being done to us through inadvertence or mistakes, **the whole course is deliberately planned and carried out; its purpose is to destroy the Constitution and our constitutional government**; then to

bring chaos, out of which the new Statism, with its slavery, is to arise, **with a cruel, relentless, selfish, ambitious crew in the saddle, riding hard with whip and spur, a red-shrouded band of night riders for despotism…**

…If we do not **vigorously fight for our liberties**, we shall go clear through to the end of the road and become another Russia, or worse…(*Church News*, 25 Sep 1949) (Emphasis added.)

To confirm the accuracy of President Clark's statement, one must only look around the world and observe the conditions in those nations under Marist governments. President Clark was indeed a genius in his understanding of such matters. We would be wise to study his counsel seriously.

What Marxism/Communism/Socialism Really Is

Marxism is one huge collection of lies. It is lies from start to finish. It is NOT a government to free the working man of his chains. Just the opposite. Communism enslaves the working class as does no other form of government. Should that be a surprise to any of us, knowing that the Devil is the instigator and organizer of Communism and Communist countries?

Marxism, with its sister ideologies, evolution and secular Humanism, completely, yes-completely, rejects God and Jesus Christ and His gospel. Should we be surprised, then, that the promises of Marxism do not result in benefits for the working class? Should we be surprised that the writings of Marx, which urge the "…working men of the world, [to] unite! You have nothing to lose but your chains!" actually tricks the working man to support a form of government that enslaves him? We need not trouble ourselves with theories. Just look at the reality of Communism. How does the working man live in Russia? China? Venezuela? Cuba? Any Communist country? Yes, I believe that Marxism was and is inspired by the Devil and the results that it is producing is exactly what Marx intended to produce.

The fact that Marxism and its sister ideologies completely reject God and Jesus Christ and His gospel is indisputable evidence that Marxism is the result of the influence of the Devil. For any who might doubt the reality of the existence of the Devil, I offer this from the *Bible Dictionary:*

…The Devil is the enemy of righteousness and of those who seek to do the will of God……Latter-day revelation confirms the biblical teaching that the Devil is a
reality and that he does strive to lead men and women from the work of God. One of the major techniques of the Devil is to cause human beings to think they are following God's ways when in reality they are deceived by the Devil to follow other paths…

The Ten Points of the Communist Manifesto

1. Abolition of [private] property and [private] land and application of all rents of land to public purposes.

2. A heavy progressive or graduated income tax.

3. Abolition of all right to inheritance.

4. Confiscation of all property of all emigrants and rebels.

5. Centralization of credit in the hands of the state, by means of a national bank with State capital and an exclusive monopoly.

6. Centralization of the means of communication and transport in the hands of the state.

7. Extension of factories and instruments of production owned by the State, the bringing of cultivation of waste-lands and the improvement of the soil generally in accordance with a common plan.

8. Equal liability of all to labor. Establishment of industrial armies, especially for agriculture.

9. Combination of agriculture with manufacturing; gradual abolition of the distinction between town and country, by a more equitable distribution of the population over the country,

10. Free education for all children in public schools. Abolition of children's factory labor in its present form. Combination with education and industrial production.

The reality of Marxism is that it is, plainly, a government of raw, unrestrained power structured so that the few ruling elites can rule over the rest of the people with brutal, unrestrained power. The Ten Points of the Communist Manifesto constitute the means by which the Marxists, et. al., plan to wrest the control of the wealth, businesses, education and government from its rightful owners to themselves. That explains the nature of Marxism and the method they use to convert free countries to Marxist ones.

The Marxists/Socialists/Communists/Globalist advocates plan to convert America to the America described by President Clark using, among other things, the Ten Points of the Communist Manifesto.

Please study the Ten Points of the Communist Manifesto. Please note Number 1, the "Abolition of property and land..." This means that the citizens cannot own homes, nor automobiles, nor dogs nor shotguns. Nothing. Certainly not a business. That is certainly the way to enslave people and to keep them enslaved. Note that many of these have been incorporated into our federal government. Especially, # 2, # 5 and, especially, # 10. The Communists certainly do not want to allow the people the right to teach their own children. After all, they might teach them about God, about Jesus Christ, about owning property, about freedom and all that kind of stuff.

Now, please take a really good look at the Ten Points of the Communist Manifesto.

When one examines the Ten Points carefully, he can understand how they can be used to change the structure of a government and convert a free country to a Marxist dictatorship.

Marxism and a Football Game

A Christian American cannot be converted to a Marxist in one step. So the Marxists do it a step at a time. Kind of like the blockers taking down the tacklers so the QB can make his run or pass. The Marxists first take out a person's belief in Adam and Eve, leading him to believe in evolution. Then they destroy his belief in the principles of Christianity and the principles of Americanism one at a time, leading him to believe in the principles of secular Humanism. The intended victim is then ready to be seduced to become a Marxist. In a group of Christians, no Marxists are to be found. Among a group of Marxists, no Christians are to be found.

The Powerful and Wealthy of Marxist Countries

Communist countries are not without their rich, however. It's just that wealth is restricted to the top bosses of the Party. The average working man is robbed of his labor so as to make the Party bosses rich.
- Dictator Putin (1952-) of Russia now has wealth totaling $ 70 BILLION
- Nicolae Ceausescu, (1918-1989) former Communist boss of Romania, had a total wealth of $ 2 Billion. He and his wife lived in opulence while the people lived in poverty.
- Manuel Noriega, (1934-2017) former Communist boss of Panama, had $ 300 million while his people went hungry.

- In Venezuela, former boss Hugo Chavez (1954-2013) had $ 2 billion.
- Present boss Nicolas Maduro Moros (1962-   ) has $ 2 million.
- The net worth for Barack Obama for year 2020 is given as $ 70 million. Before he entered politics, his salary as a community organizer was (average) $36,793/year.

Putin — Russia — Public Domain
Ceausescu — Romania — Public Domain
Noriega — Panama — Public Domain
Chavez — Venezuela — Public Domain
Maduro — Venezuela — Public Domain

It is the same in every dictatorship. There is very little difference in the structure of governments in dictatorships that claim to be non-Communist and those that are Communist. A dictatorship is a dictatorship. And the governments of all Communist countries are dictatorships. Note that the "liberal" media NEVER identifies them as such. Example, when Fulgencio Batista was ruling in Cuba, the media labeled him as the "right-wing (which he was not) dictator." (Which he was.) But when Castro assumed power, he was NEVER called the "left-wing dictator" nor the "Communist dictator" (which he was.) Mind conditioning. Thought control.

Two Contending Forces

Please recall the statements presented previously by the First Presidency in 1941, then those of Presidents Romney, Clark and Benson about Communism being a counterfeit gospel plan. This really is a battle between the forces of Christ and the forces of Satan. It is interesting to note that The Constitution was ratified in 1787 to give America time to get established and an atmosphere of liberty for the gospel to be established. Then, Joseph Smith was born in 1805. Karl Marx was born in 1818. The book of Mormon was published in 1830. The Communist Manifesto was published in 1848. Since then, the battle has been raging. This very definitely is a battle between the forces of Christ and those of the anti-Christ.

When we observe a person doing something to promote the Communist cause for no apparent reason, it must be because *it is his religion! It is his faith! It is his core belief!*

The *Nomenklatura*—the Ruling Elite Wealthy Marxists

At this point, we should introduce those who plan to be the *nomenklatura* of the United States. They plan to rule over us as our masters. Those dictators of Marist countries listed above would be the *nomenklatura* of their countries. And, there are many wealthy and powerful people here in the USA who support Marxist programs and plan to be *nomenklatura* ruling over us.

It comes as a real surprise-or shock- to most Americans to learn that the Communist revolution of 1917 in Russia received financing from some of America's Wall Street financiers. It is true.

This is one of the most difficult things for most people to accept about Marxism. All of our lives, we have been taught that the poor are represented politically by the Left, or the Socialist Democrats. . And the rich are represented by the capitalists or free market Republicans. Today, almost all, if not all, of the Democrats in Congress vote for Marxist laws as do some of those who call themselves Republicans as well. Their agenda, unbeknown to most Americans, is to dissolve the Constitution of the United States so that the U. S. can be merged economically and politically with Mexico and Canada, which would be called the USMCA and then into a world government. This world government would be of a Marxist structure and nature. The elite would rule over us but would not be accountable to us. Just like President J. Reuben Clark described. This explains the riddle of why some of the wealthy support Marxist programs. Some of the rich and powerful groups involved in this world government, are the members of the Council on Foreign Relations, (CFR), the Bilderbergers (BB) and the Trilateral Commission (TC).

The *Nomenklatura* of America

The nomenklatura of America? Sounds like the ultimate oxymoron, does it not? Here we live in the land of the free and the home of the brave, the land of capitalism, free enterprise and the greatest prosperity enjoyed by any people in the history of the world. So how could there be more than a handful of freakish *nomenklatura* in this great land? It took me years to figure out the answer to this (all by myself!) The answer is that the rich and powerful are not exempt from being greedy and power-hungry. Worse yet, it seems that the more wealth and power that some people accrue, the more they crave. Desire? Crave? Become ravenous for? The wealthy, especially those who control the media, have great influence over elections. Then they have millions for lobbyists to "influence" unscrupulous politicians. So the wealthy few have much more influence and control over elections and elected officials than do the masses of the poor and the middle class.

Now, what is the easiest way for the rich and powerful to accrue more wealth and power? The honorable and legal way is for them to produce something that everybody else wants to buy. If they produce a million widgets and can sell them and make a million dollars, or ten million, or whatever, then everybody is better off. The free enterprise system, the Constitution and freedom are preserved. But Alas! Far too few of the wealthy and powerful (the nomenklatura) willingly accept such restraints upon their investments of wealth, power and influence. Q: So what is the fastest and easiest way for the wealthy and powerful to accrue more wealth and power?

A: Why, with laws that favor themselves, of course. Or better yet, laws that favor their cartels and restrict competition with them. (Remember, John D. Rockefeller stated, while accumulating his wealth, "Competition is a sin.") And while these wealthy nomenklatura are busily engaged in increasing their wealth and power, they heartily embrace and advocate the principles of Marxism, as found in the Ten Points of the Communist Manifesto. These Ten Points result in the centralization and collectivization of power in order to render special privileges to the privileged few. This centralization of power, by definition, is collectivization, which is, by definition, socialism, whose origin is Marxism. This centralization of power, of course, constitutes corruption of constitutional government. As the transformation of the government moves from constitutional to fully corrupted, it goes first from constitutional to socialism and then, when the corruption is complete, to Communism. The tyranny and the misery begin. As President J. Reuben Clark Jr. stated that the "red-shrouded band of night riders, riding hard with whip and spur," begin their reign of tyranny.

The wealthy of this country have sufficient assets to squash the movement toward Marxism at any time. But they do not, because they support the Marxist movement and are part of it. They plan to benefit from it. Just check out the list of multi-millionaires and billionaires who are members of the CFR, which supports the destruction of the Constitution and the move to merge the U. S. into a world government.

But the above is only an abbreviated version of the process. There is more. Much more. In the process, while the rich and powerful are accruing more wealth and power, they are avidly coming to advocate (whether they believe them or not) those principles of government that favor themselves. At the expense of their fellow man, of course. In this process of accruing more and more wealth and power, the nomenklatura must gain control over media and education to convince the masses that this scheme of power that the wealthy are promoting is in their (the masses) best interests. This is where religion comes in. Now please remember the words of Presidents Grant, McKay, Clark, Benson and others[39] when they warned that the Communists were introducing a new religion—Satan's religion?

Yes, this religion of greed has attraction for the wealthy, the middle-class and the poor. And, the government that the deluded poor, middle-class and wealthy are seduced to support, finance and build serves, at the end, to

---

39. Please refer back to the Introduction.

enslave them all, physically and mentally. This seduction of corruption includes everyone. No one is excluded. In the manipulation of the minds of the masses, the control of the media and education is necessary. This new worldview that the nomenklatura wishes to inculcate into the minds of all Americans involves (but is not limited to) the origin of man, the nature of man and the government of man. (Does not the gospel of Jesus Christ cover these same topics?) Is that not true to the way that Satan works? We must not consider it a mere coincidence that the ideology involved in the building of socialism/ Communism is exactly the opposite of that of the gospel of Jesus Christ.

On whose side will we each commit our time, our resources and our energies? Whose ideology will we support? That of Christ and political freedom or that of Satan and tyranny?

The Redistribution of the Wealth

The redistribution of wealth is a key feature of Marxism. It appeals to the rabble in the streets because they anticipate that much of the wealth that is to be taken from the wealthy and redistributed will be distributed to *them*. For this reason, Marxism appeals to the masses. Now, if the wealth is going to be redistributed, *somebody* has to do the redistributing.

This is what appeals to the wealthy. They anticipate that *they* will be the ruling elite handling the redistributing. So from top to bottom, the **attraction of Marxism is pure greed. Lust for power and wealth.**

The problem is, as is well demonstrated in every single Marxist country in the world, there simply is not enough wealth to go around to these greedy masses and the greedy ruling elites. So the Nomenklatura live in luxury but the masses live in poverty and misery. No theory or speculation is needed. The evidence is abundant and overwhelming.

Marxist ("Liberal," "Progressive" etc.) Politicians and the Right to Bear Arms (Second Amendment)

There is a clear, definite and unmistakable correlation in the voting records of the members of the U. S. Congress and the movement to restrict the use of and then deprive ownership of private firearms by citizens of the United States. That is, those who want to deprive U. S. citizens of the right to own and to legally bear private firearms are the very same ones who vote for "liberal," "progressive" or Marxist legislation. An undeniable correlation. It is clear that the economic and political government that these politicians plan for us is to be an oppressive one, just as President Clark warned. They know that when oppression reaches a certain point, the people would rise up in resistance, just as our forefathers did in 1776. This is why they want to disarm us. They want to deprive us of the ability to defend ourselves or to resist the imposition of an oppressive government that they plan to impose upon us.

The Coming New World Religion—Membership Mandatory

On 11 September, 1991, President George H. W. Bush addressed the Congress and in his speech **twice mentioned** the term, "New World Order." What he conveniently failed to mention is that part of this NWO movement is also a movement to develop a new world religion. I believe it is called, at this time, **the "United Religious Initiative Project."**

Just as the sovereignty of all nations is to be obliterated as all nations are absorbed into the NWO, all religions are to be obliterated and replaced by the world religion. I believe it safe to predict that this "religion" will be a combination of evolution, secular Humanism and Marxism and forced upon the people with Marxist-like powers. Its principles will be the opposite of Christianity. Definitely anti-Christ. Should we be surprised that some members of the secret combinations are the same ones who are launching the attacks against Christianity these days?

If the proponents of the United Nations and the *United Religious Initiative Project* continue as they have been performing for decades, when can the UN use its full political force and finances to favor this World Church and to persecute all Christian churches. Leopards do not change their spots.

HOWEVER:

> First: please recall the above about liberation theology (Marxism) being taught to the poor people of all Latin America.
>
> Second: please recall from above the reference to the World Council of Churches and
>
> Third: please recall what Pacepa said about the Black Liberation movement here in the United States.

Building Hatred Toward Christians and Christianity

Because Christians and Christianity are good, it is illogical and irrational for most people to hate them. So the Devil must figure out some trickery and deception to cause people to hate that which is good. (To perceive that which is good to be evil.) One way is for him to entice them to believe in and then embrace that which appears to be good (or neutral toward good and evil) but which is evil. (Maybe like a vivacious but promiscuous young woman or a handsome, rich but predacious young man.)

But mostly it is done by labeling Christians and Christianity with pejorative-sounding adjectives in order to project a very unfavorable image to the public. No matter that there is absolutely no evidence to support the smear.

Are Christianity and Marxism Compatible?

Thus far, Marxism has never worked (for the people. It has worked for the ruling elite) in real life—and, without exception, in the places where Marxism has been the governmental model, Christians have been persecuted. Marxists hate us Christians because we stand in the way of their objectives. We promote liberty for all. We stand for the rule of law. For justice. Not social justice but real American justice. We want to make men free. The Marxists want to enslave all men, physically, mentally and spiritually. This scripture explains the natural antipathy between Marxists and Christians (2 Cor 3:17:)

> Now the Lord is that Spirit: and **where the Spirit of the Lord *is*, there *is* liberty**.

It is for this reason that the Marxists want to suppress, then extinguish, Christianity in the land, because it is a barrier to their scheme for political conquest and for subjugating the minds of the people.

There are several aspects of Marxism, as a philosophy, that put it at odds with the Christian faith. Here are a few:

Marxism is, at heart, an atheistic philosophy with no room for belief in God. Karl Marx himself was clear on this point: "The first requisite of the happiness of the people is the **abolition of religion**" ("A Criticism of the Hegelian Philosophy of Right," 1844).

Christianity, of course, is rooted in theism and is all about God. In the Marxist model, the state becomes the provider, sustainer, protector and lawgiver for every citizen; in short, the state is viewed as God. Christians always appeal to a higher authority—the God of the universe—and the politicians of Marxist governments despise the idea of there being any authority higher than themselves.

Fundamental to Christianity is that the human race started with Adam and Eve. This is in direct conflict with the theory of evolution and with the Humanist Manifesto I, II and III. Completely incompatible. This is another reason that the Humanists and Marxists hate us and consider us an enemy to be eliminated.

(Deuteronomy 5:19) "Neither shalt thou desire thy neighbour's wife, neither shalt thou covet thy neighbour's house, his

> Marxism is an ideology used as a tactic to trick the working man to build up a government that ultimately enslaves him. This government is collectivist and is ruled from the top by the super-rich. It denies to the worker the right of self-government and the right to property.

field, or his manservant, or his maid-servant, his ox, or his ass, **or any thing that is thy Neighbour's**." (Deut. 5:21)

The utopia that Marxism promises is earthly and man-made; Christians look to the Lord Jesus to establish a heavenly, perfect kingdom some day. Believers understand that, given man's sinful nature, there is no perfect system in this world. Greed and abuse of power and selfishness and laziness will taint even the purest motives.

Even if it were possible to have a perfect government, it would not be possible for it to be administered perfectly, for the administrators would be, naturally, mortals.

Some people attempt to combine Christianity with Marxist philosophy. Their attempts may be well-meaning, but they are impractical. The Puritans in the New World tried communal living for a while. When the Plymouth Colony was founded, there was no private property and all food was distributed equally amongst all, regardless of one's job (or work ethic). But that system, lacking any incentive to hard work, was soon abandoned as a complete failure. See "Of Plymouth Plantation" by Plymouth Colony Governor William Bradford for the full story. Following is a table to show the contrast between constitutional government and regional/Marxist government.

Constitutional Government	Regional/Marxist Government
1. The ultimate source of authority is our Creator.	1. The source of all authority is with the ruler; the person at the apex of power.
2. Our Creator bestows upon us our rights and a certain amount of authority.	2. The people have no rights. Only limited privileges, bestowed by the government, often called "rights."
3. We, the People, by the Constitution, bestow limited authorities upon certain agents of government to perform certain specified functions.	3. The flow of authority does not flow from the people, as all authority originates with the supreme ruler.

4. The powers of government are limited by these two methods: A. to those powers authorized by the Constitution and, B. are further limited by the Bill of Rights; the First Ten Amendments to the Constitution.	4. The powers of government are not limited.
5. The federal government has one specified purpose and that is to defend the states from enemies foreign and domestic.	5. There is no division of powers.
6. The powers of government are divided into legislative, executive and judicial to avoid tyranny. Each branch of government is prevented from exercising powers delegated to another branch.	6. The supreme ruler holds all powers; legislative, executive and judicial. This is the very definition of tyranny.
7. When a citizen is charged with a crime, he has all of the protection of the Constitution. The government must prove his guilt. He is considered to be innocent until proven guilty. The citizen is guaranteed the full protection of due process of law.	7. A citizen can be charged and convicted without due process of law. If tried, he is tried under the rules of procedure as proscribed by his accuser. In the worst tyrannies, there is not even the pretense of a trial.
8. The federal government is restricted, by the Ninth and Tenth Amendments, from oppressing the citizens since it has no authority to meddle in matters regarding their lives, liberties or properties. Such matters are reserved to the states and to the people, respectively.	8. The power of the government is not limited.

9. The officers of government are elected by and accountably to the people. All officers of the state, county and city governments that legislate, execute and adjudge the laws are accountable to the people.	9. All officers of government are accountable only to the supreme ruler. They are not accountable to the people in any way.

The structure, purpose and procedures of this regional government is very similar to a Marxist government. All it needs to be a Communist government is just more time to continue destroying the Constitution and more time to further strengthen this regional government. As the regional government is strengthened, the Constitutional government is rendered impotent. So with a little more time, the United States will be completely regionalized. Or call it Marx-ized.

This regional government was created by Executive Order # 11647 by President Richard Nixon on February 14, 1972. Nixon had absolutely no authority to create this regional government. It is not a part of the Constitutional government. It is completely incompatible with the Constitution. I consider this act by Nixon to be treason of the worst kind. Watergate wasn't even "chicken stealin'" compared with this.

Executive Order 11647 Issued on February 14, 1972 by Richard Nixon Created a New Government. A radically different kind of government!! A government with the characteristics of a tyranny that is designed to eventually supplant our constitutional government. Think of the ramifications of that!!!

This act by President Nixon was completely unconstitutional. Yes, I know, presidents had been and have been using such executive orders for years. But the repetition of an unlawful act does not make it lawful. Here is the truth about executive orders: A president may initiate all of the executive orders that he wants to, as long as they pertain to the administration of his executive branch of the government. He may NOT (legally) execute executive orders that affect the lives, liberties or properties of the citizens. The Constitution states that all (meaning ALL) legislative powers are vested in the Congress.

> **The Constitution of the United States, Article I, Section 1:** All legislative powers herein granted shall be vested in a Congress of the United States, which shall consist of a Senate and House of Representatives.

No legislative powers are vested in the executive branch. None. Every executive order that has ever been issued that involves the lives, liberties and/or properties of the people is unconstitutional, null and void for any legal purpose.

This regional government violates the separation of powers doctrine of the Constitution as it exercises legislative, executive and judicial powers. The exercise of these three powers constitutes the very definition of tyranny. It also violates the distribution of powers doctrine as it usurps jurisdiction over matters intended to be governed by the states. Here is the definition of, "tyranny":

> **Tyranny:** Arbitrary or despotic government, the severe and autocratic exercise of sovereign power, either vested constitutionally in one ruler, or usurped by him by breaking down the division and distribution of governmental powers. (*Black's Law Dictionary*)

The agencies administered under this regional government (hereinafter RG) exercise legislative, executive and judicial powers. This constitutes the very definition of tyranny. When the Congress enacts a law to give the federal government more power over certain matters that were previously under the jurisdiction of the states, the jurisdiction of these matters is now shifted from the states to the RG of the federal government. When the matters were under the states, they were under state law, which included the legislative, executive and judicial branches, which operated under the Constitution of each respective state.

Therefore, the citizens enjoyed liberty, the absence of abuse of their lives, liberties and properties because 1: The federal government was prevented by the Ninth and Tenth Amendment from touching the lives, liberties and properties of the people and, 2: the state governments were prevented from touching the lives, liberties and properties because of the limitations and restraints upon the powers granted to each branch of the state government by its respective constitution.

That is the best system ever devised by man to protect the lives, liberties and properties of the people.

When the jurisdiction over matters are shifted from the state governments to the federal RG, there is a drastic change, to wit:

1. The regulations, enforced as "laws" are created in these RG bureaucracies by unelected bureaucrats. They are not known by the people nor are they accountable to them.

2. These regulations are administered and enforced by unelected bureaucrats who are in no way accountable to the people over whom they have power.

3. When a citizen is charged with the violation of a regulation, he must appear in an administrative tribunal, sometimes called a "court" in an agency of the executive (NOT JUDICIAL) branch of the government. In these tribunals, the citizen has NO protection of the Constitution, since the Constitution is not allowed in these tribunals. The accused are allowed certain privileges, sometimes referred to as "rights," that have been drawn up by some bureaucrat in the agency of his accuser! **By his accuser!**

> All that is necessary for a government to be a tyrannical dictatorship is for the government to have unlimited control over the people and the people have no control over the government.

The fact cannot be evaded that the "laws" in the regulatory agencies of the RG are created, enforced and judged in the executive branch of the federal government. This fits the definition of "tyranny" exactly.

Please study and ponder the above until you can envision all the ramifications.

All that is necessary to transform a free country to a Marxist dictatorship is to make the necessary changes where the people have no control over the government and the government has total, unlimited power over the people and the people are not allowed to own property, especially guns. When and if the transition to the federal RG is fully completed, the result will be a tyrannical Marxist dictatorship.

Another huge problem with this RG is the shift of loyalties with the expansion of the RG. In constitutional government, the loyalties of the state employees remains generally to the respective state constitutions, the governors and the people of their states. With the growth of the number of employees in the RG, the loyalties of these employees tends to be not with the people but to the president. More tendency toward one-man-rule. As of 2020, the number of federal employees was two million. The number in the RG not found. Under constitutional government, these two million and their political loyalties, would be mostly dispersed throughout and employed by the various states. But the RG exacerbates our problems of runaway federal government since the majority of these federal employees will always vote for more and more government. Just any kind of government just so it is more.

Is the Regional Government Really a Tyranny?

The RG fits the definition of "tyranny" perfectly. If anyone tries to defend it by the claim that "we are getting along just fine now," just explain that the RG has not reached its full maturity. Once it has, the tyrants will wait for, or create, a crisis of some kind and then, at midnight some night, make the move to consolidate their totalitarian control. Governments structured like a tyranny are not created that way for no reason.

Following are two maps: one to depict the United States under constitutional government and the other to depict it under regional/Marxist government. Please see the following page.

Map A: Constitutional Government

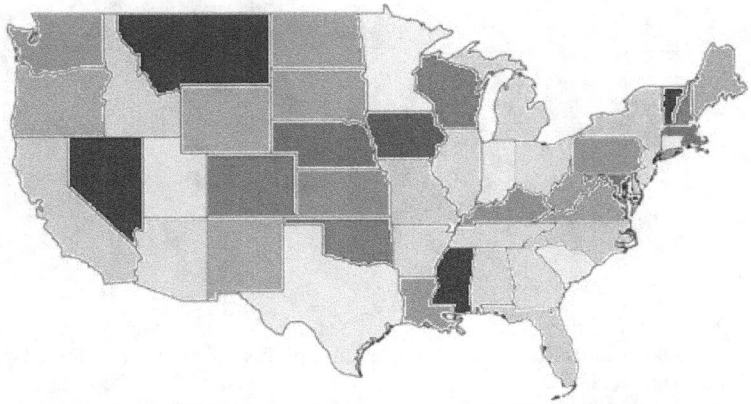

Map A depicts a United States with a government derived of definite and limited powers from the people through the Constitution. The powers are divided into federal and into state. These powers of the federal government are then separated into three different branches-legislative, executive and judicial-with the powers of each branch limited to those specified in the Constitution.

The people are protected in their inalienable rights by two methods:
1. The powers authorized to the federal government are limited; they do not authorize the federal government to assault the lives, liberties or properties of the citizens and,
2. The 9th and the 10th Amendments further and very specifically limit the powers of the federal. The borders of each state **constitute a tyranny-proof barrier** to acts of federal tyranny. Thus, Map "A" depicts a government which will preserve and respect, in perpetuity, the lives, liberties and properties of the people, as long as the provisions of the Constitution are held inviolate.

Map B: Regionalized, Marxist Government

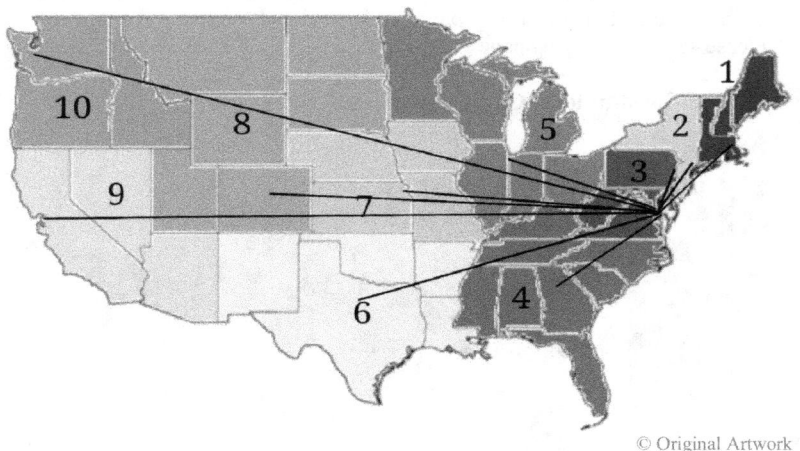

© Original Artwork

Map B depicts a United States divided into ten regions. The powers of this government are **unlimited**.[40] The "regulations" of this government, enforced as laws, originate in Washington, D. C. and are enforced in all of the states, reaching across all state lines. These "laws" are written by unknown federal bureaucrats, enforced by unknown federal bureaucrats and judged by unknown federal bureaucrats. None of them are elected by the people. They are not accountable to the people. All three functions of government are combined in these regulatory agencies, constituting the very definition of "tyranny." This government is designed to replace our constitutional government.

As the Constitution is violated and an increasing number of federal "regulations" or "laws" are enforced upon the citizens, this very effectively disempowers the state governments and empowers the regional government.

Thus, it is easy to visualize the inevitable result of such usurpation of power by the regional government. What remains is just feeble state governments and a regionalized federal government with unlimited powers. That is no way accountable to the citizens.

Under this regionalized government, the citizens have no unalienable rights but only limited privileges (mistakenly called "rights") bestowed by the regulatory agencies.

Thus, in the administrative tribunals (called, mistakenly, "courts" by the agencies) the only rights an accused citizen has are those extremely limited

---

40. If their powers have limits, please show them to me.

ones bestowed upon him by the agency itself, by his accuser. The ultimate objective (of the SCs) is to merge the U.S. with Mexico and Canada to constitute one region, or the "North American Union," and then merge this union into a world government of regions, with its own world religion, with the government having no accountability to the people. In other words, the people (that's us) will be slaves.

These regulatory agencies have none of the characteristics of constitutional government and all of the characteristics of Marxist government. Don't believe it? Make the comparison yourself. For a comparison of Constitutional with Marxist (and regional) governments, please see the table on approx. p. 90.

Richard M. Nixon was a member of the Council on Foreign Relations (CFR). Probably, there never has been a constituency more betrayed than that betrayed by Richard Milhaus Nixon. In 1968, Nixon campaigned on a solidly conservative (constitutionalist) platform. I remember. I worked to help get him elected. After being elected, Nixon turned on his supporters and friends and pushed through a Socialist agenda. They didn't call him "Tricky Dicky" for no reason. The creation of this regional government to eventually replace the Constitutional one can justifiably be called pure treason. Richard Nixon was certainly loyal to the CFR and definitely a domestic enemy of the Constitution and of conservative Republicans.

As we proceed, please keep in mind that this is serious business. We are talking about the Lord's form of government and liberty on the one hand and the Devil's and tyranny on the other. Yessir, serious business.

Putting the Pressure on Businesses

This RG is designed so that it can be used to put the pressure on businesses that might resist oppressive regulations. What business owner does not cringe at the threat of an OSHA inspection, or a charge by the EPA or some other regulatory agency? Such business owners, even if they are completely innocent of any wrongdoing, might have to send tens of thousands or hundreds of thousands in legal costs just to prove his innocence. The ability to make such threats constitutes a dangerous weapon in the wrong hands.

This regionalized government is exactly the type of government that would serve the purposes of the secret combinations. Therefore, we can safely assume that the members of the combinations were involved in its planning. I believe that we are on the right track.

The two maps depicted above are for two entirely different types of government. Yet, a succession of presidents, senators, representatives and federal judges have pretended that the Marxist RG is compatible with the

Constitution. If we are going to restore constitutional government and save our liberties, we have to know the difference. Even though the politicians and judges are too dumb to know, (or just do not care) we must know. We must understand.

The Structure of a Marxist Government Marxist governments are structured so that all power originates from the apex-at the very top and then is delegated to various persons of lesser power. The ruler at the top can give orders regarding all production, all distribution and any person.

Understanding the Fundamentals of Constitutional Government The structure and purpose of the U. S. Constitutional government is the exact opposite of that of a Marxist government. Let's look at this illustration of the flow of power in our constitutional government. It starts with our Creator, who bestows rights upon each of us. (Note: This principle is VERY important but badly violated and neglected. The government does NOT have the authority to bestow rights to any person or to any group. Not the Executive, not the legislature and not the judiciary.) We then can unite and form a government for our protection. By the Constitution, we delegate certain limited and just (we are not authorized to delegate unjust powers to the government, although we certainly do. This is a very important but badly neglected principle) powers to certain positions in the government. The government is separated between federal and the states. The federal government is divided into three separate branches and no branch is authorized to exercise the powers delegated to another branch. To do so would be usurpation.

Final Definition of Marxism

Here is a brief synopsis of the definition of Marxism:

> Marxism, with socialism and Communism, is, in finality, robbery, theft, imperialism, brutality, inhumanity, lies, deception, infidelity, betrayal, murder, treason, genocide, debauchery, Humanism, atheism and tyranny institutionalized. It is the collectivization and centralization of economic and police power for the benefit of the ruling elite at the expense of the working class. For verification of this definition, just examine any Communist country, past or present. Marxism is the exact opposite of constitutionalism. (Joe H. Ferguson 01 Sep 2019)

The Hoaxes of Marxism

> 1st. The hoax that Marxism is intended to free the working man from his chains. Examining the working and living conditions of the working men in every Marxist country in the world proves that this promise to the working men is a gigantic hoax.

2nd. Teaching high school and university students to believe in Marxist ideas and programs *without explaining to them* that IT IS Marxism. This is a horrendous cruel hoax.

3rd. Marxism is really an ideology to build governments to deliver total power and wealth to a certain ruling elite, usually called the *nomenklatura*. The working people are serfs. This is another huge hoax.

4th. The Congress passes Marxist legislation and calls it "constitutional". A hoax. The President signs this legislation and calls it "constitutional". A hoax. The Supreme Court judges this legislation and pronounces it to be "constitutional". Such rulings are pure hoaxes. Hard to believe that people in authority in our government would commit such treacherous acts, but absolutely true.

5th. The regional government created by President Richard Milhaus Nixon in 1972 is obviously intended to replace the Constitutional government of the United States. That is very easy to prove because that is exactly what has been happening since 1972. As more laws are passed that violate the Ninth and Tenth Amendments and which further empower the federal bureaucracies, the powers and jurisdictions of the fifty states are diminished. All that is necessary for the United States to be transmogrified into a Marxist dictatorship is for this present trend to continue to its logical conclusion.

A Government Built by Liars on Lies and Hoaxes Cannot Possibly Be Friendly to Christianity.

Because congressmen, presidents and judges often invert the meanings of "constitutional" and "unconstitutional, I wish to present here the definition of both and also a little story to help us all get the definitions of the two straight.

Constitutional: Consistent with the Constitution; authorized by the Constitution; not conflicting with any provision of the Constitution or fundamental law of the state. And

Unconstitutional: That which is contrary to the Constitution. The opposite of "constitutional." (Both from *Black's Law Dictionary*)

Suppose you are walking along the waterfront by a shipyard and you observe that something is under construction. You call down to the foreman and ask, "What are you building?" He responds, "A Boeing 747." But you see them laying what appears to be a keel for a ship. You are puzzled—but do not feel that you should question authority. A few days later, you can see that a hull of a ship is taking place. Then in a few days, a conning tower and a periscope.

You ask again, "What are you building?" "A Boeing 747." Indeed puzzling.

A few days later, you observe the launching. The object is launched into the water. It submerged and went away, with only a periscope showing. If it is a submarine and not a Boeing 747, the authority, the foreman, lied to you. Who and what are you going to believe? Was it a Boeing 747 or a submarine? This is what we are faced with in analyzing some of the rulings of the SCOTUS regarding "constitutionality" and "unconstitutionality." The people in authority lie to us.

The reality is that some sources of authority are also sources of disinformation[41]; of lies. Yes, some sources of authority are liars. Discomfiting, but true. We must be cognizant of this reality.

Please note that the meanings of "constitutional" and "unconstitutional" are exactly the opposite. They are not just a little bit different. Neither can one be honestly substituted for the other. I know this sounds overly simplistic. But keep this in mind, as this will become the crux of our argument and our allegations against some very malicious judgments of the SCOTUS.

What is the Attraction of Marxism?

When looking at the conditions of life of the working people of Communist countries, it is obvious that Marxism is a terrible form of government. Then why do Marxist governments exist?

The first attraction is power. There are plenty of power-hungry people in every country, including the United States, who covet power over all else. They care not who they hurt in the abuse of that power. They know that among the lower class, there are those who will vote for any politician who will promise them something for nothing; even if the promises turn out to be empty ones. Then there is the use of force and the threat of force. Then there is the use of deception, deception and more deception, as is explained herein. Further institutionalized deception. Which is professional deception with armies of agents of influence to activate it.

There is the use of corrupt government being directed by corrupt politicians using corrupt laws. All of this is used to conquer a free people. Then there are all of the tactics, strategies, sophistries and stratagems used against a confused populace. Now, as to these tactics.

The Wealthy Use Marxism to Deceive and Enslave the Working Class

The membership of the Council on Foreign Relations is comprised mostly of the wealthy, such as David Rockefeller. It was the CFR that pushed for the

---

41. About which more later.

organization of the United Nations in 1945, with Alger Hiss, a member of the CFR and also a proven Communist, a former agent for the Soviet Union during World War II, while occupying a position high in the U. S. State Department. Hiss *supposedly* represented the United States during the formation of the United Nations. Right from its inception, the objective of the CFR has been to weaken the Constitution of the United States so that the United States can be merged into a Marxist-like world government. That is the very same objective as is that of the Communist Party, USA. So the Communists and the very wealthy are all working for the same objective—a world totalitarian Globalist government, with the government having total power and the people having no rights.

The Council on Foreign Relations has the same goal for a one-world Socialist government as does the Communist Party USA and the United Nations that was organized by Alger Hiss, a Communist, to be a world government and NOT just a debating society! (ELLIOTT GRAHAM)

This explains how perilous our situation is.

Note that Antonio Gramsci's soldiers are marching right through the institutions of America. Right on schedule. Media, education, entertainment, health care, government at all levels. We are brought face to face with the reality of what we are facing as President J. Reuben clark, Jr. compares our situation with that of the Jaredites when their morality, societal values and rule of law broke down:

President J. Reuben Clark, Jr.:[42]

> **"Prophecies, Penalties and Blessings"** We are not given the step-by-step backsliding of this Jareditic civilization till it reached the social and governmental chaos the record sets out, but those steps seem wholly clear from the results. Put into modern terms, we can understand them. First there was a forsaking of the righteous life and the working of wickedness, then must have come the extortion and oppression of the poor by the rich; then retaliation and reprisal by the poor against the rich; then would come a cry to share the wealth which should belong to all; then the easy belief that society owed every man a living whether he worked or not; then the keeping of a **great body of idlers**; then when community revenues failed to do this, as they always have failed and always will fail, a self-helping by one to the goods of his neighbor; and finally when the neighbor resisted, as resist he must, or starve with his family, then death to the neighbor and all that belonged to him. **This was the decreed "fulness of iniquity."**

---

42. Alynski, Saul, Rules For Radicals a Pragmatic Primer for Realistic Radicals, Vintage books, New York, 1971, no page number. In Front of book.

This is being written in June of 2020. We are witnessing the breakdown of the rule of law, of law and order, of civilization. Riots in the streets. Mayors refusing to order the chiefs of police of many cities to quell the riots; to arrest the criminal rioters. We must presume that some sinister political force is ordering, enticing or threatening the mayors. Whatever the reason, we can see, with chilling reality, how our condition compares with that of the Jaredites as their civilization deteriorated. The deep state and the secret combinations of the Devil are gaining control of our governments at all levels.

The Transition from Freedom to Marxism (Socialism, Communism, etc.)

Communist military takeovers are quick, noisy and bloody. Communist legislative takeovers, such as the one in which we find ourselves and as described previously by Senator Jenner and as forewarned by President J. Reuben Clark, Jr., are silent, insidious and lengthy. Ours started in about 1912 with the election of Woodrow Wilson and the passage of the graduated income tax (Amendment XVI), the method of selecting U. S. senators (Amendment XVII) and the passage of the Federal Reserve Act. Then WW I then FDR and his New Deal with its massive federal programs, which constituted changes in the type of government.

Then WW II. Wars are perfect times for changes in the structure and purpose of government, since nobody is paying attention to politics. They are focused on the war. In 1947, the SCOTUS passed the *Everson* ruling, outlawing God from the classrooms and all governmental intercourse. Then the Korean war, with U. S. troops fighting the Communist North Korea (and China and Russia) while *under the command of the Communist-dominated United Nations!*

All of this about regional Marxist government sounds un-American, does it not? Well, if that is what you are thinking, you are absolutely right, because it is! Richard Nixon had absolutely zero authority to create this new government. To do legally what he did illegally would have required the calling of a constitutional convention. That did not happen. Check the Constitution. There is no provision for regional government. This regional government creates laws, enforces laws and judges laws. This consolidation of powers constitutes the very definition of tyranny, which is:

> **Tyranny:** Arbitrary or despotic government; the severe and autocratic exercise of sovereign power, whether vested constitutionally in one ruler, or usurped by him by breaking down the division and distribution of governmental powers. (*Black's Law Dictionary,* 5th Ed., West, St. Paul, 1979.)

This regional government was birthed, nourished and empowered for the specific purpose of depriving American citizens of their God-given natural rights and merging the United States into a Marxist, global government, to be dominated by Communists or Marxist-thinking dictators.

All the while the above was taking place, starting way back when with John Dewey and Horace Mann, our public education system was being transformed to teach the students to not only not oppose these changes but to accept and embrace them. Then, in 1947, came the *Everson* case, which outlawed any mention of God or the Ten Commandments in our classrooms or public discourse and installed, de facto, secular Humanism as the national religion of the United States. All of this has been done illegally. In violation of the Constitution, which is supposed to be the Supreme Law of the Land.

And back in about 1920, J. P. Morgan and crowd effectively gained control of the media.

While the above has been taking place, there has been an increasing imposition of Marxist ideas into our educational system at all levels. Some of the members of Congress have become militantly Marxist.

All Tyrannies Employ Huge Bureaucracies to Enforce Their Will

Tyrants find it impossible to force their will upon the millions of people whom they rule. Therefore, they must employ (none excepted) huge cadres of bureaucrats to enforce their will. Hitler did it. Stalin did it. Castro did it. They all do it. The Regional Government is the huge bureaucracy in our government that one man, the president, can use to enforce his will upon every citizen in America. Please give the threat that this imposes very serious thought.

All of the above, plus much more, can be considered to be "Gramsci's Long March Through the Institutions." That is what Marxism really is. Deception, fraud, usurpation of power, abuse of power, treachery, violation of trusts, pride, ego and self-aggrandizement and self-enrichment at the expense of others. Marxism is an ideology that produces a government that is structured to subjugate and enslave the people and to give the ruling elite total and absolute power over the people.

The Nature of Most Politicians

Most politicians are considerably different from the average American. Their desire for approval and for the lusts for the perks of public office usually exceed all else. So when someone approaches them and promises them the support of the masses and ALSO finances from the wealthy if they will only support certain legislation, they go for it immediately. This legislation is that which is designed to convert free America to a Marxist dictatorship and put these wealthy Marxists in positions of advantage and power.

That is what Marxism really is. For more on Marxist tricks, see the Appendix, "Communist/Leftist/Globalist/Marxist Fronts and RIOTS."

Globalists and Internationalists

The use of the terms "Globalist" and "internationalist" to describe one's political bent has become trendy in some segments of today's society. But in reality, the agenda of the Globalist and internationalist movement is to violate and weaken, then destroy the Constitution. Then, to merge the United States into a world government, which would be Marxist in nature. Mostly, the Globalist movement is comprised of the wealthy and powerful. And they LOVE the United Nations (U.N.)

When the UN was organized in 1945, the man supposedly representing the United States was Alger Hiss, later proven to have been a Soviet agent. A traitor to America. For those who still believe the UN to be what it claims to be, a peace-keeping body, please consider this statement by the UN itself: https://thenewamerican.com/great-reset-imf-to-redistribute-u-s-wealth-via-proto-global-currency/ "We must build entirely new foundations for our economic and social systems" such as no more private property. (1976 UN Declaration on Human Settlements. 1992 Agenda 21, 2015 UN Agenda 2030)

Please consider, very carefully, the above statement by the UN to "…redistribute U S. wealth…such as no more private property." This is fundamental Marxist doctrine.

We must be alert to the development of this "Great Reset" and be prepared to expose and oppose it.

Marxism is Wickedness and Wickedness Never Brings Happiness

Alma tells us, **"…Behold, I say unto you, wickedness never was happiness."** (Alma 41:10). Everything about Marxism is wicked. Its deprivation of free agency, its confiscation of the property of the workers, its lies, its deception, its murders and all the misery that it inflicts upon mankind. Just look at the state of misery of the working people in Communist countries.

And Alma, above, was directing these remarks to us as individuals. But this also applies to nations as well. Nations with wicked government never bring happiness!

Chapter Nine - Communist/Leftist/Globalist Tactics and Tricks

> When you have an immoral society that
> has blatantly, proudly,
> violated all of the commandments of
> God, there is one last virtue they insist
> upon; <u>tolerance for their immorality</u>
> Dr. James Kennedy, Ph D[43]

We are now only one chapter away from the subversion of the law and the Supreme Court.

Lest one be confused by the above chapter title, it is made so in order to emphasize the fact that the Communist rabble in the streets, the Marxist professors, all Leftists and the super-rich Globalists whose objective is to merge America with Canada and Mexico then a Globalist (world) government **all use the same or similar tactics**. This applies also to those attacking Christianity-the other side of this battle.

Conspiracy, Conspiracy, Conspiracy The Lord has warned us repeatedly and clearly about the threat of secret combinations, which are conspiracies. So we who are aware of conspiracies and know how to detect them are, obviously, on the Lord's side. On the other side of the political spectrum, however, there is a constant cacophony that, "Anybody who believes in conspiracies is a wacko! Conspiracy theory—nonsense. No such thing as a conspiracy!":

So they are NOT on the Lord's side (so *guess whose side they are on!!*) Now, to whose advantage is it to convince the public that conspiracies do not exist? Why, the conspirators, of course. One tactic is to use the power of the media to deny that a conspiracy exists. Another tactic is for the conspirators **to produce and distribute several different false conspiracy theories** (disinformation) so as to confuse the public. The conspirators can then select one of these false theories, expose it, hold it up to ridicule and ridicule *all* conspiracy theories, including those that are based on facts and are true! Thus, we see how difficult it is to accurately identify the real conspirators. It requires a lot of serious research and study.

The objective of all conspiracies and combinations is for them to manipulate the laws and the government so that they gain a disproportionate amount of influence, power and/or wealth.

---

43. I have found this on line but have not been able to document it as being from Alynski. It certainly fits the Marxist plan and the Ten Points of the Communist Manifesto.

Divide and Conquer The Left is very organized but we, although being the majority, are splintered and fragmented. This is not by accident. The Left has divided us into categories. We do not think as Americans, we think as blacks, as Latinos, as Asians, as female, as male, as LGBT, as straight, as Christians, as Secular Humanists and a dozen other ways. When we go to vote, our fragmentation is reflected in our voting. We do not vote as Americans committed to preserving the integrity of our Constitution and our American system of law and justice.

We must, somehow, get Americans to shift their focus and priorities. It is fine for us to maintain our individuality, but we should be united in our dedication to the Constitution. You can bet that our enemies are united and organized. Just look at the riots by ANTIFA and BLM in 2016 and 2020. They are well organized and **well-financed.** The majority of the rioters might be ignorant as boxes full of rocks, but those manipulating them are well organized and committed.

ANTIFA, BLM AND Racism : Since the 1960s, all Communist revolutionaries have known the maxim: "The issue is never the issue. The issue is always the revolution." That is why the "white" Antifa and the "black" BLM — work together as one. They understand that race may be the apparent 'issue' but the real goal is Communist revolution [under the banner of socialism]. -G. Edward Griffin

This Matter of "Tolerance" The anti-Christians show zero tolerance for our moral values but demand that we not only be tolerant of theirs but yield to them and even accept them!

The irreligious will choose a lifestyle that includes practices that are abhorrent to God then glorify that lifestyle as if it were normal, acceptable and even superior to any set of values which it violates. Then, when Christians stand to defend their values, they are accused of being "intolerant". Example: same-sex marriage. This constitutes sodomy, a practice severely condemned by the Bible.[44] But when we defend traditional marriage of one man and one woman and condemn or criticize same-sex marriage, we are accused of being intolerant. The irreligious have zero tolerance for our values. So by their demanding that we be totally tolerant of their values and them being totally intolerant of ours, they move the boundries of what is "acceptable" behavior. This is a serious factor in the decline of morals in our society and the diminishment of respect for Christian values and the increased acceptance of degenerate values by the general public.

---

44. Clark, J. Reuben Jr., of the First Presidency, Imrovement Era, 1940, Vol. Xliii, July, 1940, No. 7.

Homosexuals Intolerant of Christian Values, Tolerant of Coprophilia

If we are going to face reality in dealing with the LGBT attack upon Christian values, we are forced to consider this practice of coprophilia practiced by some or many homosexuals. It is so filthy that I will not explain it here. You will have to look up the definition. Anyhow, the enemies of Christian values glorify coprophilia by keeping deathly silent about it, as if it did not exist. But it does. It is also an extreme health risk. By glorifying a lifestyle that includes coprophilia but keeping silent about coprophilia itself, they are, in effect, glorifying coprophilia. Must we be tolerant of their practice of coprophilia? Should we be criticized or vilified if we are not?

When someone insists that the LGBTs are "normal", ask them if those practicing coprophilia among the LGBT are "normal". Ask them if anal sex between two males is "normal."

The irreligionists will select a principle of Christianity, such as being against homosexual practices or same-sex marriage or abortion and champion and glorify that practice. With the media on their side, they can sway public opinion and generate considerable sympathy for these practices. Then, when Christians defend their centuries-old beliefs and principles, the anti-Christians (irreligionists) come back with accusations of intolerance, racist, homophobes, misogynistic and such. The Christians, taken off guard, tend to retreat and to abandon their Christian principles. Now, I wish to address a weakness that we Christians have that we absolutely must correct. That is, we have a strong aversion to contention. It is good, of course, to not be contentious. But there are times when we have to stand our ground and defend the principles of Christianity.

> If we do not stand our ground, they (the irreligionists) will push and push and push until we have no ground left to stand on. We must stand fast to defend our Christian principles and resist the pushing and intimidations of the Left.

The irreligionist people use contention as a weapon against us in this war. The LGBT are, at times, certainly contentious. They are also pushy, when pushing their agenda, which is generally in conflict with Christian principles. In fact, it does seem as if the Marxists and all other anti-Christians and anti-Americans are using the LGBT as their political battering ram. If we do not stand our ground, they will push and push and push until we have no ground left to stand on.

We must let them know that, while we wish them well, we do not intend to yield any of our sacred beliefs, that we would be betraying Jesus Christ if we were to do so.

When they demand tolerance of their positions, they are not demanding only tolerance. They want us to be tolerant to the point of yielding our principles. That is the way that they wage war. It is psychological warfare. Unless we want to yield our Christian beliefs entirely (for that is what they are after), we must stand firm, even if we have to absorb a little abuse. From journalist Rebecca Terrell:[45]

> These [anti-Christian] arguments assume that Christians are, as a rule, intolerant of views or lifestyles different from their own. There is truth to that accusation. A moral life presupposes intolerance of immorality. In the past, this was known as having standards. But the modern definition of intolerance includes a specious insinuation that Christians' personal morals pose a direct threat to everyone else's personal freedom. Newfangled "tolerance" demands that Christians not only put up with perversion but also agree with, endorse and promote it. That would be yielding to evil.

I highly commend to you Rebecca's entire article.

Those Crying for Tolerance are Extremely Intolerant Rebecca Terrell gives another example of extreme intolerance by those who scream for tolerance of their practices:

> While LGBT is promoted and defended, Christian causes are stifled. Last year administrators at a Florida high school thwarted student attempts to form a pro-life club and even threatened to fire the teachers who had volunteered to serve as faculty advisors.[46]

Before I retired, I was flying as a pilot on international routes on the DC-10 with 7 flight attendants. Many of the male F/As were gay. I once asked a female F/A how many of the males were gay. She said, "all of them." That might be (or might not be) be an exaggeration, but it clearly demonstrates that when a gay gets into a position of power, such as doing the hiring, that he is tolerant only of gays when he is hiring.

America's Moral and Cultural Decline and the Anti-Christians (Irreligionists) The decline in American morality can be traced directly to the Far-Left and the anti-Christians. It is very simple. They vilify and attack that which is pro-Christian and glorify that which is anti-Christian. Our Creator and Eternal God gave to us some standards to live by. They are known as the Ten Commandments. They are the best set of standards in existence. They

---

45. Terrell, Rebecca, "The War On Christianity", The New American Magazine, Appleton, April 6, 2020, p. 11

46. See Bible, Topical Guide: Homosexuality, Chastity, Sexual immorality: Gen 19:5, Lev 18:22, Deut. 23:17, Isa 3:9, Rom 1:27, 1 Cor 6:9, Tim 1:10, Jude 1:7,

were the best four thousand years ago, they were the best four hundred years ago, they were the best forty years ago, they are the best right now and they will be the best into the indefinite future. Yet the anti-Christians have outlawed them from our schools and public discourse and it appears that they want to eradicate them completely. So let the world know what the enemies of Christianity are for and what they are against. They are against that which is good and are for that which is evil, corrupt and dirty.

For some reason, the mainstream media of the U. S. seems to consistently support the anti-American, anti-Christian of every issue. It certainly does favor homosexuals and therefore homosexuality. It certainly does favor Marxism over constitutionalism. It favors Leftist and Marxist politicians over "conservative" ones. In fact, it seldom misses an opportunity to vilify and demean conservative elected officials. For an excellent read on this subject, see *The Enemy Within* by David Horowitz.[47]

Choosing to be Offended It is one thing to be offended by something offensive. It is entirely another to pretend or feign being offended or to choose to be offended by something innocent of the intention to offend. The Left knows that Christians make every effort to avoid offending others. So, they have devised the tactic of pretending to be offended, to take offense, when Christians are defending Christian values. For example, some irreligionists feign being offended when listening to a prayer. Offended by listening to a prayer!!! Talk about being intolerant. This is about the ultimate in intolerance. This borders on bigotry. Or maybe it crosses the border.

Feigning Mental Damage Taking the "feigning offense" syndrome further, the Left uses the tactic of feigning mental harm by a Christian. Like the two lesbians who were refused a wedding cake by a Christian baker in Oregon. They claimed that they were mentally and emotionally harmed by being refused and were awarded $135,000.00 in "damages" by commissioner Brad Avakian of the Oregon Bureau of Labor and Industry (BOLI).

Character Assassination. To the Extent that Good People are Vilified, to that Extent We Can Realize that There is Evil in the Land. Another favorite tactic of the Left—from the "liberal" to the KGB, is to attack, with disinformation, the character of their targets. Since the Left cannot support their positions and arguments with facts, truth and logic, they must resort to some other tactic. So they go to smearing their opponents with lies of various sorts to destroy their image and credibility. One of their favorites is to accuse their opponents of being "racist", "narcissist," "white supremacist", "misogynistic" or of sexually molesting some woman 20 or 30 years ago. With the media and many judges on their side, they often make the defamation tactic work, regardless of how innocent the accused might be.

---

47. Terrell, ibid. p. 11

Labels, Labels and Labels For decades, the Left, especially the Left-biased media, has used mis-named labels to smear and discredit honest people. Since before I can remember, the Left has labeled Americans who defend the Constitution as "right-wing extremists." Sounds bad, doesn't it. Would you like to be known as a "right-wing extremist"? Yet have you ever heard of them describe a Socialist or Communist as being a "left-wing extremist"? Never! Also, the Leftists just could *never* stand for their adversaries being described accurately as "Patriotic American activists." or "American patriots." See how that works? That's psychological warfare.

The Left labels Christians who stand by their beliefs, enduring the criticism and smears of the Left as "religious fanatics"! Yet they *never* label Secular Humanists, evolutionists or Marxists as "atheistic fanatics"! More psychological warfare.

We must understand these tactics and avoid being caught off guard by them. When we understand the Left, we understand that they are a very sleazy, dishonest bunch of people.

False Accusations It matters not to the Left that the accusations are false as long as they do damage to those whom they are accusing. The Leftists seem to believe that any accusation made by the Left is true. It becomes their truth. They know that no matter how false an accusation might be, a certain percentage of the population will believe it. So, in their minds, it is effective. To the Left, if it works, it is good. In their political warfare against the public, the Left uses disinformation extensively. All disinformation is designed to deceive. If it serves their purpose, it becomes their *truth*! More psychological warfare.

The Left Glorifies its Own Furthermore, they just lie. Example: If you are as old as I am, you can remember when Fidel Castro was taking over Cuba. He *denied being a Communist!* He was even on Ed Sullivan's CBS TV program in 1959 where Sullivan proclaimed him to be "The George Washington of Cuba"! Sullivan asked Castro, "Tell me, Fidel Castro, are you concerned about the Communist influence in Cuba"? To which Castro lied, "I am not worried because, really, there is not the threat of Communism here in Cuba". Then an interview between Sullivan and Castro that was made January 11, 1959 in Cuba was aired. Then, Sullivan told the audience, of Castro:

> A fine young man and a very smart young man. And with the help of God and our prayers and with the help of the American government, he will come up with the sort of democracy...!

Yet, shortly after the complete takeover, Castro began executing opponents, nationalizing industries and expropriating property, much of it American-owned. Castro had been a Communist all along and he displayed the true nature of a Communist. More psychological warfare.

Intimidation Intimidation is a favorite tactic of the political far-left. Just the fact that they constantly use the tactic of accusing their opponents of being "racist," etc causes anyone who is going to participate in any kind of debate to fear that they will be attacked with such pejoratives. This results in intimidation. More psychological warfare.

The Left Vilifies its Adversaries. With its control/influence in the media and education, the Left villifies its adversaries. This includes all Americanist/Christian elected officials, educators, public speakers and writers. And when one speaks or writes a particularly sensitive truth, they attack him vehemently. It seems that they do not have to be told. They seem to act like a flock of a million starlings. When one turns, they all turn as one.

For example, a white male, father of four, hard-working, honest, reliable, church-going Christian, faithful to his wife, charitable, patriotic, a veteran, kind and considerate would be labeled by the Left as, "Racist, misogynistic, bigoted, womanizer and, if he is running for office, would be accused (with no substantiation whatsoever) of molesting four or five women thirty or forty years ago. With NONE of the (alleged) accusers stepping forward to face the accused. That's the way they do it. And the mainstream media gives them PLENTY of FREE assistance. More psychological warfare.

Only Two Options-Both of them Favoring the Left

We Christian constitutionalists often find ourselves involved in a controversy between ourselves and the Left with the narrator presenting us with only two options, with both options favoring the Left. A perfect example was at the end of WW II when we were given the option of invading Japan with the probability of a million American casualties or to use the atomic bomb. Those were the only two options considered and we were bombarded with the idea that an invasion of Japan would cost us a million American lives.

The truth is that Japan had offered to surrender well before the atomic bombs were dropped. Besides that, Japan had already been obliterated by conventional bombing. Her navy was decimated. The two huge ships, the battleship Yamato was sunk April 7, 1945 and the supercarrier Shinano was sunk Nov 29, 1944. Japan had no raw materials and was at that point unable to import any. She was no longer able to wage war. She was no longer a viable enemy. The reality was that we were not restricted to the two options of invasion or the A-bombs. The first A-bomb was dropped on Hiroshima Aug 6, 1945. The second was dropped only three days later, giving the Japanese government no time to renew the offer to surrender.

Here are two other very viable options that were never discussed: (1) We could have accepted the Japanese offer to surrender or (2) Since Japan's navy was nearly destroyed and since she depended entirely on imports to survive, we could have merely stopped the war and blockaded Japan. She would have been helpless! The action taken was not in the best interests of the United States. Harry Truman was the president and it is evident that he was operating under the orders of the CFR. Or the United Nations. Or both.

Leftist Laws and Courts Reward Leftists, Penalize Conservative Christians

Leftist (sometimes referred to as "liberal" or "progressive", etc.) laws are structured so as to favor the ideological Left. Such laws are most dealing with "discrimination", as it is a foregone conclusion that the plaintiffs in such cases will be of the ideological and political Left. Thus, coupled with Leftist-leaning judges and administrative "judges", are designed to put the Christian conservative American at a very distinct disadvantage. Example # 1: Melissa Klein (Sweet Cakes by Melissa.) was penalized $135,000.00 for nothing more than refusing to bake a wedding cake for two lesbians. The commissioner of the Oregon Bureau of Labor and Industries (BOLI) Brad Avakian awarded the two lesbians $135,000.00 for suffering "mental rape" and "88 symptoms of emotional stress". Must we not suspect some bias against Christians when Commissioner Avakian imposed this outrageous penalty?

Environmental Impact Statements When a citizen wants to do something on his own property, he is often required to obtain an "Environmental Impact Study". The property owner then has to engage some business or person who writes up these studies. These studies seldom contain any useful purpose. Their main purpose is, it seems, is to extract money from property owners and give it to those who write the EPA impact studies. It is a legal racket that costs the average American and enriches those of the Left.

Intimidation, Intimidation and Intimidation. Another trick that the Left use is intimidation. They are bullies—especially when they have education and the media on their side. So if one of them accuses you of being a racist, quickly demand that he define the word. Most of them do not even know what it means. But it throws most people off guard. Be ready for it.

"If Communism is such a brutal, oppressive type of government, why do such governments exist," you might ask. It is by lies, deception, treachery and brute force. The KGB/FSB are known as the sword and shield of the Communist Party in Russia. It serves to force the Communist agenda and also to protect the Communist party leaders. The KGB tactics have proven to be so effective that they have been imported to America.

Corrupting the Law in order to Attack Christians Financially Waging any war requires finances. The Left and the anti-Christians have been working assiduously to corrupt the laws so that pro-Americans and Christians are put at a disadvantage in any legal dispute. This is an old-old-old tactic of the Left and anti-Christians. This will be dealt with in the next chapter. Also, consider the SCOTUS case of *Everson,* (which will be addressed in Chapter Eleven) which corrupted the law extensively in order to do harm to all Christianity.

The KGB/FSB in Russia and in America There are lots of similarities between the Leftists here in America and the KGB/FSB of Russia. In fact, I suspect that the Leftists here study the KGB/FSB. Once a person studies up on the Active Measures, Disinformation, Agents of Influence and Useful Idiots, he can recognize them quite readily. The Leftists here are taking us down the exact same path toward where the Russian people now find themselves. Here is a warning from Senator William Jenner (1908-1970):[48]

> Today the path to total dictatorship in the United States can be laid by strictly legal means, unseen and unheard by the Congress, the President, or the people...Outwardly we have a Constitutional government. We have operating within our government and political system, another body representing another form of government, a bureaucratic elite which believes our Constitution is outmoded and is sure that it is the winning side...All the strange developments in foreign policy agreements may be traced to this group who are going to make us over to suit their pleasure....This political action group[49] has its own local political support organizations, its own pressure groups, its own vested interests, its foothold within our government and its own propaganda apparatus.(Feb 23, 1954)

The powers spoken of by Senator Jenner had been at work for over 30 years at the time of his statement. They have been at work constantly in the intervening 66 years. But-we have not heard a peep about this threat from the controlled MSM or by the controlled academia.

Helaman's warning to us reinforces the statement by Senator Jenner, in Helaman 6:

> **38** And it came to pass on the other hand, that the Nephites did build them up and support them, beginning at the more wicked part of them, until they had overspread all the land of the Nephites and had seduced the more part of the righteous until they had come down to believe in their works and partake of their spoils and to join with them in their secret murders and combinations.
> **39** And thus they did obtain the sole management of the government, insomuch that they did trample under their feet and smite and rend and

---

48. Terrell, ibid. p. 12

49. Horowitz, David, The Enemy Within, Regnery Publishing, Washington, D. C. . Hardbound, 205 pp,

turn their backs upon the poor and the meek and the humble followers of God.

40 And thus we see that they were in an awful state and ripening for an everlasting destruction.

There are several groups who work together to comprise this "...another form of government..." spoken of by Senator Jenner. There are the Council on Foreign Relations (CFR), the Bilderbergers (BB), the Trilateralist Commission (TC), the Skull and Bones (Bones) and others. All of these are comprised of the wealthy and all of them strive to merge the United States with, first, Mexico and Canada and then into a world government. Although they are the wealthy of our country, they use Marxist tactics to work toward their objectives. An excellent book to explain the workings of the CFR is *The Shadows of Power* by Perloff. Some information about the late David Rockefeller, who was one of the driving forces for world government and the Bilderbergers, will be found in the chapter on the media, chapter Seven, above.

To show the political power of the CFR, the majority of the cabinet members of most every president in the past 50 years have been members of the CFR. Also, at one time, three of the nine justices of the SCOTUS were CFR. They were Sandra Day O'connor, Breyer and Ginsburg. Now, talk about political power, THAT IS POLITICAL POWER!!! No matter who is elected president, the administration is dominated by members of the CFR. This is true even in the Reagan and Trump administrations. In the Reagan administration, the vice-president was George H. W. Bush, a member of the BONES and the CFR. Trump's man pushing through this USMCA (US, Mexico and Canada) legislation, which is a huge step toward a political and economic union of the US, Mexico and Canada, is CFR member Robert Lighthizer. Most Trump supporters presume that Trump has never read the bill. This is a bill made especially to fit the agenda of the CFR.

Senator Barry Goldwater explains[50] the grip that the CFR has on our government:

> When a new president comes on board, there is a great turnover in personnel but no change in policy. Example: During the Nixon years Henry Kissinger, CFR member and Nelson Rockefeller's protege, was in charge of foreign policy. When Jimmy Carter was elected, Kissinger was replaced by Zbigniew Brzezinski, CFR member and David Rockefeller's protege.

Admiral Chester Ward[51] was a member of the CFR for sixteen years, but who did not share the political views of the majority in the CFR, has written:

---

50. Phoebe and Kent Courtney, America's Unelected Rulers: The Council on Foreign Relations (New Orleans: Conservative Society of America, 1962) pp. 1-2.
51. This group to which Senator Jenner is obviously referring will be identified in Chapter VII

The most powerful cliques in these elitist groups have one objective in common: they want to bring about **the surrender of the sovereignty and national independence of the United States**. They differ only as to the entity into which our sovereignty should be merged. Some dream of taking the United States into a one-world all-powerful global government-possibly a vastly strengthened United Nations, or possibly limited to the Atlantic community. They consider that this objective is at once so idealistic…and so urgent…their end justifies any means.

These rich elitist people working to merge America into a world government are not considered to be Marxists. Yet their agenda, objectives and tactics are very closely akin to Marxism. This really does lend credence to the idea that Karl Marx's intent was to create an ideology and revolutionary scheme that would create a dictatorship and put the select wealthy into positions of top power over the working class in the target government.

This information about Marxism and other anti-American groups is very targeted to our subject of the Supreme Court attacking Christianity. Because all attacks on Christians and Christianity will come from the Political Left, including the one world government crowd. The United Nations has created a new religion called the *United Religions Initiative* which will definitely NOT be Christian or even benign to Christianity. It will be subversive and hostile thereto.

How the Marxists use Active Measures, Disinformation, Agents of Influence and Useful Idiots: The KGB/FSM in America

One thing is necessary for any secret combination to succeed and that is to, either by force or by trickery, compel the people to believe in and support or comply with programs of the government that are contrary to their own best interests. In America, the combinations must seduce the people to scorn the principles of Christianity and of liberty and to believe and support principles that build a government which will enslave them. To be more specific: To scorn the *principles* of Christianity, the Constitution and liberty (even while continuing to believe in all three) and to support and believe in the *principles* of Marxism (even while continuing to scorn Marxism and Communism). We live in a time of deception. A time of the greatest ironies. A time of the greatest paradoxes.

Understanding how the KGB/FSB of Russia works is MOST helpful to us in our quest to identify who might be initiating attacks against our religious liberties. The KGB/FSB is the "Sword and Shield" of the ruling elite of Russia. In addition to oppressing its own people, the KGB/FSB infiltrates and subverts other nations. Our enemies in America use exactly the same tactics as does the KGB/FSB against the Russian people and against us. For them to implement their Marxist programs, they must have a plan; a plan which includes lies to deceive, a plan to disseminate these lies and agents to carry it out. Our enemies got their ideas, evidently, from the KGB/FSB. Here they are: active measures, disinformation, agents of influence and oh yes "useful idiots." This is the method employed by domestic Marxists to trick and deceive us Americans into supporting Marxist ideas and Marxist programs that are contrary to our own best interests.

In planning their active measures and disinformation, the KGB/FSB exploits our every weakness-our greed, our ignorances and, especially, our tendency to "go with the crowd". We all do. With control of the media under the CFR people, whose agenda is also a collectivized America, they have been very successful. We must, one by one, cease to go with the crowd and think independently.

John Barron, (1930-2005) former senior editor for the Reader's Digest, with the help of former KGB Major Stanislav Levchenko, wrote of this subject. I wish to pay tribute to John. He provided Americans with some exceptionally fine works on the KGB of great value to Americans. Also, his articles and books are not only very informative, they are very interesting to read. Here it is from Barron and Levchenko:

Active Measures (Aktivnye Meroprlyatiya):

> By Soviet definition, Active Measures consist of a diversity of tactics including overt and covert propaganda,... disinformation, forgeries, use of Agents of Influence ... committed for psychological effect. Any of these tactics may be invoked individually for a limited purpose, such as defamation of a foreign leader or a powerful anti-Soviet figure like Aleksandr Solzhenitzyn. In strategic or global campaigns, all or most forms of Active Measures are employed in concert to propagate a general theme that plays upon natural human fears and yearnings.
> All Active Measures, however couched and conducted, aim at perverting perceptions of reality. To the extent that they succeed, they cause popular attitudes and public policies to be formulated on the basis of specious or unrealistic premises. Grounded in illusions rather than reality, the thought and behavior induced can secure benefits for the Soviet Union unobtainable through rational debate, reasonable negotiations or even force. As will be shown, Active Measures have persuaded millions upon millions of honorable, patriotic and sensible people who detest Communist tyranny nevertheless to make common cause with the Soviet Union...(Barron, John, 1983, *KGB Today, The Hidden Hand,* Reader's Digest Press, New York, pp 251, 252.)

> Few people who understand the reality of the Soviet Union will knowingly support it or its policies. So by Active Measures, the KGB

distorts or inverts [perceptions of] reality. The trick is to make people support Soviet policy unwittingly by convincing them that they are supporting something else...That's the art of Active Measures, a sort of made-in-Moscow black magic. It is tragic to see how well it works. (Barron, John, October 1982, "The KGB's Magical War for `Peace'", *Reader's Digest*, p. 207.)

Active Measures is **the seduction of the mind.** It is leading someone to believe something without his knowing why he believes it (or its purpose) or who it was that led him to believe it. Active Measures, incorporating disinformation and administered by Agents of Influence, is an insidious method for altering the worldview of one person or of millions. Now that they have a plan, they must have some false or incomplete information, or some just plain lies to confuse or disinform their targets. The KGB calls it "dezinformatsia." We call it "disinformation." It is nothing more than cleverly concocted lies.

Dezinformatsia (Disinformation)

Since deception is the objective of Active Measures, it necessarily employs the use of inaccurate, incomplete or misleading information or just plain lies. The use of such is a common practice with the KGB and the phrase they use to describe such is "Dezinformatsia," or "disinformation." One dictionary provides a very brief description of "disinformation":

> **Disinformation.** Incorrect and deliberately misleading information leaked especially by an intelligence agency as a means of negating and discrediting authentic information that an enemy has obtained. (The American Heritage Dictionary, 2nd College Ed.)

However, our study deserves a more comprehensive definition:

> **Disinformation** is comprised of ideas prepared for the purpose of confusing or deceiving the target(s), which might be one particular individual, a segment of the public, or the entire general public. Whether directed to one individual, or disseminated by the means of selected publications or by the mass media, disinformation will contain these characteristics: (1) it contains factual errors and/or omissions of pertinent facts which are construed to lead the target(s) to a false conclusion, (2) The result will bring benefits to those who planned its dissemination and (3) the result will be harmful to the individual or general public being deceived. (Joe H. Ferguson, October 1985)

Disinformation has become the international plague of our time. It was used by Lenin, by Stalin, by Hitler, by Goebels and it has been used by every President and by the MSM against the American people consistently all during my lifetime. Which began in 1931. Former Romanian Chief of Intelligence Ion Pacepa (about whom more later) says that Russia's "Andropov's disinformation turned the Islamic world against the United States and ignited the international terrorism that threatens us today. Disinformation has also generated worldwide disrespect and even contempt, for the United States and its leaders…" [52]

Remember-anybody, absolutely anybody, can gain access to the journalists, editors and commentators of the American media. We must be very selective in what we choose to believe, especially from the MSM.

Since the Left relies extensively upon disinformation (lies), does it surprise us that the Left is under the control of the Devil?

Agents of Influence

Just as Active Measures necessarily incorporate Disinformation for its success, certain agents must be employed to activate it. Such are called, "Agents of Influence." Now we have a plan; Active Measures and we have some disinformation to be used in that plan so we must have "agents of influence" to put it into play. John Barron explains the role the "agents of influence" play:

> We have long been aware of spy efforts in stealing information. But individuals under the control of the KGB or some other power being used to shape or influence public opinion and attitudes of people in their own countries has largely caught everyone in the Free World unawares.
> The classic Soviet espionage agent steals secrets. An agent of influence strives to affect the public opinions and policies of other nations in the interests of the Soviet Union. His or her advocacy may be open or concealed, direct or subtle. Always, though, the Agent of Influence pretends that he or she is acting out of personal conviction rather than under Soviet guidance…
> In all nations the KGB attempts to recruit agents within the political system, press, religion, labor, the academic world who can help shape public attitudes and policies to Soviet interests. (Barron, John, "The KGB's Magical War for 'Peace,'" *Reader's Digest*, Oct, 1982, pp 211, 212.

The foundation of the ideologies of the "liberals" and "progressives" of today is secular Humanism and Marxism. Just watered down a little. It is the "liberals" and "progressives," who Lenin might classify as "useful idiots" who carry the water for the agents of influence. Those doing the deceiving must have someone to deceive before their plan will work. The great majority of the Communists call themselves "liberals." That means that, among the

---

52. Goldwater, Barry, With No Apologies, William Morrow and Company p. 279

"liberals," there must be a large number of Communists. It is these "useful idiots" who do all the work for the professional agents of influence.

The Communists and others on the Left disguise their propaganda in many different forms. Elder Ezra Taft Benson warned us: "No matter whether they label their bottle as liberalism, progressivism, or social reform—I know the contents of the bottle is poison to this Republic and I'm going to call it poison."[53]

Useful Idiots

These active measures, disinformation and agents of influence would be useless if it were not for the targets of the disinformation who actually believe this stuff! This disinformation is all lies, distortions or half truths designed to deceive. That is the only purpose they serve. So whether the target of this disinformation is one person or the entire population, those who believe these lies are referred to in the bar where the KGB guys hang out as "useful idiots." They are the people who act on this disinformation and behave in a manner that is in the best interests of the KGB, but to the detriment of the people in the target country. Unfortunately, their numbers are many.

While Agents of Influence are willing and knowing operatives under the control of and on the payroll of the KGB or some other subversive group, there are always, among the targeted public, a certain number who believe, embrace and espouse the disinformation spread by the Agents of Influence. These "useful idiots," a term attributed to Vladimir I. Lenin, are those who make the plan work. They are doing the work of the KGB and for no pay.

---

53. Schlafly and Ward, Kissinger on the Couch, Arlington House, New Rochelle, NY, p. 129

"The Liberal"

as defined by

John A. Widtsoe

Unfortunately, the word liberal is not always properly used. It has been used, or misused, for so many purposes that its original meaning has largely vanished. Word-juggling, making a good word cover a doubtful or an ugly cause, is an age-old pastime. Words are too often used as shields to hide or disguise truth. Many men are inclined to hide their true motives behind a word.

The self-called liberal is usually **one who has broken with the fundamental principles or guiding philosophy** of the group to which he belongs. **He is an unbeliever**. He claims membership in an organization **but does not believe in its basic concepts** and sets out to reform it by changing its foundations. He is forever entangling his unbelief with his membership. **He wants the protection of the organization, therefore refuses to admit frankly that he rejects the fundamental beliefs of the cause and seeks truth elsewhere.**

It is a species of cowardice. In the United States, Communists, Nazis, or fascists would probably insist that they are liberals. In a church, **the liberal refuses to accept the doctrine of the church or the way of life that it enjoins upon its members**. It is an undeserved compliment to designate such men by the noble word liberal; **they are apostates from a cause**, engaged in building their own cause under false colors, whether in the state or the church. They are often without basic convictions, rudderless mariners, victims of every passing wave. Such men, whatever they may call themselves, are **dangerous to human happiness**. Certainly they are not entitled to be called liberals within the organization of which they are members. **Their chief pastime is to sow the seeds of anarchy in the hearts of others.**

Widtsoe, John A., 1943, *Evidences and Conciliations,* First Edition, Bookcraft, Salt Lake City, pp 37-39.)

The term is so appropriate. **Useful Idiots are suckers for an idea that is attractively packaged,** regardless of how false or flawed it might be. With some of them, it might be that the falseness of the idea itself attracts them.

That is what is so alluring to them. Some people reject the simple truth for the specific reason that it so simple! Such holds no attraction for them.

The Foundation of "Liberalism"

While there might be some Christianity mingled in with some "liberal" thought from time to time, there is none to be found in the foundation of "liberalism." The foundation of "liberalism" is pure evolution, Humanism and Marxism.

"Liberals," "Progressives" and "Useful Idiots"

The above brings to mind the typical "liberal" and "progressive" of today. The foundation of their ideologies is comprised of the theory of evolution, of secular Humanism and of Marxism. Just analyze any "liberal" idea. This also brings to mind the following definition of "The Liberal" by John A. Widtsoe as seen above. An excellent definition.

Without the support of "useful idiots," "liberals" and "progressives," (collectivists all) the hard-core evolutionists, secular humanists and Marxists would not be able to achieve their objectives. "Liberals," "Progressives," and "Useful Idiots" carry the bucket for the hard-core agents of influence, Marxists, Communists and wealthy collectivists. For it is always the former who disseminate, without pay, all of the disinformation and do the dirty work for the latter, the paid professionals.

We encounter Marxist ideas everywhere. Yet we never ever encounter any Communists. It is because all Communists claim to be "liberals" or "progressives." It follows then, that some of these "liberals" or "progressives" MUST BE Communists in disguise. So the next time you hear someone spouting off some "liberal" dogma, you might want to carefully and friendly-like explain to him that his idea is really only watered-down Marxism, a very false and pernicious dogma.

This matter of the enemy (any enemy) manipulating useful idiots to aid them in achieving their sinister objectives deserves serious consideration. Not only the KGB but other subversive groups have unlimited access to influential people in our media, educational system, government and entertainment.

It seems that the efforts of such groups to influence the thinking of our society began seriously **in the 1930's**. Because the American people have been unaware of these efforts, such have proven to be both effective and destructive. All manner of disinformation has been spread, dedicated to attacking and breaking down morality, Christianity and constitutional government. It is understandable and we must recognize this fact, that a certain number of the population have accepted these political concepts and philosophies that are hostile to Americanism and its foundation, the Constitution and constitutional government. Certain members of the legal profession, it is evident, have been the most willing to believe disinformation that is destructive to our system of law and our Constitution.

Are those who play the role of "useful idiot" intellectually challenged? Ponder the question seriously. A person might be very intelligent in one area but badly misinformed on some other issue. Any person who passes on information that is false and harmful to his society or country classifies as one of Lenin's "useful idiots." Let the "useful idiot" be recognized for what he is-a misguided and dangerous advocate of concepts and philosophies hostile to freedom, to justice, to Christianity, to civilization and to America.

We must remember this one very important fact: without "useful idiots," the agents of influence **could never make their "disinformation" believed** and their "active measures" effective. Furthermore, let us all be very careful to do our homework and make sure that everything that we choose to believe and to repeat is true and accurate.

How does one recognize a "useful idiot"? It is by this method: "By their fruits ye shall know them." They can be **recognized by the cultural and political philosophies** that they espouse and movements they support. Who can be a "useful idiot?" The answer is, "anyone!" Anyone, that is, who allows himself to be tricked into believing and espousing false ideas and concepts which are contrary to his own best interest and/or to the best of his neighbors and his country. Whenever we pass on information that is false and damaging to our culture or society, we are playing the part of a "useful idiot".

Active Measures, Disinformation and Agents of Influence in America

The above applies to the Russian KGB and also to any other subversive group in the U. S. that might want to mislead the American people. Is it not inevitable that Marxists in America would employ the identical same KGB tactics against the American people as the Russian KGB uses against the Russian people? Inevitable! It would be insanity to think otherwise! The direct connection between Russian Marxists and American Marxists was clearly demonstrated when the Russian Communists (Stalin, we presume) selected John Dewey to conduct the trial of Leon Trotsky in Coyoacan, Mexico in 1937.

Communists Deny Being Communists

It is amazing. Some people defend Communist arguments, defend Communists, attack anti-Communists, support Marxist legislation, support Marxist legislators, lionize Lenin and Mao and support foreign aid to Communist Russia yet they vehemently deny being a Communist! Like this creature that brays like a mule, eats what mules eat, looks like a mule and kicks like a mule but he denies being a mule! Beware of those who call themselves "liberals" or "progressives".

If they talk like Communist and do the work of a Communist, they are either a Communist or worse—they talk like Communist, think like a Communist and do the work of a Communist but are too dumb to know that they are a Communist!!! It is not necessary for a person to be an official member of the CPUSA in order to be, de facto, a Communist. The reality is that millions of Americans repeat the party line simply because they do not know any better. They are innocent of malice but guilty of ignorance. They need to use the brain that God gave to them and do their homework.

None of the justices who voted for *Everson* or *Obergefell* would admit to being Marists (I would venture to say) but both *Everson* and *Obergefell* are anti-constitutional, Marxist rulings!!!

Nothing to Prevent KGB or Other Subversives from Buying Influence in American Media

The above topic about disinformation and active measures also applies to the mainstream media, owned by members of the CFR or others having an agenda to mislead us. Be very cautious of the MSM. Also-there is absolutely NOTHING to prevent the KGB or other subversives from contacting and buying influence with anyone in the media, education or entertainment. NOTHING.

In Chapter Eight we read about a textbook case of active measures and disinformation involving the disappearance of Korean Air 007 on September 1, 1983 and the succeeding "news" reports. In Chapter 15 you will find another textbook case of active measures, disinformation and agents of influence in American media. It happened in 1970 and I was personally involved when the Communist agents of influence in the mainstream media launched an attack against the Church of Jesus Christ of Latter-day Saints (Mormon) church. I think that you will find it interesting and informative.

Previously, I mentioned that the Marxists use the carrot and the stick method. They are the experts at it. When the Honorable (one of the few) (late) George V. Hansen was a congressman for southeastern Idaho, he was one of the few brave enough to take on the IRS for its brutal and anti-constitutional tactics. Very few politicians will *tackle the IRS because they are afraid of them.*

George authored a book (Hansen, George V., 1984, *To Harass Our People,* A Positive Publication Book, 222 pp, Washington, D.C.), to explain the tactics of the IRS. I know George as being not only courageous but a very honest man, as is (not "was" as I believe George and his wife Connie still live even though they have departed this mortal life). I believe the information in his book is accurate. If it is, the IRS is a powerful agency operating as a threat to Americans and to Americanism.

After all, the IRS is built on the Second Point of the Communist Manifesto: "A heavy progressive or graduated income tax." So it is only natural that the IRS would behave contrary to the interest of liberty and justice.

Just recently, we have seen congressional hearings on the IRS for its abuse of conservative citizens and organizations. I was audited three different years by the IRS. It turned out in at least one year that they owed me money! I am firmly convinced that I was audited because I am a constitutional Republican and not a Marxist Democrat. In my campaign for U.S. Congress in 1976, I said many critical but truthful things about the IRS. One thing that we should never forget is that the IRS **was set up to collect a graduated income tax, which is one of the planks of the Communist Manifesto**. It is also structured so that it can selectively target, without just cause, political enemies of the administration.

It is Always, Always Their Intent to Deceive Us

Remember this about Communists, Socialists, Marxists, Secular Humanists, evolutionists, "liberals," and "progressives,"-They are constantly scheming on how to deceive us into believing their ideology. They want to trick us into giving up our freedoms, our liberties, our properties and our belief in Christ and His teachings. There is no deviation or exceptions from this rule.

As you review the information above about disinformation, active measures, agents of influence and useful idiots, just consider that this is exactly how the Devil works to deceive us into falling into his many snares. It seems to me that the Devil himself must have inspired the KGB in developing these tactics. Understanding how the KGB operates has been very helpful to me. Many times, I have seen something in the media that appears to have been developed as active measures, with disinformation designed to misinform the audience. These are particularly frequent as election time approaches.

Edward Bernays and Shaping the Minds of the Public

Edward Bernays (1891-1995) was not known (to my knowledge) to be a Marxist but he was a double nephew of Sigmund Freud and was possibly a Secular Humanist. Anyhow, Bernays was in the public relations business. I bring up Bernay's name at this point not because I want to associate him with the subversive workings of the KGB but because of his ability to use the mainstream media to sway the perceptions of millions. Sometimes in ways contrary to the best interests of those who believed his propaganda. His name is known to few today but he was named by *Life Magazine*[54] as one of the "100 most influential Americans of the 20th Century." Now, that's being influential! Some of Bernay's successes were:

---

54. Ion Mihai Pacepa, Disinformation, WND Books, p. 351
55. Ezra Taft Benson, "Stand Up For Freedom," given at the Assembly Hall at Temple Square, Feb 11, 1966 to the Utah Forum for the American Idea.

(1) In 1929, he had some beautiful models march in the Easter Parade in Manhattan, smoking Lucky Strike cigarettes. This was perceived as a great blow for "feminist liberation" and started the women of America to smoking.

(2) In the 1950s, the United Fruit Company, a client of Bernay's, dominated the governments of many of the "banana republics" in Central America. When a president was elected in Guatemala who wanted to reform and improve the working conditions and pay scale of the workers of United Fruit, Bernays started a propaganda campaign that resulted in a war in Guatemala. United Fruit got their way.

These two accomplishments do not merit our praise, but we must admit that Bernays was a master at manipulating the minds of the masses. In his book, he explains how the masses (that includes you and me) are manipulated. Bernay's tactics can be compared to those of the KGB, although for different objectives. Anyhow, we can learn from Bernays. From his book *Propaganda* [55]:

> **Bernays, Pp 37, 38**: The conscious and intelligent manipulation of the organized habits and opinions of the masses is an important element in democratic society. Those who manipulate this unseen mechanism of society constitute an invisible government which is the true ruling power of our country. We are governed, our minds molded, our tastes formed, our ideas suggested, largely by men we have never heard of. This is a logical result of the way in which our democratic society is organized. Vast numbers of human beings must cooperate in this manner if they are to live together as a smoothly functioning society...
>
> ...it remains a fact that in almost every act of our daily lives, whether in the sphere of politics or business, in our social conduct or our ethical thinking, we are dominated by the relatively small number of persons—a trifling fraction of our hundred and twenty million [as of 1920] who understand the mental processes and social patterns of the masses. It is they who pull the wires which control the public mind, who harness old forces and contrive new ways to bind and guide the world...
>
> P 48, 9: ...The minority has discovered a powerful help in influencing majorities. It has been found possible so to mold the mind of the masses that they will throw their newly gained strength in the desired direction. In the present structure of society, this practice is inevitable. Whatever of social importance is done today, whether in politics, finance, manufacture, agriculture, charity, education, or other fields, must be done

with the help of propaganda. Propaganda is the executive arm of the invisible government.

Small groups of persons can and do, make the rest of us think what they please about a given subject. But there are usually proponents and opponents of every propaganda, both of whom are equally eager to convince the majority...

P 71: ...So the question naturally arose: If we understand the mechanism and motives of the group mind, is it not possible to control and regiment the masses according to our will without their knowing it?

P. 73: If you can influence the leaders, either with or without their conscious cooperation, you automatically influence the group which they sway. But men do not need to be actually gathered together in a public meeting or in a street riot, to be subject to the influences of mass psychology. Because man is by nature gregarious he feels himself to be a member of a herd, even when he is alone in his room with the curtains drawn. His mind retains the patterns which have been stamped on it by the group influence...
...concluded that the group mind does not think in the strict sense of the word. In place of thoughts it has impulses, habits and emotions. In making up its mind, its first impulse is usually to follow the example of a trusted leader. This is one of the most firmly established principles of mass psychology. It operates in establishing the rising or diminishing prestige of a summer resort, in causing a run on a bank, or a panic on the stock exchange, in creating a best-seller, or a box-office success...

public domain image

"In almost every act of our daily lives, whether in the sphere of politics or business, in our social conduct or our ethical thinking, we are **dominated by the relatively small number of persons**...It is <u>they</u> who pull the wires which control the public mind." – Edward Bernays

Edward Bernays a Master at Manipulating Public Opinion

Although Bernays might never have heard of the KGB, the tactics that he used to influence the thinking of the masses were remarkably similar. What we can learn from Bernays is that every newspaper, every TV and radio broadcast contains some information that is designed to shape our worldviews; our paradigms; our perceptions and that it might very well be contrary to our own best interests!

We must be careful. I suggest the following guidelines to avoid being tricked by the media or by politicians: Establish some thoroughly reliable guidelines by which to make decisions. First, the Ten Commandments. Also learn about Secular Humanism, the opposite of Christianity. Second, understand the Constitution of the United States and also its opposite, the Communist Manifesto. Third, learn the ideologies and the tactics of the evolutionists, the Secular Humanists and the Marxists. This will stand you in real good stead. Fourth, know the enemies of Christianity and how they operate. Understand that your church will NOT, because of reasons heretofore presented, warn you of these dangers or teach you about them. We must prepare ourselves for this battle ourselves and fight this battle ourselves.

When the mask of pretense is ripped away, there is nothing good about Marxism. It is totally evil, as is every idea that supports it. This is not surprising considering the fact that its author hated God. Marxism is diametrically opposed to liberty, justice, unalienable rights, civilization and Christianity. So if liberty, justice, unalienable rights, prosperity, civilization and Christianity are good, then Marxism must be evil.

When we are fighting this evil, we are truly fighting, as Paul said, the rulers of darkness:

> For we wrestle not against flesh and blood, but against principalities, against powers, against the rulers of the darkness of this world, against spiritual wickedness in high places. (Ephesians 6:12)

Understanding the evil nature of Marxism, we should commit a good portion of our time, energy and resources to exposing Marxism for what it is and those who promote it for who and what they are.

President David O. McKay of the Church of Jesus Christ of Latter-day Saints included this in his Statement on Communism in April of 1966:

> ...The position of this Church on the subject of Communism has never changed. We consider it the greatest satanical threat to peace, prosperity and the spread of God's work among men that exists on the face of the earth...

That is powerful counsel. No equivocating there. Even for the non-LDS reader, I suggest that the above is excellent counsel. "...the greatest satanical threat to peace, prosperity and the spread of God's work among men..." That's enough to shiver me timbers! If President McKay was correct and I certainly believe that he was, then he has identified one of the main components of our enemies. "...greatest satanical threat to peace, prosperity and the spread of God's work..." Yes sir, my vote says that Marxists are going to constitute a significant chunk of the people who are and will be attacking the Constitution and also Christianity. Satanic...deception...manipulation of the minds of people...arbitrary governmental power...deprivation of liberties...Of course, President McKay said "Communism" instead of "Marxism." For those wanting to split fine hairs, though, "Communism" is built on the writings of Marx and certainly qualifies as being "Marxism" also.

The scripture from II Corinthians about liberty:

> 3:17 Now the Lord is that Spirit: and where the Spirit of the Lord is, there is liberty.

The above is only one verse, but it tells a powerful story. Liberty results from the spirit of Christ. Conversely, tyranny and compulsion result from the spirit of the Devil. For this reason, the Marxists realize that they must extinguish the spirit of the Lord in order to destroy the Constitution and impose Marxism. It is easy for Americans to recognize Marxism in Russia, where Marxism is total, but very difficult for them to recognize Marxism in America. That is because: (1) Marxism in America is being imposed not in its entirety but incrementally and: (2) Marxist legislation, agencies and programs are never labeled as Marxist. The Congress enacts a Marxist law and calls it "constitutional"; the President imposes a Marxist Executive Order and calls it "constitutional"; the Supreme Court hands down a Marxist ruling and calls it "constitutional". Marxism in increments is still Marxism and it will eventually result in total Marxism; total dictatorship and the total abolishment of Christianity. While this incremental Marxism is being imposed, the Marxists and their comrades are busy in their attacks on Christianity.

It is no accident that we are seeing attacks against Christianity becoming more blatant as the thinking of the people; the "cultural hegemony," and the government are becoming more tolerant of and favorable to Secular Humanism and Marxism.

Remember-extinguishing the Constitution in increments eventually results in its total and complete extinction. It is being extinguished by the SCOTUS ignoring it and also by enforcing anti-constitutional rulings. We have studied this previously and will study it further.

More Differences Between Americanism and Marxism

In any battle, it is necessary to understand the enemy, the enemy's ideology and the enemy's tactics. There is only one "ism" that is congruent with Americanism and that is "constitutionalism." Government under the Constitution of the United States of America, the Constitution, is unique; it was designed to protect the lives, liberties and properties of the people. Constitutionalism is the ultimate in liberty on the earth and is the opposite of Marxism. What is the difference between the two? The Marxists want us to believe that Marxism taught in our schools and Marxism in our government is

Americanism. It is not. We must learn to recognize Marxism regardless of what label somebody might put on it.

In a free country, the laws are designed to protect the lives, liberties and properties of each and every individual; their natural rights. The citizens are allowed to make choices; to choose; to discriminate as long as they do not harm another person.

God-Given Natural Rights vs. Marxist-Bestowed Privileges

Under American law, our rights are bestowed upon us by our Creator (called "natural rights") and the purpose of the government is to protect those rights. Under Marxist law, there are no natural rights since there is no Creator. Therefore, the Marxists teach that all privileges from government are "rights." Tragically, this is what is being taught in American public schools today.

The laws in a dictatorship are called **"ruler's law"** and are designed to benefit the ruler(s) at the expense of the people. Ruler's law restricts the activities of the people to only what the ruler permits them to do. Ruler's law has laws for penalizing the people for exercising their natural rights; for making choices; for discriminating; for doing anything that the ruler forbids.

Important Important Important Important

Four Hoaxes Within a Hoax

Marxism contains not one but (at least) four hoaxes. They are:

1. Putting their faith in Marx and his slogan, "Working men of the world, unite! You have nothing to lose but your chains", working men of the world have voted for, fought for and died for Marxist politicians and supported Marxist legislation that is designed to eventually enslave them, their family and all of their posterity.

2. Marxism is not really the "dictatorship of the proletariat." It is, in reality, the "dictatorship of the bourgeoisie", the ruling elite. In any Marxist state, the dictators are the "nomenklatura", or the rich. And not just a little bit rich but multi-millionaires, having stolen their millions from the working class. Marxist propaganda is designed to trick the working class into supporting Marxist programs that builds the dictatorship that enslaves them.

3. In America, members of the secret combinations constitute the ruling elite; the super rich and yet they support Marxist programs because Marxist programs allows them to control the working class. Reliable sources report that the ignorant rabble rioting in the streets and at the

universities are being financed by multi-billionaire George Soros[56] and others. So the ignorant rabble and billionaire Soros have, in the end, the same political objectives. The difference is that in the proposed government that they both support, Soros will be one of the "ruling elite" and the ignorant rabble will then be the enslaved ignorant rabble. Let's say that the ignorant rabble are doing Soros' dirty work. The difference is that the ignorant rabble have no idea of the ultimate results of their rioting. Soros knows exactly what he is doing.

4. And the grandest and cruelest hoax of all is Marxist laws being enacted by the Congress, signed by the President and pronounced "constitutional" by the Congress, the President and the Supreme Court of the United States. Marxism is being taught to our school children but not identified as Marxism. Our students graduate from our high schools and universities thinking that they are Christians and Americans but believing in the principles of Secular Humanism and in Marxism.

In government, the Congress enacts Marxist legislation and calls it "constitutional", The President signs it and calls it "constitutional." The Supreme Court rules on it and pronounces it to be "constitutional." Our young men and women go to law school and are not taught to understand the Constitution as it is written. They are taught that, if a supreme court has pronounced something to be "constitutional" then it is "constitutional." And do not ask questions; especially embarrassing questions; questions the answers to which might expose the Supreme Court.

This form of education and this form of political culture does more to confuse us than to inform us.

So here we are in 2020 A heavy cloud hangs over our nation. Half of the people realize that something is very seriously wrong. They can see some of the symptoms but are unable to diagnose the cause of them. The other half are brain dead. If they vote at all, they vote for whomever will promise them the most welfare handout. They understand not and they care not about anything else. They are and always will be part of the problem. That means that if Christianity, America and civilization are going to be saved, it is going to be up to us, the half that cares.

I suggest that we start with gaining an understanding of the Constitution, as recommended by the Lord in D&C 98:

> 6 Therefore, I, the Lord, justify you and your brethren of my church, in befriending that law which is the Constitutional law of the land;
> 7 And as pertaining to law of man, whatsoever is more or less than this cometh of evil.

---

56. Life, Aug 31, 1990

8 I, the Lord God, make you free, therefore ye are free indeed; and the law also maketh you free.
9 Nevertheless, when the wicked rule the people mourn.
10 Wherefore, honest men and wise men should be sought for diligently and good men and wise men ye should observe to uphold; otherwise whatsoever is less than these cometh of evil.

That is very sound and very powerful counsel. I consider it to be infallible. The bedrock upon which we should build our studies. We should uphold constitutional law. What kind of law should we oppose? President McKay has stated it very plainly when he told us that Communism is the greatest threat to God's work that exists. That is plain enough. I suggest that we first learn the fundamentals of constitutional law and the structure of government that results from using the Constitution as the blueprint. And then study the fundamentals of Marxism and the structure of government that results from using the Communist Manifesto as the blueprint. Then we will examine the reason that Marxism can be such a threat in America, the land of the free and the home of the brave.

The Subversion of American Law

Unknown to most Americans, the federal government has undergone radical changes. It conforms very little to the Constitution. It conforms more to the Communist Manifesto than it does to the Constitution. More on the graphic presentation of this in Chapter X. The Ten Points of the Communist Manifesto are presented previously. To understand how the SCs operate, we must understand the structures, powers and purposes of both the Constitutional form of government and the Marxist form of government.

The Collectivists Objective: Extinguish Christianity and the Constitution

The public school system is failing our students in many ways and this is a major one. It is teaching the students to believe, accept, embrace and support programs that will be part of a Humanist-Marxist government that will deprive them of all of their constitutional rights and then enslave them.

Marxism is promoted on lies and force. Its advocates make utopian promises to the ignorant masses. The masses cheer the Marxist liars. Such is the history of Marxism. History is clear on the subject. At least, if you select the right source. Merely look at the presidential race today.

Another tactic of the Left is to play the victim, especially of being "discriminated against". A perfect example of the Left employing this tactic and achieving a major victory is exemplified in the case of *Obergefel v. Hodges* in which two male gays complained that they were denied their "rights" because they were denied the opportunity to marry each other.

Marxism-The Promises and the Reality

If there ever was a theory or a movement of which its theory can be so vividly contrasted with its reality is that of Marxism. The theory of Marxism is that it would improve the conditions of the working class and take care of the poor. "Working men of the world, unite!" Was Marx's cry. But the reality of Marxism is a long, long way from what Marx promised.

The Allure of Marxism

While an economy still has enough of the free market functioning to provide a gross national product sufficient to feed everybody and pay the bills, it can pay for some Marxist programs. Thus, the profits from free market are used to subsidize Marxist programs. So the politicians promise the voters LOTS of goodies that will cost them absolutely nothing. Free food, free housing, free medical care, free lots of things. Loans that you never have to pay back. Buying out failed corporations so that the top executives can still get their golden parachutes. Subsidizing solar energy programs. Never have to pay it back. How wonderful! The people get lots of free goodies. The politicians who vote for all these Marxist goodies get LOTS of votes from people who want something for which they pay nothing. These voters have absolutely no concern for the inevitable consequences involved in such a scheme. Eventually, this house of false promises come to a point where the giveaway totals more than the free market system can produce. It all comes tumbling down. We are headed for such a collapse. We are headed for a Venezuela-style collapse, unless we can bring about some *meaningful* changes.

When we examine the system necessary to redistribute the wealth and to control all people and all industry, both manufacturing and distribution, we see a huge structure. A huge bureaucracy. Who runs a bureaucracy? It is the ruling elite, who are never mentioned in the theory of Marxism. But such is absolutely necessary for a Marxist government. Those who comprise the ruling elite are called the Nomenklatura. Russia has it. Romania had it. All Marxist countries have the ruling elite. The rich in the U.S.A. who support Marxism must want to be part of the ruling elite and Nomenklatura if and when America goes totally Marxist.

One who gets serious about studying this situation can see hundreds of the super-rich here in America supporting Marxist programs. For one thing, Marxism is one way of **restricting competition.** John D. Rockefeller, possibly the richest man in America in his day, said, **"Competition is a sin"**. Rockefeller wanted monopolistic laws that favored him at the expense of his competitors. Was he a Marxist? It is difficult to believe that a very wealthy person could be a Marxist. But once you study Marxism in this chapter you will get a good understanding of Marxism and you will be able to identify Marxist programs in our government and you will be able to identify individuals who support Marxist programs.

We must note here, with all the emphasis that we can muster, **that the politicians who vote for these Marxist programs <u>NEVER identify</u> themselves as Marxists.**

If anyone were to ever to describe them as Marxists they would deny it vigorously. They would identify themselves as "progressive" or "liberal." So just remember that the ideological foundation of the "progressives" and "liberals" is comprised of the theory of evolution, of Secular Humanism and of Marxism.

This applies not only to the politicians who promote and vote for these laws but to the unseen bureaucrats or contract writers who write them. And I forgot to mention the insanity of many of the richest of the rich in Hollywood who support Marxist candidates and who demonize candidates who would vote more in line with the Constitution and protect our freedoms. They are hugely successful in their field and hugely rich. But on the "sane" to "insane" definition, they rank very low in some areas.

These "non-discrimination" laws are completely anti-constitutional and are totally Marxist in that they are against freedom and justice.

The Reality of Marxism

To understand the reality of Marxism, we need no fancy and expensive surveys conducted by self-proclaimed "experts" at huge fees. All that is necessary is to look at the news coming from Venezuela right now, the 08 of June, 2020. The Marxist government has collapsed. The economy has collapsed. Businesses have failed. Some have disappeared. Squeezed to death by Marxist regulations and laws. Jobs have vanished. The shelves of the stores are empty.

The people are fighting over any scrap of food. Looters are stopping trucks coming into town with food. The food never gets to the stores. There is no doubt much misery being suffered by the people that is not being shown to us by the controlled and manipulated mainstream media.

The irony of this situation is that, with the disaster and misery clearly visible to us as the result of a Marxist government for the past several years, there are two candidates for the presidency of the United States (as of June, 2020) whose platform is clearly Marxist and yet they are getting a lot of support. It is obvious that the people supporting these two candidates are either not able to think or not willing to. They deny reality. By my definition, they are, to a large degree, insane. They refuse to deal with reality. They believe promises that are clearly lies. It must be that, when being taught Marxism in school, they somehow become completely enraptured with the glowing promises of Marxism.

At the same time, they become completely blind to the inevitable disastrous results of Marxism. And furthermore, they were taught to despise or even hate the Constitution and the principles that would protect their freedoms. To better understand Marxism, let's take a look at the Ten Points of the Communist Manifesto. These are the programs which the Marxists plan to use to convert America to a completely Marxist nation. They are being very successful. We are on our way to meeting the same disastrous fate that Venezuela is suffering right now.

Surprisingly, the backbone of Marx's plan, "the redistribution of the wealth" is not stated, per se, in the Ten Points. However, it is very effectively accomplished by # 2, the graduated income tax, coupled with the many and various huge welfare schemes of the federal government.

Regarding numbers 6, 7, 8 and 9 above, to control is to own. The definition of to own something means the legal right to control it. To the extent that the federal government controls a farm, a ranch or any business through regulations, it, de facto, owns it. To the extent that the federal government extracts taxes from the above entities over and beyond the amount needed to protect them, the fed-gov then, de facto, owns the profits of those enterprises. We might call this "invisible ownership" but it is very, very real. Just ask any owner of a business or any farmer or any rancher. There seems to be no limit to the greed and lust for power of the Marxists. There is no limit to the regulations that Marxist-thinking bureaucrats in the regulatory agencies can think up to impose upon the producing segment of America. After all, the bureaucrats have to do something to attempt to justify their salaries and perks. And that is the reason that our economy has slowed to a crawl. Insane government regulations.

Now, why do the American people condone Marxist government laws when they are contrary to our best interests? Maybe it is because we have been "conditioned" to accept them and perhaps even to condone them by the process known as "thought manipulation." Crazy? Here in America? Well, let's take an intelligent look at how the Marxists impose "mind control" over an entire population. Their objective is to invert perceptions of reality. To make people perceive that good is evil and that evil is good. It is amazing to realize how successful they are. An understanding of Marxist tactics is necessary.

Constitutionalism vs Marxism

Constitutionalism and Marxism are the exact opposite. Constitutionalism results in justice, freedom and prosperity. Marxism results in tyranny, oppression and misery. Yet politicians, law school professors and judges pretend that they cannot tell one from the other. Let's see if we can help them.

Just remember that Marxism is total control over the people by the ruling elite. Most politicians want power. More and more power. Thus they vote for Marxist legislation even though they might recognize that it is Marxist.

It is really very simple, once a person sets himself to understand it. Constitutionalism comes from the Constitution. Marxism comes from the works of Marx, including the Communist Manifesto. The structure and the purpose of the two types of government are entirely different. Let's start with Constitutionalism. The first thing to remember is that our rights, all of them, come from our Creator, as stated in the *Declaration*. The purpose of the government is to protect those rights. Under the Constitution of the United States, the source of all authority for government is our Creator who bestows upon us our rights.

We, the People, then authorize certain agents of government to perform certain functions. We, the People, have only the authority to bestow just powers upon the government. We do not possess the authority to bestow unjust powers. If We, the People, restrain ourselves to bestowing only just powers upon the government then the government will always be just. Except for usurpation.

It will not have the authority to exercise unjust powers. Please study the picture above very carefully. It tells a very important message regarding government. Understanding the flow of authority in a government is essential to being able to analyze a government and to be able to determine what part of it is constitutional and what part is Marxist.

In understanding Marxism, remember: (1) the purpose of a constitutional government is to protect your liberties, (2) the purpose of a Marxist government is to enrich the ruling elite—at the expense of your liberties. This means taking from you a large part of your property and earnings. It has laws to punish you for making decisions (that you would have every right to make in a free country) contrary to the laws of the rulers. The penalties might be a fine, it might be imprisonment or it might be death. The structure of the two governments are different, as depicted below. If you learn the ten points of the Communist manifesto, the information presented above and the information to be gained from the two maps on p.84, you will have a good understanding of Marxism and how it differs from constitutionalism.

It is All About Sovereignty

The objective of the SCs is to deprive us of our sovereignty. All of it. So far, they have been doing a pretty good job of it. Let's examine the definition of sovereignty:

Sovereignty: The supreme, absolute and uncontrollable power by which any independent state is governed; supreme political authority; paramount control of the Constitution and frame of government and its administration; the self-sufficient source of political power, from which all specific political powers are derived…

There are two forms of government; one is which considers the laws of God to be supreme. The other is where the laws of man are considered to be supreme. There is no other option.

The government of the United States of America is very unique in that it is the only nation in the world whose government was originally established on the premise that the supreme authority was God, that same Creator who bestowed our rights upon us citizens as declared in the *Declaration*. We citizens then authorize the officers of government to exercise certain limited and defined powers.

That is the way it was originally. It was intended that the people would keep the government pure (comprised only of the laws of God) as in the *Declaration* it is stated: "…That to secure these rights, Governments are instituted among Men, deriving their just powers from the consent of the governed." (Emphasis added). We are supposed to deliver to the government only *just* powers. Should we deliver to it unjust powers or condone its exercise of unjust powers, then the government becomes corrupted. We are guilty of both.

© Custom Artwork

But we are being robbed of our sovereignty. It is done so insidiously the average person is not aware of it. We citizens are being robbed of our sovereignty and our county and state governments are being robbed of their sovereignty. They want to change the government so that we citizens have no sovereignty and all laws ignore God's law and all originate with man.

Communist Russia, Nazi Germany and Communist China are examples of governments based solely on the laws of man. It is the objective of the SCs to transmogrify our government from one based on God's law to one which denies the laws of God and is based solely on the laws of man. The problem with this is that without the laws of God as the supreme measure by which to judge all laws made by man, the carnal nature of man prevails (emphasis on power and greed) in the making of the laws.

Important Important Important

The great danger that faces us today is that while most Americans are opposed to Marxism, they are not able to recognize the PRINCIPLES of Marxism. Marxist ideas, theories, programs, legislation and acts of government that are Marxist because they are not labeled, "Marxist." So our government is being converted to a Marxist dictatorship in small increments by acts and laws that are labeled as "constitutional."

Few citizens recognize this since they are busy making a living, raising children and all the other things that occupy our time. So please study the information in this chapter and apply it to various branches of government, the various bureaucracies and all legislation until you can readily recognize Marxism when you see it and can explain it to your family and friends.

Under Constitutional Law: 1. Constitutional law, 2. Criminal law, 3. Contract law and 4. Tort law.

The proponents of this regional-Marxist bureaucracy claim that regulatory agencies are necessary to keep things in order. That without it, confusion, mayhem and disorder would reign. Such people obviously do not understand the free market system or a constitutional form of government. With very few exceptions, all matters of law can be handled within these four different types of law:
1. Constitutional law,
2. Criminal law,
3. Contract law and
4. Tort law.

I concede that there might be a very small segment of law cases that would need to be handled by regulatory law. But it would be a small fraction of that being regulated by the present regional bureaucratic system. Here is the difference: Under constitutional law, all officers of government are elected by and accountable to the citizens they are governing and any citizen charged with a crime is due the full protection of due process of law as stated in their state constitutions. The federal government would be involved in very few criminal cases.

Under regional law, none of the agents of government are accountable to the citizens they are ruling and citizens charged with crimes are not afforded the protection of their state constitutions or the United States Constitution. Huge difference. The difference between liberty and tyranny.

Marxist-World Government-Globalist

Please for give the duplication, but the following fits here as it did in Chapter 8, "NEVER Trust the Media". This chapter is to explain the overlapping of tactics and objectives of the Marxists and the wealthy elite and Globalists. Whatever difference their might be in their tactics, their objectives are to destroy our constitutional government and to build in its place a totally centralized one, with the states and the people having no sovereignty. (see Map "B" and the explanation for it in Chapter Nine).

The centralized government would have total control and would not be accountable to the people in any significant way. Here are Rockefeller (not our friend) and friend Goldwater again.

David Rockefeller, the Bilderbergers and the Trilateral Commission

Rockefeller later (after the Bilderberg Conference of 1991 where he admitted that the media had accommodated his requests for non—coverage) admits, in print, to being part of a secret cabal conspiring with others to integrate the United States into a one world government. This world government, of course, can be accomplished only after the nullification and/or dissolution of the Constitution of the United States. Here it is from Rockefeller himself:

Some even believe we [the Rockefellers] are a part of a secret cabal working against the best interests of the United States, characterizing my family and me as 'internationalists' and of conspiring with others around the world to build a more integrated global political and economic structure—one world, if you will. If that's the charge, **I stand guilty and I am proud of it**." (David Rockefeller, *Memoirs,* Jan 1, 2002, Random House, 518 pp Hardcover, p. 405)

David Rockefeller — Public Domain

Rockefeller's confession, in his own words; in his *Memoirs* certainly does lend credence also to the report by du Berrier regarding Rockefeller's statement at the Bilderberg Conference, in Germany in 1991, about the media maintaining its silence about Rockefeller's efforts to merge the United States into a Globalist government, which would require the destruction of the Constitution and the freedoms of all Americans.

U.S. Senator Barry Goldwater, in his memoirs, gives us some good information regarding how the super wealthy perpetuate their control over the U. S. government, using Marxist tactics:

When a new president comes on board, there is a great turnover in personnel but no change in policy. Example: During the Nixon years Henry Kissinger, CFR member and Nelson Rockefeller's protege', was in charge of foreign policy.

Barry M Goldwater
U.S. Senator and Pilot
Creative Commons

When Jimmy Carter was elected, Kissinger was replaced by Zbigniew Brzezinski, CFR member and David Rockefeller protege'.[57]

The powerful European banker Anselm Rothschild once said, "Give me the power to issue a nation's money, then I do not care who makes the laws." History is more than a record of man's struggle for physical survival. Food and shelter are elementary needs, but in the minds of many, the acquisition of power is more important.

In the world of nature the predator stalks his prey, killing to satisfy hunger. In the society of man the predators pursue sovereignty, not sustenance. If successful, they find easy access to every material indulgence.

The universally recognized power structures are: (1) the state—police power flowing from political control; (2) wealth—economic power flowing from monopoly control; (3) the academy—intellectual authority; and (4) the church—ecclesiastical dictum.[58]

Senator Barry Goldwater gives us his evaluation of the Trilateral Commission:[59]

> In my view, the Trilateral Commission represents a skillful, coordinated effort to seize control and consolidate the four centers of power—political, monetary, intellectual and ecclesiastical. All this is to be done in the interests of creating a more peaceful, more productive world community. Throughout my public life and in these pages I have

---

57. Bernays, Edward Louis, 1928, 1955, 2005, Propaganda, Ig Publishing, Brooklyn. P 57: 57

58. William F. Jasper, "George Soros' War on America: Time to Prosecute the Billionaire's Global Crime Spree," The New American, Sunday, 20 November 2016
59. Goldwater, Barry, With No Apologies, William Morrow, New York, 1979, p. 279

refrained from judging other men's motives. I have no such hesitancy about judging their wisdom and the results of the actions taken...

What the Trilaterals truly intend is the creation of a worldwide economic power superior to the political governments of the nation—states involved. They believe the abundant materialism they propose to create will overwhelm existing differences. As managers and Creators of the system they will rule the future.

What Rockefeller inadvertently admitted and what Goldwater confirmed, is how secret combinations manage to accumulate and concentrate into their hands a disproportionate amount of control over the centers that mold opinions and of the power of governments so as to use this power for their own benefit and advantage.

We should be grateful that Rockefeller (definitely *not* our friend) inadvertently "spilled the beans" and that Goldwater, as our friend, confirmed what Rockefeller had spilled and provided his assistance in identifying the enemies of America. I wish to add to Goldwater's statement, above, that these managers plan to rule not only the future but every person under this "worldwide economic power". That means us. You and me. To rule, not to govern. There is a great difference.

The super—rich realize that a Marxist government gives them exactly the structure they need to accomplish their goals—to control all industry, all distribution, all workers and all people. Meanwhile, the American people continue to believe that Marxism is for the poor. After all, did Marx not proclaim, "Working men of the world unite! You have nothing to lose but your chains"!?

It makes me wonder if Marx was not financed by the Rothschilds or Weishaupts or by one of that crowd a couple of hundred years ago. Worthy of note is that Marx's partner and benefactor, Frederick Engels, was one of the wealthy elite. No doubt, Engels had much influence on Marx's thinking and writing.

Here is an excerpt from an article by James Perloff in The *New American Magazine* of July 23, 2009 that sums up the "powers that be" that control American politics, the media and education:

Ronald Reagan – Public Domain

> (Candidate Ronald Reagan speaking:) "I don't believe that the Trilateral Commission is a conspiratorial group, but I do think its interests are devoted to international banking, multinational corporations and so forth. I don't think that any Administration of the U.S. Government should have the top nineteen positions filled by people

from any one group or organization representing one viewpoint. No, I would go in a different direction."

Yet after his election, President Reagan picked 10 Trilateralists for his transition team and included in his administration such Trilateralists as Vice President George H. W. Bush, Defense Secretary Caspar Weinberger, U.S. Trade Representative William Brock and Fed Chairman Paul Volcker. Yet the entire North American membership of the Trilateral Commission has never numbered much over 100.

Council on Foreign Relations

James Perloff, in his article, "Council on Foreign Relations"[60] stated the following:

> The reason that presidential candidates' promises of "change" go largely unfulfilled once in office: they draw their top personnel from the same establishment groups — of which the Trilateral Commission is only one. Chief among these groups is the Council on Foreign Relations (CFR), the most visible manifestation of what some have called the American establishment. Members of the council have dominated the administrations of every president since Franklin D. Roosevelt, at the cabinet and sub-cabinet level. It does not matter whether the president is a Democrat or Republican. As we will later see, Barack Obama is no exception to CFR influence.
> Power Behind the Throne
>
> In theory, America's government is supposed to be "of the people, by the people, for the people." While this concept rang true in early America and many individuals still trust in it, the last century has seen the reality of power increasingly shift from the people to an establishment rooted in banking, Wall Street and powerful multinational corporations. Syndicated columnist Edith Kermit Roosevelt, granddaughter of Teddy Roosevelt, explained:
>
>> The word "Establishment" is a general term for the power elite in international finance, business, the professions and government, largely from the northeast, who wield most of the power regardless of who is in the White House. Most people are unaware of the existence of this "legitimate Mafia." Yet the power of the Establishment makes itself felt from the professor who seeks a foundation grant, to the candidate for a cabinet post or State Department job. It affects the nation's policies in almost every area.

---

60. Goldwater, Barry, 1979, With No Apologies, William Morrow and Company, Inc., New York, p. 282

Edith K. Roosevelt added that this group's goal is "a One World Socialist state governed by 'experts' like themselves."

Evidence of Powers Behind the Scenes'

Felix Frankfurter, (1882-1965) an associate justice of the SCOTUS from 1939 until 1962, once stated, "The real rulers in Washington are invisible and exercise power from behind the scenes."
Another bit of evidence that the Congress does not rule is the fact that seldom, if ever, is a piece of proposed legislation written by a congressman or his/her staff. Furthermore, legislation is seldom even read by the congressmen who vote on it. Often, legislation of several hundred pages is presented to the congressmen only hours before the vote. They have not read it nor do they know the contents thereof. The big question, then, is "who wrote the legislation"? and "For whom were the authors of the legislation working"? "By whom were they paid"? What are their names? What are their political ideologies?

Agencies of the U. S. Government Designed to Convert America to a Marxist Dictatorship

It is difficult for most Americans to accept the reality that the government of the country that we love has been corrupted to be, mostly, a Marxist dictatorship. But when we study the corruption of the law, in Chapters Eleven and Thirteen, we will see that the evidence is plain and irrefutable. Most Americans are so busily engaged in making a living, raising children, church functions, etc. that they have never made a special study of this situation. Since the MSM strives to keep us misinformed and confused, a special study is required to understand this problem. This book that you are now reading can be considered to be part of this "special study".

Let's start with the **Environmental Protection Agency.** The EPA is not a constitutional agency. It cannot be. It is not authorized by Article One Section Eight of the Constitution. Then, it is a federal agency operated in violation of Articles Nine and Ten of the Bill of Rights. It is administered through ten regions (See Map "B", Chapter Nine) into which the United States is divided. It is operated under the executive branch of the federal government, yet within the EPA, legislative, executive and judicial functions are performed. (This is the very definition of "tyranny".) When a citizen is charged by the EPA, he is hauled into one of its judicial tribunals, in which the citizen does not have the protection of the Constitution. Also, citizens can be, charged with violations of EPA regulations when they have done absolutely no harm to any person or property.

Furthermore, when a citizen wants to do something on his own property, he is required to obtain an "Environmental Impact Study". The property owner then has to engage some business or person who writes up these studies. These studies seldom contain any useful purpose. Their main purpose is, it seems, is to extract money from property owners and give it to those who write the EPA impact studies. It is a legal racket that costs the average American and enriches those of the Left.

This is part of the overall plan of the Left to deplete the resources of conservative Americans and enrich the Left. Another part of their "redistribution of the wealth).

Then there is the **Internal Revenue Service.** It is more than an agency to raise taxes. MUCH more. It is part of the "Redistribute the wealth" and "Graduated income tax" scheme of the Marxists. (See the Communist Manifesto, Chapter Nine). It is structured so that it can selectively attack citizens and seize their property, without a court order, at any time.

Then there is the **Homeland Protection Agency.** Hastily enacted after the 911 attack, when all America was in a state of trauma and presented to the Congress with insufficient time for it to be read and evaluated before the vote. In the right hands, it can serve the right purpose. But in the wrong hands, it is like any other agency, such as the SCOTUS-(as we shall see shortly) can serve as the means to destroy a free nation. It is constructed so as to serve as a national police force in the wrong hands. Suggesting the possibility that the wrong hands designed it in the first place.

The World's Greatest Irony

This practice of intolerance and the Left might be an example of the world's greatest irony. One of the Left's most-used tricks is that of accusing their adversaries, no matter of how baseless their accusations might be. The irony is this: The most tolerant are regularly accused of being intolerant by those who are in reality the least tolerant. (Those on the Left regularly accuse those on the Right of being intolerant.)

There is More-MUCH More

There is no limit to the quantity nor type of stratagems that the Left uses against us. For more, see Chapters 8, 11, 14, 17, 18 and 19. Also see Appendix "N".

SECTION TWO

Chapter Ten - Corrupting the Law to Persecute Christians

But we know that the law is good if a man use it lawfully 1 Timothy 1:8

Pure, Undefiled Uncorrupted Law vs Corrupted Law

What is meant by "pure, undefiled, uncorrupted law" is the Constitution as intended by its framers. It is as close to the law as given by the Great Lawgiver as has been found on earth. Up until Langdell came along at Harvard, the SCOTUS pretty much judged by the Constitution, by "original intent." Meaning, that if the justices had any doubt about the meaning of any part of the Constitution, they referred back to the writings of the Framers.

As long as the law remains uncorrupted, the Christians and other innocents remain protected from persecution. It is when the law becomes corrupted that this corrupted law can be used by corrupt politicians to persecute innocent people. Corrupt law is usually created by corrupt judges, but also by the legislature and the executive. When it is done by judges, it is called "judicial activism." Meaning, that justices apply some meaning other than original intent to the Constitution.

Is it Not Strange That Some People Choose to Attack Christianity?

Of all the things in the world that need to be addressed, exposed and opposed, is it not strange that some people choose to attack Christianity? Christianity is the most powerful force for good in this world that serves as an inward restraint to prevent people from committing crime—from doing harm to others. It is also probably the greatest motivator of charitable causes—to prompt people to come to the aid of others who are in need. Then why, oh why, do some people want to attack Christianity? I cannot provide the answer to the motives of all of them. But I can bring to light their actions and the result thereof. The minds of such people must be very perverted. Their worldviews must be very distorted. Whatever motivates their behavior, we must stand to defend Christianity and Christians against it.

Why the Leftist Irreligionists Corrupt the Law

Herein it will be noted that I often refer to the laws being corrupted in order to be used to persecute the Christians. This is because uncorrupted laws under the uncorrupted Constitution could not be used to persecute Christians nor anybody else. These uncorrupted laws protected the natural rights of all citizens, Christians and non-Christians alike. If we suppose that the law has been corrupted in order to persecute Christians, we must understand the foundation of that law which was corrupted and also the foundation of the law into which it was corrupted. That is, respectively, "the laws of nature and of nature's God" as the original law and "positivist law" or "revisionism" as the corrupted law. This information will be very helpful in separating the Christians and their laws from the irreligionists and their laws. After a while, it will become easy to ascertain which side is the Devil's.

Corrupt government is and always has been, the greatest threat to Christianity and to civilization. Just consider the trial of Jesus.

The Trial of Jesus from a Lawyer's Standpoint

Walter M. Chandler (1867-1935), a New York lawyer, wrote a most elucidating book entitled *The Trial of Jesus From a Lawyer's Standpoint*.[61] The account of the corruption of the law involved in the trial of Jesus is very germane to our study of the corruption of the American system of law today. I highly recommend Chandler's book to you. Christ was murdered in order to silence him and his message. America's system of law has been corrupted for the specific purpose of suppressing the history and message of Jesus Christ. Those justices on the SCOTUS who are complicit in this are just as guilty, in my mind, as those who put Jesus to death. They did it for the same purpose.

In this battle between good and evil involving civil law, we need to understand both natural law and positive law.

The Laws of Nature and of Nature's God

Thousands of "liberal" university professors will claim to the contrary, (they lie about other things, too) but this nation was founded upon the laws of nature and of nature's God. Such law is also called "natural law". As we study the laws of nature and of nature's God and its opposite, "positivist law", we can better understand why the enemies of Christ disdain constitutional ("natural") law and embrace positivist law. Here are a few statements from some of the founders of our nation and the founders of our Constitution:

---

61. Goldwater, Barry, Ibid, pp 284, 5.

Noah Webster: [The] "Law of nature" is a rule of conduct arising out of the natural relations of human beings established by the Creator and existing prior to any positive precept [human law] ....These...have been established by the Creator and are, with a peculiar felicity of expression, denominated in Scripture, "ordinances of heaven." (David Barton, *Original Intent,* Wallbuilders, 1996, 4th ed., p.225.)

Noah Webster – Public Domain

John Jay – Public Domain

John Jay (First chief justice of U.S. Supreme Court) [T]he...natural law was given by the Sovereign of the universe to all mankind. (Ibid, p. 225.)

James Wilson (Signer of the Constitution, U.S. Supreme Court justice.) God...is the promulgator as well as the author of natural law. (Ibid, p. 225.)

James Wilson – Public Domain

Richard Hooker: (The Founders drew heavily upon the writings and wisdom of English legal and theologians and philosophers such as John Locke and Richard Hooker) And because the point about which we strive is the quality of our laws, our first entrance hereinto cannot better be made than with consideration of the nature of law in general..namely, the law whereby the Eternal Himself doth work. Proceeding from hence to the law, first of Nature, then of Scripture, we shall have the easier access unto those things which come after to be debated. (Ibid., p. 220.)

Richard Hooker – Public Domain

Richard Hooker: (On the stability offered to civil government by the inclusion of God's Law) [L]et polity [civil government] acknowledge itself indebted to religion....So natural is the union of religion with justice that we may boldly deem there is neither where both are not. (Ibid. p. 220.)

Samuel Adams: In the supposed state of nature, all men are equally bound by the laws of nature, or to speak more properly, the laws of the Creator. (Ibid., p 224.)

John Quincy Adams: The laws of nature and of nature's God…of course presupposes the existence of a God, the moral ruler of the universe and a rule of right and wrong, of just and unjust, binding upon man, preceding all institutions of human society and of government. (Ibid., p. 224.)

The Laws of Nature and of Nature's God Foundational to American Law

What God loves the enemies of Christ Abhor. The enemies of the Constitution shriek and wail at the mention of the laws of nature and of nature's God. The first two paragraphs of the *Declaration of Independence* declare the justification for our nation's existence and also the origin of our rights. (Our rights do NOT come from the government):

God's laws, the laws of nature's God, are immutable, infallible and unchangeable. They cannot be changed by man. This is why the Secular Humanists and all enemies of justice hate the laws of nature's God. When God gave His law to Moses, he did not call them "The Ten Suggestions." They were and are, ten absolute and unchangeable laws. They have not changed one bit in the last 3,500 (my estimate) years since handed down to Moses. Unchangeable laws make it much more difficult for the enemies of justice to "misinterpret," and corrupt the law using various stratagems. They make it much more difficult for domestic enemies of the Constitution such as Justice Charles Evans Hughes to declare the Constitution to be "…the Constitution is what[ever] the judges say it is."

Excerpts from the *Declaration of Independence*

> When in the course of human events, it becomes necessary for one people to dissolve the political bands which have connected them with another and to assume among the powers of the earth, the separate and equal station to which the **Laws of Nature and of Nature's God** entitle them, a decent respect to the opinions of mankind requires that they should declare the causes which impel them to the separation. (Emphasis added). We hold these truths to be self-evident, that all men are created equal, that **they are endowed by their Creator with certain unalienable Rights**, that among these are Life, Liberty and the pursuit of Happiness.—That secure these rights, Governments are instituted among Men, deriving their just powers from the consent of the governed. (Emphasis added).

Note: Our rights are unalienable, because they are bestowed upon us not by man or man's government but by our Creator. This is very important when we start to examine the difference between uncorrupted law and corrupted law.

Positive Law-Relativism

Positive law posits that the the state and the lawmakers thereof, (man) constitutes the ultimate authority for civil law. There is no superior authority.

No Ten Commandments. No God. There are no rigid guidelines. Everything is changeable. This is the foundation of Humanist and Marxist law. At least, they want everything changeable. When the law is fully Marxist, then the Marxist no longer want it to be changeable. That is the political belief of Humanists and Marxists.

Although our Constitution has never been legally amended to accommodate such wholesale change, our laws now are, arguably, more positive law than natural (constitutional) law. In the law schools, positive law is emphasized and lauded. Natural law is mostly ignored and, usually, demeaned. We shall now study the process by which our government was changed from natural law to positive law and those culpable for this transition.[62] Because of the changes these people made, our government is being changed to a Marxist state. It is solely because of these changes that the SCOTUS was able to enact the *Everson* case (to be addressed in the next chapter) and others, to persecute Christianity and Christians.

Suppose You Were the Devil

In the previous chapter, Devil, we addressed two of the principle features of your religion, evolution and Secular Humanism. You are not satisfied with the little amount of success that your soldiers have been having. Persuasion alone is not getting the job done. You have to have something with more force to it. Yes, what you need is the LAW to help you in your proselyting. You are in luck. Just recently, in 1870, one of your soldiers, one Christopher Columbus Langdell, was appointed to be dean of the law school at Harvard. You have been mentoring Langdell on a couple of ideas that appear promising. Now, in his new position, you might be able to put these ideas to work. "Things are looking up," you say.

Christopher Columbus Langdell

If the law was going to be used to persecute Christians and Christianity, then there had to be some changes made. Some MAJOR changes. The structure, wording and purpose of the Constitution was entirely unsuited to be used to persecute the Christians. The American people would not stand for these changes to be made the legal way—by Article V amendment—so it had to be made surreptitiously. So, enter one Christopher Columbus Langdell, This takes us back to Harvard, in about 1870 to 1895, when Langdell (1826-1906) was the dean of the law school. It is absolutely amazing how much damage one man can do to a nation's system of jurisprudence, or to the nation itself. Langdell created, first, the idea that the law should evolve, hence the "positivism' method of law. Then, the case-history method of judging, meaning that a judge can base his ruling on a prior case and call it

---

62. Perloff, James, "Council on Foreign Relations" The New American, 23 Jul 2009

"constitutional" regardless of how it conflicts with the Constitution. Thus, it provides judges with excuses to violate the Constitution yet giving their rulings the *appearance* of propriety and constitutionality. Very devious. Very insidious. And very dangerous, as we shall see.

Langdell - Public Domain   Pound - Public Domain   Mann - Public Domain   Dewey - Public Domain

First Langdell, then Pound, then Mann, then Dewey

Four players figure prominently in the Humanist takeover of the American legal system and the American education system, all of whom figure prominently in attacks against Christians, Christianity and Christian religious liberty.

The first is Christopher Columbus Langdell (1826–1906), who had nothing to do directly with the public school system of America but who had everything to do with corrupting the American system of law so that the law could be made to favor the Secular Humanists. Changes in the American system of jurisprudence, by justices who favor Secular Humanism, would later have a direct and revolutionary effect upon education. Langdell was the dean of the Harvard Law School from 1870 until 1895. Understanding Langdell's story is prerequisite to understanding how the Humanists managed to capture and revolutionize American education.

David Noebel Describes Langdell's Effect Upon the Law:

> Langdell, of course, was the key personality behind the evolutionary interpretation of the law. He became dean of Harvard's Law School in 1870 and proceeded to move Harvard from its Christian foundation to law based on the theory of evolution. Instead of law based on the law of nature and of nature's God, law is based on ever-evolving principles determined primarily by judges. Law no longer has an absolute base, but a relative one. Langdell encouraged his students to abandon William

Blackstone's *Commentaries* on the Common Law primarily because he could not accept Blackstone's non-evolutionary interpretation of law.[63]

Roscoe Pound followed Langdell as dean of the Harvard Law School and carried Langdell's theory of evolutionary law forward, to further the destruction of the true meaning of the Constitution.

Langdell and Pound very effectively corrupted the American legal system so that judges did not have to refer to the Constitution when pronouncing a judgment to be "constitutional." This corruption was not insignificant. It was sufficiently radical to allow the SCOTUS to invert the meaning of the Constitution and to, eventually, by the rule of judges, change the government of the United States from a constitutional republic to a (nearly) Marxist dictatorship.

Then there was Horace Mann (1796–1859) It is necessary to note that Mann's religion is listed as Unitarian, which is very different from Christianity but very compatible with Secular Humanism.

Then there was John Dewey, who figured prominently in the development of the public school system, was a prominent Humanist and also had strong Marxist connections. Dewey was extremely influential back in the early days of American education in determining the direction it would take. He set it off on the wrong course. Dewey was a committed Humanist. He was a signatory to the Humanist Manifesto I in 1933. He must have been a Marxist also, since he was chosen by Stalin (we must presume) to preside over a commission to try Leon Trotsky in Coyoacan, Mexico in April of 1937.

I do not have the full story of how and why Dewey came to be chosen to preside over this commission, but it must be an interesting one. But to be chosen by someone in Moscow, Russia to preside over this commission, in Mexico, is a strong indication that Dewey was a favorite of the most powerful people in the Communist party of Russia. Also, Dewey made a trip to Russia in 1926 and wrote a book, *Impressions of Soviet Russia and the Revolutionary World.*[64] The evidence leaves little room for doubt that Dewey was either a Marxist or was very sympathetic to the Communist revolutionaries.

Now to Langdell, who was (it appears) an evolutionist and a Humanist, whether or not he ever publicly admitted it.

---

63. Chandler, Walter M., The Trial of Jesus From a Lawyer's Standpoint, 2 vol. The Empire Publishing Co., New York, 1908.

64. For more on this subject, see David Noebel, Understanding the Times, pp 508-515
65. David Noebel, Understanding the Times, 1991, Harvest House, p. 506

Christopher Columbus Langdell: Legal Revolutionary, Dean of Harvard Law

It is absolutely amazing the damage that one person can do. Remember Hitler. Remember Tojo. Remember Stalin. Remember Mussolini. Now I should like to refer once again to Dave Breese's excellent book, *Seven Men Who Rule the World From the Grave*, which explains how the ideas of Charles Darwin, Karl Marx, John Dewey, and four others still rule the world.

When closely examined, our government, our educational system and our culture are heavily influenced by Darwin, Dewey and Marx. I just wonder why Dave did not include Langdell, whose destructive influence still rules our part of the world even though he is long in the grave. Anyhow, Langdell had a tremendous influence on American law, none of it good. All of Langdell's influence has proven to be contrary to our best interests. Langdell probably had more to do with the destruction of the true meaning of our Constitution than did any other one single person. Constitutional scholar and author David Barton explains this succinctly:[65]

> ...**This Philosophy ("positivism") Was Introduced** in the 1870s when Harvard Law School Dean Christopher Columbus Langdell (1826–1906) applied Darwin's premise of evolution to jurisprudence. Langdell reasoned that since man evolved, then his laws must also evolve; and judges should guide both the evolution of law and the Constitution. Consequently, Langdell introduced not only evolutionary law, "positivism", but the case-law study method under which students would study judges' decisions rather than the Constitution. Under this case-law approach, history, precedent and the views and beliefs of the Founders not only became irrelevant, they were even considered hindrances to the successful evolution of a society... Langdell's case-law approach was gradually embraced by other law schools and the result was a *diminishing belief in absolutes. In fact, within a few short years (by the 1930s), Blackstone's commentaries on the* Law had been widely discarded. Blackstone's was deemed to present an outdated approach to law since it taught that certain rights and wrongs particularly those related to human behavior did not change.

Roscoe Pound (1870-1964) strongly endorsed the positivistic philosophy introduced by Langdell. As a prominent twentieth-century legal educator, Pound helped institutionalize positivism. Having served as a professor at four different law schools and as dean of the law schools at Harvard and the University of Nebraska, his influence was considerable-and his vision for law was clear:

> We have...the same task in jurisprudence that has been achieved in philosophy, in the natural sciences and in politics. We have to ***rid ourselves of this sort of legality*** and to attain a pragmatic [evolutionary], a ***sociological*** legal science (emphasis added) (Roscoe Pound, *Columbia Law Review*, vol. 8, no. 8, December 1908, p. 609) (Emphasis added)

According to Pound, no longer should it be the mission of jurisprudence to focus on the narrow field of legal interpretation; the goal should be to become a sociological force to influence the development of society. [Please remember this when we later get to consider judging by "social justice" rather than by the Constitution. Joe]

For all practical purposes, what Langdell introduced into American jurisprudence was judging by something other than the Constitution, but still calling it "constitutional." In our day, 2020, we are coming to the point where this sort of judging has destroyed the all-important rule of law. As far as the federal courts are concerned, they seem to abandon the rule of law at their every convenience. Langdell, it seems, was following the Gramsci plan even before Gramsci wrote it.

Rogue Justices and Rogue Courts

We need a way to identify judges and courts who do not perform as they should. Merriam Webster defines "rogue" as: "...to behave in an independent or uncontrolled way that is not authorized, normal, or expected." That seems to be the proper adjective to describe a judge or a court that does not judge according to the law. So hereinafter we shall identify judges and courts that violate the law as "rogue judges" and "rogue courts."

Before taking office, most officers of government take an oath to "...protect the Constitution against all enemies, foreign and domestic.".So a judge who violates the Constitution can also be classified as a "domestic enemy of the Constitution."

Violate the Constitution Yet Call it "Constitutional"

> **Case law** allows a court to (illegitimately) substitute an unconstitutional ruling of a previous court for the Constitution. Thus nullifying part of the Constitution and making a previous unconstitutional ruling the Supreme Law of the Land.

Langdell might be classified as the "master rogue" or "master domestic enemy of the Constitution".. He derived the very effective, if not perfect, plan to abandon the Constitution and, eventually, to render it entirely null and void. First, his "positivist" law allowed judges to add to, delete from or change the law as they saw fit. Then, the "case law" method allowed them to use prior cases that violated the Constitution as precedent instead of the Constitution itself. In both cases, they still called it "constitutional." This would keep the general public confused, passive and placated.

When a court rules by case law, it puts no value on the Constitution and instead puts full value to the pronouncements of a previous court that has ignored the Constitution and ruled by its own will. Then, to cover its malfeasance, the court pronounces its own ruling to be "constitutional," even though it has obviously ignored the Constitution and based its judgment on a prior anti-constitutional ruling of some court. Judges who look to case law instead of the Constitution as the measure by which to judge make of themselves domestic enemies of the Constitution. Their act serves to violate the Constitution and therefore to render it impotent. These are domestic enemies of the Constitution. How else can they honestly be described?

Please understand that changing the law by this method, in increments, can eventually result in the government being changed from one of a free nation to one of a complete Marxist dictatorship.

Extreme Arrogance of Some Justices

Regarding "constitutionality," Charles Evans Hughes[66,67] (1862-1948), chief justice of the SCOTUS from 1930 to 1941, stated his attitude (and that of many other justices) toward the Constitution and toward "constitutionality":

Charles Evans Hughes
Wikipedia

> We are under a Constitution, but **the Constitution is what the judges say it is.**

Justice Charles Evans Hughes definitely falls into the category of being a "rogue justice" or a "domestic enemy of the Constitution." The corruption of our laws today result from justices with attitudes like that of Justice Charles Evans Hughes. The average honest American is staggered by the dishonesty and arrogance of such people. At least, I am.

Simply Stated, "Case Law" is Treason

Both of Langdell's methods have inflicted lethal wounds on what the federal courts declare to be "constitutional" or "unconstitutional". After Langdell, the

---

66. John Dewey, Impressions of Soviet Russia and the Revolutionary World. 1929, New Republic, Inc. New York
67. Barton, David, 1996, 2000, Original Intent, Wallbuilder's Press, Aledo, Texas, p 228

definition of "constitutional" no longer meant constitutional and the meaning of the word "unconstitutional" no longer meant unconstitutional. Langdell caused the definitions of these two words to be transmogrified into, as "Case law", nothing more, as we shall see hereinafter, than an excuse for the legal sophisticates to violate and negate the Constitution. Some judges feel perfectly justified in ignoring the Constitution and judging by some other means. Subsequently, judges feel justified in ignoring the Constitution and basing their judgments on "precedent". "Precedent" is supposed to be supreme in a system of law whose fundamental premise is that the Constitution, which is organic law, is the Supreme Law of the Land. After ignoring and violating the Constitution to follow "precedent," judges never seem able to ignore "precedent" to return to the Constitution.

When it comes to justices violating the Constitution, how else can such justices be described than as "domestic enemies" of the Constitution or as "rogue" judges?

Case Law and Stare Decisis

Langdell's "case law" subsequently became dignified by the Latin term, "stare decisis." *Black's Law Dictionary* (5th ed.) describes "stare decisis" as: "Policy of courts to stand by precedent and not to disturb settled point." The legal profession now seems to revere the practice of stare decisis as something sacred, or holy. That it cannot be compromised or violated. That "precedent" is something to be rigidly adhered to while the Constitution is something to be ignored and violated.

> **Case law constitutes a gross violation of the Rule of Law. For proof, study the Rule of Law.**

Is it not extremely strange that the courts can consider it so easy to depart from, or violate, the Constitution and rule by some other standard and call it "constitutional?" They then consider this new anti-constitutional court ruling to be "precedent," as having "settled" a particular matter. They label it "stare decisis" and seem to hold it sacred. Thereafter, they consider it difficult to impossible to depart from this court-"settled" matter and return to the Constitution as a standard by which to judge.

Why Can the Legal Professionals Not See This?

All men are born with some amount of intelligence and with some conscience. The stratagems employed to violate the Constitution are so thinly-veiled, so obvious, that it would seem that any person with even a modicum of intelligence or of a conscience, would readily see the treachery involved. Yet, for some reason, the majority of SCOTUS justices, such as those who voted in the majority in *Everson* (coming up) and other such law cases just don't seem to get it.

I know that they are not that stupid. It must be their ego, pride, lust for station and glory. Or something. I have never been to law school. I have not been trained in the ministry of the law.

Yet, to me, it is as clear as a clear winter night after a storm. I have discussed this with others, both lawyers and non-lawyers alike, people of somewhat above average intelligence and they can EASILY see it. So what is it with these judges, law school professors and lawyers who cannot see it? Another one of life's unresolved mysteries.

The above clearly, if not thoroughly, explains the subversion of our law schools, legal system, government and, to a great degree, our society. Now, I encourage you to go back and read the above again very carefully. There is a powerful meaning there. Other law school professors adopted Langdell's approach and it spread like a virulent disease through the law schools, legal community and courts. It should be noted here that politicians thirsting for more power than the Constitution grants would love judges who would apply Langdell's approach and ignore the Constitution.

So it naturally follows that lawyers who embraced the "revisionism" or "positivism" approach to law and who held disdain and contempt for the Constitution would be nominated by some presidents and confirmed by some senates to be Supreme Court justices. Conversely, those who held to the view that the Constitution should continue to be held as the supreme law of the Land would be neither nominated nor confirmed. That is another part of the story of the subversion of our judiciary from 1875 to the present.

The reason that the majority of the legal sophisticates are totally incapable of understanding the treason involved in these violations of the Constitution must be laid to their carnal nature. This carnal nature blinds their eyes and sears their tolerance to the point that they are unable to determine right from wrong. Or is it that they just don't care? It also explains why many lawyers nominated and confirmed to be justices are neither the most intelligent nor do they possess the highest integrity. This is why, we must suppose, that they are confirmed by politicians of the lowest caliber.

The vicious fight to block the confirmation of Judge Robert H. Bork, a very competent justice who would have judged by the Constitution, in 1987 is proof that the honest judges or lawyers are too often neither nominated by the President nor confirmed by the Senate. This is also proof that the SCOTUS has become highly politicized and has strayed from its judicial duties. This also confirms that the U. S. Senate contains too few members who are both intelligent enough and honest enough to (consistently) confirm intelligent and honest nominees to the SCOTUS.

Eidsmoe Explains "Positive Law"

If we are going to defend Christianity, i.e., the words of Christ, we are going to have to understand what weapons the enemies of Christ are using against us. When applied in law, "relativism" is called "legal positivism." According to constitutional scholar and law professor John A. Eidsmoe,[68] this philosophy is characterized by the following five major theses:

> 1. There are no objective, God-given standards of law, or if there are, they are irrelevant to the modern legal system.
> 2. Since God is not the author of law, the author of law must be man; in other words, the law is law simply because the highest human authority, the state, has said it is law and is able to back it up.
> 3. Since man and society evolve, therefore law must evolve as well.
> 4. Judges, through their decisions, guide the evolution of law.
> 5. To study law, get at the original sources of law-the decisions of judges.

What the SCOTUS *Really Means* When it Proclaims "Constitutional"

Please study very seriously the explanation of the effect that Langdell had upon the law and the use of "positive law" and "case law" instead of the Constitution itself. Now, what the SCOTUS really means when it pronounces its ruling to be "constitutional" or "unconstitutional" is that the case is in congruity with or in conflict with, a vast collection of anti-constitutional cases which it, unofficially and unknown to the public, considers to be their (secret and unpublished) "Constitution". This is what the SCOTUS substitutes for the Constitution of the United States when it hands down its anti-constitutional rulings. This is true, to the best of my knowledge, of cases tried in all federal courts.

Whether by the use of case law or by "social justice," what the SCOTUS means by "constitutional" is whatever the Court wants the law to be. What it means by "unconstitutional" is whatever the judge does NOT want the law to be. At least, this prevails in too many cases.

Secular Humanists, "Evolving Law," and Humanist Law

Humanists are different from Christians also in the form of law that they advocate. To the Humanists, there are no absolutes, so the law must be in a constant state of flux. To them, the law evolves. There can be no absolutes; no Constitution. Change in the law is not limited to those made by the legislature or by amendment. It may be changed by the courts or by the chief executive. Constitutionally speaking, of course, this is called "usurpation." The

---

68. Charles Evans Hughes, The Autobiographical Notes of Charles Evans Hughes, , Cambridge: Harvard University Press, 1973, p 144, speech at Elmira on May 3, 1907.
69. Quoted in David Barton, Original Intent, Wallbuilders, 4th ed., 1996, p. 230

importance of understanding this will become clear as we learn how the courts have favored Humanists by changing the law. Here is what Nobel[69] says about Humanist law:

> The concept of evolution so permeates Humanist legal thinking that it can be stated, without contradiction, that evolution ultimately determines Humanistic legal principles. Man is evolving. Man is becoming. Everything is in flux. Nothing is permanent. There are no absolute legal standards. There are no permanent Ten Commandments; there is no permanent Constitution...

Please remember the above description of Humanist legal thinking when we address the issue of "separation of church and state" and how it is a serious threat to Christianity, to America and to civilization.

Please keep in mind that when judges are Secular Humanists, their attitude toward the law is as described by Nobel, above. They consider the law to be changeable and to be whatever they want it to be. So a Secular Humanist judge is going to change the law towards Secular Humanism. Just like a rattlesnake is going to strike you if he gets a chance. That is just the way they are. And, lest we forget, Secular Humanism is exactly the opposite of Christianity. It is the religion of the anti-Christ. Secular Humanists naturally hate Christians, Christianity and Christian law.

The evidence is very persuasive that Christopher Columbus Langdell was an evolutionist and probably a Secular Humanist and that his legal thinking was thoroughly permeated with the concept of evolutionary change. At the risk of being guilty of repetition, I am presenting this wisdom from Jay Liechty[70] here, because if fits here as well:

> Religion constitutes a major part of the foundation of government, because the religious beliefs of the individuals who are in power will be reflected in the government's attitude toward individual freedom. *Persons who make the rules cannot avoid reflecting their religious convictions when they enact laws and they cannot escape setting the moral tone for a nation through those laws.* The laws enacted and the moral tone set, inherently reflect the religious views of those persons who dominate government and their religious views define the moral values, motivations and acceptable behaviors for society and consequently the level of personal peace and domestic tranquility.

The Secular Humanists, along with the evolutionists and Marxists, absolutely abhor absolutes. Absolutes like the Ten Commandments and the Constitution of the United States. The reason is clear. The entire program of the

---

70. John A. Eidsmoe, Christianity and the Constitution, (MI: Baker Book House, 1987) P. 394.

evolutionists, secular humanists and Marxists is to change Americans and America by the means of subversion and deception. If the people were to believe in the Ten Commandments and the Constitution, which are absolutes, then such people would be very difficult to impossible to trick and deceive into believing that they should CHANGE into believing the principles of evolution, Secular Humanism and Marxism. So teachers in public schools that seduce and trick students to believe in the principles of evolution, Secular Humanism and Marxism can be truly classified as CHANGE AGENTS and as domestic enemies of the Constitution. Also as domestic enemies of the Bible and of Christianity.

Separation of Church and State-as per Jefferson Then the Corrupted Version

Now, before we proceed to study how Langdell and the Devil's other disciples proceeded to corrupt the American system of law so that it can be used to persecute Christians, we need to gain an understanding of the origin and the true meaning of the metaphor, "Separation of Church and State." Prior to the Revolution, King George had taxed the colonists to support his favorite church, the Anglican Church. So, the Danbury Baptists wrote to President Jefferson inquiring whether the new federal government would be a threat to their church. He replied, on January 1st, 1802. He stated that the Constitution, especially the First Amendment, constituted a "Separation of Church and State" that would protect them and their church from the intrusion by the federal government. Especially, that the government would not favor any church (any one denomination) over any others. This did not state nor imply the exclusion of the Christian religion or any mention of God from any public function or discourse. The First Amendment was ONLY a restriction of the powers of the federal government. It in no way serves as a grant of power of any kind. The first part of the *First,* called the "Establishment clause", restricted the powers of the federal government. The second half of it guaranteed to the citizens freedom of speech.

Most Americans agree with Thomas Jefferson's statement in his letter to the Danbury Baptists in 1802 regarding "Separation of church and state," so few were alarmed when the SCOTUS expropriated the statement for its own purposes. But the SCOTUS, when it applied "Separation…" to court cases, inverted its meaning to be the opposite of what Jefferson intended. Furthermore, it inverted the meaning of the First Amendment to the Constitution, which was intended to protect our religious liberties, to mean exactly the opposite of what its framers intended. The SCOTUS, by doing so, made of itself the greatest enemy of Christianity and to America that exists. To understand how this can be, we must look into the details of the situation. As they say, "The Devil is in the details." He sure is in this case.

Jefferson's Letter to the Danbury Baptists

> Believing with you that religion is a matter which lies solely between Man & his God, that he owes account to none other for his faith or his worship, that the legitimate powers of government reach actions only, & not opinions, I contemplate with sovereign reverence that act of the whole American people which declared that their legislature should 'make no law respecting an establishment of religion, or prohibiting the free exercise thereof,' thus building a wall of separation between Church & State. Adhering to this expression of the supreme will of the nation in behalf of the rights of conscience, I shall see with sincere satisfaction the progress of those sentiments which tend to restore to man all his natural rights, convinced he has no natural right in opposition to his social duties. (01 Jan, 1802)

Now, we will study the corruption of "Separation of Church and State" and learn how the Humanists managed to get their religion adopted as the official religion of the federal government and adopted as the official (de facto) dogma of the public school system. It is obvious that the principles of Christianity are exactly the opposite of those of Secular Humanism. Not just a little bit but exactly the opposite. And it is obvious also that the principles of Secular Humanism are perfectly compatible with those of the theory of evolution. Gramsci's troops are marching right along in their "Long March Through the Institutions".

Helaman Warns us About Laws Becoming Corrupted

In Helaman, we are warned of exactly the same type of situation in which we find ourselves, of the laws being corrupted. This is certainly evidence that the Book of Mormon was written for us in our day. Here it is, in Helaman 4, written by Helaman, great grandson of Alma the Elder:

> 22 And they had altered and trampled under their feet the laws of Mosiah, or that which the Lord commanded him to give unto the people; and they saw that their laws had become corrupted and that they had become a wicked people, insomuch that they were wicked even like unto the Lamanites...
> 25 Therefore the Lord did cease to preserve them by his miraculous and matchless power, for they had fallen into a state of unbelief and awful wickedness;...

Judge Robert Bork Explains More Dangers of Corrupt Law

Judge Robert H. Bork is one of the few judges whom we can thank for his efforts to defend the true Constitution and our liberties. Here he explains that corrupt laws corrupt the thinking and behavior of the people:

Law is a critical battleground because, like the arts and humanities, like sociology, history, political science and other areas that have become politicized, law has the capacity to impact the values of our people and of our culture through its educative and symbolic influence. When a court, especially, the Supreme Court, pronounces in the name of the

Judge Robert Bork- Public Domain

Constitution upon the meaning of racial justice, sexual morality, or any other subject, a cultural lesson is taught. Most people revere the Constitution as a basic compact that defines American civic morality. A decision does more than decide a case; it adds weight to one side of our cultural war, even when the decision is in fact not supported by the actual Constitution. But law, unlike other politicized fields, such as literature and philosophy, has the power to coerce and when the law in question is the Constitution, the coercion is absolute: The people and their democratic institutions are, for all immediate practical purposes, helpless before the authority wielded by judges. Herbert Schlossberg, writing about the influence of the new class on the bureaucracy, makes a point that applies as well to its influence on judges. Through constitutional decisions that are not related to the historic Constitution, that class "has found a vehicle for giving its values the force of law without bothering to take over the political authority of the state." (Robert H. Bork, *The Tempting of America,* Simon and Schuster, New York, 1990,. pp 137,8.)

Constitutional Interpretation is not "Mere Law"

When the gavel comes down on a law case, often times more is decided than "mere law." The case usually adds weight on one side or the other of the great cultural war that rages. (American Constitutionalists on one side- Gramsci and Marx's hordes on the other.) Consider the words of constitutional scholar John A. Eidsmoe:

> ...the debate over constitutional interpretation is no mere academic or legal matter. Rather it is a major battle between two conflicting philosophies, two conflicting religions and two conflicting worldviews.

> [Supreme Court] Justice [William] Brennan openly acknowledged this in his Georgetown address ["The Constitution of the United States: Contemporary Ratification," Teaching Symposium, Georgetown University, Washington, D. C., October 12, 1985, p. 51], declaring that "...our society must continue its upward progress unbounded by the fetters of original intent or the literal words of the Constitution, though an evolutionary process is inevitable and, indeed, it is the true interpretative genius of the text."

This attitude toward the Constitution expressed by Justice Brennan is typical of all those justices whom we categorize as "rogue". They hold in contempt the original intent and true meaning of the Constitution.

Yes, this matter of the law is inseparably connected with the battle that rages between two opposing cultures; between Christianity and the anti-Christ.

Justice Samuel Alito and How the Law Affects Public Opinions

Justice Alito, speaking to the Federalist Society,[71] explained how changes in the law produce changes in public worldviews. Prior to the case of *Obergefell*, (to be addressed in Chapter Twelve) the prevailing view was that marriage was between one man and one woman. Explains Justice Alito, *Obergefell* changed all that:

> **You can't say that marriage is the union between one man and one woman. Until very recently, that's what the vast majority of Americans thought. Now it's considered bigotry.**

So when a people take their eyes off of God as their chief law-giver, they turn to the only other source of law: man-made laws. They then begin to use corrupt man-made laws to support personal wickedness. They no longer ask, "What does the Bible say?" They instead ask themselves, "what does the law allow?"

So we see that corrupt laws corrupt the people and corrupt people corrupt the laws. Thus, a self-perpetuating situation is set up that can take a nation past the point of no return to its destruction.

Applying Common Sense and Proven Legal Theory to Judgments of Rogue Courts

The final argument comes down to "can those stratagems employed by various courts be considered "constitutional ?" Let us begin with the meaning of the word "constitutional." When the suffix "al" is attached to a noun to transform it into an adjective, that adjective takes on the qualities of the noun of origin. Fundamental.

Following Christopher Columbus Langdell

Fifty two years after Langdell finished corrupting the law and the minds of his law students, the stage was set for some very serious and violent corruption of the law. The time is now 1947.

Chapter Eleven - The *Everson* Case and "Separation of Church and State"

> **For we wrestle not against flesh and blood, but against principalities, against powers, against the rulers of the darkness of this world, against spiritual wickedness in high places** (Eph 6:12)

> **Everything is too important ever to be entrusted to professional experts, because every organization of such professionals and every established social organization becomes a vested-interest institution more concerned with its efforts to maintain itself or advance its own interests than to achieve the purpose that society expects it to achieve.**[72]

> **For it is a truth, which the experience of all ages has attested, that the people are commonly most in danger when the means of injuring their rights are in the possession of those of whom they entertain the least suspicion.** (Alexander Hamilton, *The Federalist,* No. 25.)

The worst acts of treachery are committed by those who pretend to be benefactors to those whom they plan to victimize

Before we Begin

Before we begin this chapter, let us never allow ourselves to be intimidated by the legal professionals because we have not been through the ministry of the law. For let us remember that those who have corrupted the law so badly to this point are the **professional lawyers and judges!**

Suppose, Again, That You Were the Devil

In a previous chapter, Devil, we discussed your anti-Christ religion of Secular Humanism and before that, your anti-Christ theory of evolution, both of which constitute important parts of your religion, we must presume. Now let's go back to 1947. You are so unhappy with the successes that the Christians are having up there on earth. You do have your soldiers, but they just are not making very good progress. You must devise some stratagem to make your religion more popular and Christianity unpopular. Your soldiers have not been very good with their proselyting. Those darn Christians are so

---

72. Jay Liechty, America's State Church, Calder Press, 1995, p. 23.

stubborn! You just can't get your religion through their thick skulls! So you start scheming on how to get your religion more exposure and how to make it more compelling and popular. You have to find some way to show those Christians who's boss and that your religion is the law of the land and that Christianity is going out of style.

If you are going to subvert and weaken those Christians, you have to find some way to diminish their belief in Christ and their understanding of the Christian religion. You must find a way to substitute the principles of your religion for the principles of Christianity.

You look around and discover the perfect distribution system for your religion. It is the public school system of America. But there are problems. There are a lot of really good teachers and they teach subjects in harmony with Christianity. You can't possibly get all those teachers converted over to your religion in a thousand years. And also, there are *laws* against what you want to do. Laws? Then you remember your disciple Langdell and you observe his work. Perfect! Not only that, your soldiers have been busy getting some lawyers, trained in the "Langdell Method" and definitely sympathetic to your point of view, appointed to and confirmed to the U. S. Supreme Court. These rogue judges, who do not consider themselves bound by the Constitution, will just change the law to accommodate your plan. You get your plan all worked out.

For years, your comrades had been gaining influence in the education system and planned to take it over completely whenever the opportunity presented itself. Indeed, the tenth point of the Communist Manifesto includes control of the education system. And your comrade William Z. Foster, in *Toward Soviet America*, published in 1932 stated the Communist objective of infiltrating education. The enemies of America and of Christianity know that in order to capture the minds of the Americans, they must capture control of the American educational system. Here is how they have done it.

John Dewey- Wikimedia Commons

During this interim, the ranks of lawyers and judges adhering to Langdell's form of law had increased. Here it is from John Dewey in 1927:[73][74]

---

73. 12 November, 2020
74. Carroll Quigley, AZ Quotes

The belief in political fixity, of the sanctity of some form of state consecrated by the efforts of our fathers and hallowed by tradition, is one of the stumbling-blocks in the way of orderly and directed change. [Dewey meant "orderly and directed change *toward the diminishment of the Constitution and toward a centralized government and a Soviet America.*]

To hurt Christianity and Christians, the worldviews of the majority of Americans must be turned from pro-Christian to anti-Christian. This means mass education. How is this to be done? Well, in the public school system, of course. Your soldiers, Devil, will turn the students against, first: the principles of Christianity, then, second, against Christian tradition, then against Christianity itself and then, finally, against the Christian people.

You'll show those Christians and their Constitution! You have waited long enough. Now, everything is in place. The year is 1947. You get one of your soldiers to bring a case to the U.S. Supreme Court. It is cited as: *Everson v. Board of Education*, 330 U.S. 1, 12 (U.S. 1947)
Hyperlink to this case. https://caselaw.findlaw.com/us-supreme-court/330/1.html

How they voted:
In the majority (aye) (Your soldiers): Black, Vinson, Reed, Douglas and Murphy.
Dissenting (nay): Jackson, Rutledge, Frankfurter and Burton.

Learning to Understand Insane Court Rulings

In this chapter, we will examine the *Everson* case of 1947, which has done tremendous damage to the cause of Christianity, civilization and to civility. To help us to understand what we are up against in trying to understand some court rulings, here is some wisdom from Judge Robert H. Bork:[75]

> To read the literature is to have one's worst fears confirmed. The sense that something in constitutional theory has gone high begins with the style of argumentation. The older constitutional commentators, secure in their commonsense lawyers' view of the Constitution, wrote prose that remains clear, to the point, self-confident and accessible to the nonprofessional reader.[76] The modern theorists are different. Their concepts are abstruse, their sources philosophical, their arguments

---

75. John Dewey, The Public and its Problems, (NY: Henry Holt and Company, 1927), p. 34.
76. Quoted in David Barton, Original Intent, 4th Ed., Aledo, TX, Wallbuilders, 1996, p. 228
77. Bork, Robert H., The Tempting of America, Simon and Schuster, NY, p. 134.
78. See, e.g., J. Story, Commentaries on the Constitution of the United States, (Carolina Academic Press, 1987) (1833) T. Cooley, Constitutional Limitations (2nd ed., 1871)

convoluted and their prose necessarily complex.[77] These writers are in fact undertaking what Justice Story forswore, the alteration of the Constitution by "ingenious subtleties," "metaphysical refinements," and "visionary speculation" to make it not a document "addressed to the common sense of the people" but one addressed to a specialized and sophisticated clerisy of judicial power.[78]

Everson v Board of Education of Ewing Township

This case began as a very minor issue involving one citizen v the small township of Ewing, New Jersey. The issue was whether the township could provide transportation to students who attended parochial schools and not public schools. Nothing more. That is all. It was a local matter the jurisdiction of which was limited to the State of New Jersey Supreme Court. Yet the SCOTUS expanded this case (and its own powers) to affect every schoolroom and every public function in America and with disastrous results. To do so, it had to perform contortions with the law that would have put Houdini to shame. This is a case that every American needs to understand. Especially, every Christian American. More on *Everson* within.

Now, forewarned, we return to address our adversary, the Devil:

Devil, the results of this case are, to your point of view, stupendous! It meets all of your fiendish expectations. Even better than you had ever dreamed! First, those nice judges changed the Constitution of the United States from being totally opposed to you and your scheme to being totally in favor of you and of it. At least, they changed it as it is perceived by Supreme Court justices. That "Separation of church and state" that your soldiers worked out is a work of genius! Fraudulent, of course, when examined closely, but a work of genius in how effective it became. From your point of view, that is.

Your disciple Langdell must be turning handsprings down there in your domain. From the point of view of the Christians and the pro-Constitution Americans, however, it was skullduggery and treason. The work of domestic enemies of the Constitution. *Everson* is cited as: https://caselaw.findlaw.com/us-supreme-court/330/1.html.

In *Everson,* your obedient disciples on the SCOTUS accomplished the following:

---

79. See, e.g., Chapter 9, infra.

1. Using Langdell's idea that the law should "evolve" and the idea of positive law, the SCOTUS added something to the Constitution. It was an excerpt from a letter by Thomas Jefferson, "separation of church and state," that was written ten years *after* the First Amendment was ratified and therefore could never have been considered to be part of the *legitimate* law of the land[79] and,

2. Then, the SCOTUS "constitutionalized" this metaphor to make it, effectively, (as they presumed) a part of the Constitution. (Constitutionally speaking, of course: How ridiculous)!

3. But-it gets worse. Not only did they hijack "separation of church and state" from Jefferson and "constitutionalize" it, they inverted its meaning. Jefferson intended that it would mean that the Congress would be barred from passing any laws that would give one denomination an advantage over the others. The SCOTUS nullified the *First* and then reconstructed it to mean that the federal government would have the authority to prevent religious ideas of any nature (except, of course, those of the Secular Humanist religion) from being taught in public schools and discussed in public discourse. The reconstructed *First* having an entirely different meaning than the original *First*.

4. To make this corrupted "law" apply to all the states, the SCOTUS applied the thoroughly anti-constitutional "incorporation doctrine". In using the First Amendment as justification for their ruling, the SCOTUS took the *First*, which is plainly written to be a restriction upon the powers of the federal government and corrupted it into being a *grant of power to themselves*! Then, with this arrogated power, they applied the *First* and the phony *Separation of Church and State* to every individual state. This is in direct and violent contradiction with the fundamental concept of division of powers between the federal government and the states, which is fundamental to the functioning of this Republic. Fundamental! This stratagem of "incorporation doctrine" is thoroughly hostile to Constitutional government. Then, there are the Ninth and Tenth Amendments, which state:

Amendment IX The enumeration in the Constitution, of certain rights, shall not be construed to deny or disparage others retained by the people.

Amendment X The powers not delegated to the United States by the Constitution, nor prohibited by it to the States, are reserved to the States respectively, or to the people.

There!!! How much more clear and concise could it be worded than that? It seems like everybody except lawyers and judges can understand it.

5. In forbidding the use of any material in the classroom that exposes or opposes evolution, secular Humanism or Marxism, The SCOTUS violated that part of the *First* that reads, "...or abridging the freedom of speech,..."

6. In outlawing the Ten Commandments and any mention of the Bible in the schoolrooms of America, the SCOTUS essentially legislated, which it has no authority to do.

7. In outlawing anything relating to Christianity, the SCOTUS did, de facto, impose the religion of Secular Humanism on every public school and caused Secular Humanism to be adopted as the official state religion of the government of the United States and of every state. This is exactly what the Framers of the *First* intended to prevent.

8. In *Everson* in 1947, the SCOTUS obviously ignored the Constitution and ruled by "social justice."[80]

9. This "Social Justice" is very vague and using it, a judge can construe a point to mean absolutely anything. Social Justice is Marxist in nature, not constitutional.

10. The SCOTUS completely corrupted the *First Amendment*, to wit: The *First Amendment* was originally intended to be a limitation on the power of the federal government. The SCOTUS, instead, made it into a grant of power. In applying the "incorporation doctrine," the SCOTUS made the corrupted *First* into a grant of almost unlimited power for themselves.

11. In forcing "separation of church and state" on the states, the SCOTUS clearly and blatantly violated the Ninth and *Tenth Amendments* to the Constitution.

12. In cases regarding "Separation...." subsequent to *Everson*, the SCOTUSes obviously abandoned the Constitution and resorted to the Langdell "case method" for their judgments.

---

80. J. Story, Supra, note 1, at vi.

In *Everson,* the SCOTUS Inverted the Meaning of the *First Amendment*.

The true meaning of the *First* is to restrict the powers of the federal government. Note that the Framers of the *First* did not restrict the Supreme Court from making laws as the SCOTUS never had and never has had the authority to make law anyhow. Note also that the *First* does not authorize the exercise of any power. It strictly prohibits the exercise of power. Here is the *First,* with the "establishment clause" in bold for emphasis.

> **Congress shall make no law respecting an establishment of religion,** or prohibiting the free exercise thereof; or abridging the freedom of speech, or of the press; or the right of the people peaceably to assemble and to petition the government for a redress of grievances.

What the framers of the *First* meant by "establishment of religion" was a *religious denomination,* like Baptists, Methodists, Catholics, etc. They did not mean any mention of God or the Ten Commandments or the Bible or anything of a religious nature.

> Corrupt judges corrupt the law, then use this corrupted law **against us**, the people. Yet these corrupt judges call this corrupted law "constitutional."

There is a huge difference.

In *Everson,* the SCOTUS proclaimed the following:

> The First Amendment has erected a wall between church and state. That wall must be kept high and impregnable. We could not approve the slightest breach.[81]

What the SCOTUS misinterpreted the words "establishment of religion" to mean was God, the Ten Commandments, the Bible or anything relating thereto. A HUGE difference from the intent of the Framers of the *FIRST*. One thing must be noted at this point is that, since 1947, the SCOTUS has enforced ITS CORRUPTED VERSION OF the *First Amendment* meticulously and with extreme fervor, while it has violated, ignored and trampled all over other very important parts of the Constitution such as the Ninth and *Tenth Amendments*. That tells everything about the hostile intent toward the true meaning of the Constitution by some justices of the SCOTUS.

---

81. This letter from Jefferson was indeed an authoritative source of information, as he was President at the time, but it was never under any stretch of the imagination to be considered to be law; part of the Constitution.

82. Social justice" definition: justice in terms of the distribution of wealth, opportunities and privileges within a society. "individuality gives way to the struggle for social justice"

This *Everson* decision has among its many critics many highly qualified legal scholars. Justice Potter Stewart observed:[82]

> I think that the court's task, in this as in all areas of constitutional adjudications, is not responsibly aided by the uncritical invocation of metaphors like the "wall of separation," a phrase nowhere to be found in the Constitution.(*Engel v Vitale,* 370 U.S., 421, 445-446 (1962), (Stewart, J. dissenting).

Justice William Rehnquist described this phrase as a "misleading metaphor", then noted:

> But the greatest injury of the "wall" notion is its mischievous diversion of judges from the actual intentions of the drafters of the bill of Rights....The "wall of separation between church and state" is a metaphor based on bad history, a metaphor which has proved useless as a guide to judging. It should be frankly and explicitly abandoned.[83] (Wallace v. Jaffree, 472 U. S. 38. 92[1984]) Rehnquist, dissenting.

Constitutional scholar David Barton explains the error of the SCOTUS as follows:[84]

> [In *Everson,* the SCOTUS] ...first divorced the First Amendment from its original purpose and then reinterpreted it without regard to other historical context or previous judicial decisions. The result was that the Court abandoned the traditional constitutional meaning of "religion" as a single denomination or system of worship and instead substituted a new "modern" concept which even now remains vague and nebulous, having changed several times in recent years. By this substitution, the court created a new and foreign purpose for the First Amendment and completely rewrote its scope of protections and prohibitions.

The understanding (actually, misunderstanding) of the religious provisions of the First Amendment, an extremely important part of the law of our nation, has been shaped by a metaphor which does not even appear in the Constitution! By this malicious malfeasance, the SCOTUS has done much damage to our constitutional republic.

---

83. Everson v Board of Education, 330 U. S. 1, 18 (1947)

84. Engel v Vitale, 370 U.S. 421, 445-446, (1962) (Stewart, J.. dissenting)
85. Quoted in David Barton, Original Intent, Wallbuilders, Aledo, TX, 1996, p. 20

What could be more malicious and damaging to a nation and to its people than to remove from the document that determines for that nation what is right and what is wrong, a provision that protects the religious freedoms of the people and inserts in its place one that deprives them of these freedoms?

It is most interesting to contrast the opinion of Thomas Jefferson with that of the SCOTUS of *Everson* regarding the scope of its power regarding the First Amendment:

> I consider the government of the United States [the federal government] as interdicted by the Constitution from intermeddling with religious institutions, their doctrines, discipline, or exercises. This results not only from the provision that no law shall be made respecting the establishment or free exercise of religion [the First Amendment], but from that also which reserves to the States the powers not delegated to the United States [the Tenth Amendment]. Certainly, no power to prescribe any religious exercise or to assume authority in any religious discipline has been delegated to the General [federal] Government. ***It must then rest with the States.*** [85][86](emphasis added)

The violation of the Constitution by the *Everson* Court included (but not limited to) the use of positivist law", the corruption of the First Amendment, "incorporation doctrine", the practice of "to constitutionalize", "social justice," the use of a corrupted version of the Fourteenth Amendment and the violation of the Ninth and Tenth Amendments.

We cannot place too much emphasis on the fact that there is NO LEGAL FOUNDATION for outlawing the Ten Commandments solely because the view of them might prove offensive to someone! Just to be sure, we had better examine, very carefully, the foundation of American law from which this "Separation of Church and State" is alleged to have originated. We need to determine whether the First Amendment itself might be un-American and bigoted or, if the First Amendment has been misinterpreted, could it be the SCOTUS itself that is un-American and bigoted? How about those, like the American Civil Liberties Union (ACLU) who brought the suits to court suing for prayer in schools to be outlawed? This is getting serious. Let's take a serious look at the First Amendment and the origin of "Separation of Church and State." Well, I have just stumbled onto something that fits right in here. It is **the Ninth Plank of *Humanist Manifesto II*.** Should we be surprised? Here it

---

86. Barton, Ibid, p. 21

is:

> **NINTH:**[87] **The separation of church and state** [As the SCOTUS misinterprets it—NOT as Jefferson meant it.] and the separation of ideology and state are imperatives. The state should encourage maximum freedom for different moral, political, religious and social values in society. It should not favor any particular religious bodies through the use of public monies, nor espouse a single ideology and function thereby as an instrument of propaganda or oppression, particular against dissenters. (Emphasis added)

This strongly suggests that the SCOTUS got their idea for the misinterpretation of "separation of church and state" from the Humanist Manifesto, or from the Humanists. Or perhaps there were one or more Humanist justices on the *Everson* court.

The History of the First Amendment and the SCOTUS's *Corrupted* "First Amendment"

We who plan to expose and defeat the Devil's plan need to understand, very clearly, the history of the true First Amendment and then the history of the corrupted "First Amendment" that his minions manufactured and are using so effectively against Christianity. Here it is:

Background: Prior to the Revolutionary War, King George III imposed a tax on the colonists to support his favored church, the Anglican Church. The result of this of course was to use the government to advantage the denomination of the Anglican Church to the disadvantage of all other denominations. The colonists fought the war to put a stop to this and other abuses. So when they were drafting the First Amendment, this kind of abuse is exactly what the Framers wanted to prevent. It is important that we understand each of the following points:

1. The issue of the First Amendment was debated in the Congress from June 7th to September 25, 1789. The *Annals of Congress* (now the *Congressional Record*) for those dates reflect the debates of the ninety Founding Fathers. There is nothing to be found therein regarding "Separation of church and state".

2. The First Amendment to the Constitution of the United States was ratified December 15, 1791. It reads:

---

87. Jefferson, Memoir, Vol. IV, pp 103-104, to Samuel Miller on January 23, 1808

<u>Congress[88] shall make no law respecting an establishment of religion, or prohibiting the free exercise thereof</u>, or abridging the freedom of speech, or of the press...[89], [90] (Establishment clause underlined.)

3. On January 1, 1802, President Thomas Jefferson, in response to a letter from the Danbury Baptists inquiring as to whether their freedom of religion was in jeopardy, wrote:

Gentlemen, - The affectionate sentiments of esteem and approbation which you are so good as to express towards me on behalf of the Danbury Baptist Association give me the highest satisfaction....Believing with you that religion is a matter which lies solely between man and his God; that he owes account to none other for his faith or his worship; the legislative powers of government reach actions only and not opinions, I contemplate with sovereign reverence that act of the whole American people which declared with their legislature should "make no law respecting an establishment of religion or prohibiting the free exercise thereof," thus building a wall of <u>separation between Church and State</u>. Adhering to this expression of the supreme will of the nation in behalf of the rights of conscience, I shall see with sincere satisfaction the progress of those sentiments which tend to restore to man all his natural rights,...[91] (Emphasis added)

Please note the date of Jefferson's letter. It was ten years *after the ratification of the First Amendment. It could not possibly have been a part of the FIRST when it was drafted!*

Jefferson's "Wall of Separation" Contrasted With *Everson's*

Jefferson intended for the "Wall of separation" to protect religion from the state. "*Everson,*" however, protects the state from religion. Or, perhaps better said, "The corrupted 'Wall of Separation' in *Everson* serves as the sword and the shield of the irreligionists, the enemies of God and of Christ, in their

---

88. Found also in Barton, David, Original Intent, Wallbuilders, p 25
89. Humanist Manifesto II, 1973
90. The Congress did not include "The Supreme Court shall make no law" since the Supreme Court was never delegated powers to legislate nor to amend the Constitution. They considered no such language necessary. To honest courts, it would not be.
91. Note the wording of the First is, very clearly, a restriction on the powers of government. Nowhere is there found therein a grant of power
such as the Court attributed to the CORRUPTED version of the First which they created in 1947 in Everson

propagation of lies and false ideas in the educational system and in their other nefarious schemes." (Joe H. Ferguson 12 Oct., 2020.) In their new and excellent book, *The Three Cs That Made America Great-Christianity, Capitalism and the Constitution,* the illustrious Mike Huckabee and Steve Feazel brought out a point that the Framer of the First Amendment NEVER intended for the *First* to be misinterpreted the way the SCOTUS did in *Everson* nor the way the liberals, Socialists and Communists do today:

> At the time of the adoption of the Constitution and the amendments, the universal sentiment was that Christianity should be encouraged....In this age there can be no substitute for Christianity....That was the religion of the founders of the republic and they expected it to remain the religion of their descendants.[92]

4. Justice Joseph Story on the Original Intent of the First Amendment

The comments of Justice Joseph Story,(1779-1845) author of *Commentaries on the Constitution of the United States*[93] on the original intent of the First Amendment are most enlightening:

> § 991. ...The real object of the [First] amendment was, not to countenance, much less to advance Mohammedanism, or Judaism, or infidelity, by prostrating Christianity; but to exclude all rivalry among Christian sects and to prevent any national ecclesiastical establishment, which should give to an hierarchy the exclusive patronage of the national government. It thus sought to cut off the means of religious persecution, (the vice and pest of former ages,) and the power of subverting the rights of conscience in matters of religion, which had been trampled upon almost from the days of the Apostles to the present age...
>
> § 992... It was impossible, that there should not arise perpetual strife and perpetual jealousy on the subject of ecclesiastical ascendancy, if the national government were left free to create a religious establishment. The only security was in extirpating the power... But this alone would have been an imperfect security, if it had not been followed up by a declaration of the right of the free exercise of religion and a prohibition (as we have seen) of all religious tests. <u>Thus, the whole power over the subject of religion is left exclusively to the state governments, to be acted upon according to their own sense of justice and the state

---

92. For a short while after the ratification of the First, various individual states continued the practice of having a state-approved religion, but the practice gradually died out

constitutions; (Emphasis added) Note: For more on this, go to: http://www.belcherfoundation.org/Joseph_story_on_church_and_state.htm

5. In 1833, in Barron v. Baltimore, the Court correctly ruled that the Bill of Rights is... ...not applicable to and do[es] not bind the State https://study.com/academy/lesson/barron-v-baltimore-in-1833-summary-significance.html

Prior to the ratification of the Fourteenth Amendment and the development of the "incorporation doctrine," the Supreme Court in 1833 held in Barron v. Baltimore that the Bill of Rights applied only to the federal, but not any state governments.

> The Courts "incorporating" the Bill of Rights **to apply to the States** was clearly in violation of the Ninth and Tenth Amendments and hostile to the original intent of the Constitution

Even years after the ratification of the Fourteenth Amendment, the Supreme Court in United States v. Cruikshank (1876) www.quimbee.com/cases/united-states-v-cruikshank still held, correctly so, that the First and Second Amendment did not apply to state governments. However, beginning in the 1920s, a series of United States Supreme Court decisions (mis)interpreted the Fourteenth Amendment to "incorporate" most portions of the Bill of Rights, making these portions, for the first time, enforceable against the state governments.

It is most important to note that between the date of ratification of the *First* and the 1920s, there was NO amendment to the Constitution to justify the SCOTUS using "incorporation doctrine." The SCOTUS merely arrogated to itself the power to create and exercise this "incorporation doctrine." An outrageous example of usurpation and arrogation of power. Constitutional authority is totally absent.

6. 1933. Humanist Manifesto I published. The Secular Humanists will prove to be a very effective enemy of Christianity and of America. From 1947 on, it appears that the U. S. Supreme Court has been under the control or at least the influence of the Secular Humanists. On the cases involving "separation of church and state" and in *Obergefell*, Secular Humanist footprints are all over them. The characteristics of the Secular Humanist religion are exactly the opposite of the characteristics of Christianity.

7. 1947. The metaphor "Separation of Church and State" burst upon the stage of jurisprudence in 1947. Prior to that time, the Court had seldom ruled upon religious matters because such were (properly) reserved to the courts

of the individual states. Such was (and still is) properly a matter for the states in accordance with the Ninth and Tenth Amendments. It was only when the Court invoked the twisted misinterpretation of the Fourteenth Amendment to include the states was the twisted interpretation of "Separation..." brought to the federal courts. Here is the SCOTUS ruling that started the Secular Humanist, Marxist, anti-Christian anti-American revolution in the United States:

Ruling: (#1) "The First Amendment has erected a wall between church and state. That wall must be kept *high and impregnable. We could not approve the slightest breach..." EVERSON V. BOARD OF EDUCATION,* 330 U.S. 1, 18 (1947). https://www.law.cornell.edu/supremecourt/text/330/1

With *Everson*, the United States government outlawed Christianity from public schools and public discourse and adopted, de facto, Secular Humanism as the official religion of the United States federal government and forced it upon every state. Completely unconstitutional and absolutely outrageous!

8. On the basis of this *corrupted version* of the *First Amendment,* the SCOTUS has outlawed prayer in schools, outlawed the Ten Commandments from schools and public discourse, outlawed the teaching of anything except the theory of evolution regarding the origin of life and started the United States on a precipitous slide toward a degradation in culture, society, education, elected officials, judges, government and economy.

9. In dissenting in the *Wallace v. Jaffree* case, Chief Justice William Rehnquist wrote the following concerning the "constitutionalizing" in the *Everson* case of "wall of separation...": https://supreme.justia.com/cases/federal/us/472/38/

Chief Justice Rehnquist[94] on "Separation of Church and State:"

There is simply no historical foundation for the proposition that the Framers intended to build the "wall of separation" that was constitutionalized in *Everson* ....But the greatest injury of the "wall" notion is its mischievous diversion of judges from the actual intentions of the drafters of the Bill of Rights...No amount of repetition of historical errors in judicial opinions can make the errors true. The "wall of separation between church and State" is a metaphor based on bad history....It should be frankly and explicitly abandoned....Our perception has been clouded not by the Constitution but by the mists of an unnecessary metaphor.

For we who plan to defend our religion against the attacks that are being waged and those that will be waged in the future, an understanding of Humanism is absolutely necessary. Also, we need to know that the ideology of the LGBT is anathema to Christianity but fits perfectly with Secular Humanism. The LGBT, the Marxists and the Secular Humanists work together to accomplish their agendas. So if a justice is an LGBT, a Marxist or a Secular Humanist, we must expect that he is going to disregard the Constitution and hand down a "social justice" ruling.

10. In corrupting the meaning of the *First*, the SCOTUS, in order to force it on the states, had to corrupt the meaning of the *Fourteenth Amendment*. Here is the uncorrupted Fourteenth (Sec. 1 of 5 Secs.) as it is worded:

Chief Justice Rehnquist
Wikimedia Commons

> ...No state shall make or enforce any law which shall abridge the privileges or immunities of citizens of the United States; nor shall any state deprive any person of life, liberty, or property, without due process of law; nor deny to any person within its jurisdiction the equal protection of the laws.

An interesting point: The Fourteenth was never legally ratified. It received approval from only 21 states, when the approval of 28 states was necessary. It was merely proclaimed as being ratified by the Secretary of State on July 20,

---

93. This letter by Jefferson is certainly to be considered to be authoritative counsel, since Jefferson was President at the time. HOWEVER it certainly in no way can be considered to be law. Note that the date of the ratification of the First Amendment was over TEN YEARS prior to the date of Jefferson's letter. The letter was not, nor could it ever be considered to be, part of the American system of law; of the Constitution.
94. House Judiciary Committee report, March 27, 1854, as quoted by Bill Bailey, "Religion and Government, Are We a Christ-ian Nation"?,"The Federalist Papers Project, accessed February 10, 2016, http://www.thefederalistpapers.org/history/religion-and-government-are-we-a-christian-nation

1868. The Secretary of State does not possess the authority to proclaim anything to be an amendment to the Constitution unless the requirements in Article V are satisfied. Another fraud perpetuated on the American people. The SCOTUS has corrupted the meaning of this unratified amendment to mean just anything that it wants it to. Even if it were legally ratified, the intent of its Framers and its wording gives no authority to the SCOTUS to apply "separation of church and state" on the states. This issue is a pernicious fraud in more ways than one. Is that not consistent with the way that the Devil works?

11. In 1973, in *Humanist Manifesto II:*

> NINTH: The separation of church and state and the separation of ideology and state are imperatives…It should not favor any particular religious bodies through the use of public monies,…

The *Everson* case came before the Manifesto II. However, this metaphor (separation of church and state) could have been circulating in the Secular Humanist circles prior to *Everson* in 1947. So in *Everson,* the Court, no doubt under the influence of the Secular Humanists, hijacked it from Jefferson, corrupted it and gave to it an entirely different meaning to accommodate their agenda.

12. And Last BUT NOT BY ANY MEANS LEAST: The SCOTUS violated the Ninth and Tenth Amendments. These are two very important amendments to the Constitution and have never been repealed. Although they have been ignored, scorned and violated by various SCOTUSes, they are still legally in place. Every time the SCOTUS invokes "incorporation doctrine" or the *Fourteenth,* it violates the *Ninth* and the *Tenth.* This demonstrates very clearly the extent to which the SCOTUSes hold in contempt the supreme law of the land; the Constitution of the United States.

The Ninth and Tenth Amendments to the Constitution constitute organic law.

> **Organic Law.** The fundamental, or constitution, of a state or nation, written or unwritten. That law or system of laws or principles which defines and establishes the organization of its government. (*Black's Law Dictionary* , 5th ed.

Organic law is superior to all other types of law. The Ninth and Tenth Amendments constitute Organic Law. Yet, the SCOTUSes consider something that they have dreamed up like "incorporation doctrine" is superior to and overrides the Ninth and Tenth Amendments. Such grandiose chicanery and fraud!

Note also that the First Amendment was intended to apply only to the federal government. The practice of state governments supporting certain churches continued for a brief time after the ratification of the Constitution, then died out. According to the original intent of the Constitution and of the *First Amendment,* the First was not a grant of power; it was clearly a restriction upon the powers of the federal government. Furthermore, the *Ninth* and the *Tenth* have never been repealed. [95]Only held in contempt and violated by various SCOTUSes.

Please note in # 4, above, by Justice Story: "...the whole power over the subject of religion is left exclusively to the state governments,..." Very important. VERY IMPORTANT! That says it ALL! The intent of the First as described above by Justice Story stood until 1947, when there was an abrupt change in the rulings of the Court regarding the First. The metaphor "Separation of church and state" was created by the SCOTUS and America has not been the same since. What was the reason for this abrupt and radical change? Was there an amendment to the Constitution? No! Was there a change in the wording of the First Amendment? No! Was there a change in the Supreme Law of the Land? Absolutely not! The change was not in the law. It was in the judges. Judges were selected by Presidents and the Senates who would accomplish certain *political* objectives. Lawyers who would deliberately misinterpret the Constitution were selected to be judges.

Perhaps we should say that they were selected to do a "politically correct" job. The evidence indicates that one of the (unwritten but employed) prerequisites for the selection of certain justices was that they be Secular Humanists or if Christian, be not more than "nominal Christians" which is Christian in name only. Now let's examine the origin and the real meaning of "Separation of Church and State." What is its origin?

The Metaphor "Separation of Church and State" is Completely Without Legal Foundation

In summary, here are reasons that the metaphor, "Separation of church and state" is completely without legal foundation:

(1) It is not found in the Constitution,
(2) There is no mention of "Separation of church and state" in the *Annals of Congress* covering the time when the First Amendment was being debated,
(3) It was taken from a letter from Thomas Jefferson which does not now, nor did it ever have, status in the organic law of the United States; in the Constitution of the United States,
(4) The Court twisted the metaphor to mean exactly the opposite of what Jefferson obviously intended in his letter,

---

95. Joseph Story, justice of SCOTUS 1811-1845, professor of law at Harvard Law School, published Commentaries on the Constitution

(5) Jefferson's letter was written over ten years *after* the First Amendment was ratified, therefore,
(6) The current application of "Separation of church and state" is completely a creation of the Court.
(7) The court does not possess authority to create law; to legislate or to amend the Constitution. Therefore, there is no legal substantiation or foundation for the Court's (mis) interpretation of or creation of "Separation of church and state" as law.
(8) To bludgeon the states into submission to this anti-constitutional ruling, the SCOTUS egregiously misinterpreted the *Fourteenth Amendment*. Nowhere in the *Fourteenth* does it give the SCOTUS this power. Furthermore, contributing to the illegality and the egregiousness of the matter, the *Fourteenth* was never legally ratified.
(9) The SCOTUS obviously employed the "incorporation doctrine" to apply the First Amendment to the states. This is completely anti-constitutional.
(10) The Court ignored and violently violated the Ninth and Tenth Amendments to the Constitution.
(11) In employing the "incorporation doctrine," the SCOTUS forced the de facto change of every Constitution of every state. It is outrageous to think that the SCOTUS possesses such legitimate authority.

The misuse of "Separation of church and state" by the Supreme Court constitutes one of the most grandiose, sinister and most destructive (to Christianity, to America and to civilization) hoaxes ever perpetrated upon mankind. This constitutes a giant hoax within the giant hoax of Secular Humanism. It is completely illegal and its effect upon mankind persecutes Christians and Christianity and benefits the causes of the Secular Humanism and Marxism. The anti-constitutional ruling of *Everson* has resulted in the oppression of the Christian religion and degradation of the culture, morality and, definitely, the quality of government in the United States.

Explanation of the *Fourteenth* by Professor Raoul Berger

The corruption of the *Fourteenth* is such a violent violation of the Constitution and such a threat to our stability and security that books have been written about it. So I shall not offer my explanation but offer excerpts from the writings of Law scholar, Professor Raul Berger:[96]

> It is the thesis of this book that the Supreme Court is not empowered to rewrite the Constitution, that in its transformation of the Fourteenth Amendment it has demonstrably done so. Thereby the Justices, who are virtually unaccountable, irremovable and irreversible, have taken over from the people control of their own destiny, an awesome exercise of

---

96. William Rehnquist (1924-2005) was appointed justice by President Nixon in 1971 and chief justice by President Reagan in 1986

power. When Chief Justice Marshall stated that the function of the legislature is to *make* the law, that of the judiciary to *interpret* it, he echoed Francis Bacon's admonition two hundred years earlier.

Much less are judges authorized to revise the Constitution, for as Justice Black, deriding the notion that the Court was meant to keep the Constitution "in tune with the times," stated, "The Constitution makers knew the need for change and provided for it" by the amendment process of article V, whereby the people reserved unto themselves the right to change the Constitution. Having created a prepotent Congress, being well aware of the greedy expansiveness of power and knowing that power can be malign as well as benign, the Founders designed the judiciary to keep Congress within its prescribed bounds, what James Bradley Thayer and Learned Hand later called "policing" the Constitutional boundaries. *Within* those boundaries, stated justice James Iredell, one of the ablest of the Founders, the legislature was to be free of judicial interference.

Unlike the academicians' current infatuation with a revisory judiciary, the Founders had a "profound fear of judicial independence and discretion." They were influenced by the English Puritans' fear that "the laws' meaning could be twisted by means of judicial construction"; they feared the judges' imposition of their personal views.

An important brake on such arrogation of the rule that a document is to be construed in light of the draftsmen's explanation of what they meant to accomplish, the so-called original intention. Jefferson and Madison attached great weight to the rule and Chief Justice Marshall declared that he could cite from the "common law" the most complete evidence that the intention is the most sacred rule of interpretation." Here law and common sense coincide. Who better knows what the writer means than the writer himself? John Selden, the preeminent seventeenth century scholar, stated, "A man's writing has but one true sense, which is that which the Author meant when he writ it."

Such were the views of Hobbes and Locke. To maintain the contrary is to insist that the reader better knows what the writer meant than the writer himself. To recapitulate, anti-activists (originalists) maintain that judges are not authorized to revise the Constitution and that it is to be construed in light of the Founders' explanations of what they meant to accomplish, no more, no less…

…In their zeal to ameliorate social injustice, academicians undermine the Constitutionalism that undergirds our democratic system. Their defense of the Justices' substitution of their own meaning for that of the Founders displaces the choices made by the people in conventions that ratified the Constitution and it violates the basic principle of government by consent of the governed.

The people, said James Iredell, have chosen to be governed under such and such principles. They have not chosen to be governed or proposed to submit upon any other." Academe has forgotten Cardozo's wise caution: the judges' "individual sense of justice…might result in a benevolent despotism if the judges were benevolent men. It would put an end to the reign of law.?

There is more. Much more. But I suggest that you apply common sense to the idea that the SCOTUS has the legitimate authority to change the intent of the *Fourteenth*.

I submit that the transmogrification of the Fourteenth by the SCOTUS is equally as legitimate is their application of "positive law", "social justice", "constitutionalizing", "incorporation doctrine" and any and all other stratagems that the SCOTUS might apply in a vain attempt to excuse away their violations of the Constitution.

Since prayer in schools and the public display of the Ten Commandments are matters properly reserved to the states, the Court had to invent some disingenuous method to nullify, even if done without the authority to do so, the Ninth and Tenth Amendments. They did this by misinterpreting the Fourteenth

1. The wording of the The *First Amendment* is very clear. Its intent is to be a limitation on the powers of the U.S. Congress. The SCOTUS, however, corrupted the *First* to grant powers to itself found nowhere in the *First*. With this power arrogated to itself, the SCOTUS:

2. Took the metaphor, "Separation of Church and State", from a letter from Thomas Jefferson, dated 01 January, 1802, to the Danbury Baptists. This date was ten years after the signing of the First Amendment, so it could not possibly be considered to be part of the *First*. Using the stratagem of evolutionary law, they made this metaphor part of the law by "constitutionalizing" it. There was not then nor is there now a legitimate process for amending the Constitution by the SCOTUS "constitutionalizing" anything. The act was and is pure usurpation.

3. **By use of the "incorporation doctrine", the SCOTUS in *Everson:***

4. Ordered the public schools and all public entities, whether state, county or local, to banish any mention of the Ten Commandments or any mention of God or Christianity.

5. Stretched the *First* to apply to the states and counties, which the framers of the Bill of Rights never intended. The U.S. Constitution and the Constitutions of the various states are separate constitutions; separate

compacts.

6. Violated the Ninth and Tenth Amendments to the Constitution, the *Fourteenth Amendment* and the "incorporation doctrine" notwithstanding.

7. Violated the Free Speech clause in the First Amendment when it ordered schools and teachers to not teach "intelligent design" or any thing that would disprove or challenge the theory of evolution.

8. In outlawing the Ten Commandments and any mention of Christianity in the schoolrooms, the SCOTUS surreptitiously but very effectively made the religion of Secular Humanism (paganistic irreligion) the de facto official religion of the United States government. This is in spite of the fact that the motto "In God We Trust" was and still is the official motto of the United States and the fact that the legal system of the United States was created on a Christian foundation.

9. The SCOTUS overrode the will of the people of the fifty states from now into the indefinite future regarding their ability to control the education systems of their states.

10. Instead of judging the law, the SCOTUS created the law. It legislated. The SCOTUS does not possess the authority to legislate. This constitutes an act of usurpation and the violation of separation of powers. It is completely anti-constitutional. The SCOTUS broke the law!

11. These acts are obviously designed to oppress Christianity and favor the religion of secular Humanism (irreligion.)

12. In *Everson* and subsequent cases, the SCOTUS claims as its authority the *First Amendment.* However what they are actually using is the corrupted, anti-constitutional version that the court itself created and to which it refers to as the "First." The *First Amendment (the legitimate First Amendment)* does not give them the authority to rule as it has done in *Everson* and subsequent cases.

If God and Christianity are Outlawed from the Classroom, What Must we Assume Would Take its Place? Why, the Opposite of Christianity, of Course, Which is Secular Humanism.

Subsequent to *Everson* in 1947, here are some excerpts from various cases dealing with "separation of church and state.["][97]

---

[97]. As stated by Berger, "…the reservation to the States in the Tenth Amendment of powers not delegated to the federal government calls for a clear showing that the successor amendment was designed to curtail these reserved powers. Over the years the Supreme court, to be sure has steadily eroded these reserved powers, but this simply represents another of the usurpations the bestrew the path of the court…No trace

Ruling: (# 1) "The First Amendment has erected a wall between church and state. That wall must be kept high and impregnable. We could not approve the slightest breach." *Everson v Board of Education*, 330 U. S. 1, 18 (1947).

(Note: The First Amendment did NOT erect a wall...it was the *corrupted First*, fabricated by the SCOTUS, that did.)

Ruling: (#2) "A verbal prayer offered in a school is unconstitutional, even if that prayer is
both voluntary and denominationally neutral."*ENGEL v. VITAE*, 1962. *Commissioner of Education v. School Committee of Leyden*, 267 N.E. 2nd 226 (Mass. 1971), cert. Denied, 404 U. S. 849.

Ruling:(#3) The SCOTUS declared it unconstitutional for copies of the Ten Commandments to be posted in a classroom because, "...If the posted copies of the Ten Commandments are to have any effect at all, it will be to *induce the schoolchildren to read, meditate upon, perhaps to venerate and obey, the Commandments.*"(Emphasis added) *Stone v. Graham*, 449 U.S. 39, 42 (1980).

Note: Oh my goodness! The students might obey the Ten Commandments! This would mean that they would not rob, kill, lie or defraud! Or riot! They might even stay out of jail! This shows the fanaticism that some SCOTUS justices have against the Christian religion.

Ruling: (#4) "The Ten Commandments, despite the fact that they are the basis of civil law and are depicted in engraved stone in the U.S. Supreme Court, may not be displayed at a public courthouse.". *Harvey v. Cobb County*, 811 F. Supp. 669 (N.D. Ga 1993); *affirmed*, 15 F. 3rd 1097 (11th Cir. 1994); cert. *denied*, 511 U.S. 1129 (1994).

Note: The issue of whether the Ten Commandments can be displayed at a county courthouse, according to the Ninth and Tenth Amendments, is strictly a matter for the states to decide. The SCOTUS had no legal authority for the above ruling.

Note: "...despite the fact that they are the basis of civil law..." This proves without a doubt that some justices of the SCOTUS (and, no doubt, some unseen force or forces) are determined to remove the Ten Commandments and Christianity from the foundation of American law. This would mean, of

---

of an intention by the Fourteenth amendment to encroach on State control—for example, ...is to be found in the records of the 39th Congress. (Raoul Berger, Government by Judiciary, 1997, Liberty Fund, Indianapolis, p. 16)

course, not just a slight change but a drastic change in our law and legal system. Drastic. Radical. Revolutionary. Treasonous. From freedom to totalitarian, we must presume. The SCOTUS has outlawed prayer in schools and the public display of the Ten Commandments on the basis that one person (out of a hundred or five hundred or a thousand) might be offended by hearing the prayer. *Might be offended by hearing a prayer*! Think about that for a minute. What should an attitude be labeled that would be offended by hearing, of all things, a prayer? Does "intolerance" fit? What is "intolerance" carried to the extreme? Is that not "bigotry?" Could it be that the Court is forcing the will of the very few bigots in our society upon all other Americans? What an outrageous idea! It would just seem so un-American for it to do such a thing! But, obviously, it is doing that very thing.

Everson, A Huge Victory for the Forces of Darkness

When the SCOTUS outlawed God and the Ten Commandments from the classrooms and public discourse, it stigmatized anything related to Christianity in the minds of the students and many of the general public. What could be worse than to put anything relating to God, the Ten Commandments or Christianity in the same legal category as murder, theft and other crimes? It has had its deleterious effect upon our people and our culture. Must we not presume that this was exactly the intent of the *Everson* SCOTUS and subsequent SCOTUSes?

Note: The above court rulings and many others, are cited in *Original intent,* by David Barton, pp 14-16. I highly recommend this excellent book to you and to all who want to better understand how the SCOTUS is waging war against Christianity.

Well, Devil, you and your disciples pulled off a HUGE victory for the forces of darkness. With this court ruling, you shoved any mention of God, Christ or the Ten Commandments right out of the public school classroom. Then, you didn't have to do anything at all to get your religion of secular Humanism adopted. When Christianity was outlawed, your religion moved right into the vacuum that was created. And you didn't have to spend one dime of your own money. You made those suckers-those Christians-pay for it all. You managed to get your entire scheme taxpayer-financed. You clever Devil, you.

With this corrupted version of the *First,* coupled with the very corrupt "incorporation doctrine," you managed to gain a tremendous amount of leverage; of disproportionate amount of political power; over your Christian adversaries. Poor dumb slobs. They have not found out a way to get a working arrangement with the SCOTUS like you have. They are so innocent. They would NEVER have thought of such a clever scheme to use against you. They are just too.... well..... too *honest!* It has been 73 years and still most of the Christians are blissfully unaware to what you have done and are doing to them. I guess you are to be congratulated. By somebody. We suppose that your buddy Langdell down there is congratulating you.

And, Mr. Devil, we must congratulate you, albeit reluctantly, on the methods that your justices employed in performing their duty (to you-not the People). You have trained them well. True to your MO, the justices employed stratagems, sophistries, chicanery and committed violations of their oaths of office, violations of the Constitution and just plain lies. They made of themselves domestic enemies of the Constitution! But-for you,-mission accomplished. A great success for you and your side, Mr. Devil. A coup, one might say.

Since the *Everson* case was to forever change the law of the United States, we need to examine and thoroughly understand the chicanery employed by the SCOTUS to make this change, to wit: 1. "Positive law". 2 To "constitutionalize," 3. "Social justice," and 4. The "incorporation doctrine." These tricks were used to turn American jurisprudence upside down.

Positive law posits that the the state and the lawmakers thereof, (man) constitutes the ultimate authority for civil law. There is no superior authority. No Ten Commandments. There are no rigid guidelines. Everything is changeable. This is the foundation of Humanist and Marxist law. At least, they want everything changeable during the time of transition from constitutional law to Marxist law. When the law is fully Marxist, then it is no longer changeable. That is the political belief of Humanists and Marxists. (Joe H. Ferguson, June 1, 2020)

To "Constitutionalize:" Means for the Court to make something "constitutional" that was theretofore unconstitutional. This is obviously a practice in illegal sophistry, as the SCOTUS does not possess the authority to constitutionalize" anything. Any such practice, then, of "constitutionalizing" something is obviously a case of violating the Constitution; of usurpation. To "constitutionalize" means to change the meaning of the Constitution without going through the process described in Article V, which is the only *legal* means of amending the Constitution. Consequently, to "constitutionalize" clearly means, to any honest and intelligent person, to "usurp". (Joe H. Ferguson, June 1, 2020)

> Using the stratagems of "Incorporation Doctrine," "Positive Law," "to Constitutionalize," "Social Justice" and "Case Law," the Courts can do anything— *absolutely anything* to the law, including converting America to a Marxist totalitarian state.

Through this *Everson* decision and all of the future decisions that you will get in your favor using the corrupted "separation of church and state," you have found a vehicle for giving your values (evolution, Secular Humanism, Marxism, etc.) the force of law without having to go to all that inconvenience of having to take over the political authority of the United States. You did not have to convince 51% of the voters of the entire country. What a beautiful scheme, you clever Devil you. And you more than likely will be able to keep the Supreme Court on your side from now on. Or at least until the Christians wake up and get organized and decide to defend Christ and his gospel and the TRUE Constitution.

Yessir, Devil, you have certainly stepped all over those Christians and cheated them out of their right to influence their congressmen and their government in this matter. You and your Supreme Court have just plain disenfranchised, to a great degree, every Christian in the country. And you have managed to get shoved anything Christian, like those Ten Commandments that you hate so much, right out the back door of every schoolhouse in America. And marching right in the front door, to replace everything Christian, are new school books and curricula just full of your special ideas-evolution, secular Humanism and Marxism. Now, let's look at "social justice:"

> **Social Justice:** Justice in terms of the distribution of wealth, opportunities and privileges within a society. "individuality gives way to the struggle for social justice."

Note: By its very definition, "social justice" is a specious stratagem to convert constitutional law into Marxist law, since it is obviously based on the Marxist scheme to "redistribute the wealth." "Social justice" is obviously a violent contradiction to constitutional law. The use of "social justice" subverts the American system of jurisprudence. It robs the American people of justice. The SCOTUS has absolutely no authority to substitute "social justice" for the Constitution.

The above speaks volumes to one who can understand it and its ramifications: "justice in terms of the distribution of wealth, opportunities and privileges within a society." This replaces the concept of protecting the rights to wealth, opportunities and privileges of that individual to the concept of distributing them according to the Marxist concept of redistributing the wealth. "…individuality gives way to the struggle for social justice…." The only way for a government to protect the rights of the people is for it to protect the rights of every individual. That is the way the Constitution is structured. The above portends the change in the intent and purpose of our form of government from the Constitution to the Communist Manifesto…all to be accomplished by the judges. Remember the above definition of "social justice." Think through its implications. Be able to recall and to explain it when necessary. Explain it to your friends. It is very important that as many Americans as possible should understand this subversive concept to our friends."Social Justice" is pure Marxism and it is being used in our courts as superior to the Constitution.

This use of "social justice" is definitely part of the plan to convert the United States to a Marxist dictatorship.

Devil, we must presume the probability that you enlisted the aid of your fellow Humanist, Marxist and educator John Dewey in this "Separation of Church and State" scheme, although you have left no tangible evidence to support it. "Separation of Church and State." This appears to be the work of the hand of unseen but powerful and stealthy Humanists. This metaphor even shows up on the Humanist Manifesto II in 1973. But how, in a Christian nation, under a Constitution which was founded upon Christian principles and with every judge swearing an oath to uphold the Constitution in all of their rulings, did the Humanists manage to get anything Christian or even congruent with Christianity (such as the teaching of intelligent design) outlawed in American education and get their anti-Christian doctrine forced in in its place? Very cleverly. And very deviously. By wholesale violations of the Constitution of the United States; by treachery. By lying. By lying to the American people.

> **A Lie[98]:** An untruth deliberately told; the uttering or acting that which is false for the purpose of deceiving; intentional misstatement. (*Black's Law Dictionary*).

We need to thoroughly understand this "incorporation doctrine" that the SCOTUS used in *Everson* and which it continues to use to corrupt our law: It is to take an amendment to the U.S. Constitution and apply it to the states:

> **The "incorporation doctrine:"** [an incomplete definition—from the internet] in U.S. law, is the process by which SCOTUSes have applied portions of the U.S. Bill of Rights to the states. Prior to 1925, the Bill of Rights was held only to apply to the federal government. Under the incorporation doctrine, most provisions of the Bill of Rights now also apply to the state and local governments. (Definition not found in Black's Law Dictionary)

The above definition, is an *incomplete definition* of the "incorporation doctrine" that the SCOTUS uses when it takes an amendment to the U.S. Constitution and applies it to the states. The above definition *condones* the practice. It omits one very important thing. For a more complete definition, see below:

> **The "incorporation doctrine", a More Comprehensive Definition**: In U.S. law, it is the process by which SCOTUSes have applied portions of

---

98. Berger, Raoul, Government by Judiciary The Transformation of the Fourteenth Amendment, Liberty Fund, Indianapolis, 2nd ed., 1997,pp 18-23

the U.S. Bill of Rights to the states. Prior to 1925, the Bill of Rights was held to apply only to the federal government. Constitutionally, that still holds true. The Constitution has never been amended to accept the "incorporation doctrine" concept. Under the "incorporation doctrine," the SCOTUS applies (without the authority to do so) some provisions of the Bill of Rights to every state, county and local government. Such action amends, de facto, the Constitution of every state and legislates, de facto, laws affecting every state, county and local government. Furthermore, in "incorporating," the SCOTUS inverts the meaning of the Amendment to mean exactly the opposite of what it was intended to mean, to wit: The *First* was intended to be a limitation on the powers of the federal government, but in "incorporation," the SCOTUS inverted its meaning to give to itself unlimited powers not only regarding the powers of the federal government but unlimited powers to, de facto, amend the Constitutions of every state, to legislate laws for every state and for every public school in every state. Since "incorporation doctrine" has been and is being done without the authority to do so, it must be properly considered to be usurpation. Justices voting in favor of cases using the "incorporation doctrine" obviously violate their oaths of office in doing so. They make of themselves "Domestic enemies of the Constitution." Since this constitutes turning the laws of the United States upside down, it can properly be perceived as treason. (Joe H. Ferguson, Oct 2016)

The Supreme Court Makes Secular Humanism, De Facto, Official Religion of the United States

In outlawing the Ten Commandments and any mention of God or of Christianity from all public schools and from all public discourse, the SCOTUS has, de facto, made Secular Humanism the official religion of the federal government and of every state in the union. It has exercised the power to do this in the complete absence of the Constitutional authority to do so. This constitutes the arrogation of power and of usurpation on a grand scale. Furthermore, in corrupting the intent of the *First,* the SCOTUS further violated the *First* by denying Americans the right to freedom of speech. The right to have taught to the students information that would challenge or discredit the badly-flawed theory of evolution and many other false and insidious ideas taught in the public school system.

There is no such thing as a permanent vacuum of ideological thought in education, or in government, or in laws or in public discourse or in just about anything. So when the SCOTUS outlawed God and the Ten Commandments from the classrooms and public discourse of America, a vacuum was created into which the ideology of Secular Humanism rushed right in. The Christian foundation, upon which America was founded, was pulled right out from under us. This Christian foundation was replaced by a Secular Humanist foundation. Christ was very effectively replaced by the Devil. From that point on, Secular Humanism began to permeate all of education and of public discourse. America had rejected God. Or, at least, five rogue justices of the SCOTUS had. Fortunately, not all Americans had.

The SCOTUS has made it against the law for teachers to tell the truth about the history of the United States and about the Constitution to the students. Against the law to tell the truth!!!!

The SCOTUS has made it against the law for teachers to tell the truth about the flaws in the theory of evolution to their students. Against the law to tell the truth!!!!!

Just think how the students of America must think when learning that God and the Ten Commandments had been outlawed from the classrooms. The law is supposed to defend good and punish evil, right? So what were those justices who voted "aye" in *Everson* in1947 thinking?

Without doubt, a powerful stigma against God and the Ten Commandments was created in the minds of millions of Americans. We should ask every justice who voted "aye" on *Everson,*"Just whose side are you on, anyhow?"

If we outlaw God and the Ten Commandments from the classroom and from public discourse, if we deny that God is the source of moral *and* civil law, what more do we have to offer than do the Communists, the Secular Humanists and the [other] Irreligionists?

In most cases, the SCOTUS also claims that their authority to apply the *First* to the states is derived from the *Fourteenth Amendment.* This claim is as spurious as is the others. The *Fourteenth* contains five sections and is too lengthy to be presented here. Check it in the Appendix. But within all those five sections, there is NO provision for the SCOTUS to apply the Bill of Rights to the states. The proper term to use to describe this action of the SCOTUS is that they have bamboozled the legal community and the American public.

Let's Apply Some Common Sense to This Insanity Called "Incorporation Doctrine":

The Constitution of the United States was created by a compact between the states and the federal government. Each individual state Constitution is a compact between the citizens of that state and the government of that individual state. The ONLY authority possessed by the U.S. Supreme Court is that given to it by the United States Constitution and its authority is specified and limited to deal with federal matters only.[99]

---

99. David Barton, Original Intent, 2005, Wallbuilder Press, Aledo, Texas, pp 13-17

It possesses NO authority from any of the states, much less all of the states to amend their constitutions. Therefore, it is very clear that the U.S. Supreme Court possesses NO authority to amend the Constitution of any state nor to legislate laws for any state nor for any county nor for any city.[100] When it does so, such is immoral, illegal, anti-constitutional and a legal nullity, pure usurpation and thoroughly anti-American.

Every time that the SCOTUS pronounces an anti—constitutional ruling to be "constitutional," it lies to the American people. There is NO WAY that the SCOTUS could have accidentally and innocently misinterpreted the *First* to mean the meaning given to it. The *First* is easy to read and its true meaning has a long history of meaning one thing and one thing only. The *First* is presented below, with the establishment clause underlined:

> **The First Amendment**: Congress shall make no law respecting an establishment of religion, or prohibiting the free exercise thereof; or of abridging the freedom of speech, or of the press; or the right *of the people peaceably to assemble and to petition the government for a dress of grievances. (Emphasis added)*

The SCOTUS distorted the Fourteenth Amendment and claimed that it authorized the Court to apply the First Amendment to the States. (For the Fourteenth Amendment, see Appendix "D".) For an excellent explanation of the disingenuous method and thinking employed by the Court in its application of the Fourteenth Amendment, see Stormer, *Betrayed By The Bench*, Chapter VIII. Also, for a more comprehensive explanation of this matter, see Raoul Berger, *Government by Judiciary*.

In misinterpreting (and it MUST have been deliberate) the Fourteenth Amendment to apply the Bill of Rights to the states, the SCOTUS arrogated to itself a HUGE amount of power.

The matter stood from 1791 until 1947 just as the Court ruled on it in 1833. That's 156 years. What happened to change the Court beginning in 1947? Was a statute enacted by the U.S. Congress? Was there an amendment to the Constitution which modified the First Amendment? Not at all. The change was in the hearts and the minds of certain justices of the SCOTUS. AND NO MORE! In *Everson* and succeeding cases, the Court ignored the original intent of the framers of the First Amendment, ignored established precedent and launched a revolution based solely upon its own ideology to serve solely its own will. Having done so, the SCOTUS from that point forward used *Everson* as its precedent and sole source of law and stubbornly refused to consider the true meaning of the First Amendment itself. Here is an excerpt from Raoul Berger[101] (Quoted in Stormer, *Betrayed by the Bench,* 2005, p. 95):

> It is the thesis of this book that the Supreme Court is not empowered to rewrite the Constitution, that in its transformation of the Fourteenth Amendment it has demonstrably done so. Thereby the Justices, who are virtually unaccountable, irremovable and irreversible, have taken over from the people the control of their own destiny, an awesome exercise of power. When Chief Justice Marshall stated that the function of the legislature is to *make* the law, that of the judiciary to interpret it,[102] He echoed Francis bacon's admonition two hundred years earlier. Much less are judges authorized to revise the Constitution, for as Justice Black, deriding the notion that the Court was meant to keep the Constitution in tune with the times, stated, "The Constitution makers knew the need for change and provided for it by the amendment process of Article V, whereby the people reserved unto themselves the right to change the Constitution."

In reading the works of Raoul Berger, I came to greatly admire the man. I especially admire his position that: "Repeated violations of the Constitution do not make them constitutional but merely compound the evil.[103]

Berger said it all. The Court does not possess the legitimate authority to (de facto) rewrite the Constitution, yet it is clear that this is exactly what it has done. This arrogation of power to apply any ruling it wishes and then call it "constitutional" indicates an extreme arrogance as well as a contempt, on the part of (some members of) the SCOTUS, for the rule of law and for the people. There has been no amendment to the Constitution to permit the rulings on "separation of church and state," or the such should apply to the states.[104] These rulings have come as the result of a shift in the judicial philosophy of the Court. A shift away from the Constitution as it is written and to "sociological jurisprudence", to "social justice". The Court justifies its violations of the Constitution by pretending to be ruling in the best interests of the people. In reality, the Court is arbitrarily imposing its own will upon an entire nation and its will is in direct conflict with the values which underline the Declaration of Independence and the Constitution. Justice William

---

100. Black's Law Dictionary, Fifth Edition, West
101. With certain specified exceptions provided for in Article III, Sec. 2
102. With certain specified exceptions provided for in Article III, Sec. 2

103. Berger, Raoul, 1997, Government by Judiciary, 2nd ed., Liberty Fund, Indianapolis, p. 18
104. This principle lies at the heart of the separation of powers, as Chief Justice Marshall perceived: "The difference between the departments is, that the legislature makes, the executive executes and the judiciary construes the law."

Brennan inadvertently but very accurately exposes the irresponsible (constitutionally speaking) attitude of the Court in his concurrence to *Torcaso v. Watkins* [105] 1961:

> The Baltimore and Abington schools offend the First Amendment because they sufficiently threaten in our day those substantive evils the fear of which called forth the Establishment Clause...Our interpretation of the First Amendment must necessarily be responsive to the much more highly charged nature of religious questions in contemporary society. *A too literal quest for the advice of the Founding Fathers upon the issues of these cases seems to me futile and misdirected. (Torcaso v. Watkins* , 367 U.S. 492-494 (1961). (Emphasis added)
> https://supreme.justia.com/cases/federal/us/367/488/case.html

Brennan was attempting to justify the Court's action. But what he did, if you read his statement carefully, was to inadvertently admit that the Court did not rule by the literal intent of the Framers of the Constitution. It could not be stated more plainly that the Court deliberately ignores the original intent of the Constitution and creates any kind of "law" that it wishes to, in the name of "progress,""social justice," or "sociological jurisprudence" and then calls it "constitutional."

Now that we have seen that the SCOTUS has fabricated the term "separation of church and state," treated it as if it were part of the Constitution and outlawed God and prayer in schools, let's take a look at the Humanist Manifesto to see what they have to say about church and state. This is the ninth point of the **Humanist Manifesto II:**

> **NINTH:** The separation of church and state and the separation of ideology and state are imperatives.

Whenever we see a ruling by the SCOTUS that conflicts with the Constitution and is oppressive to the Christian religion, it seems that we can always track it back to the Secular Humanists. From start to finish, this scheme of "Separation of Church and State" is illegal, anti-constitutional, sinister, low-down and dirty as it can get. It seems as if the Supreme Court was and is, owned by the Secular Humanists. This "separation of church and state" is itself a gigantic hoax. So what we have is a gigantic hoax wrapped up in another gigantic hoax.

Supreme Court and Humanists Refuse Freedom of Speech

By false interpretation of "Separation of church and state," a lie in itself, which will be explained hereinafter, the Secular Humanists and evolutionists have managed to, by the force of (corrupted) law, cause to be excluded from the classroom any theory or information that disproves or challenges their theory of evolution. This is, in effect, censoring. It is in direct violation of the clause in the First Amendment that was designed to protect the freedom of speech: (This clause pertains to freedom of speech:) "...or abridging the freedom of speech,..."

Louisiana Legislation Struck Down by Rogue U.S. Supreme Court

The Louisiana state legislature, in attempting to correct the censoring being done in the classroom, enacted a statute to allow Intelligent Design to be taught along side evolution. The U.S. Supreme Court struck it down. The case was *Edwards v. Aguillard*, 482 U.S. 578 (1987). Here is the syllabus as written by the SCOTUS: Louisiana's "Creationism Act" forbids the teaching of the theory of evolution in public elementary and secondary schools unless accompanied by instruction in the theory of "creation science." The Act does not require the teaching of either theory unless the other is taught. It defines the theories as "the scientific evidences for [creation or evolution] and inferences from those scientific evidences." Appellees, who include Louisiana parents, teachers and religious leaders, challenged the Act's constitutionality in Federal District Court, seeking an injunction and declaratory relief. The District Court granted summary judgment to appellees, holding that the Act [107 S.Ct. 2575] violated the Establishment Clause of the First Amendment. The Court of Appeals affirmed. Held:

1. The Act is facially invalid as violative of the Establishment Clause of the First Amendment, because it lacks a clear secular purpose. Pp. 585-594.

Note: The SCOTUS claims, in the above paragraph, that it based its ruling on the Establishment Clause of the First Amendment. What it REALLY did was to base its ruling not on the First Amendment but on the corrupted, fabricated law which *they use in place of* the First Amendment and which they *call* the "First Amendment." Here is what we are faced with: It does not matter to the SCOTUS what type of legislation the states come up with to counter the "Separation of...," the SCOTUS is going to strike it down as "unconstitutional." It matters not what the Constitution says, what justice demands, what the American people want or anything! The SCOTUS is fanatically determined to protect its big-guns against Christianity: "Evolution" and its corrupted version of "Separation of Church and State."

Here is a similar case which occurred in Dover, PA where the school district allowed the presentation of information on Intelligent Design to balance the teaching of evolution. Again, the federal court pretended to use the First Amendment as the justification to rule against the teaching of intelligent design. Please note in (1) below that the Court alleged that the policy "...amounted to an endorsement of religion in violation of the Establishment Clause;" Note that the Court failed to be specific in which religion that this policy was allegedly endorsing. If it did indeed endorse a religion, it would have been very easy for the Court to specify which religion. The Court in this case ruled for "Separation of Church and State" for exactly the same reason as the SCOTUS ruled in the *Edwards* case above. See information below about the *Kitzmiller v Dover Area School Dist*:

*In 707KITZMILLER v. DOVER AREA SCHOOL DIST.*Cite as 400 F. Supp.2d 707 (M.D.Pa. 2005)
Tammy KITZMILLER, et al., Plaintiffs, v. DOVER AREA SCHOOL DISTRICT, et al., Defendants.
United States District Court, M.D. Pennsylvania. Dec. 20, 2005
Background: Parents of school-aged children and member of high school science faculty brought action against school district and school board, challenging constitutionality of district's policy on teaching of intelligent design in high school biology class, which required students to hear a statement mentioning intelligent design as an alternative to Darwin's theory of evolution. Holdings: The District Court, Jones, J., held that:

(1) policy amounted to an endorsement of religion in violation of the Establishment Clause; [Note: It was NOT in violation of the Establishment Clause. It was in violation only of the *corrupted version of the Establishment Clause created by the Everson Court in 1947.*]
(2) policy violated the Establishment Clause under the Lemon test; and
(3) policy violated freedom of worship provision of the Pennsylvania Constitution. Ordered accordingly.
1. Constitutional Law O84.5(3)
Both the endorsement test and the Lemon test applied in determining whether school district's policy on teaching of intelligent design in high school biology class violated the Establishment Clause. U.S.C.A. Const.Amend. 1.
School district's policy on teaching of intelligent design in high school biology class, which required students to hear a statement mentioning intelligent design as an alternative to Darwin's theory of evolution, amounted to an endorsement of religion in violation of the Establishment Clause; policy imposed a religious view of biological origins into the biology course. U.S.C.A. Const.Amend. 1.
''Endorsement test'' used to determine whether there has been an establishment clause violation emanates from the prohibition against government endorsement of religion and it precludes government from conveying or attempting to convey a message that religion or a particular religious belief is favored or preferred. U.S.C.A. Const.Amend. 1.

''Endorsement test'' used to determine whether there has been an Establishment Clause violation consists of the reviewing court determining what message a challenged governmental policy or enactment conveys to a reasonable, objective observer who knows the policy's language, origins and legislative history, as well as the history of the community and the broader social and historical context in which the policy arose. U.S.C.A. Const. Amend. 1. School district's policy on teaching of intelligent design in high school biology class, which required students to hear a statement mentioning intelligent design as an alternative to Darwin's theory of evolution, violated the Establishment Clause under the Lemon test; policy's primary purpose was to change district's biology curriculum to advance religion and it had the primary effect of imposing a religious view of biological origins into the biology course. U.S.C.A. Const.Amend. 1. Under the Lemon test, a government-sponsored message violates the Establishment Clause of the First Amendment if: (1) it does not have a secular purpose; (2) its principal or primary effect advances or inhibits religion; or (3) it creates an excessive entanglement of the government with religion. U.S.C.A. Const.Amend. 1.

I suppose that if we were to look up a hundred similar cases involving citizens attempting to unlock the monopoly that the SCOTUS has given to the Secular Humanists, we would find identical results and probably identical wording. We must realize this hard reality (although we do not have to take it sitting down) that the SCOTUS, as presently constituted, is not going to give up this big gun against Christianity FOR ANY REASON. In every case, the SCOTUS claims to be basing its ruling on the Establishment Clause. But what it is REALLY doing is basing its case on the corrupted and misinterpreted version of the Establishment Clause.

In addition to relying upon the distorted and corrupt version of the *First,* the courts in the above and all similar rulings violated the *Ninth* and the *Tenth* Amendments, which are still legally in effect. Violated, ignored, scorned and overrun. But never repealed. Still legal, on paper, but not enforced.

The Clashing of Two Metaphysical Worldviews

Intelligent Design (ID) is not scorned because it is illogical or because it is bad science or because it is in conflict with the First Amendment. It is scorned (by the irreligionists) because it illuminates the flaws in the theory of evolution and because it gives the students an option. If there is anything that the evolutionists and the SCOTUS do NOT want is *for the students to have an option to evolution.* ID is scorned because it is one metaphysical worldview (Intelligent Design) that challenges another metaphysical worldview (evolution) and in the eyes of many who have beheld both, they perceive ID to be superior to the theory of evolution.

Yet, the Supreme Court and some educators desperately want to protect the theory of evolution and deny, with the force of government, (not logic and science) Intelligent Design. The Supreme Court and (some) educators are fanatically determined to deny the students an option to choose for themselves. After all, if ID were to be taught, many of the students might come to realize the lack of intelligence and or honesty on the part of the educational system that is forcing evolution on them.

Imagine Yourself the Defendant in a Murder Trial

In order to arrive at the truth in any dispute, one must have access to and properly evaluate, the complete arguments from both sides of the dispute. Imagine yourself innocent, but being the accused in a murder trial. The prosecutor is given unlimited time but your defense attorney is not allowed to speak. Would you be getting a fair trial? Neither is the theory of creation science being given a fair trial in the public schools. This must be because the Secular Humanists and the Supreme Court are terrified that some of the students might see the truth in it and believe it!

To censor or to deliberately omit vital information is to lead someone to a false conclusion; to tell a lie! The withholding of evidence that is vital to the students' developing an accurate worldview of the origin of man is a very serious offense. The same with withholding of evidence to help the students to understand how to maintain a free nation and to recognize and resist laws and programs alien to the Constitution. The education of young people is a very, very serious matter.

Evidently, the Supreme Court, the Secular Humanists, the evolutionists and the public school educators do not believe in that part of the First Amendment which would, if enforced, guarantee freedom of speech.

Teachers Not Allowed to Point Out the Flaws in the Theory of Evolution

Q: What happened to freedom of speech? After all, that is a very prominent part of the *First:* "...or abridging the freedom of speech, or of the press;..." The SCOTUS consistently ignores and violates that part of the Constitution that conflicts with its evil agenda.

The repetition of a lie will not make it true, but it can certainly give it the appearance of truth, especially when any opposing viewpoints are suppressed in the education process.

The most devious way to promulgate a lie is to withhold the truth. The most sinister and evil way to promulgate a lie is to have it forced upon the public by the government and preventing, by the force of government, the truth to be told which would expose the fallacy of the lie. Let's again take a look at the definition of a lie:

> An untruth deliberately told; the uttering or acting of that which is false for the purpose of deceiving; intentional misstatement. (Black's Dictionary, 5th ed. West Publishing Co. St. Paul)

So if one side of an argument is presented and the opposite argument is forbidden, such as the way that evolution is taught in the classroom, that is indeed the promulgation of a lie. Evolution has many flaws which put it into the "unproven theory" category. Yet, in many classrooms, Darwinism is taught as if it were true science; as if it were withouts flaws. Or, if flaws are admitted, they are minimized. Minimized to nothing or to almost nothing. What is worse is that the opposing theory, "intelligent design," is withheld from the students. They are not given the opportunity to consider it. Thus, this very flawed theory of evolution has been used very effectively to cause millions to disbelieve the principles of Christianity.

Here is a quote from former Democrat President Harry Truman which bears on this issue:

> Once a government is committed to the principle of silencing the voice of opposition, it has only one way to go and that is down the path of increasingly repressive measures, until it becomes a source of terror to all its citizens and creates a country where everyone lives in fear. (Special Message to the Congress on the Internal Security of the United States, August 8, 1950).

Whatever we might think about "Old Harry" regarding other issues, he sure told the truth that time.

In "Intelligent Design," nothing is said about God nor Adam and Eve nor about any denomination of religion. It just advocates that it appears that some intelligence was involved in designing man and other living things. Yet the teaching of this theory is adamantly forbidden by the SCOTUS and by the NEA and many of the local educators.

Evidence will be presented herein to show the compatibility of evolutionism with Humanism and Marxism, all of which are hostile to Christianity. That should cinch it for most people that evolutionism is completely incompatible with Christianity.

My message is that evolution is a pseudo science, built more on imagination, artwork and showmanship (that would give P. T. Barnum an inferiority complex). With such huge unproven gaps in the theory, evolutionism cannot honestly be considered to be a proven or even a provable theory.

The REAL Purpose of the Theory of Evolution

Evolution is advanced not because it is true but in spite of the fact that it is false. In spite of its flaws, the evolutionists, Humanists and Marxists see a very definite purpose for teaching evolution. "Science" is only the ostensible

reason that Evolution is advanced. Evolutionism serves three very definite purposes: (1) to confuse Christians in their beliefs,
(2) to promote the religion of Humanism and
(3) to promote Marxism by tricking people to disbelieve the concept that their rights come from their Creator, as stated in the Declaration of Independence. When one disbelieves the concept that his rights come from his Creator, he becomes easy prey for Marxist ideas such as rights come from government.

Darwinism has certainly been effective in producing results (1), (2) and (3). Noting the definition of "pragmatism" above, we can see that the Darwinistas accept and use evolution as "true" for purely pragmatic reasons; because it "works for them." It produces the results that they desire. What do they care that it is badly flawed?

There is no conflict between true science and true religion. There is conflict between false science and true religion and between true science and false religion. The evolutionists strive to deceive us to believe a false science so that we will not believe a true religion. Stay strong!

As for the popularity and the perpetuation of the theory of evolution, it is not because of any profound brilliance on the part of its author. It is my belief that it is due to two things: (1) It appeals to the carnal nature of man and, (2) it serves the purpose for some with nefarious designs. Every generation has a certain percentage who look for any reason to escape the restraints of the Ten Commandments. If the theory of evolution is true, then there never was an Adam nor an Eve, there never was a Moses nor the Ten Commandments. To many, that makes them think that they are free from the restraints of the Ten Commandments.

So in spite of its many flaws, the theory of evolution continues on and on because of: (1) its built-in self perpetuation feature, that it appeals to the carnal nature of man and (2) because it serves a purpose for the Secular Humanists in helping them with their recruiting and (3) it serves a political purpose for the Marxists in that it destroys people's understanding that their rights come from their Creator. This leads people to reject the Declaration of Independence and the Constitution and to accept legislation and programs which are Marxist even though they are not labeled as such and (4) it is forced upon the students by a government-enforced monopoly.

Needed: More Separation of State From Church

The SCOTUS has it wrong in more ways than one. First, they misinterpret what Jefferson said, with disastrous results. Then, they apply a blanket of dictatorship over America in *Obergefell,* resulting in more chaos and disaster. What we really need now is more separation of state from church. That's right! More separation of state from church! Stop the federal government from meddling into affairs that rightly belong to the states and their respective churches. With the SCOTUS outlawing the Ten Commandments from our schools and our civic affairs, we get more crime in our society and a diminution of civic virtue with an increase of corruption in our government.

The simple truth of the matter is that the Supreme Court of the United States is corrupting the law and then using this corrupted law against us.

The awful reality is that we now have in place what the Founding Fathers feared most: a state religion adopted by, favored by and financed by the federal government. And put into place not by the Congress but by the Supreme Court. Nor should we suppose that this came about by accident. The SCOTUS knew exactly what it was doing when it misinterpreted the Constitution to bring about this corrupted "law."

The SCOTUS is doing exactly what Gramsci planned: corrupting the cultural hegemony so that the people will accept the corruption and modification of the law toward a Marxist totalitarian state.

The Denominational Religion of Secular Humanism

Yes, Humanism is a religion by the strictest definition of the word. Humanism is a religion that is the opposite of the Christian religion. Not only that, it is a denomination. The theory of evolution is foundational to its beliefs. Humanism has its own worldview. It takes faith to believe this worldview. It is no accident that this religion of Humanism is exactly the opposite of Christianity. We must presume that the Devil himself had a hand in its fabrication. The Humanists have their own pastors and clergy, further attesting that Humanism is an identifiable, established religion. The U.S. Supreme Court has even declared Secular Humanism to be a religion. In *Torcaso v. Watkins* (June 19, 1961), the U.S. Supreme Court[106] declared that:

> Among religions in this country which do not teach what would generally be considered a belief in the existence of God are Buddhism, Taoism, Ethical Culture, Secular Humanism and others.

The American Humanist Association "...certifies humanist counselors who enjoy the legal status of ordained priests, pastors and rabbis." (See *American*

---

105. Raoul Berger, GOVERNMENT BY JUDICIARY The Transformation of the Fourteenth Amendment, 2nd ed. Liberty Fund, Indianapolis, 1997, p. xvii.
106. Prior to the ratification of the Fourteenth Amendment and the development of the incorporation doctrine, the Supreme Court in 1833 held in Barron v. Baltimore that the Bill of Rights applied only to the federal, but not any state governments. Even years after the ratification of the Fourteenth Amendment, the Supreme Court in United States v. Cruikshank (1876) still held that the First and Second Amendment did not apply to state governments. However, beginning in the 1920s, a series of United States Supreme Court decisions interpreted the Fourteenth Amendment to "incorporate" most portions of the Bill of Rights, making these portions, for the first time, enforceable against the state governments. Note: This "incorporation doctrine" is strictly the creation of the Court and is completely anti-constitutional.
Again, a case of judicial chicanery and fraud. (JHF)

Education On Trial: Is Secular Humanism a Religion? Cumberland, VA. Center for Judicial Studies, 1987,) p. 34.

The Dogma Taught in Public Schools is NOT Neutral as to Religion

The dogma being taught to the children in public schools is not neutral as pertaining to Christianity. The dogma they are being taught is a religion called Secular Humanism. Look back at Dunphy's statement about the "new faith of Humanism." What is a faith? It is a belief-a religion. A faith in Humanism has to be a faith in a religion. The point that we must understand is that the object of the Humanists, et. al. is not to exclude religion from the public schools. Their objective is to *exclude the Christian religion* and to insert, stealthily, their own religion, which is Humanism. Humanism can be described as the religion of the anti-Christ or it can be described as atheism. Either fits. A-theism is a belief; a religion. Also, wherever there is Secular Humanism, there is also Darwinism and Marxism. They all go together.

Of the religions in the United States, they can be divided into two classes: 1. Theist and 2. A-theist or atheist. Secular Humanism falls in the atheist class of religions. It is still a religion.

Now get this. At least one court has declared Secular Humanism to be a religion. The Secular Humanists have 501(c)3 status. But other courts have declared Secular Humanism to not be a religion. So, for purposes of tax status, the courts have held that Humanism is a religion. For the purposes of prohibiting Secular Humanism from being taught in the public schools because it is a religion, the courts have held that Humanism is NOT a religion. So the courts ban Christianity from the classrooms because it is a religion but will not ban the religion of Humanism. To do this requires some extreme measure of legal contortions.

Constitutional Interpretation is Not "Mere Law"

When the gavel comes down on a law case, often times more is decided than "mere law." The case usually adds weight on one side or the other of the great cultural war that rages. (American Constitutionalists on one side-Gramsci and Marx's hordes on the other.) Consider the words of constitutional scholar John A. Eidsmoe:

> ...the debate over constitutional interpretation is no mere academic or legal matter. Rather it is a major battle between two conflicting philosophies, two conflicting religions and two conflicting worldviews. [Supreme Court] Justice [William] Brennan openly acknowledged this in his Georgetown address] "The Constitution of the United States: Contemporary Ratification," Teaching Symposium, Georgetown University, Washington, D. C., October 12, 1985, p. 51], declaring that "...our society must continue its upward progress unbounded by the fetters of original intent or the literal words of the Constitution, though an

evolutionary process is inevitable and, indeed, it is the true interpretative genius of the text."[107]

Yes, this matter of the law is inseparably connected with the battle that rages between two opposing cultures; between Christianity and the anti-Christ.

We Talk to the Devil Again:

Yessir, Devil, your disciples in the SCOTUS really did you up proud and are continuing to do so. You must consider them to be very special among your many soldiers. Now, with the principles of evolution and secular Humanism being force-fed to the innocent students of America, you can use such to pry those little fingers one at a time from around that iron rod called "the gospel of Jesus Christ" so that they can fall right into your lap. You are so clever, you Devil you.

We have studied the effect that your disciple Langdell had upon American law. Then your Humanists managed to get seated on the Supreme Court of the United States a number of justices who would ignore the Constitution and rule in favor of your scheme. Whether we want to admire them or curse them for this feat, they did it. The rulings on *"Separation..."* are entirely anti-constitutional. The SCOTUS makes a mockery of the law. It violates the rule of law every time there is a vote to uphold this hoax. We should not be surprised because after all, the way that you do business is by lying, cheating and stealing. And oh yes by violating the Constitution. Well, Mr. Devil, we shall leave you for a while. We do not, however, wish you success.

When the SCOTUS outlawed God and the Ten Commandments from the classrooms and from American public discourse, America took a huge fall. And landed hard. We are still crippled from the event. This act did not elevate us—it brought us DOWN. We are still falling and shall continue to do so until we get this situation corrected.

Now, back to the Reader: Let's examine Humanist law to see how it differs from Christian law:

Humanist Law

Humanists are different from Christians not only in their religion but also in the form of law that they advocate. Christians prefer absolutes. Like the Ten Commandments; like the Constitution. To the Humanists, there are no absolutes, so the law must be in a constant state of flux. To them, the law "evolves." Change in the law is not limited to those made by the amendments

---

107. Torcaso v. Watkins, 367 U.S. 492-494 (1961)
108. United States v. Seeger, 380 U.S. 163. Also see Welsh v. United States, 398 U.S. 333 (1970)

to the Constitution or by the Congress. It may be changed by the courts or by the chief executive. Constitutionally speaking, of course, this is called "usurpation." The importance of understanding this will become clear as we learn how the courts have favored Humanists by changing the law. Here is what David Noebel[108] says about Humanist law:

> The concept of evolution so permeates Humanist legal thinking that it can be stated, without contradiction, that evolution ultimately determines Humanistic legal principles. Man is evolving. Man is becoming. Everything is in flux. Nothing is permanent. There are no absolute legal standards. There are no permanent Ten Commandments; there is no permanent Constitution...

All schemers, liars and conspirators just hate absolutes. Absolutes make it much more difficult for conspirators to convince their intended victims to believe their lies. It is much easier to detect a violation of an absolute, like a commandment of God or the Constitution. That's the reason that they teach things like "everything is relative" in schools. Here is an example of the mindset of educator and Secular Humanist John Dewey in 1927:[109][110]

> The belief in political fixity, of the sanctity of some form of state consecrated by the efforts of our fathers and hallowed by tradition, is one of the stumbling-blocks in the way of orderly and directed change.

Change? Change, Mr. Dewey? Change by whom, Mr. Dewey and in whose favor? Obviously, by the Secular Humanist judges and in favor of the Secular Humanists, Marxists and Globalists.

The above type of legal reasoning is perfectly congruent with the type employed in Marxist-style "social justice." I believe that we can safely assume the probability that "social justice" originated with the Humanists. At least, we can until someone provides us with a concise explanation of its origin: person, date and location. The reason that the Secular Humanists support Noebel's explanation of Secular Humanist law and "social justice" is precisely because such law has no fixed limitations such as imposed by the Constitution. The justices can just rule that *anything* is "constitutional" The Secular Humanist agenda is in direct conflict with the Constitution. The strict interpretation stands as a bar to the advancement of the Humanist agenda. So, when a case is presented to a court with a majority of

David O McKay- Public Domain

---

109. John A. Eidsmoe, "Creation, Evolution and Constitutional Interpretation," Concerned Women for America, Sept/1987, p. 7

justices who are either humanists or sympathetic to Humanism, such justices will ignore the Constitution and rule by the rules of "social justice". This is demonstrated loud and clear in the *Obergefell* case, regarding same-sex marriage, of June 26, 2015, which will be addressed in the following chapter.

President David O. McKay Concerned About Supreme Court Rulings

President David O. McKay of the Church of Jesus Christ of Latter-day Saints (Mormon) expressed grave concern over the rulings of the Supreme Court regarding "separation of church and state:"[111]

> For an hundred years boys and girls born in America and they who later obtained citizenship in this great country, have felt that they are "endowed by their Creator" with certain inalienable rights; that among those are: "life, liberty and the pursuit of happiness," and that these rights are endowed by our Creator.
>
> Recent rulings of the Supreme Court would have all reference to a Creator eliminated from our public schools and public offices. It is a sad day when the Supreme Court of the United Sates would discourage all reference in our schools to the influence of the phrase "divine providence" as used by our founders of the Declaration of Independence.
>
> **Evidently the Supreme Court misinterpreted the true meaning of the First Amendment and <u>is now leading a Christian Nation down the road to Atheism.</u>** (Emphasis added.)

President McKay was not a lawyer, but he certainly understood that the Supreme Court rulings were subversive to the Christian beliefs of American students. If President McKay declared that the Supreme Court misinterpreted the First Amendment, by golly, that is good enough for me! THE SUPREME COURT MISINTERPRETED THE FIRST AMENDMENT!!! (Emphasis added)

SCOTUS Makes it Against the Law to Tell the Truth

The SCOTUS has made it against the law to tell the truth about some very critical issues.

First, they made it illegal for teachers to teach the students about the flaws in the theory of evolution.

Second, they made it illegal for law school professors to explain the flaws in the rulings of the SCOTUS regarding their ruling in the *Everson* case since

---

110. Noebel, David, Understanding the Times, p. 500
111. John Dewey, 1927, The Public And its problems, Henry Holt and Company, NY, p. 34

they would have to mention God, the Ten Commandments and other issues relating to religion.

Imagine: Against the law in America to tell the truth! They made it illegal for teachers and professors to teach, in any class, the benefits that the Christian religion and the Christians give to America! How can any bad or evil idea, ideology, practice or law be corrected if it is against the law to tell the truth about it? That is corrupt government at its worst and the people who caused the situation are the worst kind of people. Let's put the blame for our problems where the blame belongs so that we can work towards getting them resolved.

Here is how the justices voted in *Everson*:
In the majority: Black, Vinson, Reed, Douglas and Murphy.
Dissenting: Jackson, Rutledge, Frankfurter and Burton.

The results of this case are, to your point of view, Devil, stupendous! It meets all of your fiendish expectations. Even better than you had ever dreamed! First, those nine judges changed the Constitution of the United States from being totally opposed to you and your scheme to being totally in favor of you and of it. At least, they changed it as it is perceived by Supreme Court justices. That "Separation of church and state" that your soldiers worked out is a work of genius! Phony, of course, when examined closely, but a work of genius in how effective it became. From your point of view, that is. Your disciple Langdell must be turning handsprings down there in your domain. From the point of view of the Christians and the pro-Constitution Americans, however, it was skullduggery, mean-spirited and, yes, even treason.

The five justices who voted for it (Black, Vinson, Reed, Douglas and Murphy) made of themselves domestic enemies of the Constitution, enemies of all Christians and traitors to all freedom-loving Americans and, yes, to God.

In *Everson,* your obedient disciples on the SCOTUS accomplished the following:

1. Took an excerpt from a letter by Thomas Jefferson, "separation of church and state," that was written ten years *after* the First Amendment was ratified and was never part of the law[112] and,
2. Completely without authority, "constitutionalized"[113] it and forced it upon the American public. In "constitutionalizing" "separation of church

---

112. Quoted in David Barton, 2000, Original Intent, (Aledo, Texas, Wallbuilder Press, p. 228
113. McKay, President David O., Statement on the Supreme Court Ruling, Deseret News, Monday, June 17, 1963
114. This letter from Jefferson was indeed an authoritative source of information, as he was President at the time, but it was never under any stretch of the imagination to be considered to be law; part of the Constitution.

and state", the SCOTUS gave to it a meaning exactly the opposite of what Jefferson meant by it.[114]

3. To make this "law" apply to all the states, the SCOTUS applied the thoroughly anti-constitutional "incorporation doctrine".[115]
4. In using the First Amendment as justification for their ruling, the SCOTUS took the *First,* which is plainly written to be a restriction upon the powers of the federal government and made it into a *grant* of power *to themselves*! Furthermore,
5. In forbidding the use of any material in the classroom that exposes or opposes evolution, secular Humanism or Marxism, The SCOTUS violated that part of the First that reads, "…or abridging the freedom of speech,…"
6. In outlawing the Ten Commandments and any mention of the Bible in the schoolrooms of America, the SCOTUS essentially legislated, which it has no authority to do.
7. In outlawing anything relating to Christianity, the SCOTUS did, de facto, impose the religion of Secular Humanism on every public school and caused Secular Humanism to be adopted as the de facto state religion of the government of the United States and of every state.
8. In *Everson* in 1947, the SCOTUS obviously ignored the Constitution and ruled by "social justice."[116]
9. In forcing "separation of church and state" on the states, the SCOTUS violated the Ninth and Tenth Amendments to the Constitution.
10. In cases regarding "Separation…." subsequent to *Everson,* the SCOTUS obviously abandoned the Constitution and resorted to the Langdell "case law" for their judgments.

Well, Devil, you and your disciples pulled off a HUGE victory for the forces of darkness. With this court ruling, you shoved any mention of God, Christ or the Ten Commandments right out of the public school classroom. Then, you didn't have to do anything at all to get your religion of Secular Humanism adopted. When Christianity was outlawed, your religion moved right into the vacuum that was created. And you didn't have to spend one dime of your own money. You made those suckers-those Christians-pay for it all. You managed to get your entire scheme taxpayer-financed. You clever Devil, you.

With this corrupted version of the *First,* coupled with the very corrupt

---

115. This word "constitutionalized" is used to trick the unknowing into believing that the SCOTUS can make something part of the Constitutuion by merely "constitutionalizing" it. The SCOTUS does NOT possess such authority. This is another legalistic-sounding scam put over on the American people by the SCOTUS.
116. See Letter from Thos. Jefferson to the Danbury Baptists, Jan 1, 1802.

"incorporation doctrine," you managed to gain a tremendous amount of leverage; of disproportionate amount of political power; over your Christian adversaries. Poor dumb slobs. They have not found out a way to get a working arrangement with the SCOTUS like you have. They are so innocent. They would NEVER have thought of such a clever scheme to use against you. They are just too.... well..... too *honest!* It has been 73 years (as of 2020) and still most of the Christians are blissfully asleep to what you have done and are doing to them. I guess you are to be congratulated. By somebody. We suppose that your buddy Langdell down there is congratulating you.

And, Mr. Devil, we must congratulate you, albeit reluctantly, on the methods that your justices employed in performing their duty (to you-not to the People). You have trained them well. True to your MO, the justices employed stratagems, sophistries, chicanery and committed violations of their oaths of office, violations of the Constitution and just plain lies. But-for you-mission accomplished. A great success for you, Mr. Devil.

Since the *Everson* case was to forever change the law of the United States, we need to examine and thoroughly understand the chicanery employed by the SCOTUS to make this change, to wit: 1. To "constitutionalize," 2. "Social justice," 3. The "incorporation doctrine." and the corrupted Fourteenth Amendment. These tricks were used to turn American jurisprudence upside down.

> **To "Constitutionalize:"** Means for the Court to make something "constitutional" that was theretofore unconstitutional. This is obviously a practice in illegal sophistry, as the Court does not possess the authority to "constitutionalize" anything. Any such practice, then, of "constitutionalizing" something is obviously a case of violating the Constitution; of usurpation. To "constitutionalize" means to change the meaning of the Constitution without going through the process described in Article V, which is the only *legal* means of amending the Constitution. Consequently, to "constitutionalize" clearly means to usurp, or to arrogate powers. To "constitutionalize" is nothing more than a legal-*sounding* stratagem to trick, deceive and convince a naive, trusting public. (Joe H. Ferguson, 2020)

Well, Mr. Devil, your soldiers on the SCOTUS won a great battle for you when they thought up this scheme of "constitutionalizing". To do so means to change the meaning of the Constitution. The procedure to do this legally is specified in Article V of the Constitution. This requires a convention and then, to finalize an amendment, the approval of three fourths of the states. Your soldiers in the SCOTUS certainly pulled off a huge coup when they changed the Constitution by "constitutionalizing" instead of by the only legal way to do it as specified in Article V.

Mr. Devil, through this *Everson* decision and all of the future decisions that you will get in your favor using the corrupted "separation of church and state," you have found a vehicle for giving your values (evolution, secular Humanism, Marxism, etc.) the force of law without having to go to all that inconvenience of having to take over the political authority. You did not have to convince 51% of the voters of the entire country. What a beautiful scheme, you clever Devil you. And you more than likely will be able to keep the Supreme Court on your side into the indefinite future.

Yessir, Devil, you have certainly stepped all over those Christians and cheated them out of their right to influence their congressmen and their government in this matter. You and your Supreme Court have just plain disenfranchised, to a great degree, every Christian in the country. And you have managed to get shoved anything Christian, like those Ten Commandments that you hate so much, right out the back door of every schoolhouse in America. And marching right in the front door, to replace everything Christian, are new school books and curricula just full of your special ideas-evolution, secular Humanism and Marxism.

> **"Incorporation Doctrine"** No definition found in *Black's Law Dictionary.* No true definition found in any other source. Here is a partial explanation, (From *Free* Test Now):
> "...The doctrine of selective incorporation, or simply the incorporation doctrine, makes the first ten amendments to the Constitution—known as the Bill of Rights—binding on the states. Through incorporation, state governments largely are held to the same standards as the federal government with regard to many constitutional rights, including the FIRST AMENDMENT freedoms of speech, religion and assembly and the separation of church and state; the FOURTH AMENDMENT freedoms from unwarranted arrest and unreasonable SEARCHES AND SEIZURES; ..."Until the early twentieth century, the Bill of Rights was interpreted as applying only to the federal government. In the 1833 case *Barron ex rel. Tiernon v. Mayor of Baltimore*, 32 U.S. (7 Pet.) 243, 8 L. Ed. 672, the Supreme Court expressly limited application of the Bill of Rights to the federal government. By the mid-nineteenth century, this view was being challenged..."

Note: The above explanation is partly accurate but is not complete. It fails to explain that the SCOTUS , when it began to apply the :"Incorporation doctrine" had absolutely no authority to do so. None. Furthermore, it fails to explain the stratagem employed by the SCOTUS in its application of the incorporation doctrine. That is, when they applied one of the Bill of Rights to the states, it (almost invariably) changed or completely inverted the meaning of it. For example, in *Everson,* the SCOTUS changed the First Amendment from being a limitation on the powers of the federal government to a GRANT OF POWER TO THE SCOTUS. This constitutes an outrageous arrogation of power by the Court to itself by a completely illegal stratagem.

The Constitution of the United States is a contract between the states and the federal government. The constitutions of the various states are contracts between the people of those states and the governments of those states. It is completely illogical to think that the SCOTUS has the authority to: 1 Apply the Bill of Rights to the state constitutions and, 2 Invert the meanings of the Bill of Rights from intending to be a limitation of power to being a grant of power. Incorporation Doctrine is a fraudulent stratagem by the SCOTUS especially directed against the Christian people of the United States.

Congratulations, Mr. Devil

Mr. Devil, you accomplished the impossible! In one fell swoop, you have banned anything Christian from being taught in the public schools and had installed a government-enforced policy that your religion and government ideas would be taught exclusively!!! Evolution and Secular Humanism, the foundational ideologies of your own personal religion and a government-enforced edict that they be taught in every public school in America. And no competition allowed! And with evolution and Humanism being taught exclusively, Marxism would fall into place naturally. That—and a little time—is all that you need to suppress and maybe even destroy Christianity and the Constitution in America.

Rioting Thugs the Product of *Everson* and the Public School System

This is being written in **June of 2020.** Riots, looting, burning and stealing are occurring in many cities across America. Triggered, supposedly, by the death by police of a black man, George Floyd, in Minneapolis. There is more, much more, to this phenomenon than just protesting the death of one man. It involves the mentality of the rioters and the motivation of the various mayors to order the chiefs of police to stand down and allow the rioting, looting and burning to continue.

It cannot be stated with too much emphasis that the rioters and the mayors are products of the public school system, influenced by the *Everson* case. Neither the rioters nor the mayors encouraging them have respect for the lives, liberties and properties of other people. They are, by my definition, uncivilized. They are behaving like primitive animals. Or worse. All of these uncivilized thugs, rioters and mayors, are products of *Everson* and the public school system.

Neither these mayors nor the rioters have the spirit of Christ in them. It was educated out of them in the public school system, as ordered by *Everson*.

Gramsci and his Soldiers Marching Through the Institutions

Everson has proven to be a HUGE victory for Gramsci's plan to "march through the institutions" and to capture, step by step and institution by institution, parts of America until America is completely captured and dominated by the Marxists.

With *Everson*, the Rebellion Against God in America Became Institutionalized

The Final and Finalizing Argument

The final argument comes down to whether all of these radical changes to our law and our fundamental legal document, the Constitution, which, according to its own text, constitutes, "The Supreme Law of the Land," made by these courts which we consider to be "rogue," and made by the use of stratagems which we consider to be illegal, can be considered to be legitimate. In other words, are they legal or illegal? If we are going to fight for Christian Religious Liberties, we must know the answer to that question.

The Framers of the Constitution built in a provision to legally change the Constitution. Any other way of changing it would constitute usurpation. it would be illegal. This means for amendments is provided for in Article. V. If any change in the Constitution is made without meeting the requirements of Article V, it is obviously unconstitutional and illegal.

NONE of the specious reasons provided by the various SCOTUSes meet the requirements of Article V. Therefore, they are illegal. They are frauds. They are shams.

The Framers were very cautious when constructing the Constitution to protect the integrity of the Constitution from usurpation and other illegal acts. Therefore, does it seem even remotely reasonable that the Framers would approve or condone means for the SCOTUSes to give to themselves the power to amend the Constitution? That in itself seals the argument. NO person or group possesses the authority to unilaterally change the Constitution.

Therefore, the changes to our law by the stratagems discussed above are unconstitutional and illegal. Most of them are detrimental to the sovereignty of our nation and alter the structure of our government so as to accommodate being absorbed into a world government. Many of them also are restrictive to the free exercise of religious liberties and therefore constitute attacks upon religion. They are stratagems used by anti-American and anti-Christian forces against Christians and Christianity.

Here is the final proof: The names for these stratagems, "case law," "to constitutionalize," "incorporation doctrine," "social justice," etc., were created for a purpose. That purpose was to fool a naive public into thinking that a serious violation of the Constitution is actually "legal."

This appears to be the greatest and most insidious hoax or scam or stratagem ever used against the forces of freedom and of Christianity. If there is a greater one, please show it to me.

It is obvious. We Americans have been too trusting of some very scheming, conniving and treacherous domestic enemies of the Constitution in power over us.

Chapter Twelve - *Obergefell* Another Attack Against Christianity and the U.S. Constitution

> From 2 Timothy:
>
> 3, This know also, that in the last days perilous times shall come.
> 4. For men shall be lovers of their own selves, covetous, boasters, proud, blasphemers, disobedient to parents, unthankful, unholy,
> 5. Without natural affection, truce-breakers, **false accusers**, incontinent, **fierce**, **despisers of those that are good**.
> 6. **Traitors**, heady, **high minded**, lovers of pleasures more than lovers of God.

Please Remember This: That when evaluating the extent of the malfeasance of rogue judges, please remember that, no matter how inconsequential a violation of the Constitution might appear, that every part of the Constitution is an important part of the whole. If the Constitution is destroyed in an instant or in an hundred years, the **results will be the same**: an introduction of tyranny and misery such as we have never seen. For the United States to be merged into the global government, the Constitution must be destroyed (rendered impotent).

There are powerful forces at work to accomplish this. Mostly, **they finance** their nefarious work **with federal tax dollars**. Some of them work from within our government.

These forces are anti-American, anti-Christian, they are powerful and well-financed. The time for us to expose and defeat them is growing short. One of the organizations whose agenda is to destroy or weaken the Constitution so that the United States can be merged into a global government is the Council on Foreign Relations, or CFR. It must be noted that two justices of the SCOTUS that ruled on *Obergefell*, Breyer and Ginsburg, are members of the CFR.

When the SCOTUS violates the Constitution, it is empowering the secret combinations of the Devil, dedicated enemies of America, of Christ and Christianity.

Obergefell Akin to *Everson*

Voted Aye on *Obergefell*: Ginsburg, Breyer, Kennedy, Sotomayor and Kagan
Voted to Dissent: Roberts, Scalia, Thomas and Alito

The ostensible purpose of *Obergefell* case of 2015 **was to give "rights" to gays and lesbians to have same-sex marriages**. However, its "unintended consequences" (if indeed they were "unintended") serve to deliver a crushing blow to both constitutional government and to the Christian religion. The justices who voted in the majority in *Obergefell* employed many of the stratagems that were used in *Everson*. It seems that these rogue justices have devised a very clever and disingenuous set of stratagems to ignore, bypass and to violate the Constitution. These stratagems seem to fit all cases and are the favorite weapons of rogue justices.

Obergefell Makes a Mockery of the Rule of Law

Right from the outset, *Obergefell* abandoned the Constitution in favor of "social justice." When one thinks of "social justice", one normally thinks of the social attitudes of all of the people in the country. Such is not the case. For the definition of "social justice" employed by the rogue justices is their own idea of what social justice *ought to be,* even though that idea might be held by only a small segment of the population. By 2015, a few states had passed laws legalizing same-sex marriages. But the majority had not. So the rogue justices, in their construction of *Obergefell*, not only violated the Constitution seriously, they ruled against the social attitudes of the majority of the American people and also deprived the majority of Americans of the right to vote on this issue in local elections. Unmitigated arrogance, I would attribute to these rogue justices.

In the long run, however, the same-sex issue is not the most important issue of the case. By far, it is the "Unintended consequences" that are so important and so destructive to our constitutional system of law, to our culture, to our people and to our Christian religion. In fact, it is my opinion that, to the political and ideological forces driving the construction of the opinion in *Obergefell,* the "unintended consequences" are by far more important than the intended consequences. In fact, since the "unintended consequences", get far less scrutiny and publicity than does the main issue in a legal case, it can be used very deceptively. The use of such has become a favorite tool of the political Left. This decision certainly adds momentum to the Left's side in this cultural, political and religious battle. Here is a hyperlink to the entire case: *Obergefell v. Hodges 135 S. Ct. 2584 (2015)*

The arguments of the petitioners are not without merit. But we who oppose *Obergefell* do so because of its "unintended consequences" which constitute an extremely destructive effect upon American law and justice. *Obergefell* makes a mockery of the Constitution and the rule of law. It perfectly conforms to the Secular Humanist agenda and to "social justice." To view the entire case, both the majority and the dissents, please click on the hyperlink above. For an understanding of how this case is destructive to American law, please read, very carefully, the opinions of the justices who dissented. They are MOST interesting. And a real education in constitutional law. So refreshing!

Noebel explained for us, in *Understanding The Times* the Humanist approach to the law. We have looked at the definition of "social justice," which is completely compatible with Humanist law but completely incompatible with constitutional law. When "social justice" is applied, it overrides and displaces many provisions of the Constitution. This will help us to understand what is and has been going on in the Supreme Court that seems "crazy!" They are not crazy at all. They are perfectly in accord with the Humanist mind. It appears that the Humanists have captured the Supreme Court (or-five members thereof as of 2015) It is evident that, in *Obergefell,* the rogue justices involved used some standard other than the Constitution by which to judge and also had an objective in mind before the trial began.

It does appear that, at every opportunity, the rogue justices of the SCOTUS are ignoring the Constitution and substituting therefor "case law," "social justice" law and "incorporation doctrine" law to completely invert the meaning of the Constitution and the Constitutions of every state.

The substitution of "social justice" for the Constitution as the measure by which to judge is for the purpose of using the courts to effect "social engineering," to manipulate the values of society as well as effecting a paradigm shift in the way that the society perceives the law and many other values. Carried to its logical conclusion, a free nation can be transmogrified into a Marxist dictatorship by "social justice" and "social engineering" by the Supreme Court.

What are the Religions of the Justices?

They might claim to be Baptists, Methodists, Catholic, Mormon, Lutheran or anything. But they might, in reality, believe in and practice Secular Humanism. The way for us to know is easy. It is "by their fruits ye shall know them." They might be Catholics or Jews or whatever on Sundays, but when they rule in favor of secular Humanism in court cases, they are then secular humanists. If they reject the Constitution and base their rulings on "social justice" and Humanism, we can know that they are, de facto, Secular Humanists. It appears that, in *Obergefell,* the SCOTUS (or the five justices in the majority) relied entirely upon "social justice" and ignored the Constitution completely.

Using "social justice" instead of the Constitution, a Court can do just *anything* that it wants to. Not restrained by anything. Unlimited powers. "Social justice" applied by rogue justices can, in a short while, render the Constitution completely impotent and destroy America. Please study the wording of "social justice" above. It is pure Humanism and Marxism. Judging by "social justice" constitutes replacing the Constitution with Humanism and Marxism.

Obergefell—A Landmark (and Disastrous) SCOTUS Case

Ostensibly—Whether Same-Sex Couples Have Right to Marry

In *Obergefell v. Hodges*, date of 26 June, 2015, the ostensible issue was whether same-sex couples had the "right" to marry. The case affected more than that, however, as the fallout in "unanticipated consequences" was staggering. Or, the more we diagnose *Obergefell*, the more reason that we have to question whether these consequences were really unanticipated. Or were they anticipated-and desired (by the perpetrators)?

Obergefell Complies with Council on Foreign Relations Agenda

Two of the justices who sat on the SCOTUS during *Obergefell* are members of the Council on Foreign Relations (CFR). They are Breyer and Ginsburg. Both voted "aye".

All of the offenses committed in the "Separation..." cases plus: The SCOTUS intimidates (the issue of whether *Obergefell* compels county clerks, etc. to perform same-sex marriages when they might not wish to is still unclear). This would force people into a contract in which they had no desire to participate. Even if the SCOTUS were to possess the authority to create "rights" for same-sex couples to marry, it does not possess the authority to command citizens of the states to perform such marriage ceremonies.

Nevertheless, in *Obergefell,* the SCOTUS ruled in favor of same-sex marriages. Nationwide.

In doing so, the SCOTUS violates the following important characteristics of constitutional law:

1. It bestows "rights" upon a certain class of people in violation of the fundamental principle of the Declaration of Independence and the Constitution that, under the American system of law, all rights are bestowed by our Creator and it is the duty of the government to protect those rights., to wit:

> We hold these truths to be self-evident, that all men are created equal, *that they are endowed by their Creator with certain unalienable Rights*, that among these are Life, Liberty and the pursuit of Happiness.—that to secure these rights Governments are instituted among Men, deriving their just powers from the consent of the governed. (The *Declaration,* par 2.) (emphasis added)

Under the American system of law, neither the Congress nor the President nor the courts possess the authority to bestow legitimate rights upon any person or any group of persons. This is a unique system of law, far superior to any other. (I am speaking about the *uncorrupted* American system of law.) By this presumption to bestow rights, **these five justices must consider**

themselves to be gods, on an equal or higher status than our Creator who, according to the organic documents of our nation ...and our law, is the only one who can bestow legitimate rights upon us. Thus, these five justices arrogated to themselves a power not authorized by the Constitution.

2. It violates the distribution of powers between the federal government and the states in that it imposes its own laws upon the states and local governments.
3. It applies the corrupted version of the Fourteenth Amendment, "interpreting" it to mean something entirely different than its framers intended. This constitutes amending the Constitution, which the SCOTUS has absolutely no authority to do.
4. It forced its will upon all states and counties, thereby violating the Ninth and Tenth Amendments of the Constitution and nullifying the right of the people to control their own government.
5. The above violations of the Constitution constitute a serious threat to the free exercise of religion, especially Christianity. It violates the custom that is as old as man's recorded history regarding marriage consists of the union of one man and one woman. Or, in the case of ancient Biblical times, of one man and one or more women. In all of recorded civilized history, there never has been the approval of one man marrying another man nor of one woman marrying another woman.
6. It contravenes the Christian doctrine that is as old as the Bible itself regarding sodomy. Thus, *Obergefell* legalizes, institutionalizes and glorifies a practice that has been, for centuries, considered to be unclean, unsanitary, a health risk, immoral and sinful. *Obergefell* is an insult to Christian doctrine and to the highest moral values of the American people.
7. The above violations, applying the anti-constitutional practice of "social justice," advance the agendas of the Marxists, Secular Humanists and Irreligionists.
8. *Obergefell* denigrates and suppresses religion. The Christian religion, that is. It denies the American people the right to control their local governments. A HUGE matter.
9. *Obergefell* threatens all religions with the idea that they do not have the right to control their own doctrine nor to control who they employ nor to what ceremonies, practices and ordinances they can approve or disapprove. Make no mistake. Obergefell is a step toward oppressing, persecuting and, ultimately, attempting to destroy the Christian religion.
10. In *Obergefell,* the SCOTUS, in addition to the above-mentioned violations of the
Constitution, employed at least the following stratagems: "social justice", "constitutionalizing" "incorporation doctrine" and its corrupted version of the Fourteenth Amendment and the violation of the Ninth and Tenth Amendments.

The use of each and every one of these stratagems constitutes violations of the Constitution.

The SCOTUS Violated the Law in Order to Persecute Christians and Christianity

The SCOTUS might claim that they were merely "enforcing the law," and that the consequences of the "Separation…" cases and *Obergefell* are merely the "unintended consequences" of enforcing the law. Such a claim would be spurious. Completely spurious. The SCOTUS is not enforcing the law. It is corrupting the law and then enforcing this corrupted law. It is corrupting the law in order to produce the *obviously intended* consequences which could have been and should have been foreseen from the beginning. These *intended* consequences were obviously intended and planned. We can only presume that the SCOTUS fully intended that *Obergefell* would produce the consequences that it produced. Therefore, these consequences were not only anticipated but desired and planned for by the five members of the SCOTUS who voted in the majority.

In *Obergefell*, the SCOTUS used the following stratagems as excuses to themselves for violating the Constitution:

1. Social justice,
2. Evolutionary law,
3. "constitutionalizing" and
4. the "incorporation doctrine"

These justices took oaths to uphold and defend the Constitution of the United States. Yet their ruling constitutes many **gross violations thereof**. They betrayed their oaths of office and every citizen of the United States and every person who will be a citizen in the future. They made of themselves "domestic enemies of the Constitution." I do not recall any traitor in our history who has done as much damage to America as have these five justices.

Here is an Excerpt from the Majority Opinion in *Obergefell:*[117]

(Voting in the majority were Justices Anthony M. Kennedy, Ruth Bader Ginsburg, Stephen G. Breyer, Sonia Sotomayor and Elena Kagan) (Note: Breyer and Ginsburg are members of the CFR.)

---

117. The "Incorporation Doctrine" sounds so, well, "legal." But closely examined, it is but another stratagem employed by the SCOTUS to trick the American people into believing that the SCOTUS possesses the authority to, de facto, amend the Constitution; to change the meaning of the Constitution. Furthermore, it presumes the authority to amend the Constitutions of all fifty states! The SCOTUS possesses no such authority. "Incorporation Doctrine" is a scam.

These considerations lead to the conclusion that the right to marry is a fundamental right inherent in the liberty of the person and under the Due Process and Equal Protection Clauses of the Fourteenth Amendment couples of the same-sex may not be deprived of that right and that liberty. The Court now holds that same-sex couples may exercise the fundamental right to marry. No longer may this liberty be denied to them. *Baker v. Nelson* must be and now is overruled and the State laws challenged by Petitioners in these cases are now held invalid to the extent they exclude same-sex couples from civil marriage on the same terms and conditions as opposite-sex couples.*Obergefell v. Hodges*, 135 S. Ct. 2584, 2604-05, 192 L. Ed. 2d 609 (2015)

> A Judgment based on "social justice," which is Marxist in nature, produces an entirely different ruling than one based on the Constitution.

Note: The *Fourteenth* does not, nor was it ever intended to, give the SCOTUS the authority to rule on marriage cases as in *Obergefell*. By their own imagination, fabrication and usurpation, the SCOTUS has made of the Fourteenth a deep and mysterious well of undefined and unlimited powers out of which they can draw at any time they wish the terms "due process" and "equal protection of the law" to mean anything- absolutely ANYTHING that they wish it to. Using this illicit and arrogated power, the SCOTUS has morphed into a rogue oligarchy, ignoring the Constitution and the rule of law, ruling by "social justice" and illegally forcing more and more secular Humanism and Marxism into the American culture, laws of the United States and of the fifty states. Judging by its rulings, this oligarchy of five rogue justices is anti-American and anti-Christian. With the elimination of any mention of God or Christianity in the classroom, a vacuum occurs.

No vacuum remains for long. So when God and Christianity are removed, what moves in to replace them? Why, a religion called "Secular Humanism." So this "separation..." does not result in only the absence of religion from the classrooms of America; the result is the removal of anything Christian and the insertion in its place the religion of Irreligion, or Secular Humanism. So, Qui bono? (Who benefits?) Why, the Humanists and Irreligionists do. This is something very important to understand today as we strive to protect our Constitution from total destruction. The decisions of all of these cases regarding the suppression of Christian principles are structured upon "social justice" instead of the Constitution. The driving force behind "social justice" are the Humanists. At least, "social justice" is in congruity with Humanism and it is obvious that the Humanists benefit from rulings such as *Obergefell*. The five justices who voted in the majority in *Obergefell* have made of themselves "domestic enemies of the Constitution" and thus, being the majority, made of the SCOTUS a "domestic enemy of the Constitution," of

America and of Christianity. If this sounds shocking to you, just think about it for a while and you will realize that it is true.

Note: Observe the SCOTUS attitude toward marriage and human sexual behavior, such as homosexuality. It is completely contrary to that given to man by his Creator. Conversely, it is completely in harmony with the Secular Humanist belief that there is no supernatural; no God and therefore no rules for life and living from God to man. This *Obergefell* ruling is anti-constitutional and pro-Secular Humanist, as proven by the Fifth Point of *Humanist Manifesto I*:

> **FIFTH** [Point]: Humanism asserts that the nature of the universe depicted by modern science makes unacceptable any supernatural or cosmic guarantees of human values. Obviously Humanism does not deny...

Anything supernatural is rejected by the Humanists. Anything, such as the Ten Commandments or anything Biblical as a standard for human behavior. So no Ten Commandments...no Constitution built on the Ten Commandments. This explains very clearly the connection between the ideology of Humanism and the SCOTUS ruling on *Obergefell* and the rulings on "Separation of Church and State."

How *Obergefell* threatens Religious Liberty, America and Civilization

1. By overriding our state laws, *Obergefell* destroys our ability to control the laws affecting our religious liberties through our state legislatures.
2. Puts our religious liberties in jeopardy by being subject to rulings of judges in Washington, D.C. who might be Secular Humanists and/or Marxists.
3. Assaults, in its attempt to change, the definition of marriage.
4. Denigrates the traditional and long-standing Christian meaning and purpose of marriage.
5. Legitimizes and glorifies sodomy, in contradiction of centuries-old Christian values. It outlaws Christian values and criminalizes Christian practices regarding denying marriage to same-sex couples.
6. Forces county clerks and others, including ministers and clergy, to perform marriages of gays or lesbians when the religious values of same might be contrary to gay and lesbian marriages. Has absolutely no concern for the rights of these people.
7. Threatens to force the Church of Jesus Christ of Latter-day Saints and probably others, to perform marriages in their temples and other edifices considered sacred, to perform marriages of gays and lesbians, when such marriages would be in strong conflict with the policies and values of these churches, their governing bodies and their members.
8. Puts all laws, state and federal, subject to a gang of five or more rogue lawyers who have contempt for the Constitutions of both the United States

and of all of the fifty states and for the laws of all fifty states.

9. Puts all laws, state and federal, including those affecting our religious freedoms, subject to the whims of five or more lawyers who, in defying the Constitution of the United States, exercise illicit powers whose limits know no bounds. Furthermore, unknown to the public, these judges might either be Secular Humanist or Marxists or might be sympathetic to the Secular Humanists and Marxists, whose ideologies are hostile to Christianity. These judges might be disposed to ignore the Constitution and to rule according to their own ideologies, which would put Christianity and all Christians in jeopardy.

10. Threatens churches that operate universities or schools to provide rental quarters to married students, whose standards or honor code might exclude LGBT couples.

11. Defies the nature and origin of rights for all Americans. Our rights, (all of them, not just a fraction) under the American system of law, come from our Creator. Our Creator not only has never approved or condoned same-sex marriage or relationship, He has condemned such. (Leviticus 18:22, Deut. 23:17, Rom 1:27. For more see Bible, Topical Guide.)

12. By creating "rights" (in reality special privileges) for the LGBT crowd that had never before existed, the SCOTUS perverted the role of government. Under the American form of government, our rights are bestowed upon us by our Creator. The proper role for the government is to protect those rights. In *Ogerbefell,* the SCOTUS played the role of the Creator of these rights. Thus, the LGBT people will naturally perceive the SCOTUS, not our real God, as being their "god." Thus, the LGBT people are added to the millions who draw federal welfare according to "rights" to this welfare bestowed by the Congress or the SCOTUS. Thus, the Congress or the SCOTUS becomes their "god." Thus, a huge portion of the population considers as their "god" the President, the Congress or the SCOTUS. In crisis times (and crises can be natural or manufactured) these mobs (or armies) can be dangerously explosive and destructive. These people are not loyal to Americanism. Nor to the one true God. They are loyal to the false "gods" of the government.

The above might seem abstract. But I tell you that it is very real. These people do not appreciate the working, taxpaying people who make their welfare payments possible. They despise us. Explosive situation. Dangerous situation.

> **Alma 10:27 And now behold, I say unto you, that the foundation of the destruction of this people is beginning to be laid by the unrighteousness of your lawyers and your judges.**

Searching for a Motive-Qui Bono?

In examining *Obergefell,* it is obvious that the SCOTUS broke the law more times than did Bonnie and Clyde. But why? what was their motive for breaking the law? There must have been a motive! In the investigation of every crime, the detective first asks himself, "Qui Bono?" Which means, "Who benefits"?

In the cases of *Everson* and *Obergefell*, those who benefitted were the Secular Humanists, Marxists and Globalists. And these benefits came at the expense to the Christians, to Christianity and to the integrity of our constitutional government.

To emphasize the threat to Christianity, it is not only the SCOTUS. The federal judicial system at all levels has been packed with judges who are dedicated to Langdell's "case law" method of judging and who favor Secular Humanism and Marxism and who hold the Constitution and Christianity in contempt.

In clear and honest evaluations of the cases involving "Separation of..." and *Obergefell*, it is obvious that both violated the Constitution. It is also obvious that the "unintended consequences" of both severely restrict Christians and harm Christianity It is also obvious that the main text of these two case is hostile to Christianity.

None of the cases involving "Separation of..." and *Obergefell* serve any legitimate purpose since: "Separation of Church and State does not exist in the Constitution. It is not part of constitutional law. The SCOTUS does not have the authority to "constitutionalize" anything and 2. The SCOTUS does not have the authority to create "rights" for any special group of people. Therefore, the SCOTUSes involved violated the Constitution in multiple ways and for the sole purposes of persecuting Christians and Christianity and in violating and therefore weakening the Constitution of the United States.

Very similar, if not identical, **to the trial of Jesus**.

Gramsci's Soldiers are Marching Right Along

The secular humanists, following Gramsci's plan perfectly, have now captured the public education system, the U. S. Supreme Court (intermittently) and have altered much of America's law. Coincidentally, they have made HUGE changes in America's cultural hegemony. Gramsci must be very happy. So are the Secret Combinations.

Now let's examine the type of government that Gramsci's soldiers, the "ruling elite" and the secret combinations of the Devil are planning for our future: Marxism.

Should You Happen to be a Law Student, the Governor of your State, an Average Honest American citizen or the President of the United States

If you happen to be a law student enrolled in Con Law 101 and you are frantically trying to reconcile some of the law cases that you are being taught as being "constitutional" with the Constitution itself, you might as well stop trying. It cannot be done. They are irreconcilable. Incompatible. Unfixable. Incongruous. Dissonant. Diametrically opposed. Don't drive yourself crazy. Accept reality. Much of what is taught in law schools as being "constitutional" is, in reality, unconstitutional. The SCOTUS lies. Ask your law professor to prove that the use of "case law" is, truly, constitutional. Also ask your professor to prove that the use of "social justice," "constitutionalizing," and the incorporation doctrine" are constitutional. You might wish to explain to him the definitions of "constitutional" and "unconstitutional" from *Black's Law Dictionary:*

> **Constitutional:**[118]Consistent with the Constitution; authorized by the Constitution; not conflicting with any provision of the Constitution or fundamental law of the state. And
>
> **Unconstitutional:**[119]That which is contrary to the Constitution. The opposite of "constitutional."

I shall make no attempt to explain the flaws in these stratagems for two reasons:

1: The SCOTUSes have enshrouded some most of them in the mists of obfuscation and,

2: Judge Robert H. Bork can explain them much better than can I. I just ask you to compare the Constitution itself to *Everson* and to *Obergefell* and see if you can honestly come up with the same verdicts as did those justices.

Now, here is Judge Bork, a judge who was denied a seat on the U. S. Supreme Court for the sole reason that he was so intelligent, so competent and so committed to the Constitution that a senate of corrupt, inept and treasonous politicians would not confirm him:[120]

---

118. "Social justice" distribution of wealth, opportunities and privileges within a society. "individuality
gives way to the struggle for social justice" That is, we are judged as units of a mass rather than as individuals.
119. Bork, Robert H., The Tempting of America, Touchstone, New York, 1990, pp 137,8.
120. There is no fundamental right for same-sex couples to marry found in the Constitution, including the Fourteenth Amendment. Under constitutional law, all rights are bestowed upon us by our Creator. Our Creator has never stated the right of same-sex couples to marry. Judges do not possess the authority to bestow such rights. This is a clear-cut case of the use of the stratagem called "constitutionalizing,"
the act of declaring something to be "constitutional" that was not theretofore "constitutional." This constitutes amending the Constitution. The SCOTUS claims such authority, but certainly does not possess it.

...The adoption of the due process clause in the fourteenth amendment soon provided, as we have seen, a temptation to judicial constitution-making the Justices could not resist. Soon they were using the concept of substantive due process, invented in *Dred Scott* for use against the federal government, to strike down state laws in no way related to race on grounds reflecting nothing but the personal views of the Justices...The Court ultimately did incorporate most of the Bill of Rights,...but...the Court also continued to make up new rights under the fourteenth amendment...

.....The controversy over the legitimacy of incorporation continues to this day, ...Nevertheless, the application to the states of the Bill of Rights enormously expanded the Court's power. That meant making its interpretations of the various amendments the uniform law throughout the nation, which had never occurred before. This process, though it started much earlier, was completed during the years of the Warren Court and created the occasions for some of its most controversial rulings...

.....What Bickel said of the Warren Court may be said of all courts in our history that cut through procedure to substance and through substance to political outcome. They engage in civil disobedience, a disobedience arguably more dangerous, because more insidious and hence more damaging to democratic institutions, than the civil disobedience of the streets...

.....There are heavy costs for the legal system, heavy costs for our liberty to govern ourselves, when the court decides it is the instrument of the general will and the keeper of the national conscience. **Then there is no law; there are only the moral imperatives and self-righteousness of the hour.** (emphasis added)

Thank you immensely, Judge Bork.

Regarding the SCOTUS's misinterpretation of the first amendment, the Court has adopted and maintained a most strict secularist view of the establishment clause. This confirms that their motive was and is to oppress Christianity and Christians.

Robert Bork is a judge whom I respect enormously, both for ability and for integrity. If you will read the above very carefully, you will find much to explain the reasons for the SCOTUSes misinterpreting the law in order to reach the conclusions that they did. I highly recommend to you his book *The Tempting of America.* It is right on, yet written in a manner that we lay people can understand.

If you are the governor of your state and you and your attorney general and your minions of bureaucrats are trying to understand how you can enforce BOTH the Constitution of your state and some rulings of the SCOTUS such as *Everson* and *Obergefell,* just realize that it cannot be done. You must choose. I suggest that you honor your oath of office and enforce the legitimate Constitution of your state and resist the illegitimate rulings of the SCOTUS.

If you are a parent and are trying to teach your children to understand the Constitution and some of the rulings of the SCOTUS or laws of the federal government, just realize that the Constitution is right and that anything in conflict with it is wrong.

If you are President Donald J. Trump and you are wondering how to honor your oath of office and also to enforce the rulings of *Everson* and *Obergefell*, STOP WONDERING. You DO NOT have to send out the federal marshalls to enforce these anti-constitutional rulings. Honor your oath of office and announce to the American people the reason that you re not enforcing these anti-constitutional rulings of the SCOTUSes.

Synopsis of Chapter:

It is safe to predict that all the laws that will be used to persecute Christians in the future will be "positive laws" or "relativism", coupled with stratagems like "constitutionalizing", "incorporation doctrine", "Fourteenth Amendment", "social justice" and whatever other stratagems the SCOTUS might come up with. . Consequently, we should understand them.

These violations of the Constitution were done with malicious intent. They could not have been done otherwise. They were crafted to serve a specific purpose. The justices certainly were not so stupid as to have not been conscious of what they were doing. Such would have been impossible.

There are only two reasons to corrupt the law: 1. To be able to merge the U.S. into a world government or 2 to persecute the innocent. Why else corrupt the law? Why else turn the SCOTUS into an oligarchy?

Whenever the innocent are persecuted, it is because of corrupted laws and corrupted government officials. Whenever the guilty are not prosecuted, it is for the very same reason.

> *Obergefell* did more than just legalize same-sex marriages. MUCH more. It:
> 1. Legitimatized and glorified a practice that had been, since the beginning of time, condemned by God.: Sodomy.
> 2. Robbed the American people of their right to govern themselves in this very crucial matter which, according to the Ninth and Tenth Amendments, is reserved to the states and to the people.
> 3. Seriously jeopardizes the ability of all Christian churches to conduct their own affairs. Puts them financially at risk.
> 4. Further weakened our constitutional form of government by violating certain very important provisions. This moves the United States further into position to be merged into a Marxist one-world government.
> 5. Moves the United States further away from being a Christian nation and closer to being a Secular Humanist one. Of rejecting God and Christian principles.
> 6. Stigmatizes Christianity as being against something that is now institutionalized and dignified even though it is still immoral in the eyes of God.

Chapter Thirteen - That Awful Crime of Discriminating

The Freedom to Choose; to Make Choices, is the Very Foundation of Liberty
Punishing the Right to Choose is the Essence of Tyranny

This is Definitely Germane to the Subject of Religious Liberty

BOY SCOUTS OF AMERICA

Lest you wonder about why include discriminating in this book, here is why. Those who file charges of "discrimination" are invariably leftists and many times LGBT. And they are invariably against Christian pro-American people. The purposes of the "anti-discrimination" laws are two-fold: 1. They serve to take money from "conservative" Americans and put it into the pockets of the Leftists and to take from straight Americans and put it into the pockets of the LGBT and, 2. They serve to legalize and dignify practices such as sodomy, same-sex marriages, etc. Some of the charges made are "discrimination" are absolutely ridiculous. Like the couple that refused to bake a wedding cake for the lesbian couple and were fined $135,000.00. And the fact that the lesbians would file a suit over such a frivolous matter indicates a very high degree of intolerance. In fact, intolerance to the point of being bigotry. Yes, bigotry. Check the definition. They are mean-spirited.

An examination of "anti-discrimination" laws and commissions reveals that they are structured to favor the political Left and the anti-Christians. A close look at how the Boy Scouts of America is being destroyed reveals some interesting insights.

The Boy Scouts of America Destroyed by "Anti-discrimination" Laws.
The saga of the Boy Scouts is truly tragic. For over an hundred years, the Boy Scouts of America has been a force for good. The BSA motto has been:

> On my honor, I will do my best
> To do my duty to God and my country and to obey the Scout Law;
> To help other people at all times;
> To keep myself physically strong, mentally awake and morally straight.
> A Scout is trustworthy, loyal, helpful, friendly, courteous, kind, obedient, cheerful, thrifty, brave, clean and reverent.

Millions of American boys have had their ideals and their behavior elevated by their participation in the Scouts. America certainly is a better place because of the Boy Scouts.

After reaffirming its membership policy in February 2012, the Boy Scouts of America came under immense pressure from media, corporate donors and many local Council Scout executives to revise its policy regarding memberships for the LGBT. To maintain its unusually high standards of morality, the BSA naturally had to exclude homosexuals from its membership. The 100 + year membership standard that open or avowed homosexuals did not "possess the moral, educational and emotional qualities deemed necessary for leadership." (Charter and Bylaws of BSA, Article VIII, section 1).

This standard of non-admittance of homosexuals with other teen-age boys is perfectly reasonable and understandable. By definition, homosexuals are males who engage in sodomy with other males. The mainstream media has hounded us with the disinformation that homosexuals are "normal" and no different from other males. This is, tragically, completely false. Just consider that "gay" men are constantly looking for other male partners for companionship and sex. Some of these "gays" are very aggressive. They might even be classified as "predatory."

The very definition of "homosexual male" is that he is going to be seeking sexual activity with other males. Now, put these "gays" in with some young teenaged Scouts in overnight and week-long campouts and what is NATURALLY going to happen? The older homosexual males will be preying upon the

> Let us first address what it means "to discriminate." To discriminate means to choose. To make a choice. Freedom to choose, to make choices without being punished by the government, is the very foundation of liberty and justice.
>
> Let us understand, very clearly, that the Left and the LGBT are opposed to straight Americans being able to make legitimate choices without being punished.

younger males. That is as predictable as the sun coming up every morning.

Not only is this tragic, it is grossly unjust. The BSA is being faced with thousands of lawsuits, but the BSA is not the perpetrator in this case. The BSA is, along with the young boys, the VICTIM! The perpetrators in these cases are the "gay" Scouts. Yet they are not being sued nor prosecuted! Nor even condemned! Speaking legally and morally, it would be hard to find a more unjust situation. Furthermore, this did not develop by accident. The political strategists among the political Left and the Deep State without doubt recognized years ago a perfect situation for them to exploit. So, naturally, being the exploiters that they are, they proceeded to exploit! Now, they are reaping huge benefits, cultural, political and financial, by the disintegration of this once great organization.

Under <u>uncorrupted</u> constitutional law, the Scouts would have had the right to choose to whom they wished to extend membership and to whom they did not wish to. That's called "freedom to choose." If the BSA had been able to exercise this basic American right, they could have greatly minimized or possibly eliminated this whole gigantic problem.

And, it all happened because of the "anti-discrimination" laws and attitudes. Court cases and the media using "discrimination" as a means to judge by some standards other than traditional American and constitutional standards and values.

It is almost as if the destruction of the Boy Scouts of America was planned. By the Deep Left, is my guess.

Sweetcakes by Melissa in Gresham, Oregon Aaron and Melissa Klein operated a bakeshop, "Sweetcakes by Melissa," in Gresham, Oregon. One day in 2012, to women entered the bakeshop to buy a wedding cake. When they informed the owner that it was for a wedding of two lesbian women, the owner declined to fill the order, explaining that it was contrary to his religion.

The two women, Laurel and Rachel Bowman-Cryer, filed a complain with the Oregon Bureau of Labor and Industries. Commissioner Brad Avakian leveled a penalty of $135,000.00 against the Kleins. A Hundred and Thirty Five Thousand Dollars for merely saying no to baking a cake. Under constitutional law, the Kleins had every right to say no to the order for the cake. Rights. Freedoms.

That is what America and constitutional law is all about. The case went to the SCOTUS, which issued a writ of certiorari to retry the case. The $135,000.00 is in escrow (as of 06 October, 2020) awaiting final disposition. In this case, hooray to the SCOTUS! It has been said around Oregon that Avakian has a son who is gay. Must we suspect that there was some bias in Avakian's judgment against the Klein's of $135,000.00? This demonstrates the danger of allowing certain people to wield such power over others. More will be said shortly about commissions compared with courts shortly.

Masterpiece Cakeshop Harassed by Colorado Civil Rights Commission
Another case of an innocent person, a Christian, being persecuted because of the anti-discrimination laws is that of Jack Phillips, who operates the Masterpiece cake shop in Lakewood, Colorado. In July of 2012, two gay men, Charlie Craig and David Mullins, entered the Cakeshop to order a wedding cake for their forthcoming wedding. Mr. Phillips declined to take the order, explaining that it was against his religious principles. Jack explained that the couple was welcome to buy anything else in the store. Another bakery sold the desired cake to the couple. One one naturally think, "well, that solves that problem." But not so. Not by a long shot. Under the state's public

accommodations law, the Colorado Anti-Discrimination Act, Craig and Mullins filed a complaint against Masterpiece and Jack Phillips with the Colorado Civil Rights Commission.

Courts vs. Commissions that Pretend to be Courts

At this point, we need to address the issue of commissions that pretend to be courts. How are they different from state courts? Why do they exist, considering that a court system already exists in all state governments? They are special courts, so they must serve a special purpose. Here are two things to consider: 1. Under a commission rules, the accused does not have the protection of the Constitution of his state. For example, he does not have the right to a jury of his peers. And, 2. The people who seek the position of "judge" in these commissions are very likely to be ideologically disposed to favor those who are plaintiffs before the court. That is, the "judge" looks upon the defendants with disfavor. We must presume that his judgments will be affected by his ideological bent. Phillips eventually took his case to the U. S. Supreme Court and won, (In this case, hooray for the SCOTUS0 with the provision that he must make certain changes and retrain his employees. He was forced to stop baking cakes for weddings, which was 40% of his business. So he suffered considerable financial damage.
To read the entire U.S. Supreme Court case, pull up the following:
https://www.supremecourt.gov/opinions/17pdf/16-111_j4el.pdf

A must read to understand the judicial/executive moves made in the case:

https://www.lexisnexis.com/community/casebrief/p/casebrief-masterpiece-cakeshop-ltd-v-colo-civil-rights-comm-note, the commission passed the case to an administrative law judge (judge under the executive) to make the final decision.

It is interesting to note that Craig and Mullins were represented by the American Civil Liberties Union, which is quite often found on the side opposing the Constitution and liberty.[121]

Phillips was represented by Alliance Defending Freedom The ADF assists Christians who are being wrongfully persecuted by the law.

We cannot over-emphasize the fact that it is the right of any American to say "no" to a request for products or services. There is no place in constitutional law to penalize an American for refusing to enter into a contract that someone else wants to force on him. Nor can we over-emphasize the danger of commissions and bureaucracies that exercise legislative and/or judicial powers. **Extremely dangerous**. Bureaucracies and commissions **are created**

---

121. This entire paragraph is based not upon constitutional law but upon "social justice." Judging by "social justice" ignores and therefore nullifies the Constitution

specifically for the purpose of denying defendants their rights that they would have in a regular court of law in the judicial branch. One way to corrupt the law is to make it illegal for a person to exercise his legal rights.

Where is the Part About Discriminating Found in the Constitution?

Many lawyers must be scratching their heads about what the "law" means today compared to when they went to law school. Here might be part of the answer. *Somebody* in the legal scheme of things is changing the law without bothering to wait for statutes or a constitutional amendment to make the change. They just resort to a "quick and easy" change method. Slightly illegal. It seems that the political Left will stop at nothing to try to win their objectives. This one really is an all-time low. These perps of this bad deed are all lawyers and judges, who are all supposed to be the most honorable (that includes honest) professions in the country. Corrupting the law to punish Americans for doing nothing more than exercising their right to make a choice. That is what the majority, if not all, of these laws against discriminating are all about.

Another "Crime" Invented by the Lawyers and Judges: To Make a Choice; to Choose

Some years ago the act of discretion; of discriminating; of making a choice, was, by statute or by court ruling, criminalized. What is the definition of "discriminate?" Why, it means to make a choice. To choose. To make it a crime to discriminate is to make it a crime for an American citizen exercising his right to choose. Just that simple. With making it a crime to discriminate, the courts have put the basic American right to choose in the same category with murder and stealing, i.e., a crime. Let's apply a little American common sense to these court rulings.

Let us also be aware that the Left is taking advantage of our good nature. We do not want to harm anyone and if "discriminating" would harm anyone, we would refrain from doing so. So we are intimidated from exercising our legitimate rights to choose. To make choices. To be free Americans. Then, when it is a law, its force becomes more than mere intimidation. It is a very insidious way **to change the culture**; to make changes in the government.

These "anti-discriminating" laws very definitely impact the thinking of the people. It also very definitely makes changes in the hegemony. Gramsci must be very pleased. "Anti-discriminatory" laws go along perfectly with his plan to "March through the institutions." By making "discriminating" a crime, the legislatures and/or the courts can steadily but unrelentingly take away most of the rights of every American. By the use of "social issues" that are nowhere to be found in the Constitution, the courts can turn this country into a Marxist dictatorship. They are doing it. And they would do this while expanding the "rights" of the LGBT, Marxists and Secular Humanists. Where would that take us?

Making it A Crime To Exercise the Right to Choose

The fundamental purpose of the Constitution is to protect every American's right to choose; to discriminate! The fundamental responsibility of judges is to judge by the Constitution and protect these rights. By using "social justice" as the means by which to judge, judges are turning the law upside down.

Let's examine the damage being done by making it against the law to exercise the right to choose. They call this "criminal" act, "discrimination." In a Marxist dictatorship, the people's right, by law, to discriminate is very limited. That is chiefly the difference between a free government and a dictatorship. Let's see how some of these laws against discriminating affect us and our society:

Scenario A: Pete, Joe, Sam and Two Hamburger Stands: The American Way

Suppose that you, Pete, operate a hamburger stand. I come into your hamburger stand and order a cheeseburger, with fries and chocolate-banana milkshake. (My favorite) You refuse to serve me. You do not need a reason. That is your right as an American, (which would be protected by the Constitution, if it were enforced.) So I say, "Very well, Pete. Have a good day. I wish you well." I then go two blocks down the street to Sam's hamburger stand. Sam says, "Hi Joe. Come in. What'll it be?" I order a cheeseburger, fries and a chocolate-banana milkshake. He serves me the order. I pay him and he says "Come back again soon, Joe." The result? Pete is happy because he did not have to serve me a cheeseburger. Sam is happy because he sold one more cheeseburger. I am happy because Sam makes better cheeseburgers than you, Pete, do anyhow. The walk two blocks down the street did not hurt me a bit.. Besides, I needed the exercise. Everyone is happy. That is the American way. Now let's examine the results from the anti-American , Marxist way.

Scenario B: Now Pete, Joe, Sam and the LGBT:"Social Justice"; the Marxist Way

I come into your (you are still Pete) hamburger stand and order a cheeseburger. You refuse to serve me. I sue you for committing that horrible offense of discriminating. You committed that awful crime of making a choice. The judge, who is ideologically disposed to ignore the Constitution and to seek "social justice" through some "law" that might never have been passed by the legislature, rules in my favor. You have committed the awful offense of having made a choice. I choose to take offense; to pretend that I have been psychologically damaged. The judge orders you to pay to me $135,000.00 in damages for mental anguish and all sorts of imagined sufferings. That is a great injustice. But that is not all. This penalty is not limited to you. The results of this court ruling affects every person who operates a hamburger stand within the jurisdiction of this court. The law has been changed. A new law has been created. Thousands of people have lost the right to exercise their natural right to say, "no". Whether this law originated in a court or a legislature or in the U.S. Supreme Court, the result is the same. If the court happens to be the SCOTUS, it affects every American. Thus, liberty and justice are extinguished under the guise of correcting a wrong that does not exist.

I consider that the judge in this case as well as myself, if I were to file such a lawsuit, to be mean-spirited. To penalize people just because they exercise their right to refuse to provide you a service is mean-spirited. We must consider the possibility that the judge in this case is ideologically disposed to favor the plaintiffs. He cares not about justice. He is using the law to beat people into submission to his idea of what the culture should be. "Social justice."

Just consider the difference between scenario A and that of B. In B, all I would have had to do would be to go down the street a couple of blocks to Sam's Place. Would that have been such a terrible imposition upon me? None whatsoever. That's the reason that we must believe that the LGBT (lesbians, gays, bi-sexual and transgender) crowd to be mean-spirited.

It does appear that many, if not most, of the people who file this kind of a lawsuit do so not in the interest of justice but just to be mean. The corrupt law rewards them for being mean. It seems that the worldview of people filing lawsuits against others for "discriminating" is Marxist. These people hate people, especially Christians, with an Americanist worldview. They seem to hate those who own and operate businesses.

Just consider the difference in two entire societies, one that operates on the spirit displayed in Example A and the other on the spirit displayed in Example B. What a difference! It seems that some college professors, instead of educating their students, are sensitizing them so that they are spring-loaded to want to accuse somebody of being racist, homophobes or of that awful crime of discriminating against somebody just because they exercised their rights to say "no." This leads to much contention and a diminution of harmony, camaraderie, efficiency and production.

A Proposed Law to Criminalize the Right of Religions to Choose Who They Hire

In 2009, HR 3017 was introduced in the U.S. House of Representatives and a similar bill, HR 3017 in 2015. These bills were designed **to make it a federal criminal offense for Christian organizations to "discriminate" in their hiring practices; of choosing to hire people whose <u>views would be</u>**

compatible with the hiring organization, therefore refusing to hire people with hostile views! A Christian church would be forced to hire Secular Humanists, Communists, members of the ACLU or anyone else who would, obviously, be disruptive and destructive to that church. These bills did not pass, but similar ones will be back. If such a bill were to pass, the Christian-haters would be lined up a block long at Christian churches to get hired so that they could **infiltrate, agitate and disrupt** that organization's operations. It would probably deal the death blow to all Christian churches. No doubt, that is exactly what the sponsors of HR 3017 were hoping to accomplish. These are mean-spirited and evil people.

The fact that such a bill was even introduced in the U.S. House is very threatening. Please give this careful study. This "discrimination" tactic that is being used against us is very deceptive and it plays on the sympathy and desire to be tolerant of many good people. However, the result is that it deprives us of our just liberties and, in increments, serves to diminish our constitutional government and empower the Marxist government.

These anti-discriminatory laws are definitely not created or enforced in the spirit of the Constitution. They amount to the use of government to force people into contracts into which they do not wish to be a party. The right to choose to enter into a contract or to refuse to enter into a contract is basic and fundamental to liberty, justice and freedom. It is also necessary for religion to be able to exist. Most anti-discriminatory laws strike right at the heart of the Constitution, of American justice and, all too often, of the Christian religion.

Tolerance and Bigotry

This matter of "tolerance" is wonderful, if used correctly. Often, we are asked to be tolerant of the LGBT. That's ok with me. But then they sometimes take advantage of our tolerance, like asking our support for certain legislation that gives them certain "rights" but denies certain legitimate rights for others and accusing us of being "intolerant" if we do not concede to their legislation. Also, the lesbian couple in Oregon who sued a bakery couple for refusing to bake a cake for them. This is intolerance in the worst degree. Such is rightfully called "bigotry." It is mean-spirited. That's right. Intolerance to a certain degree becomes bigotry and it is not impossible for bigotry to be legalized and institutionalized. We must be careful to not offend others, but also be careful to not let them take advantage of us by pretending to be offended or that their "rights" are going to be violated if we do not yield to their demands.

The Difference Between a Free Country and a Dictatorship

In a free country, the people have a right to choose; to make choices. In a dictatorship, the people are penalized for making choices that are counter to the demands of the dictator. The dictator makes rulings regarding everything in the private lives of the people. That is the main difference between a free country and a dictatorship. With a sufficient numbers of laws penalizing "discrimination," a free country can be turned into a dictatorship.

To put it another way, in a free country the officers of government are elected by the people and accountable to them. The powers that they exercise are defined and limited. In a dictatorship, the powers of the government are undefined and unlimited. The officers of government are not accountable to the people. The people have no recourse against offensive acts of government.

In a **free country transitioning to a dictatorship**, one can judge pending legislation by this manner:

1. Does it increase or decrease the arbitrary power of the government over the people and

2. Does it increase or diminish the control that the people have over the government; the accountability of government officers to the people.

The Danger of Making It a Legal Offense to Make a Choice; To Discriminate

We have seen where the bakery couple were fined (or penalized-if it were a civil case) for doing nothing more offensive than saying "no" to a demand to bake a cake.[122] We must carry this practice of making it a legal or civil offense to make a choice to its logical conclusion. Unless we make some changes, this practice can result in a tragic social and legal condition. Similar to Communism or Naziism.

The SCOTUS, in *Obergefell,* has already made it against the law to discriminate against the LGBT by refusing to perform marriage ceremonies for them. What other mischief can the SCOTUS create by using this anti-discrimination concept? It can destroy Christianity and America. And here is how.

1. It could make it against the law for a church to "discriminate" against adulterers by teaching that such is a violation of the word of God and for excommunicating or disfellowshipping its members found guilty of such practice.
2. It could make it against the law for a church to "discriminate" against sodomites by teaching that the practice of sodomy is in violation of the teachings of God.
3. The same can apply to teaching against fornication, thievery, lying and every other sin. It would require some imagination, but the SCOTUS

---

122. This is a crafty stratagem. They are not excluded from one of civilization's oldest institutions. They are just as free to marry a person of the opposite sex. This oldest institution has never included the marriage of two of the same-sex.

seems to be long on that. Considering the fact that the Oregon bakery couple was forced to pay $135,000.00 in "emotional damages" for refusing to bake a cake, think what a church could be penalized for teaching that adultery is a sin and having a thousand adulterous members file a lawsuit against it for teaching that adultery is a sin, thereby "discriminating" against adulterers.

Please stop for a minute and give the above very serious thought and see where this practice of criminalizing the right to make a choice is taking us. Look into the future. Look at the potential for damage. This use of criminalizing the right to make a choice can completely destroy our liberties, beginning with religious liberties.

> The right to choose, liberty, is the foundation of all civilizations. Criminalizing the right to choose; to make a choice, is the foundation of all tyrannies.

It is necessary to note that adultery, fornication, sodomy and all sort of sexual promiscuity is perfectly approved and encouraged by the religion of Secular Humanism. Please refer back to Chapter Three and the excerpts from the Humanist Manifestos.

If a court can order a couple operating a small bakery to pay $135,000.00 for refusing to bake a cake for a lesbian couple, that the lesbians suffered "irreparable emotional damages" Consider how vulnerable to lawsuits a church would be for teaching that sinners will go to hell for lying, stealing and adultery if they do not repent.

This is How You Can Determine If I Am Right

In writing this book, I know that I am tackling some extremely sensitive subjects. If I am wrong, I will be leading people astray, which is a grievous sin. So I am extremely careful. The reason that I know that I am right is that everything that I am writing is in harmony (as close as I am able to make it) with what the Lord has told us through his prophets. I cannot think of anything found herein that is contrary thereto. (If you find something, please inform me immediately by email.) If you will put everything in this book to the test of concentrated study and serious prayer, I believe that you will come to the same conclusion.

Anti—Discriminatory Law=Rule by a Tyranny of the Minority

By the use of anti-discriminatory and similar laws, the courts have found a way to circumvent the Constitution and the will of the majority and rule in favor of a small tyrannical minority including, usually, the LGBT, the Secular Humanists and the Marxists. This means, of course, that it is detrimental to Christians and Christianity. Anti-Discriminatory laws are definitely not neutral toward justice, the Constitution and Christianity. In fact, anti-discriminatory laws discriminate against all those being forced to give up their freedom to comply with them.

We have seen clearly how legitimate freedoms can be taken away under the guise of "protecting the rights of minorities" by the use of "anti-discrimination laws." Is there any limit to the number or amounts of our legitimate rights that can be taken away by more and more-and more and more-laws against "discrimination"? This is a very dangerous weapon employed by the Marxist and Humanists.

Protecting the LGBT with Anti-Discriminatory Laws Promotes Sodomy

How many politicians advocating anti-discriminatory laws to "protect the rights" of the LGBT have described the sexual habits of the LGBT? Yet, such laws not only protect "rights" that do not exist, they protect the practice of sodomy, previously criminalized and give the LGBT special privileges in the courts. In providing the practice of sodomy the protection of the law, the government in effect dignifies and glorifies this practice and also homosexuality. This is, of course, contrary to Christian teachings.

By denying us the right to choose, Gramsci's soldiers are making a powerfully negative impact upon our cultural hegemony.

Justice Samuel A. Alito on Discrimination[123]

> One more example, consider what a member of the Colorado Human Rights Commission said to Jack Phillips, the owner of the now notorious Masterpiece Cake Shop, when he refused to create a cake celebrating a same-sex wedding. She said that freedom of religion had been used, quote, to justify all kinds of discrimination throughout history, whether it be slavery, whether it be the Holocaust, we can list hundreds of situations where freedom of religion has been used to justify discrimination, you can easily see the point. **For many today, religious liberty is not a cherished freedom. It's often just an excuse for bigotry and it can't be tolerated, even when there is no evidence that anybody has been harmed**. (Emphasis in original)

That is how the Left misinterprets the word "discrimination" and uses it to their advantage. They put the label of "bigotry" on it, then corrupt the law to make this "bigotry" against the law. Choosing the principles of Christianity on which to attach their labels of "bigotry," they proceed to use the media, the

---

123. Not true. An outright lie. They ask for special privileges, the creation of special "rights" that do not exist under the Constitution.

public education system and the courts to attack and persecute Christians and Christianity.

The Conclusion

The Danger of Anti-Discriminatory Laws and Court Rulings

In cases involving "discrimination," activist Leftist judges accomplish by stratagem that which they could never accomplish by proper interpretation of the Constitution. By pretense, they pretend to be protecting the "rights" of a certain group of people. But in reality, they bestow upon this group special privileges, which they (erroneously) call "rights." These special privileges, or illegitimate "rights" give advantages to this group which automatically results in disadvantages, whether by design or by "unforseen consequences," to the rest of the citizens and encroaches upon their legitimate rights . Such action:

1. Denies to the citizens the right to make legitimate choices in certain matters. The government has no such authority to deny to citizens the right to make legitimate choices and
2. Forces citizens into contractual arrangements in which they do not wish to become involved.

No authority is found in the Constitution for such action. The Founders recognized that the right to make contracts by private citizens is essential to liberty. Article I, Sec. 10 says: "No State shall enter into any Treaty, Alliance…ex post facto Law, <u>or Law impairing the Obligation of Contracts,</u>…" Just consider. The right to make or to not make contracts, unimpaired by the powers of government, is essential to a free society. (Emphasis added)

Small wonder that the word "discrimination" is nowhere to be found in the Constitution. Nor is its origin rooted in the Constitution. Its usage in today's courts is in complete violation of the true intent of the Constitution. It is unconstitutional. It is illegal. It it is not law. It is another stratagem. And it is dangerous. It allows the courts to do illegitimately what the Constitution does not allow them to do legitimately.

The right to make choices is **the essence** of freedom. Each case involving "discrimination," punishing citizens for making choices, diminishes our legitimate freedoms. The continued use of this manufactured, corrupted law is a severe threat to our freedoms and, especially, to our religious freedoms. In the interest of justice and freedom, this stratagem of "discrimination" should be discontinued.

We should always remember that "to discriminate" means "to choose." The ability to choose is the essence of freedom. In every case (as far as I have been able to determine) where a law has been enacted to outlaw some kind of perceived discrimination, a certain group of people have been granted some special privileges, called "rights" while the rest of the people have been denied a portion of their legitimate natural rights.

In other words, **all anti-discriminatory laws serve to punish Americans if they exercise some particular natural right**. With enough anti-discriminatory laws, we could be in a quasi-dictatorship. These anti-discriminatory laws seem to me to be anti-constitutional. Whether they are or not, they certainly **aid the Marxists and the irreligionists.** I would imagine that Gramsci's soldiers spend a lot of time working for "anti-discriminatory" laws.

How the Left uses Corrupt Law Against Christians

The Left knows that, according to the Bible,[124] sodomy is a serious sin. So, they start a campaign in the media and in public education to glorify and generate sympathy for gay men. Then, they enact laws or hand down court rulings penalizing anyone who discriminates against sodomy or gay men. In this manner, they use the law to attack a sacred Christian principle.

Next, the Left knows that the concept of woman lying with or marrying a woman or two men doing the same is an abomination in the sight of God. So the Left starts a campaign with their influence in the media and the public education system to glorify same-sex marriages. Then, in *Obergefell,* the SCOTUS legalizes and legitimatizes same-sex marriages. Nationwide! One more example of using corrupted law to strike at an established principle of Christianity. See how it's done?

So, attacking one Christian principle after another, SCOTUS has attacked Christianity itself and all Christians. There is no indication that the SCOTUS plans to discontinue this practice (except for the confirmations of the three new justices). The danger is that they will continue until every principle of Christianity is attacked and made "illegal."

The Left is very adept at corrupting the law then using this corrupted law against Americanism and against Christian principles. In fact, the use of corrupted law is one of the primary weapons that the soldiers of Gramsci use in their march through the institutions of America.

---

124. For more of the majority opinion, see Appendix A

Chapter Fourteen - The SCOTUS-Greatest Threat to Christianity and to America

> For we wrestle...against powers, against the rulers of the darkness of this world, against spiritual wickedness in high places (Eph 6:12)

> **Everything is too important ever to be entrusted to professional experts, because every organization of such professionals and every established social organization becomes a vested-interest institution more concerned with its efforts to maintain itself or advance its own interests than to achieve the purpose that society expects it to achieve.125**

> **For it is a truth, which the experience of all ages has attested, that the people are commonly most in danger when the means of injuring their rights are in the possession of those of whom they entertain the least suspicion. (Alexander Hamilton, The Federalist, No. 25.)**

Could it Possibly Be?

For those who refuse to believe that courts, or their judges, can become corrupted or can become threats to religion, please consider the following. In 2020, the governor of Nevada, Steve Sisilak, issued rulings regarding the Covid-19 "pandemic." His rulings were much more restrictive on houses of religious worship than they were with casinos. The issue was taken to court. The governor and the casinos, won. The houses of religious worship lost. Consider now the comments of Justice Samuel A. Alito[126] on this matter:

> ...a very tough call. take a quick look at the Constitution. **You will see the Free Exercise Clause of the first amendment which protects religious liberty, you will not find a craps clause or a blackjack clause or a slot machine clause**. Nevada was unable to provide any plausible justification for treating casinos more favorably than houses of worship. But the court nevertheless deferred to the governor's judgment, which just

---

125. Black's Law Dictionary

so happened to favor the state's biggest industry and the many voters it employs.

The judgment of the court regarding the Nevada case was obviously not based upon the law. What was it? Money? Power? What else?

Could it possibly be that the SCOTUS is the greatest threat to Christianity and to America that exists? Those who have not seriously studied this situation and its implications will surely perceive this allegation as being preposterous. I am being very careful to not accuse wrongfully. My allegation comes as a result of my great love for the Constitution, for those wonderful men and women who fought the Revolution, those who caused for this great Constitution to come into existence, all of those service men and women who have sacrificed and died for the cause of liberty and every other person who has done so as well.

Our perilous situation today comes from excess tolerance. We have been all too tolerant of greed, dishonesty, violations of the rule of law and, especially, of domestic enemies of the Constitution. We have been far too tolerant of those who are members of secret combinations that plot the destruction of our Constitution and the submergence of America into a Communist-like world government. We have been far too tolerant of rioters, looters and thieves. We have been far too tolerant of those in positions of trust whose duty it is to maintain law and order but who fail to do so. In view of the above, I consider my allegations to be well studied and to be fair and just.

For These Reasons, the Supreme Court Became so Corrupted

Many languages are spoken within the Beltway. But the ones that effect the most moving and shaking are, no doubt, known by the acronym MIP. Money, Influence and Power. By tracing the flow of money, influence and power, one can usually evaluate a court ruling and determine who benefited and who lost regarding the MIP. Now, consider the difficulty of changing the laws of the United States regarding a certain issue. First, let us consider the effort required to change the law regarding a matter of local (not federal) nature. To do so legitimately, we would have to influence the majority of the state representatives, senators and governors of all fifty states and a considerable number of voters in those states. This, obviously, would require a huge amount of effort and money. Now, let us consider another way of accomplishing the same objective. The illegitimate but very easy and cheap way. That would be to get the approval of five out of nine of the justices of the SCOTUS. What HUGE difference ! Now we see that the SCOTUS presents a HUGE temptation to those with nefarious schemes who want to alter the government of the entire nation to suit their own agenda. And without having to change the mind of one voter or one congressman or one president or one governor or one state legislator. In this culture war, (war between the Constitution vs Marxism, morality vs immorality, good vs evil, civilized vs uncivilized and Christ vs. Satan) one such victory for our enemies has a great effect. And all this might be done contrary to the wishes or even the knowledge of the majority of the American people.

Consider, also, that those who would seek to alter the laws of our country to suit their agenda by this easy but illegal method, would naturally be the most evil and dishonest people in our nation. Thus, the use of this method to change our laws tends to allow the most evil people in our nation to gain power over us. Total power. Opportunities for easy political advantage attract corrupt people.

Yes, with enough MIP, anything can be done. We would be naive indeed to think that this avenue to political results has not been used and often.

We have not recognized this corruption because we have become accustomed to it. We have come to perceive it as, "…that's the way that things are."

In Fact, if We Do Not Get This problem Solved, None of the Others Will Matter.

Please consider the hundreds of millions who have suffered and died because of corrupt politicians and corrupt governments. Nazi Germany, Communist Russia, Communist China and many others. We must not treat this matter of corrupt government here in America frivolously.

In the balance hangs not only the future of America but of the world, of civilization and of Christianity. Please give this your serious consideration, shape your opinions and take action accordingly.

Jefferson Warns of Overly-Ambitious SCOTUSes:

In a letter to William Jarvis, Jefferson expressed the following concern:[127]

> You seem … to consider the judges as the ultimate arbiters of all constitutional questions; a very dangerous doctrine indeed and one which would place us under the despotism of an oligarchy. Our judges are as honest as other men and not more so. They have, with others, the same passions for party, for power and the privilege of their corps…. And their power [is] the more dangerous as they are in office for life and not responsible, as the other functionaries are, to the elective control. The Constitution has elected no such single tribunal. [128]

---

126. op cit

The allegation that the SCOTUS constitutes the greatest threat to Christianity, to America and to civilization that exists certainly must seem shocking to some. The SCOTUS justices are always presented to the public in their long black robes, so sophisticated and somber. As if constituting integrity beyond reproach. But we have seen in *Everson* and in *Obergefell* that some justices judge by a different measure than the Constitution. By doing so, they are crafting judgments to suppress any mention of God, the Ten commandments and the Jewish or Christian religions and have, de facto, made Secular Humanism the official religion of the United States and are converting our government to an atheistic, Marxist dictatorship.

Advice From the First Presidency:

> "Communism [Marxism] is **not a political party nor a political plan** under the Constitution; **it is a system of government** that is the **opposite** of our Constitutional government. ...
> ..."Since Communism, [Marxism} established, would destroy our American Constitutional government, **to support Communism** [Marxism} **is treasonable** to our free institutions and **no patriotic American citizen** may become either a Communist [Marxist} or supporter of Communism [Marxism]."(*Deseret News,* 03 July, 1936.)

***Everson*-the Greatest and Most Malicious Hoax Ever Perpetrated on Mankind?**

Just consider the scope and magnitude of evil perpetrated in just the *Everson* case alone. The very mention of God, the Ten Commandments or the foundation of our nation was outlawed from every public school and all public discourse in America. Furthermore, the SCOTUS violated the Constitution in many different ways in order to accomplish it. The teachers forbidden to teach their students about the flaws in the theory of evolution. The teachers forbidden to teach their students about how Christianity played such an important part in the founding of our nation! Now, that is evil! And on a grandiose scale!

In just these two cases, we have seen the SCOTUS violate the law repeatedly in order to achieve their objectives. These two cases both serve to: 1. change the structure and purpose of the government of the United States to more easily be merged into a world Marxist government and 2. to denigrate, demean, persecute and prosecute Christians, Christianity and Christian churches. We need not rely upon my opinion alone. The opinions of the dissenters of *Obergefell*, very capable justices, make very plain the extent of the malfeasance of the justices who voted for this case. I agree with those justices who dissented. So, they must agree with me. I must consider that the men and women who violated their oaths of office and violated the law in order to achieve objectives # 1 and 2, above, are, by my standards, betrayers of the people they are supposed to be serving and enemies of Christ, of America and of civilization. Hard words? They are supported by the evidence.

Could it Be—the SCOTUS is Guilty of Blaspheme?

First, let us consider the definition of "blaspheme":

Legal Definition of blasphemy. : the crime of insulting or showing contempt or lack of reverence for God or a religion and its doctrines and writings and especially God as perceived by Christianity and Christian doctrines and writings.(Merriam-Webster).

What the SCOTUS did in Everson in order to outlaw God, the Ten Commandments, the origin of man and even the discussion of these actions involved violating the Constitution several times. This shows a tremendous contempt for God, His words and for anyone who believes in Him and His words. To me, that is the epitome of blaspheme.

The Destruction of the Rule of Law: "Positive law", Case Law, "Incorporation Doctrine", "To Constitutionalize", "Separation of Church and State", Corrupted First Amendment, Corrupted Fourteenth Amendment and "Social justice".

Please study, very seriously, the effects of the above eight malevolent and specious stratagems employed by the SCOTUSes as excuses to violate the Constitution. With these in practice, what meaning is left for the Constitution? They leave it without force or effect. Without meaning. We are all too often ruled over by a lawless gang of five or more rogue lawyers. They ignore the law. They scoff at the rule of law. They sneer at the rights of the American citizens and the Constitution that was designed to protect them. They are without conscience. They hold in contempt the Ten Commandments. They perceive their powers as unlimited and unrestrained. They have their own agenda. This agenda is to continue to shape the laws so that Christians and Christianity are suppressed and oppressed and the structure and purpose of the government is modified so as to fit into a world government. This leaves us at the mercy of an oligarchy of five (or more) malevolent, rogue lawyers.

That is my indictment against all rogue lawyers, law school professors and judges from Christopher Columbus Langdell through today. However PLEASE NOTE that I have the utmost respect for those lawyers, law school professors and judges who honor, judge by and uphold the Constitution (as originally intended by its Framers.)

Yes, when the SCOTUS is comprised of five or more justices who vote as did the majority in the *Everson*[129] case (1947) or in *Obergefell*[130] (2015) regarding

---

127. Bork, Robert H., The Tempting of America, Simon and Schuster, New York, pp 130-132

the corrupted version of "separation of church and state" the SCOTUS is guilty as charged. That is, they voted to ignore and to violate the Constitution and to vote according to their own wills. Both the *Everson* and the *Obergefell* courts belong in the category of "rogue courts" because they violated the Constitution. They shaped their ruling to conform to and to accommodate the ideology of the Secular Humanists and the Globalists, which is the opposite of the Constitution. They voted to violate the Ninth and Tenth Amendments, thereby illegally forcing their anti-constitutional law upon all fifty states. It matters not what laws the states might enact or that the Congress of the United States might enact that would protect our rights. Rogue courts such as the *Everson and Obergefell* courts exercise the power (illegal though it might be) to strike them down. Such courts pay no attention to the law, to the will nor to the natural rights of the people. They are just like the judges who tried Jesus. They have their agenda and they know the verdict before the trial begins. Such courts can direct the power of the government to force Christianity right out of existence. Furthermore, it appears that they have the will to do so.

Now let me issue another caveat regarding the title of this chapter. That is, that the SCOTUS *CAN* BE the greatest threat to Christianity and to America that exists. It WAS in 1947 in the *Everson* case and in 2015 in *Obergefell*. Since then, three new justices, Gorsuch, Kavanaugh and Barrett. have been confirmed who we hope will shift the balance of power back to the Constitutional side. But if the balance should ever shift back to the other side, then the SCOTUS would then again become the greatest threat to Christianity and to America that exists. We cannot be oblivious to this danger. Here is why and how the SCOTUS can constitute such a threat.

Now that the SCOTUS is more favorable (or less hostile) to the Constitution, it still has not undone the anti-constitutional rulings by previous SCOTUSes. The damage they did continues to plague us.

Under this set of circumstances, the Supreme Court of the United States is the most (or one of the most) dangerous threats to Christianity, to civilization and to America that exists on the face of the earth.

---

128. The 1943 "Report of the California Senate Fact-Finding Subcommittee on Un-American Activities" stated: "The American Civil Liberties Union may be definitely classed as a Communist front or 'transmission belt' organization. At least 90% of its efforts are expended on behalf of Communists who come into conflict with the law. While it professes to stand for free speech, a free press and free assembly, it is quite obvious that its main function is to protect Communists in their activities of force and violence
in their program to overthrow the government."
129. An interesting note: The OR Labor Commissioner, Democrat Brad Avakian, was the one who waged a one-man jihad against Aron and Melissia Klein, the bakery couple and ordered them to pay the lesbian couple $135,000 in damages for "emotional damages." Avakian ran for OR Secretary of State in 2016 and was soundly defeated. In an election where the state went 11% for the Democrat candidate for president, Avakian was soundly defeated by 4.4%. Sweet victory.
130. In an address to the Federalist Society, 12 Nov, 2020

The evil stratagems serve to nullify the Constitution, thereby removing practically all, if not all, restraints on the powers of the SCOTUS. Starting in 1947, the SCOTUS has arrogated to itself an increasing amount of powers until now there is practically no limitation on its powers. This is an extremely dangerous situation.

This is being written the 5th of October, 2020. Ginsburg is now gone. That is definitely an improvement, from the Constitutionalist point of view. Justice Barrett has been nominated. It will remain to be seen how she will vote.

Some justices, such as the five who voted for *Everson* in 1947 and the five who voted for *Obergefell,* in 2015 seem to recognize no limitations to their powers. They have no respect for the Ninth and Tenth Amendments. They certainly do not consider that the Constitution serves as a limitation on their powers. And if the Constitution does not limit their powers, then nothing does. Now, consider that the ideology of these justices is (or seems to be) Humanist and Marxist and that they issue their rulings in disregard of the Constitution and in congruity with Humanism and Marxism and they thereby change not only the federal law and government but they override and change the laws and governments of every state as well. Very soon they could have the entire government of the United States changed to be a Marxist, Humanist government which would be completely hostile to liberty and to Christianity. **This constitutes a problem to us of such magnitude that, if we do not get it fixed, none of the other problems threatening us will matter.**

Here is why the SCOTUS (when comprised of five or more rogue judges) is such a threat:

1. When the Constitution was ratified and this nation was founded, the government created was one of limited and specified powers. Only those powers given to the federal government by the people through the Constitution.
2. Since dictatorships are structured so that the dictator has the power to control, tax or confiscate the property of all citizens, the Framers of the Constitution structured our government to minimize this threat. They did this by dividing the state governments from the federal government and leaving the governing of all or most of the property of the citizens under state control. Then, they added more protection by adding the Ninth and Tenth Amendments to the Bill of Rights.
3. The SCOTUS ignores the Constitution and rules by some other agenda. When analyzing its ruling, it can be readily seen that the ruling was made in conformity with Marxist and Humanist principles, which are exactly the opposite of the Constitution. The Ninth and Tenth state:

The Ninth Amendment

> The enumeration in the Constitution, of certain rights, shall not be construed to deny or disparage others retained by the people.

The Tenth Amendment

> The powers not delegated to the United States by the Constitution, nor prohibited by it to the States, are reserved to the States respectively, or to the people.

The Ninth and Tenth Amendments are clear and unambiguous. Furthermore, they are not just "somewhat important" to the integrity and futurity of this Republic. They are absolutely and unequivocally essential! The Ninth and Tenth are as necessary to the futurity of this Republic as wings are to an airplane. Without the division of powers between the federal government and the states, this ship of state just will not fly! Yet, the Congresses, the Presidents and the SCOTUSes have violated the Ninth and Tenth to the point that, at present, our Republic is breathing its last gasps of breath. Please see Map "B" and the explanation that goes with it in Chapter Nine. We are in the last stages of a Communist/Marxist/Globalist revolution and takeover. Note the riots in June of 2020. Riots are the sure signs of the breakdown of law and order. This signals the decay of the present government in anticipation of a takeover or coup of a different force. You probably will not believe this, because the public school system and the media teach us that Marxist programs are "constitutional". So you are not alarmed. To understand this situation, one must commit himself to considerable study and thought.

The SCOTUS Corrupts the Law Then Uses this Corrupted Law Against Us

The evidence is overwhelming that the SCOTUS has deliberately corrupted the law in (but not limited to) *Everson* and *Obergefell*. These corrupted cases serve to: 1. Modify the structure and purpose of the government of the United States so that it can be merged into world government. This plan for world government is part of the agenda of the very politically powerful Council on Foreign Relations (CFR). It must be noted that two of the justices who sat on *Obergefell,* Breyer and Ginsburg, are or were members of the CFR and, 2. Hinder, persecute and prosecute Christianity, Christians and Christian religious denominations.

Consider "Social Justice"

The use of "social justice" instead of the Constitution might have appeal to some. After all, we were all taught in school and college that the Constitution is so-well-so *antiquated.* But just consider-"Whose idea of "social justice?" It just might be anybody's. After all-we are never advised of this in the opinion of the majority. It is a deep, dark secret. Social justice usually proves to be, under close analysis, "justice" according to Karl Marx.

Ignorance or Malicious Intent?

It is obvious that the results of *Everson* and *Obergefell* are perfectly designed to harm Christianity and to change the structure and purpose of the government of the United States. The only question remaining to be resolved is: "Was this done by bumbling incompetence or by malicious intent"? If it is by accident, then the justices who caused it must be very ignorant. As for me, I cannot believe that they are that ignorant. I must believe that the results are exactly what the justices who voted "aye" on them planned for the results to be. I do not accuse them of ignorance nor incompetence. Therefore, the only option remaining is malicious intent on the part of the justices. Do we really want to be ruled over by just anybody's opinions? Just between you and me, I very much prefer the Constitution.

9. Let it be known to all people that, in the absence of evidence to disprove the allegations **above, that the SCOTUS constitutes the most diabolical threat to the Constitution of the United States, to America, to the American people, to Christianity and to civilization that exists on the earth.**

Any Question?

If there is any question in your mind about whether the Supreme Court is or could be the greatest enemy to Christianity and to America that exists, please study carefully the excerpts from both the majority and from the dissents, from *Obergefell*[131] found herein. Note that the arguments from the majority are not based on the law-from the Constitution. They are based on sociological factors (social justice) and emotions.

Here are excerpts from *Obergefell*. Please read the opinions of both the majority and of the dissents very carefully. Therein is an excellent study in constitutional law. In this case are found many threats to Christian freedoms.**(You may pull up the entire case by using the following link:**
https://www.supremecourt.gov/opinions/14pdf/14-556_3204.pdf
Similarities Between *Everson* and *Obergefell*: How *Both* Courts Violated the Constitution

There are some distinct similarities between *Everson* and *Obergefell* in how they both used the same stratagems to violate the Constitution. Obviously, both courts had their agendas and their conclusions in mind before the court convened. Very interesting study in corrupted law *and* in human nature.

---

131. See Bible, Topical Guide, "Homosexuality." Lev 18:22(20:13) Deut 23:17, Isa 3:9. More

As you read through this case, try to catch instances where the following stratagems are employed: "Evolutionary law," "Social Justice," "Incorporation doctrine," 14th Amendment and "Constitutionalizing."

Please note particularly the majority ignore the Constitution and base nearly their entire case on "social justice." Try to detect how the SCOTUS corrupted the law and visualize how this corrupted law can be used against us Christians. After the case, a few examples will be presented of how this case presents a huge threat to Christian freedoms.

How Should American Citizens Judge Judges who Violate the Constitution?

Judging judges rightfully might be the greatest test for us who have been commanded to judge rightfully, for to judge wrongfully is a great sin. For in the case of judges, we are judging men and women who are held by society to command the utmost respect. For us to judge judges rightfully, we must not only be exceptionally honest, we must be exceptionally well informed and correctly informed on the law. That is, if we are going to judge the Lord's way. Which is the only correct way. To judge too harshly or too leniently is to judge wrongfully, as explained in Moroni 7:14:

> Wherefore, take heed, my beloved brethren, that ye do not judge that which is evil to be of God, or that which is good to be of the Devil.

Let's start out by judging those judges who judge by the ONLY way that is the American way to judge-and that is, they very simply judge by the Constitution of the United States. These judges serve to keep America what it should be-the land of the free and the home of the brave. We can consider all such judges as our heroes. We should let them know that we respect them and we honor them.

Now we have some housecleaning to do in order to save America and to save Christianity. If we were to judge all judges equally, it would be the supreme insult to the good and honest judges. So we dare not do that. Therefore, let us judge honestly. Judges who violate the Constitution do thereby violate their oaths of office, which is a most serious breach of trust. When they pronounce an anti-constitutional act to be constitutional, (or vice-versa) they are pronouncing a lie, a lie to be enforced by the sword. Furthermore, they are making of themselves domestic enemies of the Constitution.

When I was sworn in to the United States Air Force as a second lieutenant in 1953, I took a solemn oath to uphold and defend the Constitution of the United States against all enemies, foreign and domestic. I had to learn what a domestic enemy of the Constitution was. It is the very worst kind of enemy.

An enemy from within. One pretending to be a friend but who is in reality an enemy.

Domestic Enemies of the Constitution

Foreign enemies are readily recognizable. They attack us with guns, ships, tanks and planes. They wear the uniforms of their nation. They make no pretense. Their hostility is readily apparent. It is deadly.

Yet domestic enemies of the Constitution can be even more deadly than foreign enemies, since their hostility is concealed. They feign loyalty to the country in which they live. Yet they have broken with its founding principles. In America, they disbelieve, yes, even hold in contempt and scorn the principles upon which this nation was founded. They disdain the Biblical, moral and ethical principles which serve as the foundation of the organic documents of this nation, i.e., the Declaration of Independence and the Constitution of the United States. They might feign allegiance to the Constitution. They might even swear an oath to uphold and defend it. They might hold high office. They might even wear the solemn robes of the Supreme Court of the United States. Yet they condemn, attack and violate the Constitution and the principles embodied therein.

Many such enemies belong to powerful organizations, recognized by many as secret combinations of the Devil, whose objective is to weaken, violate and render impotent the Constitution of the United States.

They might own or control the instruments of the media-TV, radio, newspapers, etc. In such, they glorify politicians and others who support legislation and programs that violate the Constitution and support the Deep State and efforts to merge the United States into a world government. On the other hand, they report with disdain anything that is congruent with the Constitution. They demean, vilify and attack any public figure or citizen who supports and defends the Constitution and all efforts to expose and oppose those who would weaken, violate or destroy the Constitution.

Domestic enemies of the Constitution range from the high and the mighty down to the most common citizen. They might go to church, go to parades, salute the flag and swear allegiance to it. Yet they support ideas, ideologies, legislation and programs that are hostile to the principles of the Constitution.

To save this constitutional republic of America, let us recognize the domestic enemy of the Constitution for what he really is. Whether by malice, greed or by ignorance, he is dangerous to the security, peace and economic stability of this great nation. He must be recognized for what he is, exposed and opposed.

The domestic enemy of the Constitution constitutes The Enemy Within.

(Joe H. Ferguson May, 2020)

A judge who judges to violate the Constitution acts to transmogrify the government of the United States from a constitutional republic into a Marxist dictatorship. He/she judges to transmogrify the government from one that protects the religious freedoms of the citizens to one that assaults and infringes upon those freedoms.

Therefore, judges who violate the Constitution do not deserve respect and honor. They deserve to be recognized for what they are: rogue justices, domestic enemies of the Constitution, enemies of mankind, enemies of liberty, enemies of civilization, enemies of justice and enemies of God. They deserve to be exposed for what they really are and to be removed from office.

Conversely, those justices on the SCOTUS who support and defend the Constitution and its principles deserve our highest praise. Let us make it known far and wide, loud and clear, that these justices are loyal friends to liberty and justice, friends to liberty-loving Americans and friends to America. They deserve our greatest admiration and support.

Conclusion

This threat is of such magnitude that if we do not get it fixed, none of the other threats to Christianity, to America and to civilization will matter.

SECTION THREE

Chapter Fifteen - Warnings of Ancient Prophets Regarding Our Day

Vision From 600 B.C. until Today

The purpose of this chapter is to emphasize:

1: The ancient prophets had a perfect vision of our day and our problems and
2: Their evaluations of our problems and our times were right on the money and
3: These prophecies were given to us to help us to avoid being deceived by our adversaries.

Reading words of the prophets in the Book of Mormon and the Bible is like looking through a window into the future.

Many years ago, I thought that I believed the Book of Mormon prophets. But when I look back, I realize that I had several of those "except for" gaps in my faith. I now have had 55 years to seriously study the social and political situation in America. Now, let's take those prophetic warnings of two thousand years ago and see how they square up with the cultural and political conditions of today. Let's start with Helaman 6:

> 38 And it came to pass on the other hand, that the Nephites did build them [the Robbers of Gadianton] up and support them, beginning at the more wicked part of them, until they had overspread all the land of the Nephites and had seduced the more part of the righteous until they had come down to believe in their works and partake of their spoils and to join with them in their secret murders and combinations.

Wow! Today, the Marxists have taken over the Congress and dominate nearly all levels of government. And the Marxist (liberal, progressive, Globalist, etc.) ideology dominates education. Most Americans have come to believe in evolution, Humanism and Marxism without realizing it. They have been, shall we say, "seduced," as Helaman said of the Nephites many years ago? And let us not forget-this was the *more part of the righteous*. This causes us to pause for some serious self-evaluation. Each of us can ask ourselves, "Have I been seduced to believe in the works of the evil forces? I consider myself to be a righteous person and I live in a community of righteous people. But our media and our government is saturated with Marxism and its attending philosophies. Have I managed to escape this deluge or have I been seduced? Now let us proceed on to the next two verses:

> 39 And thus they [Gadianton Robbers] did obtain the sole management of the government, insomuch that they did trample under their feet and smite

and rend and turn their backs upon the poor and the meek and the humble followers of God.

The Marxists do dominate the Congress, the executive branch (excepting the President) and the SCOTUS, as we have seen by examining the *Everson* and the *Obergefell* cases. And in both these cases, the SCOTUS does turn its back upon the humble followers of God.

How could Helaman have said it any more accurately? Remember, he was writing not only a history of his times but a message specifically to us who live in these times. And now, for a sobering thought:

> 40 And thus we see that they were in an awful state and ripening for an everlasting destruction.

Are we in an awful state and ripening for destruction? I will not venture a guess. But I know for a fact that there are several Globalist groups who are organized, powerful and well-financed who are determined to destroy the Constitution and merge the U. S. into a Marxist-like world government. If this happens, it would be like unto us being conquered by an alien, hostile foe.

Now let us proceed to Helaman Chapter 7:

> 4 And seeing the people in a state of such awful wickedness and those Gadianton robbers filling the judgment-seats-having usurped the power and authority of the land; laying aside the commandments of God and not in the least aright before him; doing no justice unto the children of men;

It is as if Helaman were describing our times above instead of his. We do have some people in a state of awful wickedness. We definitely do have judges filling the judgment-sets who have usurped the power and authority of the land and have laid aside the commandments of God, since they have violated the Constitution which was founded on the Ten Commandments and the laws of nature and of nature's God. Then, they have supplanted the Constitution with their own ideologies, which are based on Secular Humanism and Marxism, which are the philosophies of the Anti-Christ. That is wickedness. Furthermore, We, the People, have tolerated them doing it. That is also wickedness.

> 5. Condemning the righteous because of their righteousness; letting the guilty go unpunished because of their money; and moreover to be held in office at the head of government, to rule and do according to their wills, that they might get gain and glory of the world and, moreover, that they might the more easily commit adultery and steal and kill and do according to their own wills—
> 6 Now this great iniquity had come upon the Nephites, in the space of not many years; and when Nephi saw it, his heart was swollen with sorrow within his breast;...

One way that the federal government condemns the righteous because of their righteousness is to enforce the provisions of the *Everson* case. Then, "Letting the guilty and the wicked go unpunished…" We have certainly seen plenty of cases at the very top levels of government where the guilty and the wicked have gone unpunished. Now, how about the rioting in the streets of America that have gone unpunished for months? (This is being written in October of 2020). Is not the burning of buildings, the destruction of property and the killing of people not to be considered wicked? And what about the mayors of the cities where rioting continues who have given orders to the chiefs of police to stand down and to allow the rioters to go unpunished? Is that not wickedness?

For the past 90 years there has been an unprecedented attack and smear campaign against the Constitution and against anyone who would stand up to defend it.

We Christians have a fault and that is, we are too timid. We especially **do not wish to offend anyone**. So when the Left pretends to be offended by the words of Jesus Christ, we tend to back off and shut up. We do not wish to offend. But one of the favorite tactics used by the political Left is to feign or pretend to be offended when no offense was intended. So if the enemies of Christ are going to choose to be offended, let them go ahead and be offended! The proper defense against that Left-wing tactic is simple. Just let them be offended!

We should not ignore the warning from the Lord in Doctrine and Covenants 60:

> 2 But with some I am not well pleased, for they will not open their mouths, but they hide the talent which I have given unto them, because of the fear of man. Wo unto such, for mine anger is kindled against them.

This brings us to *Current Events:* to rioting in the streets of American cities. This matter is even more serious than one might suppose. There is evidence to support the idea that some of these rioters are not local. They are bused in. And that they are paid. It also appears that the mayors of the rioting cities are acting in unison. Are they being ordered to order their Chiefs of Police to stand down? This certainly does encourage the rioting and the rioters. This strongly suggests that whoever giving the orders to the mayors and to the rioters has an agenda and this agenda is definitely contrary to the best interests of the United States. What this suggests to me is that we are in the last stages of a revolution. A Communist revolution. Call it Marxist or call it Globalist or whatever kind of revolution that you wish. Its intent is to negate the Constitution and install a Marxist-style dictatorship.

These people who comprise the rioters are not just temporary rioters. They constitute a standing army, living off of government dole between riots. They have never prepared themselves to have a marketable skill. Many of them do not want a job. Too much like work. They stand ready in an instant to riot, burn, loot and steal. They hold a Humanist-Marxist worldview so they naturally hate working, responsible people. Like those who own businesses, homes and things like that. Because of their Humanist-Marxist worldview, they hate all Christians and property owners. Furthermore, the public school system is cranking out thousands more just like them every year. These people and those in the Deep State in the federal government, constitute a rogue force that could pull a coup and take complete control of the federal government and many state governments. More on this in Chapter 17.

These rioters described above are criminals. They are also uncivilized.

We never had to worry about our country becoming uncivilized until 2008. Now, it is a very serious matter. It threatens our entire system of government. Without law and order, without the rule of law, we cannot operate and prosper as a nation,. These permanently unemployed people have plenty of time to be organized by community organizers to do all sorts of things that disrupt our society and commerce.

This brings us to our present situation and the Communist rioting all over America.

Chapter Sixteen - The 2020 Election and the Blocking of Justice

> "Use This Sword Against my Enemies, if I Give Righteous Commands;
> But if I Give Unrighteous Commands, Use it Against Me."
> Roman Emperor Trajan

The Future is Here

It is now May of 2021. The election of 2020 is behind us, but not the *unanticipated consequences* thereof.

A large segment of the population is under the understanding that the election was "very problematic" at best. Many have been providing evidence that this "problem" is **not even a new occurrence**. But, that Donald Trump's massive popularity broke the machines made to keep the Globalists in power in 2016 and again in 2020.

People like Mike Lindell are actually presenting proof of the "problem" through several documentaries. And in each documentary, there is a sense of GRATITUDE TO GOD, for allowing this evidence to be collected and presented to the people. For **without** the breaking of the machines, **nobody would have known**. It would have been the proverbial…"Oh well, better luck next time. See you in 2 or 4 years."

Not this time. The fight is "ON." So be it.

This chapter is not about the much debated and censored 2020 election. It is about the Supreme Court's complete evil negligence in stonewalling the lawsuits that ensued afterward.

There were 100s of suits brought by regular people, businesses and U.S. States because of this 2020 election. All brought between November 2020 and January 2021. There were many more even after that. But, this period of time is when most of the damage was done.

Very little evidence, to **ZERO evidence** was ever presented to any court at any level during this time. The court system would not touch the subject.

There was scant evidence entered into any level of Federal court record **even after** January 2021.

The Supremes Do the Dirty Work of the Globalists to Change Society

So how did this happen?

The Globalists working in synergy put a stop to any evidence being able to be entered into Federal Court record, by simply blocking the attempts at the suits of regular people and businesses. The judges would simply throw them out. It didn't matter the reason.

But, what about a State suing another State?

Now THIS is more interesting.

In the U.S. Constitution it states:

> (U.S. Constitution: Article III, Section 2, Clause 1)
> "The Judicial Power shall extend to all Cases, in Law and Equity, arising under this Constitution,… to Controversies to which **the United States shall be a Party**;—to Controversies **between two or more States**; between **a State and Citizens of another State**; between **Citizens of different States**,"

The Federal court system has jurisdiction to decide these types of cases:
1. Controversies to which **the United States shall be a Party** – Many of the suits did contain the United States itself as a party.
2. Controversies **between two or more States** – States were suing other States that did not perform their elections up to their own legal code.
3. Controversies between **a State and Citizens of another State** – Citizens, businesses and organizations of one State were suing Another State for improperly holding elections against their own legal code.
4. Controversies between **Citizens of different States** – This was happening with citizens, businesses and organizations suing businesses of other States, namely Dominion Voting Systems were getting lots of suits against them. Plus other electronic voting system private companies.

To specifically clarify what the Founding Fathers wanted to happen when States VS States are the parties…just to add a point so that they couldn't be misunderstood:

> (U.S. Constitution: Article III, Section 2, Clause 2)
> "In all cases affecting ambassadors, other public ministers and consuls and **those in which a state shall be party**, the **Supreme Court shall have original jurisdiction.**"

When a State of the United States is a party in a lawsuit, either being sued or bringing the suit…the Supreme Court of the United States **IS the only court with original jurisdiction to adjudicate that case.** No lower Federal Court has any jurisdiction whatsoever. The case can't be tried in any lower Federal Court, or any other court, except the Supreme Court.

This Constitutional Concept Has Been Shredded in the Past

Case law comes to destroy the framers original intent once again.

In Alabama v. Arizona (1934) – The States had a controversy involving the sale of convict made goods. Yet, the Supreme Court DECLINED JURISDICTION. And wouldn't hear the case.

Yet, the Supreme Court went **well beyond** claiming "no jurisdiction." It actually went ahead and stated, **AND SET THE FUTURE PRECEDENT** and indicated that **its jurisdiction of suits <u>between states</u>** will be exercised **only when** absolutely necessary. Further, that the threatened injury to a plaintiff state **must be of great magnitude and imminent** and that <u>**the burden**</u> **on the plaintiff state** to establish all the elements of a case **is greater than the burden generally required by a petitioner seeking an injunction in cases between private parties**.

Thus, for a good while now, the Supreme Court has been DECREASING the States Rights. By making the burden of proof to take the case much higher, than normal suits.

Now Comes Texas and 27 States /Versus/ Pennsylvania, Michigan, Wisconsin, Georgia, Arizona and Nevada for Election Law Irregularities

Starting on December 7th, 2020 Texas brought suit against Georgia, Michigan, Pennsylvania and Wisconsin. The case was filed directly with the Supreme Court, just like it should be as per the U.S. Constitution.

(See: https://www.breitbart.com/politics/2020/12/07/texas-sues-georgia-michigan-pennsylvania-and-wisconsin-at-supreme-court-election-rules/)

Texas' grounds for the suit was the these 4 States violated the Electors Clause of the U.S. Constitution because they made illegal changes to their voting rules through courts and state governor actions, RATHER than through the Constitutional appropriate method of voting laws into existence through the state legislators.

Which of course, those 4 states did actually violate their own laws and the U.S. Constitution…issuing those "emergency declarations" to do mail-in voting in a haphazard way…because of the corona virus pandemic, that was being blasted to every television by the news 24 hours a day at the time.

In only 2 more days, the case was joined by 17 MORE STATES. And I think over the next few days, there were even more states than that, that joined as Plaintiffs in this "Texas v Pennsylvania case."

(See: https://news.yahoo.com/texas-joined-17-red-states-210909190.html)

Then, just a few days later on December 11, 2020, the U.S. Supreme Court declined to hear the case because "Texas lacked standing to challenge the results of the election held by another state."

Yet, there was a rumor that escaped via a simple court clerk to the offices of the Supreme Court just 1 week later.
It is stated like this:

> "He said that the justices, as they always do, went into a closed room to discuss cases they're taking or to debate. There's no phones, no computers, no nothing, no one else is in the room except for the nine justices. It's typically very civil. They just debate what they're doing.
>
> But when the Texas case was brought up, he said he heard screaming through the walls as Justice Roberts and the other liberal justices were insisting that this case not be taken up. And the reason — the words that were heard through the wall when Justice Thomas and Justice Alito were citing Bush versus Gore — from John Roberts were 'I don't give a (brief pause to omit obscenity) about that case. I don't want to hear about it. At that time, we didn't have riots.'"

This rumor was stated on the Texas House floor during the meeting of electors for the State of Texas. And they voted 34-4 in a resolution to damn the U.S. Supreme Court for "moral cowardice" for throwing out the Texas v. Pennsylvania suit.

(See: https://www.statesman.com/story/news/columns/2020/12/18/texas-electors-defense-damning-supreme-court-acting-moral-cowardice-damningly-inaccurate/3958103001/)

This information seems to be had on the Hal Turner Radio Show. But it doesn't appear to have originated here.

(See: https://halturnerradioshow.com/index.php/en/news-page/news-nation/loud-arguments-in-us-supreme-court-chambers-over-texas-lawsuit-court-intimidated)

This information was debunked on Left-controlled fact-checking websites.

However, just a few days later on December 19, 2020, I found this article that George Soros himself **congratulated** Justice John Roberts for doing the exact thing, that the debunkers claimed never happened.

(See: https://www.thegatewaypundit.com/2020/12/going-supreme-court-chief-justice-john-roberts-even-soros-cheered-roberts-davos/)

Plus, the Supreme Court itself actually responded to the claim.

(See: https://www.theepochtimes.com/supreme-court-responds-to-claim-that-john-roberts-shouted-at-other-justices-over-texas-lawsuit_3624378.html)

So now in 2021, the Supreme Court has set a very odd future precedent, by NOT taking the case. The individual States can adopt at-will any election procedures they like. Through any means they like; Constitutional or not. And swing national elections however they want. And use that newfound power to whip the other states into subjection.

With this defacto elimination of the Electoral College; the BIG STATES with the most electoral votes can make easy election laws and use those public votes, legitimate or not, to push the electoral votes of their state to any candidate of their choice in national elections.

The Blue States usually vote blue and the Red States usually vote red. But, what about the purple swing states. If a few of these States pushed through lax election laws, the national elections would favor the Socialists forever more.

The Position Where We Find Ourselves

There is no exaggeration in the above. We are in a perilous situation. Our enemies are among us. Our enemies are in positions of power **over us**.

If the election system isn't straightened out in a hurry, there is no more voice of the people in the United States of America. If there is no voice of the people, America is lost to Socialism forever.

Rulers law would have taken hold and strangled the once free people of America. There is no way to vote these types of powers out of existence. Only God can fix this situation now.

I wait on His hand and pray mightily for His favor to bless this promised land of America. That the work of freedom will continue in the world. I wait.

Chapter Seventeen - The Deep State

> If ever a time should come, when vain and aspiring men shall possess the highest seats in government, our country will stand in need of its experienced patriots **to prevent its ruin**. (Samuel Adams, Letter to James Warren, Oct 24, 1780)

All Tyrannies Need Bureaucracies to Enforce Their Rule

Our Situation Becoming Perilous

The secret combinations, Communists and allied forces have acquired sufficient strength to be more forceful and also more brazen. That is, the members of the SCs in the government refuse to take orders from our duly and lawfully elected President Donald Trump. Trump is the first president in my lifetime (and I am 88) that has challenged the conspiratorial and viciously anti-American forces within our federal government. Being challenged, they are resisting by refusing to obey legitimate orders. They obviously take their orders from SOMEBODY ELSE. That somebody else is the subject of this book, the numerous secret combinations. These rebel forces (whom I perceive as traitors to America and to the American people) have earned the sobriquet of the "DEEP STATE." They have been operating for over a century, gaining strength and power with every year. They have never previously been forced to the surface because, until now, no president has challenged them and their power. But now, along comes President Donald John Trump.

Please consider the extremely serious nature of this situation. Employees in a government who rebel at taking orders from the chief executive. This calls up the image of a ship being commandeered by those who are not authorized to do so and being put on a course other than that which the owners of the ship had intended it to follow. In the language of the sea, this is called, "mutiny." It is also "rebellion," "theft" and "treason." It is also, literally, a "coup." It is taking over the control of the government of and, ultimately, everything in the United States. The ultimate objectives of these people constituting the "Deep State" are exactly the same as those of the Secret Combinations. Our situation today is parallel to that of the people in 3 Nephi 6:

> 29 Therefore they did combine against the people of the Lord and enter into a covenant to destroy them and to deliver those who were guilty of murder from the grasp of justice, which was about to be administered according to the law.
> 30 and they did **set at defiance the law and the rights of their country**; and they did covenant one with another **to destroy the governor** and to establish a king over the land, that the land should no more be at liberty but should be subject unto kings.

We have every reason to believe that the symptoms that we see on the surface are the direct result of the mutiny going on beneath the surface by the Secret Combinations of the Devil to take complete control of our government. And not only our government but all of our properties and of our education system and of our churches. It matters not that these mutineers are greatly outnumbered by loyal Americans. If the mutineers manage to carry the present insurrection to its logical conclusion, then they will have complete control of not only the federal government but all of our military forces and police forces. They will have ALL of the guns, ALL of the military forces and ALL of the police forces of the country! And don't think for a minute that we could vote ourselves out of such a situation.

For an explanation of the Deep State, please see the excellent article by The *New American* editor Gary Benoit below:

What Is the Deep State?
From The Editor [Gary Benoit] of *The New American*

> Until recently, "the Deep State," the subject of this special report from *THE NEW AMERICAN,* would not have been a common topic for discussion among either the talking heads on network television or everyday Americans around family dinner tables or office water coolers. But all that changed with the 2016 presidential race and the election of Donald Trump to the White House. And a subject that many Americans were once only dimly aware of, if they were aware of it at all, has become a popular topic.
>
> But what is the Deep State? Does it even exist? Is it something to be feared? What can be done about it? The articles that follow shed much-needed light on these important questions.
>
> In a nutshell, the Deep State is a state within a state—a shadow government that manipulates and shapes the policies of the visible government, without regard to the best interests of the country, the U. S. Constitution, the laws enacted by the Congress and the public policies of the president, who heads the executive branch. The evidence assembled in this special report shows that the Deep State does exist within the shadows of power and that it is working to submerge the United States in an emerging new world order (global governance), in contravention of President Trump's stated policy of "America First." The leaks from the intelligence community, which are intended to delegitimize and even topple the duly elected president, are just part of the evidence exposing the existence, machinations and clout of the Deep State.
>
> The first article in this special report is a brief introduction to the existence of powers behind the throne (page 6), not just in America today but in world history. This is followed by articles exposing the shadowy swamp creatures inhabiting the underbelly of the entrenched unelected bureaucracy within the U.S. government in

general (page 8) and within the so—called intelligence community in particular (page 13).

But there is more to it than that—there is also the "Deep State Behind the Deep State." As explained in our article bearing that title (page 19), the power elites manipulating the levers of political power are outside as well as inside government. One example is the establishment Powerhouse known as the Council on Foreign Relations, a Globalist—minded private entity.

The articles referenced above and two others, constituting almost all of this special report, were written by Alex Newman, this magazine's foreign correspondent and a knowledgeable researcher of Deep State machinations. Completing the report is a short piece by Arthur R. Thompson, the chief executive officer of The John Birch Society, who explains that the Deep State's powerful grip on our government (and on other aspects of American life) can be broken through the organized efforts of everyday citizens—simply by shining the light of day on it (page 44). In fact, not only can this be done, but it must be done, since the survival and restoration of our great country depends on it.

We encourage all readers to read this report, to place it in the hands of others and (in general) to become involved.
—Gary Benoit [Editor]

(Reprinted from the January 8, 2018 issue of *The New American* Magazine)

I highly recommend that you go to the *New American* website and pull up the following seven articles from the January 8, 2018 issue or merely click on the titles below, which are linked:

Pulling Strings From Behind the Scenes by Alex Newman

Bureaucracy vs. Trump, America, Constitution

Underbelly of the Intelligence Community by Alex Newman

Behind the Deep State: CFR

Follow the Rothschild, Soros and Rockefeller Money by Alex Newman

Secret Societies: Skull & Bones, Bohemians, Illuminati by Alex Newman

Exposing the Deep State by Arthur R. Thompson

The information contained in the above articles is vital for us to be able to defend ourselves from the Deep State, then defeat it, then begin to re-instate our Constitution and to preserve America and our freedoms.

Just as the KGB (now the FSB) is the "sword and the shield" for Communist Russia, the Deep State can be considered the "sword and the shield" for the sinister forces which we have identified that are destroying the Constitution and whose goal it is to merge the United States into a regionalized world government in which we, the people, would have no rights whatsoever. The Secret Combinations of the Devil form of government.

Do not underestimate the significance of this battle. It is a HUGE battle between good and evil. It might be THE last battle. When a segment of the government refuses to obey the law and a large segment of the public supports that rebellious and lawless segment of the government, that constitutes the disintegration of the democratic process and the genesis of general rioting and looting and of a civil war.

Please pull up the above-mentioned articles about the Deep State and read them very, very carefully.

The stunts that the enemy pulls sometimes seem to be absolutely CRAZY! If you ever feel confused, just remember that everything that the enemy does is to negate the Constitution, to merge the United States into a North American Union with Canada and Mexico, then to merge the NAU into a world government. And also to suppress or to eliminate the freedom of religion. Everything that the enemy does is to further those objectives.

Then phone your U. S. representative and your U. S. Senators and tell them to Kill THE DEEP STATE!

Joe

Epilogue

This One Commandment Which We Absolutely Must Not Ignore

When we consider the numbers, the wealth, the power and the forces arrayed against us and bent upon our submission and/or destruction, our situation appears to be hopeless. To me, it appears to be so. At least, without some direct intervention by the Lord in our behalf. I do believe in miracles. And I do believe that the Lord is very desirous to see our side prevail. The BIG question is, "Do we deserve His help?" To me, there are two messages from the Lord that bear directly upon this situation. The first is

> **1 Nephi 3:7: ...I will go and do the things which the Lord hath commanded, for I know that the lord giveth no commandments unto the children of men, save he shall prepare a way for them that they**

may accomplish the thing which he commandeth them. (Emphasis added)

Riots

As this is being written, the first of June of 2020, riots are sweeping America. These are very important *Signs of the Times* in that they signal the serious breakdown of law and order. Thousands of demonstrators and rioters are roaming the streets of, according to one report, 240 American cities. There are many tragedies in this case, but one of the main ones is that there is sufficient police personnel and resources and legal justification in every one of these cities to stop the rioters but they are not doing so. They are standing down. We must presume that, in every case, the reason is that they have been given orders to stand down by their mayors. En masse! Consider that. The primary duty of the mayors are to command the police force to protect the lives, liberties and properties of the citizens. It appears that all of the mayors have been given orders from someone at a centralized location, to stand down. Who could this be? When we had riots in about 2016, I checked about eight of the cities in which there were riots. In all eight, the mayors were Democrats. We must wonder how many of the present 240 have Democrats as mayors. The answer to that question might tell us something.

The magnitude of these riots indicate that we are in the latter stages of a coup or takeover of some kind. Whatever and whoever, a takeover would not be good.

It is important that Americans gain an understanding of the motivation behind these riots, who is financing them and who the perpetrators are. Here are three excellent articles on this subject by William F. Jasper:

The New American, "Rioting For a Reason: Civil Unrest and Political Opportunity," by William F. Jasper, Dec 15, 2014
The New American, "George Soros' War on America: Time to Prosecute the billionaire's Global Crime Spree," by William F. Jasper, Nov 20, 2016
The New American, "Anti-Trump Riots: Follow the Money, by William F. Jasper, Dec 19, 2016.

Let's begin with Jasper's article dated Dec 15, 2014, "Rioting For a Reason; Civil Unrest and Political Opportunity," regarding the rioting occurring in Ferguson, MO, Baltimore, MD and other places. Bill gives ample evidence that these riots are Communist fronts:

Rioting For a Reason; Civil Unrest and Political Opportunity

"We have nothing to lose but our chains! We have nothing to lose but our chains!" The chant erupted across the nation and around the world at demonstrations (and riots) in response to a St. Louis County grand jury's decision not to indict white police officer Darren Wilson in the shooting death of Michael Brown, a black man, in Ferguson, Missouri. It was heard again following the vote of a New York grand jury not to indict a police officer in the death of Eric Garner and again when Attorney General Eric Holder addressed a crowd in Atlanta, Georgia.

Is it merely a coincidence, a fluke, that this slogan echoes the most famous lines of Karl Marx's Communist Manifesto?

"Communists everywhere support every revolutionary movement against the existing social and political order of things," Marx declared, in the concluding lines of his revolutionary tract. "The Communists disdain to conceal their views and aims," he continued. "They openly declare that their ends can be attained only by the forcible overthrow of all existing social conditions. Let the ruling classes tremble at a Communistic revolution. The proletarians have nothing to lose but their chains….

Working Men of All Countries, Unite!"

Communist sloganeers condensed and paraphrased Marx's wordy text into a catchier war cry that has accompanied tumults, riots and revolutions on every continent since the Manifesto's release in 1848: "Workers of the World, Unite. You have nothing to lose but your chains!"

Do the young demonstrators chanting "We have nothing to lose but our chains!" realize that they are repeating Marx? Probably not, but the older revolutionaries leading them certainly do. In the forefront of the Brown/Garner demonstrations, stoking the fires of resentment, race hatred and class warfare, are 1960s veterans of the Students for a Democratic Society (SDS), the Black Panther Party, the Communist Party USA, the Revolutionary Communist Party, the Black Radical Congress, Freedom Road Socialist Organization, the Organization for Black Struggle and other more moderate-sounding "peace" and "justice" organizations. But don't expect CNN, NPR, ABC, CBS, NBC, or the New York Times to report the facts we will detail here concerning this crucially important connection to the ongoing violence and civil turmoil.

One of the other new propaganda memes in the planned race war that is currently unfolding in our cities, "Black Lives Matter," is, likewise, the product of the revolutionary Marxist-Leninists who dominate much of academe and that special class of citizens known as "community organizers," whose political cachet has soared under professional "community organizer" Barack Obama. The co-Creators of the #BlackLivesMatter slogan that has suddenly appeared on posters, T-Shirts, Tweets and protest banners, are Patrisse Cullors, Alicia Garza and Opal Tometi, three far-left, black, feminist activists who idolize Communist terrorist revolutionaries Assata Shakur and Angela Davis, as well as the Black Panther Party and the Black Liberation Movement... (William F. Jasper, "Rioting For a Reason," The New American, 15 Dec, 2014.)

I recommend to you that you pull up the article and read it in its entirety. Now let's go to Bill's article, "Anti-Trump Riots: Follow the Money" in the December 19, 2016 issue:

Anti-Trump Riots: Follow the Money by William F. Jasper:

George Soros, Alex Soros, Jonathan Soros, Tom Steyer, Donald Sussman, Herb and Marian Sandler and Michael Bloomberg: What do these and other billionaire Democratic Party donors have in common with the #Not My-President rioters who ravaged American cities following the November 8 elections? That's a crucially important question that demands answers, because a lot more anti-Trump mayhem is in the works.

Were the "protests" that quickly devolved into riots nation-wide following Donald Trump's historic upset of Hillary Rodham Clinton merely spontaneous outbursts resulting from widespread fear and anger over the Republican candidate's alleged promotion of hatred, racism, misogyny, xenophobia and intolerance? That, of course, is the narrative of the establishment media choir, which, thankfully, has been so thoroughly discredited and exposed-for lies, bias, propaganda and censorship-in this past election cycle that
tens of millions of Americans no longer believe a single word of the deceptive drivel dispensed by their scribblers and talking heads.

The riots and violence that continued day after day were the continuation and culmination of previous rehearsals in Ferguson, Baltimore, Milwaukee, Chicago and elsewhere that were instigated and coordinated by activist leaders of Black Lives Matter, MoveOn.org, International Action Center, ANSWER Coalition and other far-left, fake "grassroots" groups. They can be relied upon to perform on cue because they are lavishly funded by George Soros, the big tax-exempt foundations (Rockefeller, Ford, Carnegie, et al.) and activist "pass through" organizations such as the Tides Foundation and Democracy Alliance that bundle and launder hundreds of millions of dollars in "dark money" to the street revolutionaries.

Black Lives Matter (BLM), which has become one of the most efficient riot-making operations, has been especially blessed with largess from the billionaire elites. As The New American noted in a 2014 article ("Rioting for a Reason"), BLM was founded by Patrisse Cullers, Alicia Garza and Opal Tometi, three black lesbian Marxists "who idolize

Communist terrorist revolutionaries Assata Shakur and Angela Davis, as well as the Black Panther Party and the Black Liberation Movement." Ah, that's just the ticket for George Soros. He and his Open Society Foundations have showered BLM with more than $33 million. That's a pretty good chunk of change, but it was only seed money. The Ford Foundation announced a few months ago its plan to raise $100 million in pooled donor funds for the BLM rioters. (William F. Jasper, "Anti-Trump Riots: Follow the Money," *The New American,* December 19, 2016.)

If these people are funding Communist activities, why are they not prosecuted? Let's now go to Bill's article in the *New American* of 20 Nov, 2016:

"George Soros' War on America: Time to Prosecute"

by William F. Jasper

"Not My President! Not My President!" Day after day, in cities from coast to coast, the chanting mobs of rioters have illegally blocked streets and freeways, set fires, thrown Molotov cocktails, injured police officers, destroyed property and defaced public buildings with graffiti. Portland, Oregon, a bastion of "progressive" Democrats, has been the epicenter of much of the violent action aimed at president-elect Donald Trump. Of course, as we have previously reported, not only did most of the Portland rioters who were arrested fail to register to vote, a large percentage of them appear to be professional, paid protesters.

Many of them, no doubt, were hired in response to the advertisements for paid anti-Trump protesters that appeared on Craigslist and other media in Seattle, Portland, Chicago, Pittsburgh, Boston, Denver, Philadelphia, New York and elsewhere. Many of these "spontaneous" protests/riots would not have occurred without organized efforts involving hundreds of busses transporting thousands of protesters/rioters, many of whom appear to have traveled across state lines.

Many of the anti-Trump rioters, then, would appear not only to have violated state laws against rioting and inciting to riot, but also federal law against the same crime. Specifically, the rioters could be (and should be) charged under Title 18 U.S. Code § 2101, which provides:

(a) Whoever travels in interstate or foreign commerce or uses any facility of interstate or foreign commerce, including, but not limited to, the mail, telegraph, telephone, radio, or television, with intent -

(1) to incite a riot; or

(2) to organize, promote, encourage, participate in, or carry on a riot; or

(3) to commit any act of violence in furtherance of a riot; or

(4) to aid or abet any person in inciting or participating in or carrying on a riot or committing any act of violence in furtherance of a riot...

Shall be fined under this title, or imprisoned not more than five years, or both.

The definition section of 18 U.S. Code § 2102 defines the crime of rioting this way:

(a) As used in this chapter, the term "riot" means a public disturbance involving (1) an act or acts of violence by one or more persons part of an assemblage of three or more persons, which act or acts shall constitute a clear and present danger of, or shall result in, damage or injury to the property of any other person or to the person of any other individual or (2) a threat or threats of the commission of an act or acts of violence by one or more persons part of an assemblage of three or more persons having, individually or collectively, the ability of immediate execution of such threat or threats, where the performance of the threatened act or acts of violence would constitute a clear and present danger of, or would result in, damage or injury to the property of any other person or to the person of any other individual.

Obviously, the anti-Trump rioters who were arrested for starting fires and committing other acts of violence and public disturbance should be prosecuted under applicable state laws and those who traveled interstate to do the same should also be prosecuted under federal law as well. But what about the organizers of the riots, those who hired the rioters and transported the perpetrators across state lines to engage in this criminal activity? Are they not also culpable under the "aid and abet" provisions cited above? Are they not also liable for prosecution under the federal conspiracy statute (18 U.S. Code § 371) which provides:

If two or more persons conspire either to commit any offense against the United States, or to defraud the United States, or any agency thereof in any manner or for any purpose and one or more of such persons do any act to effect the object of the conspiracy, each shall be fined under this title or imprisoned not more than five years, or both.

The Obama Department of Justice had no problem with charging Oregon ranchers Dwight and Steven Hammond-respected, hard-working, tax-paying, law-abiding citizens-with terrorism and arson, for accidentally burning a few acres of "public land" while carrying out a controlled burn on their own land. The Obama/Lynch DOJ prosecuted these dangerous "terrorists" and threw them into federal prison. (See here and here).

When supporters of the Hammonds, led by Nevada ranching family members Ammon and Ryan Bundy peacefully occupied the Malheur National Wildlife Refuge in protest earlier this year, the Obama administration mobilized all its resources in response, including an ambush that resulted in the shooting death of Hammond supporter Robert LaVoy Finicum.

The Obama administration and its media allies were stunned a few weeks ago when an Oregon jury acquitted the Bundy brothers and their five additional co-defendants of all charges, including charges of conspiracy to use "force, intimidation and threats" against federal employees. Will the Obama/Lynch DOJ show any similar zeal to prosecute the thugs who carried out the violent riots in Portland, Oregon-or in the many other venues around the country? Will they prosecute the co-conspirators who financed and planned the riots? That is highly unlikely, since the financiers of the "#NotMyPresident" anti-Trump rallies are some of the Democrat Party's biggest donors. Heading the list of the Rioters-R-Us financiers is top Obama/Clinton fundraiser George Soros (shown at right), the Daddy Warbucks of all causes Socialist and subversive…(William F. Jasper, "George Soros' War on America: Time to Prosecute" *The New American,* Nov 20, 2016)

I encourage you to pull up the article and read it in its entirety. Very important information. Joe.

Criminal, anti-American activity, funded by the super-rich but the lawbreakers are not prosecuted. One reason is that, no doubt, the mayors of most of the cities where the riots have occurred are Democrat. These are the same mayors who have defied President-elect Trump by stating that their cities would continue to be "sanctuary cities" and would not let the criminal aliens be picked up and deported. What an attitude. In my opinion, the Democrat Party has become mostly Marxist and mostly subversive to the Constitution; to America. Any Democrats want to try to prove me wrong?

Since there is evidence that the BLM and other rioters are funded by some deep-pocket sources, should we not presume also the probability that the mayors of the cities that did not prosecute rioters/looters/arsonists were also "funded" to not prosecute the rioters?

Chapter Eighteen - Defense and Counterattack - Exposing and Defeating a Communist Front

God to Moses: "...and proclaim liberty throughout all the land unto all the inhabitants thereof ;..."[132]

A Textbook Case -The Communist Attack on the Mormons 1970

Here is a case in which I was involved back in 1970 which is a perfect example of a Communist activity, with active measures Communist fronts, agents of influence and disinformation.. On the surface, a group of riotous college students would appear wherever Brigham Young University played a basketball game and proceeded to invade the basketball court to carry out demonstrations. But in analyzing all the evidence, presence of active measures, disinformation, agents of influence all begins to surface. A well-defined, well-organized and financed operation, involving many wealthy newspaper owners and TV station owners.

The first thing that we must understand is that there is an organized, powerful, well-financed and determined force of anti-Christ people working now to destroy Christianity, America and civilization. You have seen some of them on TV. I have told you how they are organized and what their objectives are.

It's up to you and to me. We should not have to be told to do something as important as this is. We are not commanded in all things. One problem is that most good Christians are very busily engaged in making a living, raising a family, going to ball games, a fishing trip once in a while, civic duties and church assignments. They associate with their own. They are so good that they cannot believe that others would be as evil as we have described herein. They are so busy that they are not aware of this insidious wickedness that is gaining power over us and which plans to overpower us completely. Oh yes and to destroy us. I hope that the information presented herein is sufficiently clear and easy to understand. I know that it is accurate. I hereby testify to its accuracy. I hold no juris doctorate in the law, nor Ph.d in political science, nor in theology, nor in anything. (I do, however, hold an Airline Transport Pilot Rating with single and multi-engine land and single-and multi engine sea, with instrument rating, flight instructor and ground school instructor.) But I have studied this situation, diligently, for 52 years and I understand it. I will just say this: I am willing to publicly debate the contents of this book with any Ph.d, any lawyer, any law school professor, any judge, any politician, ANYBODY.

---

133. Samuel A. Alito, Jr., 12 Nov 2020 address to the Federalist Society

I have made every effort to make sure that everything in this book is accurate. But-if you do find an error, please advise me immediately at jhferg@msn.com. My plans are to revise this book every six months or so to correct whatever errors that might surface.

The following gives us excellent advice on how to construct both a defense and an offense against the SCs. *We should shine light on all the hidden things of darkness*, their ideologies, their stratagems and their tactics. Consider:

> D&C 123:13: Therefore, that we should waste and wear out our lives in bringing to light all the hidden things of darkness, wherein we know them; and they are truly manifest from heaven-

First of all, we must strengthen ourselves for the battle. This is going to get fierce. One thing I wish to explain is how the enemy takes advantage of us. It is by intimidating us and shaming us into abandoning the truth and yielding to a lie. Even good people are vulnerable to this. It was to the most humble people in the world that President Ezra Taft Benson delivered his Conference address entitled, "Beware of Pride:"

> **Pride results in secret combinations** which are built up to get power, gain and glory of the world. (See Hel. 7:5; Ether 8:9, 16, 22–23; Moses 5:31.) This fruit of the sin of pride, namely secret combinations, brought down both the Jaredite and the Nephite civilizations and has been and will yet be the cause of the fall of many nations. (See Ether 8:18–-25.) (CR Apr 1989) (General Conference of the Church of Jesus Christ of Latter-day Saints, April, 1989.)

For one thing, pride motivates those who move the agendas of the SCs. But they in turn use our weaknesses (false pride) to cause us to acquiesce to ideas and government programs that are contrary to our own best interests. Please refer back to Chapter Five on Marxism about the KGB using disinformation, active measures and agents of influence against their targets. Our enemies constantly strive to make the truth unpopular and lies popular. They also attack any person, especially a U. S. Representative or U. S. Senator, who stands up for the truth. They are very clever at it. They also attack, demean and intimidate voters who support honest candidates. When we allow our worldview to be altered because we are intimidated to reject the truth or to accept or condone a lie, that is because of pride. No matter how big, tough, mean and humble we might be. Allowing ourselves to be intimidated to reject the truth is because of pride. False pride, that is. We can all be proud of being Christians, of being Americans, of being proud of our children and grandchildren. That is a different kind of pride.

There is no people on earth who are more full of false pride than the members of the secret combinations. They hate being exposed. That is to their weakness and to our advantage, if we will but exploit it.

Be Ready to Defend Christianity

We must stand able and willing to defend Christianity from all attacks. When we are attacked, we must be ready to defend our position by articulating the value of Christian values in our society and in our public discourse. Founder John Adams[133] (1735-4th of July, 1826) stated it this way:

> We have no government armed with power capable of contending with human passions unbridled by morality and religion. Avarice, ambition, revenge or gallantry would break the strongest cords of our Constitution as a whale goes through a net. Our Constitution is designed only for a moral and religious people. It is wholly inadequate for any other.

Christians who live by the Ten Commandments are the most valuable citizens of our society. We do not fill up the jails. We work and pay taxes. We are a stabilizing influence in our society. Just witness the people who rioted in Ferguson, MO, Baltimore, Chicago, Portland and other cities. They were not just demonstrating. They broke windows and doors, turned vehicles over and set them on fire and caused all sorts of disturbances. These people are threats to our peace and stability. Just consider if all Americans were to behave as those people do. Uncivilized. Our economy would cease to function. We would be in ruins.

We Christians are restrained by our beliefs, by a force within us, from such behavior. Nobody has to tell us not to riot. They do not have to send hundreds of police to prevent us from rioting. We just naturally do not desire to behave in such manner. Referring to the statement by Adams, above, we are not driven by unbridled passions as are the rioters. Christian values are extremely important to the health and welfare of our America. Without Christian values, America would cease to be America.

Is All This Really Happening?

We are all so busy trying to make a living, raise our kids and cover all the bases that we never become aware of the symptoms of the destruction of our Constitution and of the attacks on Christianity. But they are happening. Is it not true that our borders are becoming less effective? Is it not true that our state borders have been rendered less important because of such SCOTUS decisions as "separation of church and state" and *Obergefell*? Have not the borders of every county in the nation also been violated, rendering of less importance the governments of those counties? This is evidence-or proof-of the dissolution of all governments under the Constitution of the United States in preparation for incorporating the land mass of the United States into a

North American Union and then into a world government. This constitutes an attack upon all of our liberties, including our Christian liberties.

Let me tell you a story of how exposure is effective against secret combinations.

A Rag-Tag Group of Four Exposes and Defeats a Communist Front and Active Measures

This little story is about how effective exposure is against secret combinations. In 1969-70 the Communists launched an attack against the Mormon Church through their Communist publications, the mainstream media and disruptive demonstrations at BYU basketball games by Communist front groups. (Remember-the MSM TV stations and newspapers are owned by the wealthy-not by the working men of the world uniting to throw off their chains.) They made up all sorts of false allegations.

Dr. W. Cleon Skousen – Creative Commons

They knew that some people would believe them. Also, they had their demonstrators at every Brigham Young University basketball game. Then, someone sent to Dr. W. Cleon Skousen a copy of a Communist newspaper (following shortly) that **contained the identical information** that was being put out by the mainstream media. Now, our suspicions were confirmed regarding the source of the attacks.

Dr. Skousen wrote up an analysis of the Communist article. We printed up a bunch of these using Clair Blackburn's little A. B. Dick printing press that he had in his home. We put my address on them so people could order more copies. Cleon sent copies (of the Communist article along with his own analysis) out to everybody on his mailing list and so did I. (Then) Elder Ezra Taft Benson sent out a bunch. Pretty soon the orders came rolling in from all over the country. Person to person and then on some radio talk shows, we started to get our message out. The MSM never printed or broadcast a bit of our side of the issue. Not a bit. Not that I ever heard of.

Please see, on the following page: An analysis of the contents of The *Daily World* by former FBI agent Dr. W. Cleon Skousen

W. Cleon Skousen
Salt Lake City, Utah 15 February, 1970

Anyone familiar with Communist tactics will recognize that this is no ordinary article. It is a signal to Communist "transmission belt" to go to work. There are people strategically placed in the bulk of the opinion- molding facilities of the United States who watch for signals like this in the Communist press. The Communists are looked upon as the "vanguard" or tactical leaders in the fight against the open society of the United States.

Communist signals are therefore accepted by the entire cadre of left-wing collectivists as the logical targets for a united attack. The Communists refer to this large group of fellow-travelers as their "transmission belt." By unitedly attacking an identical target, they create a syndrome of incidents which have an overwhelming impact on the thinking of the American people. This technique has been used successfully for fifty years.

This type of massive propaganda assault is designed to distort public thinking to the point where it paralyzes the effectiveness of the organization under attack. In fact, the object is not merely to discredit the victim but create an atmosphere of deep resentment or even hatred toward it.

For several months the volume and intensity of criticism against the LDS Church has been mounting. The Communist Party has apparently decided to take over the leadership of this agitation and give it financial and institutional support. If the pattern follows past incidents of this kind, we may expect to see the so-called legitimate press, radio and TV begin a whole series of "reports" on all types of subjects related to the LDS Church.

It will be explained that the LDS Church has suddenly become "news." All of these "reports" will be handled in a way which makes the Church look rich, priest-ridden, racist, super-authoritarian and conservative to the point of being archaically reactionary.

W. Cleon Skousen

That which Dr. Skousen described above was a textbook case of *active measures,* with *disinformation* being disseminated by *agents of influence* against a specific target, the Church of Jesus Christ of Latter-day Saints (Mormon) to attempt to achieve a specific objective (to demean the image and reputation of the Mormon Church in the eyes of the public.) There are several lessons to be learned from this incident. One that I wish to emphasize, however, is that it is very obvious that Communist agents infiltrated into and became employed by the newspapers OWNED BY THE VERY RICH used those newspapers for Communist purposes. Or, maybe we should say, for collectivist purposes, which include the Marxists (Communists) and some members of the Big Four (CFR, Bones, BB and TLC) and other groups, including the Globalists, working to destroy America and Christianity.

Then, the NCAA put out a tabloid-sized newspaper about the attacks on campuses and identified the agitators at the basketball games as being members of the Students for Democratic Society (SDS), Student Non-violent Coordinating Committee, (SNCC) the Black Panthers (BPP), Black Student Union (BSU), Black Student Alliance (BSA), W. E. B. Dubois Clubs, Student

Liberation Fronts(SLF) and the Youth International Party (YIP). The MSM had failed miserably in reporting this extremely vital information. Well, I had done my homework. I recognized these groups immediately as having been identified by J. Edgar Hoover, head of the F. B. I., as Communist-front groups.

I phoned the NCAA and received permission to use two pages of their newspaper. I then wrote two pages to go with the two NCAA Pages to make a four-page tabloid and had a bunch printed. Joel Dunn in Tooele at the *Tooele Transcript Bulletin* printed them for us on a rush order and at a very reasonable price. Dr. Skousen sent out copies to people on his list, so did I. Clair Blackburn sent out a bunch. Elder Benson sent out a bunch. Orders came in from all over the country. Thousands of copies. I wish that I had kept track of the number. Then suddenly, the attacks stopped. **As if they were all coordinated from one central location.** Which they were. They stopped as suddenly as if someone had drawn the window shade down. We, a little rag-tag bunch of guys, working on an almost zero $ budget, had exposed them. **They ran for their holes**, being the cowards that they were. All it cost the LDS Church was the postage that Elder Benson used. I like to brag every once in a while about us little ol' Davids whuppin' that great big Goliath. (Hope it is not the wrong kind of pride.)

The first page of the four-page tabloid that we created and distributed is shown on the following page.

Communist Front Groups

We have here a perfect example of front groups. The SDS, SNCC, BPP, BSU, BSA, W.E.B. Dubois Clubs, SLF and YIP were all pretending to be acting independently but were actually acting in behalf of the CPUSA (the Communist Party USA.) This is just as FBI Director J. Edgar Hoover had described.

> Here we have nine terrorist groups, many of which had been identified by FBI Director J. Edgar Hoover as Communist Front Groups, attacking a church-a religious institution and yet the main stream media made absolutely no mention of this fact. That certainly constituted distorted reporting and in favor of the Communists and Globalists.

It is especially worthy to note that none-absolutely none-of the information that we distributed exposing the Communist front groups was ever printed in the mainstream media newspapers. Complete blackout, even though it was VERY newsworthy. They would print everything bad about the LDS church that the Communists wanted printed, but they would not print anything to expose the agitators that we anti- Communists wanted printed. Tells us something, doesn't it?

In withholding the identities of the Communist front groups, the mainstream media protected the Communists! The same is happening today. By withholding the identities of the Communist front groups, the media is protecting and aiding them. The Lord has told us how we are to nullify the evil works of the G&A and the SCs: In D&C 123:13:

> Therefore, that we should waste and wear out our lives in bringing to light all the hidden things of darkness, wherein we know them;...

That is the answer, plain and simple. The G&A and the SCs cannot operate when the spotlight is shown upon them. They run like cowards. Like mice. Like cowardly mice.

As I reflect upon this skirmish that we had with the Communists, it encourages me to believe that we can win this great battle, notwithstanding the wealth and power that our enemies have, especially the power that they wield over the minds of many otherwise good Americans. We must win it by exposing the evil nature and designs of those who are attacking America and Christianity.

A Checklist for Defense/Offense Against the Combinations

<u>**Exposure, Exposure and more Exposure**</u>! The tactics the anti-Christ are using against us are illegal and against the law. They have misinterpreted and corrupted the Constitution, the *First* and the *Fourteenth* to arrogate unto themselves powers never delegated to them by the Constitution. We must inform a few million of our fellow Americans of this and do it in a hurry. One way is by the use of this book, which is free. Just consider:

Let's do some math. Say that 100 good people send notices about this book to ten of their friends. (I am sending out over 200 to start with) That's 1,000. Then, a week later, this 1,000 send notices to 10 of their friends. That's 10,000. Third week 100,000. Fourth week 1,000,000. Fifth week, 10,000,000. Sixth week 100,000,000. And the cost is zero! Just a little bit of effort. Now, I well realize the "bumps in the road" involved in this hypothetical plan. But you get the point of what can be done.

But even better. Suppose that 100 good people send notices out to ten of their friends this week. And ten the next week. And ten the next. And they ask all of their friends to do the same. East Coast—West Coast—Texas—Alaska—All over. Imagine the results...I can't even count that high. The thought of the potential is most interesting. And the cost would be zero. Just a little effort.

I ask you to pledge (to yourself) to send out ten notices per week for five weeks and ask your friends to do the same.

2. Send invitations not only to your friends about this book but to your United States Senator and Representative, to the governor of your state, to your state senator and representative and to your elected county officials, especially your county clerk.

We need to get our state officials to understand the danger to us in condoning the overreach and usurpation by the SCOTUS that presume to command the governor, the legislatures and county officials to replace the will of the people with the will of a rogue Supreme Court. This will destroy Christianity, America and civilization.

3. Send emails once per week to your contacts with a one or two paragraph message that you know that the U. S. Supreme Court is grossly violating the Constitution in persecuting Christians to benefit the Secular Humanists and Marxists and state how the SCOTUS is violating the Constitution. Send to every elected official named above in # 2. Once per week each one.

4. Be ready to stand in defense of Christians and Christianity. We Christians are the most law-abiding, hardest-working, most productive, most tax-paying and stay-out-of-jail citizens in the country!!!!! We honor, obey and sustain the law. Challenge any body giving you trouble to prove otherwise.

Chapter Nineteen - Defending Christ and His Words

It pains me to say this, but in certain quarters, religious liberty is fast becoming a disfavored right... (Justice Samuel A. Alito[134])

For whosoever shall be ashamed of me and of my words, of him shall the son of man be ashamed, when he shall come in his own glory and in his Father's and of the holy angels. (Luke 9:26)

Those who do not think that we are indebted to Christ just have not counted up their blessings lately. I readily acknowledge that I am MUCH in His debt and the more I think about it, the larger that I realize that this debt is. A friend once told me, "The greatest sin is the sin of ingratitude." It slowly dawned on me, over the years, that he was right and that I was GUILTY! So I have been trying to overcome my mortal weakness and be more grateful to Him to whom I owe so much.

Christians tend to shrink from politics because of its contentious and "dirty" nature. Politics is surely contentious. And it is at times dirty. Some of the people involved are greedy and very, very duplicitous. They intentionally want to drive Christians from the fray so that they can have the field to themselves uncontested. When this happens, evil wins. Evil people with evil purposes are propelled into positions of power. Power over us. Power to make and enforce laws that suppress Christians and Christianity.

Our reluctance to engage in "politics," dirty though it might be, when Christ and His words might need some defense in this arena, might eventually be perceived as cowardice.

Some go on trying to serve the Lord while trying to avoid offending the Devil.

I am now ready to stand up to defend Christ and His words (His gospel-and the PRINCIPLES of His gospel) no matter how badly we might be outnumbered or out-financed. (My life is not worth so much now, anyhow, since I am now 89 and have lived most of it.) For most of my life, I was afraid to stand up for Christ and His words. I was very deficient in gratitude and I was DUMB-very lacking in knowledge!!!!

For one thing, Christ has given me that most precious gift of liberty. **(2 Cor 3:17: Now the Lord is that Spirit: and where the Spirit of the Lord is, there is liberty.)** I consider myself somewhat a student of history and I have

---

135. Samuel A. Alito, Jr., 12 Nov 2020 address to the Federalist Society

witnessed the misery of millions of people who have lived in countries without liberty. I have lived through a period of time wherein a hundred million or more lost their lives by being in wars or being executed by Marxist-Nazi governments. I might be slow, but I FINALLY GOT IT!!! How fortunate and blessed I have been to have lived in America these past 89 years. I love this country and I love what has made it great-the Constitution of the United States and the spirit of Christ. And I love those who fought for our independence and who framed our Declaration of Independence and our Constitution. I now realize how ungrateful I have been. I realize also that the sin of ingratitude is one of the worst sins.

Attacks on Christianity Come From the Political Left

As stated earlier, we can expect that all attacks on Christians, Christianity and Christian liberty will come from the political Left. They will not come from those awful "right-wing extremists" who believe in God and the Constitution. Proof: At least five of the nine justices voted in the majority in the *Everson* case in 1947 and imposed the definitely anti-constitutional ruling of "Separation of church and state" upon us and outlawed any mention of God or the Ten Commandments in our schools and in public discourse.

These justices are in the political far Left. They have to be to violate the Constitution as they did. We of the Right are working to restore and defend the Constitution. This is proof absolute. Also, the five justices who voted in the majority in *Obergefell* in 2015 *have to be* in the political far Left. In fact, two of them, Breyer and Ginsburg, are members of the Council on Foreign Relations.

Voting in the majority in *Everson,* in 1947: Black, Vinson, Reed, Douglas and Murphy. Voting to dissent in *Everson* in 1947: Rutledge, Frankfurter, Jackson and Burton.

In his Statement on Communism in 1966, President McKay stated:

> The Russian Commissar of Education wrote: "We must hate Christians and Christianity. Even the best of them must be considered our worst enemies. Christian love is an obstacle to the development of the revolution. Down with love for one's neighbor. What we want is hate. Only then shall we conquer the universe."

Marxists of every degree, it seems, hate Christian principles and, usually, Christians also. Whether they are hard-core Communists, Socialists, Globalists, progressives or liberals, they all, in varying degrees, hate Christianity because hating Christianity naturally goes with believing in Marxism. Even those "liberals" who attend Christian churches seem to strongly oppose some of the *principles* of Christianity.

If you think that I am being unreasonable in this statement, just be observant as this battle progresses. It will become more obvious. Just see if any of the attacks on Christian liberties come from those whose political beliefs are based on the Constitution. There will be very few, if any. I predict that such will be ZERO.

Christians tend to shrink from politics because of its contentious and "dirty" nature. Politics is surely contentious. And it is at times dirty. Some of the people involved are greedy and very, very duplicitous. They intentionally want to drive Christians from the fray so that they can have the field to themselves uncontested. But then evil wins. Evil people with evil purposes are propelled into positions of power. Power over us. Power to make and enforce laws that suppress Christians and Christianity. We must enter the fray. This reminds me of an appropriate bit of prose:

> You have no enemies, you say
>
> Alas, my friend, the boast is low
>
> For those who have mingled in the fray that the brave endure
>
> Must have made foes
>
> If you have none, small is the work that you have done
>
> You have struck no traitor on the hip
>
> You have dashed no cup from perjurer's lips
>
> You have never turned the wrong to right
>
> You have been a coward in the fight
>
> (Unknown)

Corrupt laws (all Socialist laws in America are corrupt laws because they exist only because they violate and contradict the Constitution) corrupt the people. Just consider: wickedness in our government is bound to have an effect upon some people.

So part of our efforts to defend religious liberties MUST include working for just laws. That means laws in congruity with the Constitution. That means the Constitution as it is written, NOT as it is misinterpreted by some court.

A Battle for the Bodies and Souls of Man

President (then of the Quorum of the Twelve) Ezra Taft Benson[135] warned us of the serious nature of this battle:

> Today, we are in a battle for the bodies and souls of man. It is a battle between two opposing systems: freedom and slavery, Christ and anti-Christ. The struggle is more momentous than a decade ago, yet today the conventional wisdom says, "You must learn to live with Communism and to give up your ideas about national sovereignty." Tell that to the millions-yes, the scores of millions-who have met death or imprisonment under the tyranny of Communism! Such would be the death knell of freedom and all we hold dear. God must ever have a free people to prosper His work and bring about Zion.

The United Religious Initiative

There is at present developing an organization, a force, that might become a serious threat to all Christianity worldwide. It is called the United Religious Initiative. This URI is associated with the United Nations. I suppose that if the principles of this URI were known, they would be in congruity with those of Secular Humanism., evolution and Marxism. This would make them in conflict with and hostile to Christianity. They are seeking to recruit not only members but churches. Just consider that if the URI were to grow to several million and be funded by the UN, which is funded by the US, which gets its money from the US taxpayers. Then the powers and influence of the UN over the American people were to grow. This could be a very dangerous force to all Christians. Now, the URI is a reality. The rest above is my speculation. The URI might not amount to much in the future. But then it might. We should be aware of it and track its growth and activities.

In Closing, Let's Review our Situation.

1. There is an organized, determined and well-financed attack upon the Jewish and Christian Religions. It appears that the enemies of Christianity are determined to suppress and, if possible, to eliminate Christianity and Christians entirely.

2. The enemies of Christianity are found all throughout our culture, our educational system, our media and our government, including the Supreme Court of the United States. As Paul warned us, we have, "…wickedness in high places." (Eph 6:12.)

3. The enemies of Christianity include secret combinations of the Devil. Some of these individuals and organizations are very wealthy and very powerful as well as highly respected.

---

136. Mike Huckabee and Steve Feazel, THE THREE Cs THAT MADE AMERICA GREAT-CHRISTIANITY, CAPITALISM and the CONSTITUTION., Trilogy Christian Publishing, Tustin, CA, 85

4. These enemies of Christianity are also enemies of the Constitution of the United States and of America. Their objective is to destroy not only Christianity but all of the rights and liberties of the American people and merge the United States into a world government. This world government would have total power over us but would in no way be accountable to us. It would be Marxist (Communist) in nature. It would be a government hostile to God, to Christ and to the principles of Christ.

5. The stakes in this battle are as high as they can possibly be. This enemy, inspired by the Devil himself, wants to take from us not only every possession that we own but our souls as well. Our homes, our vehicles, our businesses, our boats, our books, our shotguns and our dogs. And oh yes—our children also.

6. The way to tell which side is the Lord's and which side is the Devil's is very simple. The government that protects individual liberty is the Lord's. The side that denies individual liberty is the Devil's. Consider, from 2 Cor 3:17:

7. Now the Lord is that Spirit; and where the Spirit of the Lord is, there is liberty.

8. Ancient and modern prophets have warned us about these secret powers. Their warnings have been powerful, direct and succinct. If you will read them very carefully, you will likely come to that same conclusion.

9. Some enemies of Christianity and of America are justices on the Supreme Court of the United States. They have intentionally (they can't be that stupid) misinterpreted and distorted the meaning of the Constitution and have corrupted the laws of the United States and are using these corrupted laws against Christianity and against America.

10. The forces arrayed against us are so numerous and so powerful that our fate of being conquered by them appears inevitable. In fact, it is obvious that the only chance that we have of winning is with the direct intervention of the Lord Himself. The question is, from the Lord's point of view, do we deserve it?

11. Now-a HUGE plus on our side. We are on the Lord's side. And He is on our side, if we will but do what we should do.

Opportunities are Everywhere to Fight for Christian Liberties

We need not wait for some highly visible event attacking Christian liberties to take action. Opportunities are all around us. (As the fighter pilot said when he was surrounded by enemy planes, "I was in a target-rich environment.") We can teach our children and grandchildren to recognize some of the many false ideas that are prevalent in our culture. We can teach them the truth regarding that issue. We can teach them the special scriptures and the words of modern prophets that warn us about this evil. This is VERY important. Teach them that there are some evil people and some misguided people who are threats to our religion and to our country.

You can teach them the words of the prophets and show them how accurate these prophets have been regarding our situation.

You can take many false ideas taught to your children in schools and teach them the truth. Teach them how to recognize false ideas.

If you feel so inclined, you can send out unlimited notices to your friends, family and associates introducing them to this book.

The Constitution (The original Constitution, not the one of today that has been so corrupted by judges and politicians) was a very special document and the men who framed it were very special men. We are beneficiaries of their work. Let us show our appreciation. Let us show our appreciation by fighting to restore the original intent of the Constitution. By doing so, we will be expressing our appreciation to the Lord and those who he chose for this work and we will also be blessing ourselves and our posterity with much better government. Maybe, just maybe, we can avoid the disaster and misery for which we are headed.

The Declaration of Independence is also a very special document. It states that our rights come from our Creator. Not from man nor a government. This is very special. This makes us very special people of all the people of this earth. It also states that the purpose of government is to protect those rights. Nothing else. Nothing more, nothing less.

The Laws of God and the Laws of Man

The rule of law[136] is breaking down here in America. The destruction of the rule of law leads to the destruction of a nation. Anyone who does not realize this has just not done his history. We are facing chaos and then anarchy and then a brutal Marxist (Communist) dictatorship. The proof is in history. If we do not change our political course, civilization and Christianity will not survive in America. We have two and only two options. The one is to continue on our present course following the laws of man to anarchy and to destruction. The other course is to turn to the Laws of God. We have not had to make a hard choice until recently because our laws of man were not so

---

137. Thomas Jefferson, The Writings of Thomas Jefferson, vol. 15 (Washington, DC: Thomas Jefferson Memorial Association of the United States, 1903), 277.

divergent from the Laws of God that we could not muddle along and "get by." But this is changing and changing fast.

At work are two divergent political ideologies. The one is the Constitution of the United States, built in congruence with the Laws of God. The other is Marxism, built upon the laws of man. Or, to put aside all subtleties and put it to you straight—the Laws of the Devil. The Laws of the Devil are exactly the opposite of the Laws of God, just as Marxism is exactly the opposite of the Laws of the Constitution.

The average person reading this will probably be shocked and exclaim "extremism" in his attempt to escape the obvious. But if one will examine the Constitution honestly and the Ten Points of the Communist Manifesto honestly and then examine the governmental structure and the laws of the federal and the state governments, he will come to the awful realization that our government is more Marxist than it is Constitutional. Have you paid attention to what has happened to the people of other Communist countries? Russia? China? Poland? Romania? Venezuela? Cuba? I have.

Let us never forget that America was founded by courageous and knowledgeable men and women resisting the tyranny of King George III. These brave American colonists were considered to be traitors by the British. They would have been hung if caught. These American colonists constitute a perfect example of lesser magistrates defying the tyrannical rule of a higher magistrate. By their defiance, bravery and knowledge, they made America and laid the foundation for our freedom.

Possible Solutions to Our Problems

First, for any correction to this problem to occur, there must be more understanding by the general public, by county officials, sheriffs, state legislators, state attorneys general, governors, the leaders of both political parties, U. S. Representatives, U. S. Senators and Presidents. Also lawyers and law school professors. This will have to be started by a grass-roots movement, with people like you and me doing the work.

The Doctrine of the Lesser Magistrate. There is a little-known but very legitimate, legal and moral way for citizens to countermand the illegal and tyrannical efforts of rogue politicians and judges. It was used when the **knights brought King John to Runnymeade to address abuses of power. The result was the Magna Charta It is the exercise of righteous power by lesser officials such as state governors and, especially, sheriffs, to refuse to comply with the unrighteous and illegal demands of higher officials. Such act is called "to int**erpose." Few Americans understand this principle, but if the Constitution is the supreme law of the land, then this principle of interposition and of the doctrine of the lesser magistrate is legal and moral.

Here "unconstitutional" is explained in an encyclopedia of law called *American Jurisprudence:*[137]

> *Since an unconstitutional law is void, the general principles follow that it imposes no duties, confers no rights, creates no office, bestows no power or authority on anyone, affords no protection and justifies no acts performed under it . . .*
>
> *A void act cannot be legally consistent with a valid one.*
>
> ***An unconstitutional law cannot operate to supersede any existing valid law.***
>
> *Indeed, insofar as a statute runs counter to the fundamental law of the land, it is superseded thereby.*
>
> ***No one is bound to obey an unconstitutional law and no courts are bound to enforce it.***
>
> — Sixteenth American Jurisprudence, 2nd Ed. Sec. 177. (late 2nd Ed. Sec. 256) *(*Emphasis added.*)*

If one understands this fundamental principle of constitutional law, explained above, he can then begin to understand the logic, legality and morality of interposition and the doctrine of the lesser magistrate. There is no wiggle room. Either the above is true and accurate and the doctrine of the lesser magistrate is perfectly legal and moral, or the Constitution is not the supreme law of the land, as stated in Article VI of the Constitution itself.

We must not perceive that every law issued is one that we must revere, sustain and support as if it were the Constitutional law of the land. We might be forced to obey an unconstitutional law simply because the government, even though legally and morally wrong, wields the power to enforce it. But we need not revere, sustain and support such law nor respect those who enforce it. We must vigorously oppose every unconstitutional "law," regardless of whether it originated in the executive, legislative or judicial branch. Our freedoms and the future of America and religious freedoms depend upon it.

A Lesser Authority Standing on Legitimate, Constitutional Law Wields More Authority than a higher authority standing on unconstitutional law. Thus, a sheriff can wield more authority standing on constitutional law than does the governor or agents of the federal government standing on unconstitutional law. The federal government has used bluff and the lack of

---

138. https://caselaw.findlaw.com/us-supreme-court/330/1.html

knowledge of the American people to enforce unconstitutional laws and programs.

Wisdom from Pastor Matthew Trewhella[138] and from Founder James Madison

THE IDEA that lawless federal courts, including the U. S. Supreme Court, must be obeyed-even when they write opinions that uphold injustice and murder - *is a fiction.*

The Supremacy Cause - Article 6, Clause 2 of the U. S. Constitution - *nowhere* declares that federal courts or the U. S. Supreme Court has supremacy for declaring what is constitutional. Rather, it states that the U. S. Constitution itself has supremacy. All government officials take an oath to uphold the Constitution. they do *not* take an oath of subservience to the federal judiciary.

When the Supreme Court acts outside the limits of the Constitution, it is incumbent upon the lesser magistrates, within their spheres of authority, to maintain allegiance to the U.S. Constitution and not blithely obey federal lawlessness. Nowhere are the states compelled to a suicide pact with a lawless federal government. (Matthew Trewhella)

WHEN THE FEDERAL GOVERNMENT MAKES UNJUST OR IMMORAL LAWS OR COURT OPINIONS… "…the states who are parties thereto [parties to the U.S. Constitution], have the right and **are in duty bound**, to interpose for arresting the progress of evil." (JAMES MADISON, ARCHITECT OF THE U. S. CONSTITUTION)

This Doctrine saved the lives of some innocent people. A perfect example of this principle was when a military commander defied the order of his commander to execute some innocent people The year was 1838. The place was Caldwell County, Missouri. The innocent men to be executed were Joseph Smith and several others. The general giving the order to shoot the condemned men was Major General Samuel D. Lucas. The military commander to whom the order was given was Brigadier General Alexander W. Doniphan (1808-1887). Here is the order and the response:

[To] Brigadier General Doniphan:
Sir: You will take Joseph Smith and the other prisoners into the public square of Far West and shoot them at 9 o'clock tomorrow morning.
[From] Samuel D. Lucas

---

139. https://www.supremecourt.gov/opinions/14pdf/14-556_3204.pdf

Major-General Commanding

Here is the response from Brigadier General Doniphan to Major General Lucas:

> It is cold-blooded murder. I will not obey your order. My brigade shall march for Liberty tomorrow morning at 8 o'clock and if you execute these men, I will hold you responsible before an earthly tribunal, so help me God.
> A. W, Doniphan, Brigadier General

General Doniphan did what was obviously morally and legally correct. He *interposed* on behalf of the innocent prisoners. How unfortunate that our politicians of today fail to understand either the morals involved or the Constitutional principals in our American system of law. Oh yes-General Lucas did not have the prisoners executed. General Doniphan, due to his courage and his understanding of natural law and interposition, saved them. (For more on this subject of *The Doctrine of the Lesser Magistrate*, see the Appendix)

Standing Up to Tyrannical Petty Politicians and Bureaucrats. This past and on-going "pandemic" might prove to be the most grandiose scam ever perpetrated on mankind. Here is one fact that is undeniable: no officer of government possessed the legal authority to order us to wear masks nor to order businesses to be shut down nor churches to not operate or to be restricted. This whole thing has been done by raw, unconstitutional, usurped power. No emergency authority exists to override nor negate the Constitution of the United States nor any state constitution.

Article IV Sec. 4 states: "The United States shall guarantee to every State in this Union a Republican Form of Government,..." This means that no executive has the authority to write law. Only the legislature. That applies to federal as well as state governments. No executive has the authority to create law and then enforce it. In the madness of this "pandemic," we have seen petty little tyrants, with unlimited lust for power not granted to them legally, issue orders with no constitutional authority and run roughshod over the American people.

First We Heal Ourselves

While we are working toward restoring the Constitution, we can start on smaller objectives. We can start with studying the rudiments of the Constitution and then the Ten Points of the Communist Manifesto so that we can be able to differentiate between them. Then we teach

> The healing of our land begins with each individual American. We must gain an understanding of the Constitution. Then, we must understand the Communist Manifesto, beginning with the Ten Points. Then, we must understand the difference between constitutional laws and Marxist ones.

these to our children and grandchildren. We teach them also how evolution and Secular Humanism are hostile to Christianity. We teach them that there are many things in this world that are false, yet come from "respectable" sources. Teach them that we must be selective in what we choose to believe. To search for the truth. And to reject those things that are not true. Make the education of your children the top priority in your life. Consider home-schooling them or transferring them to a (be very selective) private school. When we teach our children we surprise ourselves at what we ourselves learn. Teaching is the very best learning process.

We constantly increase our understanding by reading reliable literature.

We pray daily to the Lord to help us to increase our understanding and to help us to avoid being deceived by the adversary. We ask him to help us to be more effective in standing up to defend Him and His words (His gospel and everything related to it.)

In the near future, we might be called upon to disobey civil authorities in order to protect our liberties and to defend the gospel of Jesus Christ. This is because, in all cases where the enemies of Christ and of America use the law to persecute Christian Americans, they use corrupted, unconstitutional "law." We are, in many ways, in the same circumstance as Jesus was when he was tried by the corrupt authorities who violated the legitimate laws in order to get a conviction. Or Daniel when he was thrown into the lion's den.

For more on this subject, see Appendix "H," "The Doctrine of the Lesser Magistrates."

Just a word of caution. Although this doctrine of the lesser magistrates is perfectly legal and moral, it is not without its dangers. In any situation in which it must be deployed, those who love corrupt law and who hate legitimate law will be in power. So one must have a sufficient number of citizens on his side in order to be successful. No good is accomplished by one who becomes a martyr without results.

This battle is likely to get MEAN. In the days ahead, which might become very dark, just always remember-we have the most powerful force in the universe on our side.

A Huge Victory for Freedom of Religion

From: Mat Staver, Founder and Chief Counsel for Liberty Counsel, Orlando, FL (Rcvd 28 May, 2021):

We must never go down this road again where our freedom is trampled by tyrannical potentates. Our historic case in California is the beginning of the end to permanently quarantine these godless governors.

California Gov. Gavin Newsom must pay 1.35 million dollars for persecuting churches. Neither he nor California will ever again steal the religious freedom of Californians, thanks to a historic court order achieved by Liberty Counsel. Read on to learn more.

This is a miraculous victory, but we still have churches to free in other states, including Maine where our case defending Calvary Chapel is before the Supreme Court. *Please help us keep defending religious liberty and have YOUR IMPACT DOUBLED BY THE CHALLENGE GRANT!*

Having terrorized California churches for over a year, Gov. Gavin Newsom has now been forced to give up-*and pay up.*

Liberty Counsel has obtained a PERMANENT STATEWIDE injunction prohibiting Newsom and the State of California from EVER issuing another discriminatory restriction on ANY church or place of worship! And this is not limited to COVID restrictions.

No more church closings. No more capacity limits. No more singing bans. No more fines. No more threats of prison. NO MORE Not ever.

The California churches are once again FREE to worship and minister to people as the Lord leads, not as government dictates.

The Constitution has been fully restored and vindicated!

This is the FIRST statewide permanent injunction in the nation. Every persecuted in California benefits from this win. California had to call a cease-fire. Now the state will have to pay each church for persecuting them. The three million dollar fine on a southern California church will end!

The California churches are once again FREE to worship and minister to people as the Lord leads, not as government dictates.

Some More Good News: Judicial Watch is going state to state in the critical states assisting in the fixing of our electoral process.

Chapter Twenty - The Constitution is the Solution

The Constitution of the United States is Misunderstood, Greatly Under-Appreciated and Repeatedly Violated

Most of the problems in our country are the direct result of violating the Constitution. However, the Leftist professors and politicians blame our problems on the Constitution itself. But the problems are NOT caused by the Constitution. They are caused by VIOLATIONS of the Constitution. This nation has turned away from God and the Constitution. History proves that when people do this, there are serious consequences. If we were to turn back to the Constitution, we would turn back to God. This is because the Constitution is based on natural law, which is God's law for man.

It is difficult for us to appreciate the value of the Constitution. In our day, educators ridicule it, law school professors denigrate it, Supreme Courts misinterpret it, politicians violate it and so the general public knows little about it and what they do know is subject to gross error. We must study it and do some deep thinking. Look at the governments of the other countries of the world and how the people there suffer. The Framers of our Constitution created a masterpiece. The political and cultural problems that we are having in America today are not because of defects in the original Constitution. They are caused by violations of that Constitution. To demonstrate how special these men and women who founded our country were and the men who framed the Constitution, we are told that the Lord Himself raised them up for this very purpose. (See D&C 101:80). How many other people in the world have had men raised up by the Lord for the very purpose of creating a government for them?

In August of 1877, the spirits of some of the Founders and other important people were permitted to appear in the St. George temple to President Woodruff and asked him why had their work not been done for them. Now THAT is special. So President Woodruff proceeded immediately to baptize a live brother on behalf of several of them and some others.

ALL of the problems that we have that are political result from violations of the Constitution. They also result from the violation of moral principles. If we can restore the Constitution in our country, we can restore peace and prosperity. When we uphold the Constitution, we uphold the principles the Lord has taught us, because the Constitution was constructed on Christian principles. Consider from 2 Chronicles Chapter 7:

> 14 If my people, which are called by my name, shall humble themselves and pray and seek my face and turn from their wicked ways; then will I hear from heaven and will forgive their sin and will heal their land.

15 Now mine eyes shall be open and mine ears attent unto the prayer *that is made* in this place.

We are His people. But what are these wicked ways that we should turn from? I submit that we should turn from socialism, Communism and all the theories and ideologies that support Marxism. Many of His people have been guilty of embracing socialism, or certain principles of socialism. The Constitution is the Lord's form of government for man. Marxism is the Devil's form of government for man.

Let us now humble ourselves and pray and seek His face and turn from our wicked ways and ask for His forgiveness and for Him to heal our land.

The signs of the times indicate that we are likely to face serious times in the near future. Here is an excerpt from President Russell M. Nelson's talk, "Revelation for the Church, Revelation for our Lives," from the April, 2018 General Conference:[139]

> In coming days, it will not be possible to survive spiritually without the guiding, directing, comforting and constant influence of the Holy Ghost.

I submit that for us to have the influence of the Holy Ghost to comfort us, we must obey the Lord's commandments to defend His gospel, every principle and support His form of government and oppose the Devil's form of government. We must expose and oppose all of the Devil's works of darkness.[140]

The odds against us are staggering. But remember—the most powerful force in the universe is on our side.

Just a couple more items: First: I highly recommend that you pull up the speech Justice Alito to the Federalist Society on 12 Nov 2020 and read it very carefully. It contains much wisdom and Second: I also recommend that you read the dissents by the dissenting justices in the *Obergefell* case in Chapter 13 herein. Much wisdom therein and, Third: Home school your children, with the assistance of a good extension course from a good school. Make sure your children learn the principles of Christianity and its opposite, the principles of Secular Humanism. Make sure they learn the fundamentals of the Constitution and the fundamentals of its opposite, the Communist Manifesto.

The Righteous are Always Persecuted by the Wicked Using Corrupt Laws

---

140. Obergefell v. Hodges, 135 S. Ct. 2584, 2604-05, 192 L. Ed. 2d 609 (2015)

I close with this truism: The righteous are and always have been and always will be, persecuted and killed by unrighteous men using corrupted laws. If we allow the corruption of our laws to continue, this will further empower and encourage the wicked to inflict persecution upon the righteous. If there is no limit put on this corruption, then there will be no limit as to the persecution that the wicked will inflict upon the righteous using these corrupted laws.

If You Want to be Effective, Join an Established Group that fights for the correct principles. Such group will no doubt be in disfavor by the popular media. Those who tell the truth always are. To fight for the truth, one must always be willing to take a little abuse. But cheer up. The way to meet the finest people is to be involved in a righteous cause that has been made unpopular by the media, the unrighteous and the ignorant.

Correcting the Arrogation of Power by the SCOTUS will require a president who will nominate just -ices who will rule by the Constitution and a Senate that will confirm them. That will require MUCH effort. In the meanwhile, we must expose and oppose the evil committed by the SCOTUS. I suggest this book as one instrument to accomplish this purpose.

Exposing the corruption in the SCOTUS has some added advantages. It introduces to others the corruption in one branch of the government and also the fact that there is probably corruption in the other branches. This can be very beneficial.

I conclude with my wishes for the Lord's blessings be upon you during the coming times and, especially, upon your efforts to defend and restore liberty and the blessings of God in our land.

The End

P.S, Following are names and addresses of institutions that help us when we are attacked because of our religious beliefs. Use them when necessary. Support them financially.

Recommended Reading and Periodicals:
1. *The New American* Magazine, Appleton, WI
2. *The "Last Days" Timeline* – Volume 1, by James T. Prout
3. *The "Last Days" Timeline* – Volume 2, by James T. Prout
4. *The President Makers,* by Don Fotheringham

2. *World Affairs Brief,* by Joel M. Skousen
3. *The Deep State-Pulling Strings From Behind the Scenes*, by Alex Newman. A Special edition of The New American Magazine, Appleton, WI
Books:
1. *The Doctrine of the Lesser Magistrate,* by Matthew J. Trewhella
5. *The Shadows of Power,* by James Perloff
6. *The Threat Within,* by David Horowitz
4. *Prophets, Principles and National Survival,* by Jerreld L. Newquist
5. *Original Intent,* by David Barton
6. *Global Gun Grab,* by William Norman Grigg
7. *The Enemy Within* by David Horowitz
8. *Dark Agenda The War to Destroy Christian America* by David Horowitz
9. *A Witness And A Warning,* by Ezra Taft Benson
10. *Christianity And The Constitution* by John Eidsmoe
11. *Coercing Virtue* by Judge Robert H. Bork
12. *The Bilderberg Group, NAU Ed.* by Daniel Estulin
13. *Killing The Deep State,* by Jerome Corsi

Sources for Help in Home Schooling:
American Heritage Schools Website: "American-Heritage.org"
Admissions Office: Admissions @AHS mail.com 801 642 0055 ext 310
Hillsdale College: Key in "Hillsdale College" in your URL click on "online courses."
Liberty University: Key in "Liberty University," click on "Online Academy."
Freedom Project Academy FPEUSA.org 920 749 3793
Provost Joseph Becker, M.S., J.D., provided these links to talks given at Mises Institute that you might find interesting:
https://www.youtube.com/watch?v=3QMSDJn2wSU

https://www.youtube.com/watch?v=0sNWbiAMf80

https://www.youtube.com/watch?v=xbtrVlMqPRw

Institutions that help Christians with their legal defenses when attacked for their
religious beliefs and activities.
Alliance Defending Freedom 15100 N. 90th St Scottsdale, AZ 85260 720 689 2410
First Liberty Institute 2001 W. Plano Parkway Plano, Texas 75075 972 941 4444
Liberty Counsel PO Box 540774 Orlando, FL 32854 407-875-1776
The Becket Fund:https://www.becketlaw.org/
The Foundation for Moral Law, Montgomery, AL 334 262 1245 info@morallaw.org

APPENDIX

Appendix A: Obergefell

Link to Obergefell: www.law.cornell.edu/supremecourt/text/14-556

Excerpts from the majority opinion:

(Voting in the majority were Justices Anthony M. Kennedy, Ruth Bader Ginsburg, Stephen G. Breyer, Sonia Sotomayor and Elena Kagan)
>These considerations lead to the conclusion that the right to marry is a fundamental right inherent in the liberty of the person and under the Due Process and Equal Protection Clauses of the Fourteenth Amendment couples of the same-sex may not be deprived of that right and that liberty. The Court now holds that same-sex couples may exercise the fundamental right to marry. No longer may this liberty be denied to them. Baker v. Nelson must be and now is overruled and the State laws challenged by Petitioners in these cases are now held invalid to the extent they exclude same-sex couples from civil marriage on the same terms and conditions as opposite-sex couples. *Obergefell v. Hodges*, 135 S. Ct. 2584, 2604-05, 192 L. Ed. 2d 609 (2015)

Excerpts from Dissenting Opinions Chief Justice John Roberts, Justices Antonin Scalia, Samuel Alito and Clarence Thomas:
Obergefell v. Hodges, 135 S.Ct. 2584 (2015). Here is the link to the case with the dissenting opinions: http:///opinions/14pdf/14-556_3204.pdf
Chief Justice John Roberts, joined by Justices Scalia and Thomas: (at p. 19)

>But this Court is not a legislature. Whether same-sex marriage is a good idea should be of no concern to us. Under the Constitution, judges have power to say what the law is, not what it should be. The people who ratified the Constitution authorized courts to exercise "neither force nor will but merely judgment." The Federalist No. 78, p. 465 (C. Rossiter ed. 1961) (A. Hamilton) (capitalization altered).
>
>Although the policy arguments for extending marriage to same-sex couples may be compelling, the legal arguments for requiring such an extension are not. The fundamental right to marry does not include a right to make a State change its definition of marriage. And a State's decision to maintain the meaning of marriage that has persisted in every culture throughout human history can hardly be called irrational. In short, our Constitution does not enact any one theory of marriage. The people of a State are free to expand marriage to include same-sex couples, or to retain the historic definition.

Justice Antonin Scalia, joined by Justice Thomas: (at p. 30)
>The substance of today's decree is not of immense personal importance to me. The law can recognize as marriage whatever sexual attachments and

living arrangements *2627 it wishes and can accord them favorable civil consequences, from tax treatment to rights of inheritance. Those civil consequences--and the public approval that conferring the name of marriage evidences--can perhaps have adverse social effects, but no more adverse than the effects of many other controversial laws. So it is not of special importance to me what the law says about marriage. It is of overwhelming importance, however, **who** it is that rules me. Today's decree says that my Ruler and the Ruler of 320 million Americans coast-to-coast, **is a majority of the nine lawyers on the Supreme Court**. The opinion in these cases is the furthest extension in fact--and the furthest extension one can even imagine--of **the Court's claimed power to create "liberties"** that the Constitution and its Amendments **neglect to mention**. This practice of **constitutional revision** by an unelected committee of nine, always accompanied (as it is today) by extravagant praise of liberty, **robs the People** of the most important liberty they asserted in the Declaration of Independence and won in the Revolution of 1776: **the freedom to govern themselves.**

Justice Clarence Thomas, joined Justice Scalia: (at p. 33)
The Court's decision today is at odds not only with the Constitution, but with the principles upon which our Nation was built. Since well before 1787, liberty has been understood **as freedom from government action**, not entitlement to government benefits. The Framers created our Constitution to preserve that understanding of liberty. Yet **the majority** invokes our Constitution in the name of a "liberty" that the Framers **would not have recognized**, to the detriment of the liberty they sought to protect. Along the way, it rejects the idea--captured in our Declaration of Independence--that human dignity is innate and suggests instead that it comes from the Government. This distortion of our Constitution not only ignores the text, it inverts the relationship between the individual and the state in our Republic. I cannot agree with it.

Most Americans--understandably--will cheer or lament today's decision because of their views on the issue of same-sex marriage. But all Americans, whatever their thinking on that issue, **should worry about what the majority's claim of power portends.**

Appendix B - How Obergefell Threatens Religious Liberty, America and Civilization

1. By overriding our state laws, *Obergefell* destroys our ability to control the laws affecting our religious liberties through our state legislatures.
2. Puts our religious liberties in jeopardy by being subject to rulings of judges in Washington, D.C. who might be Secular Humanists and/or Marxists.
3. Assaults, in its attempt to change, the definition of marriage.
4. Denigrates the traditional and long-standing Christian meaning and purpose of marriage.
5. Legitimizes and glorifies sodomy, in contradiction of centuries-old Christian values. It outlaws Christian values and criminalizes Christian practices regarding denying marriage to same-sex couples.
6. Forces county clerks and others, including ministers and clergy, to perform marriages of gays or lesbians when the religious values of same might be contrary to gay and lesbian marriages. Has absolutely no concern for the rights of these people.
7. Threatens to force the Church of Jesus Christ of Latter-day Saints and probably others, to perform marriages in their temples and other edifices considered sacred, of gays and lesbians, when such marriages would be in strong conflict with the policies and values of these churches, their governing bodies and their members.
8. Puts all laws, state and federal, subject to a gang of five or more rogue lawyers who have contempt for the Constitutions of both the United States and of all of the fifty states and for the laws of all fifty states.
9. Puts all laws, state and federal, including those affecting our religious freedoms, subject to the whims of five or more lawyers who, in defying the Constitution of the United States, exercise illicit powers whose limits know no bounds. Furthermore, unknown to the public, these judges might either be Secular Humanist or Marxists or might be sympathetic to the Secular Humanists and Marxists, whose ideologies are hostile to Christianity. These judges might be disposed to ignore the Constitution and to rule according to their own ideologies, which would put Christianity and all Christians in jeopardy.
10. Threatens churches that operate universities or schools to provide rental quarters to married students, whose standards or honor code might exclude LGBT couples.
11. Defies the nature and origin of rights for all Americans. Our rights, (all of them, not just a fraction) under the American system of law, come from our Creator. Our Creator not only has never approved nor condoned same-sex marriage or relationship, He has condemned such. (Leviticus 18:22, Deut. 23:17, Rom 1:27. For more see Bible, Topical Guide.)
12. By creating "rights" (in reality special privileges) for the LGBT crowd that had never before existed, the SCOTUS perverted the role of government. Under the American form of government, our rights are bestowed upon us by our Creator. The proper role for the government is to protect those rights. In

Obergefell, the SCOTUS played the role of the Creator of these rights. Thus, the LGBT people will naturally perceive the SCOTUS, not our real God, as being their "god." Thus, the LGBT people are added to the millions who draw federal welfare according to "rights" to this welfare bestowed by the Congress or the SCOTUS. Thus, the Congress or the SCOTUS becomes their "god."
Thus, a huge portion of the population considers as their "god" the President, the Congress or the SCOTUS. In crisis times (and crises can be natural or manufactured) these mobs (or armies) can be dangerously explosive and destructive. These people are not loyal to Americanism. Nor to the one true God. They are loyal to the false "gods" of the corrupted part of our government.
The above might seem abstract. But I tell you that it is very real. These people do not appreciate the working, taxpaying people who make their welfare payments possible. They despise us. Explosive situation. Dangerous situation.

Alma 10:27 And now behold, I say unto you, that the foundation of the destruction of this people is beginning to be laid by the unrighteousness of your lawyers and your judges.

Appendix C - George Washington's Farewell Address

George Washington's Farewell Address 17 September, 1796 (Excerpts therefrom)

...It is important, likewise, that the habits of thinking in a free country should inspire caution, in those entrusted with its administration, to confine themselves within their respective constitutional spheres, avoiding in the exercise of the powers of one department to encroach upon another. The spirit of encroachment tends to consolidate the powers of all the departments in one and thus to create, whatever the form of government, a real despotism.

A just estimate of that love of power and proneness to abuse it, which predominates in the human heart, is sufficient to satisfy us of the truth of this position. The necessity of reciprocal checks in the exercise of political power, by dividing and distributing it into different depositories and constituting each the guardian of the public weal against invasions by the others, has been evinced by experiments ancient and modern; some of them in our country and under our own eyes.

To preserve them must be as necessary as to institute them. If, in the opinion of the people, the distribution or modification of the Constitutional powers be in any particular wrong, let it be corrected by an amendment in the way which the Constitution designates.

But let there be no change by usurpation; for, though this, in one instance, may be the instrument of good, it is the customary weapon by which free governments are destroyed. The precedent must always greatly overbalance in permanent evil any partial or transient benefit which the use can at any time yield.
Of all the dispositions and habits which lead to political prosperity, religion and morality are indispensable supports.

In vain would that man claim the tribute of patriotism, who should labor to subvert these great pillars of human happiness, these firmest props of the duties of men and citizens. The mere politician, equally with the pious man, ought to respect and to cherish them. A volume could not trace all their connections with private and public felicity.

Let it simply be asked, Where is the security for property, for reputation, for life, if the sense of religious obligation desert the oaths which are the instruments of investigation in courts of justice? And let us with caution indulge the supposition that morality can be maintained without religion. Whatever may be conceded to the influence of refined education on minds of peculiar structure, reason and experience both forbid us to expect that national morality can prevail in exclusion of religious principle. 'Tis substantially true, that virtue or morality is a necessary spring of popular government. The rule, indeed, extends with more or less force to every species of free government. Who that is a sincere friend to it, can look with indifference upon attempts to shake the foundation of the fabric?...

Appendix D - How to Study the Constitution

To facilitate understanding the original intent of the Constitution, keep the following in mind:
1. The Constitution means what it says, not what the Supreme Court or some lawyer or law school professor says it means.
2. The Constitution is a grant of power from the people to the federal government. The fedgov has NO legitimate authority other than that specified in the Constitution. Any exercise of power other than that specified in the Constitution constitutes usurpation,.
3. According to Article I Section I of the Constitution, All (repeat ALL) legislative Powers herein granted shall be vested in a Congress of the United States,...NOTE: No legislative powers are vested in the executive branch or the judicial branch. The president can legitimately issue executive orders to administer the affairs of the executive branch. He has NO authority to issue or to enforce executive orders that affect the lives, liberties and properties of the American citizens and which violate Amendments IX and X to the Constitution. No judicial powers, such as are exercised by the regulatory agencies, are granted to the President. None.
 It is true that, due to checks and balances, one branch may legitimately negate the acts of another, but it can never exercise the powers of another.
4. The separation of powers into the legislative, executive and judicial branches is absolute. No branch can legally exercise powers not vested in it by the Constitution.
5. According to Article I, Sec. 8, the authority to declare war is vested in the Congress. The executive branch does not possess the power to declare war. The Congress does not have the authority to delegate to the executive branch the power to declare war.
6. Any agreement that the executive branch makes with a foreign nation constitutes a
treaty and the Constitution says (Article II): "...He [the president] shall have power, by and with the advice and consent of the Senate, to make Treaties, provided two thirds of the Senators present concur;..." Note: The president does NOT have the authority to unilaterally enter into a treaty with a foreign nation. All treaties require the advice and consent 2/3 of the Senate.
7. VERY IMPORTANT to saving America, our religious liberties and all of our liberties, learn the meaning of Article III, Sec. 2, par 2 of the Constitution of the United States, which reads: "...the supreme Court shall have appellate Jurisdiction, both as to Law and Fact, with such Exceptions and under such Regulations as the Congress shall make." (Emphasis added)
8. And MOST IMPORTANT: Not only does the Constitution not empower the federal government to meddle with the affairs of the citizens regarding life, liberty and property, the Ninth and Tenth Amendments specifically forbid it. Each state should be a sovereign entity and each citizen a sovereign citizen.

H. Usurpation-Definition thereof (Black's Law Dictionary, 1979.)

The unlawful encroachment or assumption of the use of property, over or authority which belongs to another. An interruption or the disturbing a man in his right and possession.

The unlawful seizure or assumption of sovereign over. The Assumption of government or supreme power by force or illegally, in derogation of the Constitution and of the rights of the lawful ruler.

Usurpation for which writ of prohibition may be granted involves attempted exercise of power not possessed by inferior officer.

Note: The enemies of the Constitution use usurpation extensively to assume and exercise powers that they cannot gain legally. Without the use of usurpation, the enemies of the Constitution would be rendered powerless. It behooves all of us to understand the term usurpation and to recognize it when we see it so that we can expose and oppose it. George Washington's Farewell Address addresses the danger of usurpation very succinctly.

Appendix E - Excerpts from the *Declaration of Independence*

Understanding the Declaration is prerequisite to understanding the Constitution. Here are a few comments regarding some of the more salient parts of the Declaration:
> We hold these truths to be self-evident, that all men are created equal, that they are <u>endowed by their Creator with certain unalienable Rights,</u> that among these are Life, Liberty and the pursuit of Happiness. That to secure these rights, Governments are instituted among Men, deriving their just powers from the consent of the governed... (Emphasis added)

Note that the Declaration states that our rights come from our Creator. This is in sharp contrast to the current policy of the fedgov of extending special privileges and calling them "rights." It seems that the politicians want us to believe that our rights come from them and not from our Creator. As if the politicians want us to believe that they are our gods.

This is the very reason that some want to use the misinterpreted metaphor, "Separation of Church and State," to force the teaching of evolution to all students in the public schools. They do not want the children to learn that their rights actually come from their Creator.

Full Text of the Declaration can be found here.

The Declaration of Independence
IN CONGRESS, July 4, 1776. The unanimous Declaration of the thirteen united States of America,

When in the Course of human events, it becomes necessary for one people to dissolve the political bands which have connected them with another and to assume among the powers of the earth, the separate and equal station to which the Laws of Nature and of Nature's God entitle them, a decent respect to the opinions of mankind requires that they should declare the causes which impel them to the separation.

We hold these truths to be self-evident, that all men are created equal, that they are endowed by their Creator with certain unalienable Rights, that among these are Life, Liberty and the pursuit of Happiness.--That to secure these rights, Governments are instituted among Men, deriving their just powers from the consent of the governed, -- That whenever any Form of Government becomes destructive of these ends, it is the Right of the People to alter or to abolish it and to institute new Government, laying its foundation on such principles and organizing its powers in such form, as to them shall seem most likely to effect their Safety and Happiness. Prudence, indeed, will dictate that Governments long established should not be changed for light and transient causes; and accordingly all experience hath shewn, that mankind are more disposed to suffer, while evils are sufferable, than to right themselves by abolishing the forms to which they are accustomed. But when a long train of abuses and usurpations, pursuing invariably the same Object evinces a design to reduce them under absolute Despotism, it is their right, it is their duty, to throw off such Government and to provide new Guards for their future security.--Such has been the patient sufferance of these Colonies; and such is now the necessity which constrains them to alter their former Systems of Government.

The history of the present King of Great Britain is a history of repeated injuries and usurpations, all having in direct object the establishment of an absolute Tyranny over these States. To prove this, let Facts be submitted to a candid world.

He has refused his Assent to Laws, the most wholesome and necessary for the public good.

He has forbidden his Governors to pass Laws of immediate and pressing importance, unless suspended in their operation till his Assent should be obtained; and when so suspended, he has utterly neglected to attend to them.

He has refused to pass other Laws for the accommodation of large districts of people, unless those people would relinquish the right of Representation in the Legislature, a right inestimable to them and formidable to tyrants only.

He has called together legislative bodies at places unusual, uncomfortable and distant from the depository of their public Records, for the sole purpose of fatiguing them into compliance with his measures.

He has dissolved Representative Houses repeatedly, for opposing with manly firmness his invasions on the rights of the people.

He has refused for a long time, after such dissolutions, to cause others to be elected; whereby the Legislative powers, incapable of Annihilation, have returned to the People at large for their exercise; the State remaining in the mean time exposed to all the dangers of invasion from without and convulsions within.

He has endeavored to prevent the population of these States; for that purpose obstructing the Laws for Naturalization of Foreigners; refusing to pass others to encourage their migrations hither and raising the conditions of new Appropriations of Lands.

He has obstructed the Administration of Justice, by refusing his Assent to Laws for establishing Judiciary powers.

He has made Judges dependent on his Will alone, for the tenure of their offices and the amount and payment of their salaries.

He has erected a multitude of New Offices and sent hither swarms of Officers to harrass our people and eat out their substance.

He has kept among us, in times of peace, Standing Armies without the Consent of our legislatures.

He has affected to render the Military independent of and superior to the Civil power.

He has combined with others to subject us to a jurisdiction foreign to our Constitution and unacknowledged by our laws; giving his Assent to their Acts of pretended Legislation:

For Quartering large bodies of armed troops among us:

For protecting them, by a mock Trial, from punishment for any Murders which they should commit on the Inhabitants of these States:

For cutting off our Trade with all parts of the world:

For imposing Taxes on us without our Consent:

For depriving us in many cases, of the benefits of Trial by Jury:

For transporting us beyond Seas to be tried for pretended offences

For abolishing the free System of English Laws in a neighboring Province, establishing therein an Arbitrary government and enlarging its Boundaries so as to render it at once an example and fit instrument for introducing the same absolute rule into these Colonies:

For taking away our Charters, abolishing our most valuable Laws and altering fundamentally the Forms of our Governments:
For suspending our own Legislatures and declaring themselves invested with power to legislate for us in all cases whatsoever.

He has abdicated Government here, by declaring us out of his Protection and waging War against us.

He has plundered our seas, ravaged our Coasts, burnt our towns and destroyed the lives of our people.
He is at this time transporting large Armies of foreign Mercenaries to compleat the works of death, desolation and tyranny, already begun with circumstances of Cruelty & perfidy scarcely paralleled in the most barbarous ages and totally unworthy the Head of a civilized nation.

He has constrained our fellow Citizens taken Captive on the high Seas to bear Arms against their Country, to become the executioners of their friends and Brethren, or to fall themselves by their Hands.

He has excited domestic insurrections amongst us and has endeavoured to bring on the inhabitants of our frontiers, the merciless Indian Savages, whose known rule of warfare, is an undistinguished destruction of all ages, sexes and conditions.

In every stage of these Oppressions We have Petitioned for Redress in the most humble terms: Our repeated Petitions have been answered only by repeated injury. A Prince whose character is thus marked by every act which may define a Tyrant, is unfit to be the ruler of a free people.

Nor have We been wanting in attentions to our Brittish brethren. We have warned them from time to time of attempts by their legislature to extend an unwarrantable jurisdiction over us. We have reminded them of the circumstances of our emigration and settlement here. We have appealed to their native justice and magnanimity and we have conjured them by the ties of our common kindred to disavow these usurpations, which, would inevitably interrupt our connections and correspondence.

They too have been deaf to the voice of justice and of consanguinity. We must, therefore, acquiesce in the necessity, which denounces our Separation and hold them, as we hold the rest of mankind, Enemies in War, in Peace Friends.

We, therefore, the Representatives of the united States of America, in General Congress, Assembled, appealing to the Supreme Judge of the world for the rectitude of our intentions, do, in the Name and by Authority of the good People of these Colonies, solemnly publish and declare, That these United Colonies are and of Right ought to be Free and Independent States; that they are Absolved from all Allegiance to the British Crown and that all political connection between them and the State of Great Britain, is and ought to be totally dissolved; and that as Free and Independent States, they have full Power to levy War, conclude Peace, contract Alliances, establish Commerce and to do all other Acts and Things which Independent States may of right do. And for the support of this Declaration, with a firm reliance on the protection of divine Providence, we mutually pledge to each other our Lives, our Fortunes and our sacred Honor. (Emphasis added in various places above)

Appendix F - The Fourteenth Amendment

Note: The *Fourteenth* is presented here because the SCOTUS uses it as an excuse to ignore and violate the *Ninth* and *Tenth* and impose anti-constitutional "law" upon the states. In reality, there is nothing in the *Fourteenth* to justify such action.

Section 1. All persons born or naturalized in the United States and subject to the jurisdiction thereof, are citizens of the United States and of the State wherein they reside. No State shall make or enforce any law which shall abridge the privileges or immunities of citizens of the United States; nor shall any State deprive any person of life, liberty, or property, without due process of law; nor deny to any person within its jurisdiction the equal protection of the laws.

Section 2. Representatives shall be apportioned among the several States according to their respective numbers, counting the whole number of persons in each State, excluding Indians not taxed. But when the right to vote at any election for the choice of electors for President and Vice President of the United States, Representatives in Congress, the Executive and Judicial officers of a State, or the members of the Legislature thereof, is denied to any of the male inhabitants of such State, being twenty-one years of age and citizens of the United States, or in any way abridged, except for participation in rebellion, or other crime, the basis of representation therein shall be reduced in the proportion which the number of such male citizens shall bear to the whole number of male citizens twenty-one years of age in such State.

Section 3. No person shall be a Senator or Representative in Congress, or elector of President and Vice President, or hold any office, civil or military, under the United States, or under any State, who, having previously taken an oath, as a member of Congress, or as an officer of the United States, or as a member of any State legislature, or as an executive or judicial officer of any State, to support the Constitution of the United States, shall have engaged in insurrection or rebellion against the same, or given aid or comfort to the enemies thereof. But Congress may, by a vote of two-thirds of each House, remove such disability.

Section 4. The validity of the public debt of the United States, authorized by law, including debts incurred for payment of pensions and bounties for services in suppressing insurrection or rebellion, shall not be questioned. But neither the United States nor any State shall assume or pay any debt or obligation incurred in aid of insurrection or rebellion against the United States, or any claim for the loss or emancipation of any slave; but all such debts, obligations and claims shall be held illegal and void.

Section 5. The Congress shall have power to enforce, by appropriate legislation, the provisions of this article.

Appendix G - The Bill of Rights

The First 10 Amendments to the Constitution as Ratified by the States, 1791

Preamble

Congress OF THE United States
begun and held at the City of New York, on Wednesday
the Fourth of March, one thousand seven hundred and eighty nine.
THE Conventions of a number of the States having at the time of their adopting the Constitution, expressed a desire, in order to prevent misconstruction or abuse of its powers, that further declaratory and restrictive clauses should be added: And as extending the ground of public confidence in the Government, will best insure the beneficent ends of its institution
RESOLVED by the Senate and House of Representatives of the United States of America, in Congress assembled, two thirds of both Houses concurring, that the following Articles be proposed to the Legislatures of the several States, as Amendments to the Constitution of the United States, all or any of which Articles, when ratified by three fourths of the said Legislatures, to be valid to all intents and purposes, as part of the said Constitution; viz.:
ARTICLES in addition to and Amendment of the Constitution of the United States of America, proposed by Congress and ratified by the Legislatures of the several States, pursuant to the fifth Article of the original Constitution.
Amendment I: Congress shall make no law respecting an establishment of religion, or prohibiting the free exercise thereof; or abridging the freedom of speech, or of the press; or the right of the people peaceably to assemble and to petition the Government for a redress of grievances.
Amendment II: A well regulated Militia, being necessary to the security of a free State, the right of the people to keep and bear Arms, shall not be infringed.
Amendment III: No Soldier shall, in time of peace be quartered in any house, without the consent of the Owner, nor in time of war, but in a manner to be prescribed by law.
Amendment IV: The right of the people to be secure in their persons, houses, papers and effects, against unreasonable searches and seizures, shall not be violated and no Warrants shall issue, but upon probable cause, supported by Oath or affirmation and particularly describing the place to be searched and the persons or things to be seized.
Amendment V: No person shall be held to answer for a capital, or otherwise infamous crime, unless on a presentment or indictment of a Grand Jury, except in cases arising in the land or naval forces, or in the Militia, when in actual service in time of War or public danger; nor shall any person be subject for the same offence to be twice put in jeopardy of life or limb; nor shall be compelled in any criminal case to be a witness against himself, nor be

deprived of life, liberty, or property, without due process of law; nor shall private property be taken for public use, without just compensation.

Amendment VI: In all criminal prosecutions, the accused shall enjoy the right to a speedy and public trial, by an impartial jury of the State and district wherein the crime shall have been committed, which district shall have been previously ascertained by law and to be informed of the nature and cause of the accusation; to be confronted with the witnesses against him; to have compulsory process for obtaining witnesses in his favor and to have the Assistance of Counsel for his defense.

Amendment VII: In suits at common law, where the value in controversy shall exceed twenty dollars, the right of trial by jury shall be preserved and no fact tried by a jury, shall be otherwise reexamined in any Court of the United States, than according to the rules of the common law.

Amendment VIII: Excessive bail shall not be required, nor excessive fines imposed, nor cruel and unusual punishments inflicted.

Amendment IX: The enumeration in the Constitution, of certain rights, shall not be construed to deny or disparage others retained by the people.

Amendment X: The powers not delegated to the United States by the Constitution, nor prohibited by it to the States, are reserved to the States respectively, or to the people.

Appendix H - Congress Supposed to Regulate the Supreme Court

: Article III, Sec. 2, Par 2 of the Constitution of the United States
"...the supreme Court shall have appellate Jurisdiction, both as to Law and Fact, <u>with such Exceptions and under such Regulations</u> **as the Congress shall make**." (Emphasis added)

Appendix I

Appendix J - The Doctrine of the Lesser Magistrate

(Continued from previous in Chapter 20, "Defending Christ and His Gospel" Quotes from *The Doctrine of the Lesser Magistrates - A Proper Resistance to Tyranny and a Repudiation of Unlimited Obedience to Civil Government* by Matthew J. Trewhella:

> Page 28: When the lesser magistrates act, there will be those who will accuse them of anarchy and chaos. Because Americans have heard the mantra their entire lives that "We are a nation of law - we must respect the rule of law" many tend to believe the accusations. But what if unjust or tyrannical law has been made? Are we to respect it just because the State declares it to be *"the law of the land?"* Are we to passively stand by and conform?
>
> Western history exclaims a resounding -"NO!" From Thomas Aquinas who declared that "an unjust law is no law at all" to the Nurenburg Trials where unquestioned obedience to man's law was soundly condemned - Western history points out our duty to disobey when ordered to do that which is unjust or wrong, even when the civil government has made it legal. As America's founders were known to say, "Disobedience to tyrants is obedience to God." (Used by Jefferson on his personal seal.
>
> *The duty to resist unjust law is the product of Christian thought.* Our loyalty is to Christ first - not man, not the State. So when the civil government makes unjust or immoral laws or policies, we obey Christ, not the State. Christianity acts as a check to tyranny. The whole of society should be thankful for the preservation of liberty that Christianity engenders. Christians are the best of citizens. We obey the State and are productive in commerce. We disobey the State only when they make unjust or immoral law. We have a salvific affect upon society as a whole.
>
> When Christians practiced civil disobedience by blockading the doors of America's abortion clinics in the early 1900's in an attempt to protect the preborn from a brutal death, they were accused of anarchy and chaos and admonished to respect the rule of law. The truth is the U.S. Supreme Court instigated anarchy and chaos when they declared preborn babies open game to those who would kill-for-profit in their 1973 Roe v. Wade decision. Those blockading the doors were actually trying to restore order.
>
> The U.S. Supreme Court was the anarchist, not the pro-lifers. [The SCOTUS violated the Constitution in its decision of Roe v. Wade]
>
> When the lesser magistrates are accused of insubordination or anarchy because they interpose against bad law, the counterfeit man-made "rule of law" will be heralded by the Statists. They will sing and herald the mantra - "we must obey the rule of law!" But if the rule of law

itself is unjust and immoral, then what virtue is there in supporting it? To do so is to stand the rule of law on its head.

Man should not respect "the rule of law" just because "it's the rule of law," rather we respect it because as Blackstone said - it does not "contradict" the law of God. This is why Western Civilization respected the rule of law for nearly 1,500 years, precisely because it was based upon the law of God.

The Laws of God and the Laws of Man
The rule of law[141] is breaking down here in America. The destruction of the rule of law leads to the destruction of a nation. Anyone who does not realize this has just not done his history. We are facing chaos and then anarchy and then a brutal Marxist (Communist) dictatorship. The proof is in history. If we do not change our political course, civilization and Christianity will not survive in America. We have two and only two options. The one is to continue on our present course following the laws of man to anarchy and to destruction. The other course is to turn to the Laws of God. We have not had to make a hard choice until recently because our laws of man were not so divergent from the Laws of God that we could not muddle along and "get by." But this is changing and changing fast.

At work are two divergent political ideologies. The one is the Constitution of the United States, built in congruence with the Laws of God. The other is Marxism, built upon the laws of man. Or, to put aside all subtleties and put it to you straight—the Laws of the Devil. The Laws of the Devil are exactly the opposite of the Laws of God, just as Marxism is exactly the opposite of the Laws of the Constitution.

The average person reading this will probably be shocked and exclaim "extremism" in his attempt to escape the obvious. But if one will examine the Constitution honestly and the Ten Points of the Communist Manifesto honestly and then examine the governmental structure and the laws of the federal and the state governments, he will come to the awful realization that our government is more Marxist than it is Constitutional. Have you paid attention to what has happened to the people of other Communist countries? Russia? China? Poland? Romania? Venezuela? Cuba? I have. (For more on this subject, see "Attachment "H," "The Doctrine of the Lesser Magistrates." Let us never forget that America was founded by courageous and knowledgeable men and women resisting the tyranny of King George III. That is a perfect example of lesser magistrates defying the tyrannical rule of a higher magistrate.

Possible Solutions to Our Problems

First, for any correction to this problem to occur, there must be more understanding by the general public, by county officials, sheriffs, state legislators, state attorneys general, governors, the leaders of both political parties, U. S. Representatives, U. S. Senators and Presidents. Also lawyers and law school professors. This will have to be started by a grass-roots movement, with people like you and me doing the work.

The Doctrine of the Lesser Magistrate.

There is a little-known but very legitimate, legal and moral way for citizens to countermand the illegal efforts of rogue politicians and judges. It was used when the knights brought King John to Runnymeade to address abuses of power. It is the exercise of righteous power by lesser officials such as state governors and, especially, sheriffs, to refuse to comply with the unrighteous and illegal demands of higher officials. Such act is called "to interpose." Few Americans understand this principle, but this is the way it MUST BE if the Constitution is held to be the supreme law of the land. Here "unconstitutional" is explained in an encyclopedia of law called *American Jurisprudence:*[142]

> *Since an unconstitutional law is void, the general principles follow that it imposes no duties, confers no rights, creates no office, bestows no power or authority on anyone, affords no protection and justifies no acts performed under it*
>
> *. . .A void act cannot be legally consistent with a valid one.**An unconstitutional law cannot operate to supersede any existing valid law.***
>
> *Indeed, insofar as a statute runs counter to the fundamental law of the land, it is superseded thereby.*
>
> ***No one is bound to obey an unconstitutional law and no courts are bound to enforce it.***
>
> — Sixteenth American Jurisprudence, Second Edition, Section 177. (late 2nd Ed. Section 256)

If one understands this fundamental principle of constitutional law, explained above, he can then begin to understand the logic, legality and morality of interposition and the doctrine of the lesser magistrate. There is no wiggle room. Either the above is true and accurate and the doctrine of the lesser magistrate is perfectly legal and moral, or the Constitution is not the supreme law of the land!

III. Another very viable option is for the President to refuse to enforce anti-constitutional rulings of the SCOTUS. This would be perfectly legal. After all, is a President conforming to his oath of office to support and defend the Constitution of the United States if he, the chief executive, orders unconstitutional SCOTUS rulings to be enforced? NO! This protection built into the Constitution is called checks and balances. The President is not required to enforce the anti-constitutional acts of any other officer of government.

The President could send notices to the governors of all fifty states and announce to the general public the following:

> To the governors of all states and to all Americans: Attorney General _____ and I, along with several very competent constitutional scholars, have very carefully studied the court case of *Everson,* ruled on by the Supreme Court of the United States in 1947. We have found several egregious errors in this ruling. We have found many provisions of *Everson* to be in violation of the Constitution. We have agreed unanimously that I would be violating my oath of office to uphold and defend the Constitution of the United States if I were to enforce the anti constitutional provisions of *Everson.* Therefore, no federal marshalls nor any other federal agents will be enforcing the provisions of *Everson*. A more thorough explanation of our findings will be found on the following website: _____.

The principle involved in legally defying the will of a superior magistrate is that, in the United States, the Constitution is the Supreme Law of the Land. This is affirmed by Article VI:

> **This Constitution and the Laws of the United States which shall be made in Pursuance thereof and all Treaties made, or which shall be made, under the authority of the United States, shall be the supreme law of the land; and the judges in every state shall be bound thereby, any Thing in the Constitution or Laws of any State to the Contrary notwithstanding.**

This brings us to the doctrine of the lesser magistrate. How can the acts of the lesser magistrate be superior to those of the greater magistrate? It must be when the lesser magistrate is wielding more authority than is the greater magistrate. An example would be when the greater magistrate (president or governor) is attempting to enforce an act that is in violation of the Constitution and is unconstitutional, null and void, (and therefore in violation of God's Law as well) and the lesser magistrate (sheriff) is acting under constitutional law.

An example would be during the Covid 19 epidemic. Some bureaucrat in the federal government (in the executive branch, which has NO legislative authority) issued an order to close down businesses and that everybody had to wear masks. This argument is not with policy. It might have been a good policy. (Or it might NOT have been) The question that every American should have been asking was, "By what authority do you issue this order?" Every county sheriff and every governor should have been demanding of that bureaucrat to show the source of his authority. For the truth is, there was none. There is no such authority. They claim "Emergency authority." There is no such authority found in the Constitution. It does not exist. Just think, if "Emergency Powers" were to give presidents or governors sweeping and limitless powers and if this same president or the same governors were the same to declare the "Emergencies," Then such would make of every president and every governor absolute dictators. And few politicians pass up an opportunity to grab more power.

Example of Government Ignorance: The governor of Utah, Gary Herbert, issued an executive order on or about the 10 of November, 2020 ordering the closure of certain businesses and many other onerous orders. He claimed that, "The Tenth Amendment to the United States Constitutes gives me this authority…" Gary, my friend, you sure made yourself look silly to the knowledgeable citizens of the great state of Utah. Maybe nationwide.

Might be Our Only Option

The way things are going, it appears that our only chance for survival might be the Doctrine of the Lesser Magistrate. It is coming. In the distant future or near future, it is coming. Most people believe that it cannot happen here. IT IS HAPPENING HERE!!! And the only way for America, Christianity and civilization to emerge victorious is for enough citizens to understand and defend God's Law, the Constitution. If we are going to survive a military-like collision of political ideologies in the near future, we had better start preparing now. RIGHT NOW! It is most important that, especially, the sheriffs of the counties understand their authority and their responsibility. I suggest that you obtain and study the Constitution of the United States and also the book, *The Doctrine of the Lesser Magistrate,* by Matthew J. Trewhella.

One other possible option, a long shot, is for the President to announce that he is not going to enforce the unconstitutional rulings of the U. S. Supreme Court, such as the "Separation of Church and State" in the *Everson* case. Presidents do not have to enforce anti-constitutional acts of Congress or rulings of the Supreme Court. This would be a possibility under Trump. But under Biden or any other Democrat, it would have about as much chance as a snowball in hell.

Appendix K - Attacks on Religion by Politicians

by Mat Staver,

The Assault on Christians...and Your Freedom
Oct 2, 2020
There is an open assault on people of faith in many parts of the country by governors who encourage rioters and protestors while restricting, even criminally charging, pastors, churches and parishioners who gather for worship. In California, for instance, churches and pastors are now being held in contempt and fined for having worship services. ALL WORSHIP is banned for most of the state. There are many shocking developments I want to share. - Mat

California has gone off the deep end when it comes to attacks on churches. On July 6, Gov. Gavin Newsom banned singing and chanting. Then on July 13, he BANNED ALL WORSHIP and this includes Bible studies and fellowship in private homes with anyone who does not live in the home.
California has gone off the deep end when it comes to attacks on churches. On July 6, Gov. Gavin Newsom banned singing and chanting. Then on July 13, he BANNED ALL WORSHIP and this includes Bible studies and fellowship in private homes with anyone who does not live in the home.
Violations of Gov. Newsom's orders come with criminal charges of up to one year in prison and daily fines of 1,000 dollars.
These orders are now being enforced against pastors, churches and even parishioners.
All the facts below – and more – are a matter of public record...

- **Pastor** John MacArthur of Grace Community Church is facing tens of thousands of dollars in fines by Los Angeles County and this is just the beginning of the fines. The County also revoked his lease on a parking lot the church has used for 45-years. Continued meetings will increase the fines and Pastor MacArthur could go to jail.
- Pastor Ché Ahn, Harvest Rock Church, its staff and parishioners have been threatened with daily criminal charges and fines of 1,000 dollars per day. Each criminal charge comes with up to one year in prison. This threat was sent to our client in a letter from the Pasadena Prosecutor. These criminal threats also apply to the church's home fellowship Life Groups. Our case is now at the Court of Appeals.
- Pastor Rob McCoy of Godspeak Calvary Chapel was held in contempt and the church is now being fined every time it meets. The next step could be jail for the pastor and former mayor of Thousand Oaks, California. This is the same pastor who in 2018 consoled and prayed with the families of victims at the mass shooting at the Borderline Bar & Grill.
- Pastor Jack Trieber of North Valley Baptist Church has been fined 5,000 dollars per service for "singing," and now the church faces

over 100,000 dollars in fines. This church is in one of the few counties where limited worship is permitted, but no singing. The city sent spies to the church over the summer and then posted a letter at the church demanding it cease and desist, stating the church is "unlawful."

There are many more churches being attacked and likely many more fines and criminal charges to come – not just for the brave pastors and congregants I have mentioned, but for the growing number of churches that have decided to TAKE A STAND against CA Gov. Gavin Newsom's illegal and unconstitutional restrictions against religion.

Here are the *actual*, verifiable *facts* about Newsom's orders:
On July 6, Gov. Newsom issued a "Worship Guidance" document which states unequivocally, "Places of worship must therefore **discontinue singing and chanting activities and limit indoor attendance** to 25% of building capacity or a maximum of 100 attendees."
On July 13, Gov. Newsom banned **ALL WORSHIP** for any county on the County Monitoring List, which covers about 80 percent of the population. This "no worship" ban includes private homes with anyone who does not live in the home.

On August 31, Gov. Newsom issued his "Blueprint" that even more clearly reveals his discrimination against churches and worship for most of the state. In every one of his newly minted Tiers, he gives preferential treatment to nonreligious gatherings in Museums, Gyms, Fitness Centers, Family Entertainment Centers, Cardrooms, Satellite Wagering, Laundromats, Malls, Destination Centers, Swap Meets and more.
Gov. Newsom's orders affect all churches and places of worship, even home Bible studies and fellowship. It is now even worse than "no singing" because all in-person worship is banned, including home Bible studies and fellowship with anyone who does not live in the home.

Imagine this – it is criminal in California to go to your neighbor's home to pray with them or have a Bible study.

To various degrees, what I described in California is still happening in many states. The same governors who love abortion and encourage protestors suppress the church and people of faith. Their agenda is obvious.

Please, stand with us now as we defend the many churches and pastors around the nation under attack for exercising their RIGHT to worship God.

We now have six federal lawsuits pending at the Courts of Appeal against some of the most egregious anti-Church governors – those of Maine, Virginia, Kentucky, Illinois, California and Colorado. And our Illinois case involving outrageous bullying against our Romanian church clients will be the first church case presented to the U.S. Supreme Court to consider for a full review. We WILL ensure that Americans retain their unalienable, constitutional RIGHT to worship according to their consciences instead of according to the whims of anti-god governors!

This fight has proven to be extraordinarily expensive, which is why I am so thankful for the challenge grant established by one of our loyal supporters.

For a limited time, every donation will be effectively DOUBLED by this grant. Please, do not let this opportunity pass you by. Our religious freedom is far too important not to defend!

Finally, please be in prayer for the pastors, churches and faithful Christians under attack by lawless governors intent on silencing God's word and shuttering His churches.

Mat Staver
Founder and Chairman

P.S. Liberty Counsel is now fighting SIX federal lawsuits against lawless governors and anti-church bureaucrats seeking to silence God's people and shutter God's churches. This work continues even as we battle for Judge Barrett to fill the seat left open by Justice Ruth Bader Ginsburg's passing. Please, take advantage of the generous Challenge Grant which will DOUBLE THE IMPACT of your donation today.

Appendix L - Judging the United States Supreme Court by Utah Chief Justices A. H. Ellett and J. Allen Crockett

Chief Justice A. H. Ellett, Utah State Supreme Court 1977-79:
The United States Supreme Court, as at present constituted, has departed from the Constitution as it has been interpreted from its inception and has followed the urgings of social reformers in foisting upon this Nation laws which even Congress could not constitutionally pass. It has amended the Constitution in a manner unknown to the document itself. While it takes three fourths of the states of the Union to change the Constitution legally, yet as few as five men who have never been elected to office can by judicial fiat accomplish change just as radical as could three fourths of the states of this Nation. As a result of the recent holdings of that Court, the sovereignty of the states is practically abolished and the erstwhile free and independent states are now in effect and purpose merely closely supervised units in the federal *system.* (Quoted in Jerome Horowitz, *The United States Has Two Constitutions How to Identify and Promote the True Constitution*, Ch. 2, p. 3.) (TDC p. 74)

Chief Justice J. Allen Crockett, Utah State Supreme Court 1979-1981
This [usurpation] has resulted in a constant and seemingly endless process of arrogating to the federal government more and more of the powers, not only not granted to it, but expressly forbidden to it and in disparagement of the powers properly belonging to the sovereign states and the people. This development is a clear vindication of the foreboding of the founding fathers and their fears of centralization of powers. This was but natural because of the conditions out of which our form of government came into being and because history is strewn with other examples which demonstrates that undue, uncontrolled and unwieldy concentrations of power in any individual or institution tends to destroy itself. It is our opinion that this is the evil which the founders feared so keenly and tried so zealously to guard against, but which is now rife upon us. It is plainly evident that it was their desire and purpose to avoid this by providing for what they believed to be an essential and desirable balance of power between the sovereignties of the states and the federal government.

What we have just said is with the utmost respect and indeed devotion, to our system of government. This includes devotion to the founders' concept of a sovereign nation consisting of sovereign states, with the respective sovereignties so interrelated that their sovereign powers check and balance each other; which we think it is of the utmost importance to respect and maintain. Consequently, we feel impelled to voice our disagreement with the almost unbelievable arrogation of power by and to the federal government and its judiciary.
(*Utah v. Phillips,* 540 Pacific 2nd 936, p. 938.) (TDC p. 81)

About the Author

Joe H. Ferguson was born in Tyler, Texas and finished high school there. In 1948 he drove his 1931 Model A Ford coupe from Tyler to Logan, Utah where he attended Utah State for three years. He started flying in a 65 hp Aeronca Champ in the fall of 1949 and flying became his love and his profession. Fraternity brothers paid him to fly over to Afton, Wyoming and bring back two cases of 6% Wyoming beer. Joe says that , "I got my start in aviation by bootlegging." In 1952, due to engine trouble in his Luscombe, he landed at Provo, Utah and subsequently enrolled at Brigham Young University where he attended winter and spring quarters of 1952 and 1953, graduating with a degree in business administration. During the summers of 1952 and 1953 he flew 450 hp Stearmans cropdusting in Arizona and Texas. Joe entered USAF pilot training in November of 1953 and flew PA—18s, T—6s, T—28s, B—25s, B—29s and was a pilot in the 9th air to air refueling squadron at Mountain Home AFB, ID flying KC—97 air to air refueling tankers. His flight duties took him to North Africa, Japan and Alaska.

After the USAF, he flew for the airlines for 43 years. Flying was his love and his livelihood. He married and had six children. He has been a serious student of politics and the law since 1964 and developed a keen perception of forces subversive to Americanism, to Christianity and to civilization. Although a non—lawyer, Joe will debate any lawyer, any judge at any time and any place and give them plenty of time to draw a crowd. Joe's perception of government and the law is in total conflict with the worldviews of most lawyers and most judges. Joe's is in conformity with the Constitution of the United States. The worldviews of most lawyers and most judges, especially of five of the present justices of the U.S. Supreme Court, are in conformity with Marxism and Secular Humanism and with those of the secret combinations of the Devil, which is in direct conflict with the true intent of the Constitution of the United States.

"And that, my Christian American friends, is the root of our problems, religious and political." says Joe.

The justices of the Supreme Court might pronounce their rulings to be "constitutional," but they are in reality hostile to and in conflict with the Constitution and in reality are in conformity with Marxism and Secular Humanism. Just read the *Obergefell* case (a U.S. Supreme Court case. Chapter IV) about same-sex marriage. Then read the dissents of four wise and courageous justices: Roberts, Scalia, Alito and Thomas. (Presented herein) (They must agree with me. Because I certainly do agree with them.) A real education in the law. Reading the contrast between the ruling of the five justices who voted aye and the four justices who dissented is a real education. It will help anyone to understand the problems facing us.

Joe has six children scattered from St. George to Texas to Wisconsin to Montana to Idaho. He presently lives in Cedar Hills, Utah with his wife Carole.

www.ingramcontent.com/pod-product-compliance
Lightning Source LLC
Chambersburg PA
CBHW052049230426
43671CB00011B/1846